Cybersecurity and Digital Trust in Smart and Sustainable Tourism

Mohammad Badruddoza Talukder
https://orcid.org/0009-0008-1662-9221
International University of Business Agriculture and Technology, Bangladesh

Ismot Tasmary Salsabil
https://orcid.org/0009-0006-4911-502X
Engineering Institute of Technology, Australia

IGI Global
Scientific Publishing
Publishing Tomorrow's Research Today

Published in the United States of America by
IGI Global Scientific Publishing
701 East Chocolate Avenue
Hershey, PA, 17033, USA
Tel: 717-533-8845 | Fax: 717-533-7115
Website: https://www.igi-global.com E-mail: cust@igi-global.com

Library of Congress Cataloging-in-Publication Data

LCCN: 2026026466 (CIP Data Pending)
ISBN13: 9798260018507
Isbn13Softcover: 9798260018514
EISBN13: 9798260018521

British Cataloguing in Publication Data
A Cataloguing in Publication record for this book is available from the British Library.

Table of Contents

Detailed Table of Contents

Mohammad Badruddoza Talukder, International University of Business Agriculture and Technology, Bangladesh
Md. Shoeab Akhter, International University of Business Agriculture and Technology, Bangladesh
Abdullah Ebna Ashraf, International University of Business Agriculture and Technology, Bangladesh
Iftiaq Sarkar, International University of Business Agriculture and Technology, Bangladesh
Hamida Akter Ritu, International University of Business Agriculture and Technology, Bangladesh
Md. Mehedi Hasan Sawon, Daffodil International University, Bangladesh

Artificial intelligence-assisted tourism has brought in the new age of predictive travel intelligence, with travelers seeking immediate suggestions, risk forecasts, and itinerary recommendations. Smart systems analyze massive datasets ranging from user behavior to weather conditions to geopolitical threats to optimize travel. The blockchain network is a security layer that is open and rampant to prevent unwanted activities across the platform, and the chapter investigates the cyber vulnerabilities of these AI travel intelligence systems, including risks of data manipulation, adversarial AI attacks, privacy violations, and algorithmic challenges in securing the personal and behavioral data with which travel is predicted. The chapter then emphasizes the importance of data protection frameworks and transparent design algorithms that do not compromise blockchain-based authentication mechanisms in the pursuit of ensuring digital trust. The insights offered help cybersecurity practitioners, policymakers, and tourism technology startups build safer and more transparent systems.

Cybersecurity and sustainable tourism are inseparable as they lead to the achievement of the United Nations Sustainable Development Goals (SDGs). In light of cyber threats that have been ramping up along with the digital transformation related risks of the tourism market. The chapter explores the concept of cybersecurity as a key element that can safeguard digital tourism infrastructure, enforce data privacy, and improve the level of stakeholder trust. It summarizes various theoretical voices, appraises the existing studies, and presents a framework that can balance cybersecurity and sustainable tourism objectives in terms of implementation. The major challenges like cyberattacks focused on tourism platforms, breaches in the data of the travelers, and incompetent regulations are examined. The paper provides practical methods that can be employed to enhance cybersecurity resilience within tourism, in an effort to support SDGs such as decent work and economic growth (SDG 8), industry innovation (SDG 9) and sustainable urban development (SDG 11).

The digital era has transformed tourism into an intelligent ecosystem, driven by smart infrastructure and real-time services. These innovations enhance convenience and personalisation, but they also introduce significant cybersecurity vulnerabilities, including data breaches, phishing attacks, insecure IoT devices, partner-related risks, and operational disruptions from ransomware or denial-of-service attacks. Cybersecurity governance in tourism is largely generic, lacking sector-specific frameworks. This study emphasises the need for tailored and proposes a Cyber-Resilience Model built on four pillars: Technological layers, Organisational layers, Policy and Governance layers, and User-Centric layers. Practical implications will help policymakers, businesses, technology developers, academia, and tourists towards safer digital practices. As tourism advances digitally, building cyber resilience is essential for sustaining trust, operational continuity, and economic stability. By doing so, the sector can thrive in a globally interconnected and secure future.

This chapter presents a Cyber Resilient Smart Tourism Framework that combines digital forensics, Artificial Intelligence (AI), and blockchain to improve security, transparency, and trust in online tourism systems. The framework is structured into four layers preventive, detective, responsive, and adaptive each designed to detect, analyze, and mitigate cyber threats efficiently. It shows how AI helps with predicting trends and spotting potential threats, while blockchain keeps evidence safe from tampering and makes everything clear and open. Case studies, including the Collins Aerospace cyberattack and the Italy hotel data breach, demonstrate the framework's real-world applicability. The integration of forensic intelligence with AI and blockchain strengthens data protection, incident response, and cross-domain collaboration among tourism stakeholders. The chapter points out the need for proactive resilience, forensic readiness, and adaptive learning to secure the next generation of smart tourism infrastructures.

Digital transformation has reshaped tourism transportation into a Smart Tourism Transportation Ecosystem supported by Artificial Intelligence, the Internet of Things, and autonomous systems. These technologies improve operational efficiency and enable personalized travel services, while expanding cyber-physical attack surfaces that may affect safety, system reliability, and economic trust. This chapter, per the authors, analyzes the evolving cyber threat landscape across air, maritime, and land transportation sectors and examines AI- and IoT-based security mechanisms. Using a qualitative approach based on case studies and literature review, a five-layer resilience framework is proposed, consisting of Layered Defense Architecture, Zero-Trust Security Model, Resilience-by-Design, Privacy-Preserving Analytics, and Continuous Monitoring. The findings indicate that cybersecurity should be integrated as a strategic design element. The chapter provides recommendations to support secure, resilient, and sustainable tourism transportation systems.

Smart tourism, powered by technologies like the Internet of Things (IoT), artificial intelligence (AI), and big data, has revolutionized the travel industry by enhancing personalization and efficiency. However, this digital ecosystem is vulnerable to cybersecurity threats such as data breaches, ransomware, and phishing, which erode trust among tourists and stakeholders. Integrating cybersecurity with digital forensics offers a robust approach to safeguarding data, ensuring privacy, and enabling effective incident response. This chapter examines the synergy between these disciplines, analyzing challenges, proposing a conceptual framework, and offering actionable recommendations to foster a trusted travel ecosystem. Through a comprehensive literature review and case-based findings, it highlights the critical role of proactive security measures and forensic readiness in smart tourism.

As tourism evolves into an age of hyper-connectivity and immersive digital enhancement, the assurance of cybersecurity and forensic resilience has become crucial for intelligent tourist ecosystems. This chapter examines the architectural and analytical frameworks necessary to protect cyber-physical infrastructures integrated inside smart destinations. It delineates a stratified cybersecurity framework that incorporates zero-trust principles, edge-based threat detection, and secure IoT protocols to safeguard against the evolving threat environment. Focus is directed towards forensic analytics frameworks that utilize machine learning, behavioral modeling, and blockchain-based audit trails to facilitate real-time incident response and post-event analysis.

Preface

INTRODUCTION

The convergence of digital innovation and sustainability has ushered in a new era for global tourism—one defined by smart systems, data-driven decision-making, and interconnected infrastructures. As destinations increasingly adopt technologies such as artificial intelligence (AI), the Internet of Things (IoT), blockchain, and big data analytics, tourism is evolving into a sophisticated digital ecosystem. These advancements have enhanced efficiency, personalization, and accessibility while supporting broader sustainability goals. However, they have also introduced significant cybersecurity challenges, raising critical concerns about data protection, system integrity, and the preservation of digital trust.

This edited volume, *Cybersecurity and Digital Trust in Smart and Sustainable Tourism*, addresses the pressing need to secure tourism systems while aligning them with sustainable development objectives. As tourism becomes more reliant on digital platforms and smart infrastructure, the risks associated with cyber threats—including data breaches, ransomware attacks, and algorithmic manipulation—continue to grow in scale and complexity. Ensuring digital trust is therefore fundamental not only to technological advancement but also to the long-term viability and resilience of the tourism sector.

As editors, we have brought together a diverse group of scholars and practitioners who examine the intersection of cybersecurity, digital forensics, and sustainable tourism from multiple perspectives. The chapters in this volume explore how secure digital ecosystems can support the United Nations Sustainable Development Goals (SDGs), enhance stakeholder trust, and foster innovation. By integrating theoretical frameworks, empirical research, and practical applications, this collection offers a comprehensive exploration of how cybersecurity can be embedded into the design and governance of smart tourism systems.

Importantly, this book emphasizes that digital trust is not solely a technical construct but a socio-technical imperative. It encompasses transparency, accountability, privacy protection, and ethical data use. In a sector built on customer experience and global mobility, trust is the cornerstone of success. This volume aims to equip researchers, policymakers, and industry leaders with the insights needed to build secure, sustainable, and trustworthy tourism ecosystems in an increasingly digital world.

CHAPTER OVERVIEW

This volume comprises twelve chapters that collectively examine the role of cybersecurity and digital trust across smart and sustainable tourism systems.

Chapter 1 investigates AI-based travel intelligence systems, focusing on predictive tourism and the associated cybersecurity risks. It explores challenges such as adversarial AI attacks, data privacy concerns, and the role of blockchain in ensuring secure and transparent systems.

Chapter 2 examines the relationship between cybersecurity and sustainable tourism goals, particularly in the context of the United Nations SDGs. It proposes frameworks to align cybersecurity strategies with sustainable development objectives, emphasizing resilience and stakeholder trust.

Chapter 3 explores smart tourism infrastructure and its associated security challenges. It introduces a cyber-resilience model that integrates technological, organizational, policy, and user-centric layers to strengthen tourism ecosystems.

Chapter 4 presents the concept of a cybersecurity–sustainability nexus, linking cybersecurity practices with the achievement of SDGs. It offers governance and resilience-based perspectives to address digital vulnerabilities in tourism systems.

Chapter 5 provides a case-based analysis of cybersecurity in Vietnam's sustainable tourism practices. It examines how digital transformation supports sustainability while introducing new risks, emphasizing the need for multi-stakeholder collaboration.

Chapter 6 introduces a cyber-resilient smart tourism framework that integrates digital forensics, AI, and blockchain technologies. It demonstrates how these tools enhance transparency, trust, and incident response capabilities.

Chapter 7 focuses on cybersecurity in aviation and transport systems within smart tourism. It proposes a layered resilience framework incorporating zero-trust models and continuous monitoring to address evolving cyber threats.

Chapter 8 explores the integration of cybersecurity and digital forensics to create a trusted travel ecosystem. It highlights the importance of proactive security measures and forensic readiness in safeguarding digital tourism platforms.

Chapter 9 examines cybersecurity architectures and forensic analytics in digitally augmented travel ecosystems. It presents advanced frameworks for protecting cyber-physical infrastructures and enabling real-time threat detection.

Chapter 10 discusses the importance of cybersecurity and digital forensics in ensuring secure smart tourism experiences. It identifies key vulnerabilities and proposes strategies for enhancing resilience and stakeholder confidence.

Chapter 11 concludes the volume by focusing on smart agro-tourism systems and green destinations. It highlights how cybersecurity and digital forensics can protect rural tourism infrastructures and support sustainable development.

CONCLUSION

The contributions in this volume collectively underscore the critical importance of integrating cybersecurity into the foundation of smart and sustainable tourism systems. As digital transformation accelerates, the tourism sector must navigate an increasingly complex threat landscape while continuing to innovate and grow. The chapters highlight that cybersecurity is not merely a defensive mechanism but a strategic enabler of trust, resilience, and sustainability.

A recurring theme throughout this book is the necessity of adopting a holistic and proactive approach to cybersecurity. This includes embedding security into system design, fostering organizational awareness, and leveraging emerging technologies such as AI and blockchain to anticipate and mitigate risks. Equally important is the role of governance, policy alignment, and international cooperation in addressing cross-border challenges and ensuring consistent standards across the global tourism ecosystem.

Finally, this volume reinforces the centrality of digital trust in shaping the future of tourism. Trust influences traveler behavior, stakeholder collaboration, and the adoption of new technologies. By prioritizing transparency, ethical data practices, and robust security measures, the tourism industry can build resilient systems that support both innovation and sustainability. It is our hope that this book serves as a valuable resource for advancing research, informing policy, and guiding practice in the pursuit of secure and sustainable tourism in the digital age.

Chapter 1
AI-Based Travel Intelligence Systems: Cybersecurity and Digital Trust in Predictive Tourism

Mohammad Badruddoza Talukder
http://orcid.org/0009-0008-1662-9221
International University of Business Agriculture and Technology, Bangladesh

Iftiaq Sarkar
http://orcid.org/0009-0007-9314-815X
International University of Business Agriculture and Technology, Bangladesh

Md. Shoeab Akhter
http://orcid.org/0009-0004-4582-2937
International University of Business Agriculture and Technology, Bangladesh

Hamida Akter Ritu
http://orcid.org/0009-0003-3853-9247
International University of Business Agriculture and Technology, Bangladesh

Abdullah Ebna Ashraf
http://orcid.org/0009-0007-3523-1705
International University of Business Agriculture and Technology, Bangladesh

Md. Mehedi Hasan Sawon
http://orcid.org/0009-0000-2846-1018
Daffodil International University, Bangladesh

ABSTRACT

Artificial intelligence-assisted tourism has brought in the new age of predictive travel intelligence, with travelers seeking immediate suggestions, risk forecasts, and itinerary recommendations. Smart systems analyze massive datasets ranging from user behavior to weather conditions to geopolitical threats to optimize travel. The blockchain network is a security layer that is open and rampant to prevent unwanted activities across the platform, and the chapter investigates the cyber vulnerabili-

DOI: 10.4018/979-8-2600-1850-7.ch001

ties of these AI travel intelligence systems, including risks of data manipulation, adversarial AI attacks, privacy violations, and algorithmic challenges in securing the personal and behavioral data with which travel is predicted. The chapter then emphasizes the importance of data protection frameworks and transparent design algorithms that do not compromise blockchain-based authentication mechanisms in the pursuit of ensuring digital trust. The insights offered help cybersecurity practitioners, policymakers, and tourism technology startups build safer and more transparent systems.

1. INTRODUCTION

In recent years, the tourism industry has made a digital change by the Rapid Integration of Artificial Intelligence behavioral privatization, planning, and experience. The fusion of machine learning, big data analytics, and algorithm decision-making has enabled the emergence of real-time forecasting, behavioral privatization, dynamic pricing, and the emergence of capable intelligent travel platforms capable of automated service distribution. Since passengers demand rapid immediate reactions, hyper-recommendations, and spontaneous experiences, AI-based systems now serve as the backbone of modern tourism operations—from the ecological tour program to the booking apps (Hemmati et al., 2024)—from smart virtual assistants. The creation of a prepaid platform for travelling represents a breakthrough in the business: the system is not based on reactive services but anticipates vastness of any kind of data input, including past discoveries, past reservations, social media presence, weather conditions, and the jollies of passengers depending on the geopolitical surroundings. These web pages not only come up with directions, recommendations, and route modifications, but also evaluate political instability, health risks, and environmental risks. At the same time as promising unrivalled efficiency, AI generates a corresponding surge in vulnerabilities, raising cybersecurity and heightening underlying concerns of mistrust in digital applications. With tourism being data intensive, concerns are given to the secure nature of the storage, transfer, and utilization of data. Sensitive personal information such as travel history, financial credentials, biometric IDs, and even emotional behavior patterns are collected on an unprecedented scale, making tourism platforms the major targets for cyberattacks and data violations. In addition, the increasing use of the future algorithm introduces important challenges such as algorithm bias, adverse AI manipulation, data poisoning, and opaque decision-making, which threatens the credibility and fairness of AI-borne recommendations. The paradigm shift demands immediate attention from tourism scholars, cyber safety experts, policymakers, and technology developers (McStay, 2020). Nevertheless, despite this growth, the research on securing

AI-operated travel systems and installation of digital trust mechanisms remains limited and fragmented. Current educational literature has focused largely on the role of AI in service individualization and increasing operational automation, but there is a sufficient difference in studies that checks to reduce cybersecurity risks, protect user privacy, and ensure transparency and fairness in AI-based tourism applications. For example, several platforms deployed the AI model as a "black box" without a clear output, which limits the ability to understand or take travel decisions made by users. Moreover, decisions made by AI are usually influenced by the large and no uniform third-party data entry; malicious attempts at intervention, i.e., data manipulation, or disadvantageous attacks cannot be ruled out, and the present flaw in integrated data governance policies in the international tourism market further exposes them to risks.

Therefore, this chapter examines the convergence of the AI-Manufacturing Tourist System with cybersecurity challenges, with the goal of presenting a wide, evidence-based story that combines innovation with moral responsibility (Hemmati et al., 2024). This applies to three interacted dimensions: AI's functionality and scope in future tourism; Spectrum of cybersecurity weaknesses contained in such systems, and the framework required to manufacture the digital trust—inflammatory verification, privacy-by-design model, algorithm transparency, and moral AI perfection (Wongchestha et al., 2025). Ultimately, the purpose of this study is to fill an important research interval and start the discourse of scholars on how AI-based tourism platforms can be both intelligent and reliable. Since the industry continues its projection to automation and smart systems, it becomes necessary to understand the future accuracy and dual imperative of the future accuracy and digital integrity for the creation of a durable, inclusive, and safe tourism ecosystem in the 21st century (Knani et al., 2022).

1.1 Objectives

1. To detect the role of artificial intelligence in intelligence systems and future tourism on modern travel platforms.
2. To check cyber security weaknesses associated with AI-based tourism applications.
3. To suggest ways to provide digital trusts, data security, and moral rules in smart tourism systems.

2. THEORETICAL OBSERVATION: THEORETICAL APPROACH TO AI-BASED TRAVEL INTELLIGENCE SYSTEM: CYBERSECURITY AND DIGITAL TRUST IN FUTURE TOURISM

Artificial Intelligence (AI) in the tourism sector has revolutionized how the journey is planned, experienced, and managed (Pencarelli, 2020). The standardization of industry innovation and responsibility includes personal recommendations, risk forecasts, and future technologies for automated decision-making (Serban et al., 2025). However, this progress brings forward important theoretical ideas. First, we consider how emerging tourism models are becoming increasingly data-driven, raising questions about control and personalization. Next, we examine the cybersecurity weaknesses that could compromise the integrity of AI systems that travelers and businesses depend on. Finally, we look at the ethical responsibility to foster digital trust—through openness, clear consent, and fairness. Together, they provide a holistic framework to guide the responsible and safe development of intelligent tourism systems in the digital age.

2.1 Predictive Tourism Intelligence: Theoretical Foundations and Practical Dimensions

The Predictive Tourism Travel Industry is a transformative paradigm that takes advantage of Artificial Intelligence (AI) to forecast traveler behavior, reducing the disruption and disrupting the travel experiences before a journey starts. Unlike traditional reactive systems, future tourism depends on large data, Machiavellian traveler behavior, and behavioral analysis to distribute active services (Guo et al., 2024). Its theoretical foundation lies in data-operated decision-making, where real-time inputs (for example, user location, weather trends, and geopolitical events) are processed by algorithms to generate timely recommendations. For example, platforms such as Google Travel or Hopper use trained machine learning models on historic datasets to suggest optimal booking windows, predict delays, or offer alternative routes during emergency situations. The implication of the real world is a change from static to adaptive tourism planning—the travellers receive a real-time health alert, weather warnings, and destination suggestions based on the status of development. Theoretically, it aligns with the development system theory, where tourism platforms act as adaptive, intelligent systems, which respond to frequent learning and external stimuli (Yang et al., 2019). However, this refinement raises moral and operational challenges, including data abuse and algorithm opacity. As a scale of future tourism systems, balance becomes necessary between automation, privatisation, and moral rule. Thus, the future of tourism is not only an innovation in functionality but is also adapted through the imagination of travel and AI privatisation.

2.2 Algorithmic Vulnerability and Cybersecurity in AI-Based Travel Systems

The theoretical intersection between artificial intelligence and cybersecurity in tourism exposes a new risk landscape sized by adverse attacks, data poisoning, and behavior profiling. The AI model, while user, efficient in learning patterns from data, when exploited malicious actor model input or training dataset (Brundage et al., 2024), it is naturally susceptible to manipulation. From the point of view of a cybersecurity theory, these threats challenge integrity, availability, and privacy—the main principle of information protection. For example, attacks of data poisoning can corrupt the training data of an AI model to mislead tourists about a certain hotel chain or regional safety or redirect passengers towards less desirable places. Similarly, adverse disturbances—subtle changes in hills or data—can cheat the facial identification systems of the airport and compromise security and service accuracy. Such weaknesses reflect the theoretical concept of "attack surfaces" in cyber-physical systems, where each data entry point can be exploited. AI tourism platforms sensitive data – Biometric ID, financial transactions, and the gathering of an array of behavioral insights—make them attractive goals. Nevertheless, many current systems lack discrepancy, encryption security measures, or adverse testing mechanisms. The need for flexible architecture is necessary (*Artificial Intelligence and Machine Learning for Enhancing Resilience*, 2025).

2.3 Digital Trust as an Ethical Imperative in Smart Tourism Systems

The Digital Trust is the moral foundation stone of the AI-based tourism systems, including transparency, user autonomy, consent, and fairness. This refers to the belief that users keep their personal data in intelligent platforms to handle their personal data morally while providing fair, clear services. Information ethics and trust theory, which emphasise accountability, informed consent, and system transparency, theoretically contain digital trust. Tourism platforms analyze intimate user behavior—search history, geolocation, biometric data—for painful experiences. However, without strong data governance and moral design, such systems violate user rights. When the platforms collect consensus through long, unpaid conditions or vague third-party data sharing, the trust is further erased. The 2020 Marriott data breach, which highlights more than 5 million records, indicates how the data damages public belief (Tripathi & Mukhopadhyay, 2020). In response, rules such as The General Data Protection Regulation (GDPR) advocate for privacy by design, data minimalization, and user access rights. Ethically sound systems should offer visibility and control to users over how their data is used. Concepts such as explainable AI (XAI), data ownership, and celebrity design—the AI systems can operate transparently using the user, which can increase the engagement and accountability. Thus, promoting a digital trust is not just a regulatory obligation but a theoretical and practical requirement for a durable, inclusive tourism ecosystem.

3. AI IN PREDICTIVE TOURISM

Increasing integration of artificial intelligence in the travel industry has given rise to a new frontier, known as predictive tourism—where advanced algorithms begin with traveller preferences, behaviours, and possible risks even before estimating. The origin of the future of tourism is the use of numerous and diverse data sources, such as user browsing habits, geolocations, seasonal weather patterns, and global political events (Pan & Yang, 2016). These strengthen input platforms to estimate the needs, optimise experiences, and reduce disruption in real time. AI-driven travel platforms such as Google Travel, Hopper, and Kayak are already deploying these techniques to adapt to planning, pricing, and privatisation, and this section introduces the scope, data foundation, and current applications of future tourism and introduces a foundation for deep discovery in the following subdivisions (Jeetesh et al., 2024).

3.1 Introduce Predictive Tourism: Definition and Extent

The Predictive Tourism Travel and Tourism Sector refers to the integration of Artificial Intelligence (AI) techniques to estimate the needs, preferences, and possible risks of passengers before starting their journey. Unlike traditional reactive systems, where users manually require input options and preferences, future tourism platforms depend on historical data, real-time input, and advanced algorithms, which produce timely and reference-sensitive travel recommendations (Gajdošík & Marciš, 2019). This approach reflects a major paradigm change in the concept of tourism services and the way it is distributed, where the platforms do not only respond to the demand but also give it a consistent shape. Predictive Tourism empowers travel operators to distribute hyper-personalised services by analysing trends, user behaviour, seasonal demands, and global development. Does this involve recommending alternative routes due to natural disasters or suggesting off-peak travel times for better pricing, the future tourist allows smart decisions to be made that increase the user's satisfaction and operational efficiency. The system also contributes to the strategic plan to predict high-deserving seasons for tourism businesses, estimate booking behaviour, and allocate resources more effectively. From the process and housing selection for transportation planning and in-trip assistance, the future tourist end-to-end plays an important role in customising the experience. Its importance is not only increasing due to the increasing expectations of the user but also due to the increasing competition in the global tourism sector, where smart, data-operated platforms are quick to become standard. Future-stating tourism limits reach various sub-domains—hotels, destination marketing organizations, tour operators, and even National Tourism Boards—opposing its scalability and adaptability. Since the tourism industry is more digitally connected, the future of tourism is ready to become one of the basic elements of the smart tourism infrastructure, which combines the facility, security, privatization, and operational agility to meet the demands of today's passengers. This chapter examines these growing possibilities, while this AI-manual change also addresses the moral, safety, and trust-related challenges associated with them (Gretzel et al., 2015).

3.2 Data Sources Used (User Behavior, Location, Weather, Political Risk, etc.)

The effectiveness of future tourist tourism is very high; it depends on the quality, diversity, and accuracy of data sources that feed into its algorithms. These AI systems draw from a broad spectrum of datasets to analyze and estimate passenger behavior, preferences, and external conditions that can affect their journey. One of the most fundamental data inputs comes from user behavior analytics, including previous discovery, browsing patterns, booking history, and reaction to previous experiences (Albattat et al., 2025). This information helps the system to create a dynamic passenger profile, which improves the accuracy of future recommendations. In addition to behavioral data, geolocation information from mobile devices and wearable technologies allows the platform to monitor user movements in real time and provides suggestions based on closeness and availability (Gretzel et al., 2015). Weather data is also important, as many travel decisions—like going to a tropical beach, hiking trails, or skiing resorts—are seasonal and real-time climate conditions. Public health alerts and event calendars—like local festivals, conferences, or refinement of the protest-defense decision-making process—ensure that tourists are informed of potential disruption or opportunities. Political and safety risk indices, often collected from government travel advice or news monitoring equipment, are used to warn passengers about unstable areas or sudden natural disasters or sudden crises such as civil disturbances (Raleigh et al., 2023). Therefore, for future tourism, it is necessary to implement a strong data governance structure that ensures accuracy, safety, and user consent in all data channels to act morally and efficiently.

4. CYBERSECURITY THREATS IN AI-AIDED TRAVEL SYSTEMS

As AI becomes central for future tourism, the hazards of cyber security have emerged as important challenges. The purpose of adverse attacks and data poisoning is to manipulate their training or input data and manipulate the AI model, making recommendations of biased or harmful travel. In addition, user violations of privacy—such as behavior or unauthorized disclosure of financial or biometric data—raise ethical and legal concerns. In addition, the rise of AI-enabled eminent travel platforms has increased the risk of space spoofing, payment fraud, and phishing attacks, where criminals exploit the system's weaknesses or cheat users. These threats reduce confidence in the AI system and expose the immediate requirement of safe architecture, moral data handling, and global standards for the protection of both users and service providers within the developed digital tourism scenario.

4.1 Adversarial Attacks on AI-Controlled Systems Aiming to Manipulate Outcomes and Data Poisoning

Since the AI-based travel system becomes more advanced and central for tourism experiences, they are unsafe for rapid adverse attacks that want to manipulate their forecast capabilities. Adverse attacks include the machine learning models behaving unexpectedly or harmfully to the system to deliberately feed misleading or subtly corrupt data. For example, an attacker may slightly change the input data to force the AI recommendation engine in favor of specific destinations, vendors, or services—resulting in improper business advantage or misinformation (Deldjoo et al., 2021) for users. It not only endangers the integrity of travel platforms but also reduces the consumer trust. One of the most related methods used in these scenarios is data poisoning, where the attackers have compromised the training dataset that relies on the AI system. If the learning model of the system is contaminated in the training phase—such as by injecting wrong data about fake hotel ratings or fabricated tourist safety reports-This can give rise to long-term distortions in service distribution and decision-making (Nguyen et al., 2024). In terms of travel, such manipulations may redirect tourists to overhyped or exploitative vendors. Adverse attacks also expand to machine vision systems in airports, such as facial identification or automatic check-in, where microscopic image disturbances can dodge AI into wrong individuals. The implications are not only commercial but also serious safety and moral concerns. Despite the increasing use of AI in tourism, awareness of adverse hazards between platform developers and tourism operators is low; many systems are left sick to detect or reduce such attacks. Adverse training, strong discrepancy detection systems, and verification layers for input data such as counterants are still in early adopting stages. This emerging danger landscape asks for intensive cooperation among AI engineers, cybersecurity experts, and tourism technology providers, who can develop flexible architecture that can withstand manipulation, algorithms that can ensure fairness, and the preservation of the entertainment of the digital travel ecosystem (He et al., 2023).

4.2 Risks of Location Spoofing, Payment Fraud, and Phishing

As AI-aided travel platforms use location tracking, confirmation of booking, and rapid dependence on real-time data for safe transactions, they become the major goals for location spoofing, payment fraud, and phishing attacks. Location spoofing involves proving GPS data incorrect to mislead the user's actual status, which may disrupt service distribution or be exploited for fraud purposes. For example, a cybercriminal region-specific traveller may manipulate the location data to reach the deals or only to claim loyalty awards for verified passengers (Khan et al., 2021). In more dangerous scenarios, spoofing can incorrectly transport services, compromise navigation tools, or keep individuals incorrectly in or outside geo-fencing areas—increasing both protection and legal implications. Equal-related payment is an increasing risk of fraud, especially with travel platforms digital wallets, one-click purchases, and automated booking tools. The fraudsters exploited the weaknesses of the system or conducted social engineering attacks to steal the information about the credit card, bypass the payment gateway, or impersonate users. Increasing use of AI-based chatbots and virtual travel assistants can unknowingly aid in this process if they lack safe user verification protocols (Larsson et al., 2021). For example, a passenger attached to an unsafe chatbot can inadvertently reveal individual financial statements, which can then be used in fraudulent transactions. Additionally, the phishing attacks targeting passengers through email or fake websites have developed into sophistication. Cybercriminals now deploy AI-based emails or cloned interfaces that are similar to reliable travel brands, which attract users to enter sensitive data, and these attacks are often more vulnerable during extreme weather or when users are stressed and more vulnerable to deception. The result is not only a financial loss but also a rupture in confidence between users and digital travel platforms. To combat these risks, tourism companies should invest in multi-factor authentication (MFA), biometric verification, and real-time fraud detection algorithms, and they should continuously operate cybersecurity audits and educate users about phishing awareness. Blockchain-based payment verification and detection of AI-operated discrepancy may further strengthen the defense mechanism. The future travel ecosystem requires an active, multi-level approach that combines technical safety measures with human awareness and regulatory support (Halima Oluwabunmi Bello et al., 2024; Shrestha et al., 2025).

Table 1. AI-Based Travel Intelligence Systems: Cybersecurity and Digital Trust in Predictive Tourism

Component	Description	Key Data Inputs	Potential Cybersecurity Risks	Digital Trust & Risk Mitigation Measures
(1) User Behavior Prediction (Chung et al., 2019)	The passenger uses AI algorithms to predict preferences and future travel patterns.	Search history, booking records, and social media activity	Data violations, unauthorized framework, and misuse of personal data	Data encryption, transparent data policies, user consent.
(2) Dynamic Pricing Engines (Kamyab & Bahrami, 2016)	Demand adjusts prices in real time depending on forecast and customer division.	Historical demand data, competitive rates, seasonal trends	Price manipulation, unfair pricing practices, algorithm bias	Regulatory compliance, moral AI audit, clear pricing.
(3) Personalized Recommendations (Khatwani & Chandak, 2016)	Provides analogous suggestions for destinations, hotels, or activities.	Demographic data, location data, previous travel history	Targeted phishing, identity theft, unwanted data sharing	Safe storage, opt-out option, clear privacy policies.
(4) Smart Itinerary Planning (Mrazovic et al., 2017)	Real time creates customized travel plans using data and user preferences.	Flight and hotel availability, weather, local programs	System hacking, manipulation in travel system	Multi-factor authentication, regular safety update.
(5) Automated Customer Support (Degtyarevaa et al., 2024)	AI chatbots and virtual assistants handle queries and bookings.	Conversation log, user account data	Chatbot Spoofing during the conversation, data leak	Safe API, Sessions Encryption, Acquired Chatbot Identification.
(6) Predictive Risk Management (Barboza et al., 2017)	Analyze potential disruption and suggest options.	Global news feed, transport data, weather forecast	Data tampering, false alert, misinformation	Reliable data source, blockchain verification, audit trails.

Source: Authors Own based on Degtyarevaa et al. (2024)

The table 01 shows that AI-powered travel intelligence system function and the types of data they use are included in potential cybersecurity risks, and the digital trust provides observation of how the future of tourism can be maintained in tourism.

5. DIGITAL TRUST AND ETHICS CONSIDERATIONS

Ai-operated tourist systems require a strong moral foundation for the installation of a digital trust. The function and recommendations of the AI algorithm suggest that transparency in decision-making promotes the user's confidence. However, algorithm bias can reduce fairness by eliminating discrimination based on flawed or unbalanced data. To address this, moral inspection and impartiality-comprehensive design must be preferred. Equally important for the user are the principles of consent, control, and ownership of data—individuals understand and manage and maintain rights on their personal information. Together, these moral columns protect users' autonomy and trust, which promote responsible and inclusive AI integration in the tourism sector. It is necessary to balance innovation with accountability for the sustainable development of forecast tourism platforms.

5.1 Transparency as a Building Block for Trust in AI Decision-Making

Transparency is a fundamental pillar in establishing confidence within AI-operated tourist systems. Future-staging technologies shape fast travel decisions—from destination recommendations to dynamic pricing and risk alerts—and users and stakeholders require clarity about how these decisions are made. In tourism, transparency is necessary for ensuring the safety of users' trust, as intelligent systems analyze individual preferences, financial data, and behavioral insights. Tourists need to understand how their data is collected, processed, and translated into recommendations or alerts. When there is a lack of interpretation of decisions, users can question the reliability of AI output, especially in high-dot conditions such as emergency alerts or financial transactions. This user can significantly reduce engagement and system adoption. Transparency should be extended beyond the interpretation of code-level. This includes the disclosure of data sources, algorithm logic, model limitations, and decision parameters in an understandable and accessible manner. Providing users with the ability to audit or trace—either through the revelations of the AI (XAI) interface or moral design—strengthens the digital trust. In addition, transparency plays an important role in the convenience of reducing algorithm bias and compliance with data governance standards such as GDPR, which emphasizes user rights for clarification. Therefore, the cultivation of transparent AI systems in future tourism not only promotes a moral regime but also enables durable and user-centric innovation. When passengers are informed and under the control of AI-mediaeval decisions, it promotes intensive confidence in the system and increases the alleged value of intelligent tourism platforms. Transparency, thus, is not only a technical feature but also a strategic and moral requirement for trusted AI in tourism (Koo et al., 2025).

5.2 Algorithmic Bias and Discrimination

As Artificial Intelligence (AI) systems are rapidly embedded in tourism platforms, the issue of algorithm bias and discrimination has emerged as an important concern.

These biases arise when AI models—trained on historical data—existing social, cultural, or demographic inequalities increase or increase. In terms of future tourism, such prejudices may appear in various ways, including improper prioritization of sites, uneven access to travel services, or reinforcement of stereotypes based on race, nationality, gender, or socio-economic status. Algorithm discrimination does not necessarily occur with malicious intentions but with data imbalance, poorly selected prioritization, or opaque algorithm design (Favaretto et al., 2019). For example, a tourism recommendation system can suggest high-end resorts to users from rich backgrounds, keeping people with persistent prior expense patterns, which can limit inclusion. Similarly, future analytics may overlook the risk levels associated with certain passenger demographics, resulting in unclear outputs that can impact travel decisions or safety alerts. Uncontrolled, these biases can destroy the digital trust and damage the reliability of AI-competent tourism platforms. Miscellaneous and representative datasets should be preferred during model development. In addition, interdisciplinary inspection—including sociologists, moralists, and tourism professionals—can help identify and reduce discriminatory patterns before deployment. Ultimately, ensuring algorithm fairness is not only a technical requirement but also a moral imperative. To be durable and moral for AI in tourism, the system must be designed to serve a diverse population without bias, promoting an inclusive and respectable digital environment for all passengers. (Favaretto et al., 2019)

6. SECURITY STRUCTURES AND TECHNICAL SOLUTIONS

AI-based tourism platforms depend on strong technical foundations. The data ensures encryption storage and privacy during transmission, while the access control mechanism regulates authorized use. Blockchain-based certification and verification enhance the trust by providing irreversible records, safe digital identification, and automatic smart contracts (Yallop et al., 2021). Adoption, in addition to this, of the "celebrity-by-design" principles promotes algorithm transparency and user awareness, while compliance with GDPR ensures valid and moral data handling. Together, these strategies create a safe, privacy-focused, and user-centric digital ecosystem. They protect sensitive user data, are able to make transparent decisions, and ensure regulatory alignment for permanent and reliable operation of future tourist systems. Integrating these layered safety solutions confirms the flexibility of overall digital trust and AI-operated travel platforms (Hesselman et al., 2020; Malgieri, 2016).

6.1 Data Encryption and Access Control Mechanism

In the developed ecosystem of AI-based tourism platforms, data encryption and access control mechanisms are fundamental to ensure the safety and integrity of user information. As a smart tourism system, the collection of vast quantities of sensitive data and processes—such as travelling credentials, biometric identities, and practical preferences—this information needs to be secured from unauthorised access, cybercasts, and data violations, which is paramount (Youssef et al., 2024). Data encryption serves as the primary protective measure. This involves transforming readable data into encoded formats, which can only be decrypted near the correct cryptographic keys by authorised parties. The end-to-end encryption process means that it is secured both in transit and when stored; hence, the chances of data interception or modification by ill-wishers are limited. In the case of tourism applications that rely on cloud-based or mobile-based computing systems, data encryption protocols like AES-256 or RSA with high-level encryptions will be needed to protect both the stable and dynamic data sets. (Greaney, 2012) Access control mechanisms, on the other hand, restrict access to the data by limiting who can access the data and how. A framework that is common and that guarantees that authorised personalities, systems, or applications have the capability to retrieve or manipulate sensitive information includes role-based access control (RBAC), discretionary access control (DAC), and compulsory access control (MAC). As an example, the system administrator of the booking system might have increased access, as compared to a hotel receptionist or any third-party seller, restricting weaknesses. Encryption and access control, when used together, produce a multi-layered safety strategy to augment the values of protecting data privateness, integrity, and accessibility, and cybersecurity. Additionally, the mechanisms make it possible to observe such laws as general data protection regulation (GDPR), where the necessity to take high security measures is provided when processing personal information. With the integration of encryption and access control into the AI-driven tourism infrastructure, its developers and operators may contribute to the enhancement of trust and flexibility that may lead to a safer and more responsible digital travel environment.

6.2 Celebrity-by-Design and GDPR Compliance in Tourism Systems

In the development of AI-operated tourist platforms, the principle of "celebrity design" and GDPR compliance play an important role in building systems that are not only safe but also transparent, moral, and user-centric. Together, these approaches guide the creation of responsible digital ecosystems where privacy and privatization coexist. Celebrity-designed refers to a human-focused design philosophy that promotes transparency, explains the capacity within the AI system, and promotes user empowerment (Akhtar et al., 2024). The term implies that the AI system should "behave like a celebrity"—in the eyes of the public, open to investigation, and accountable for its decisions. Tourism applications include the construction of the interface where users can clearly understand why some recommendations are made, how their data is being used, and what the system follows in creating predictions. This openness helps to demolish the AI algorithm, leaving the perception of black-box decision-making and promoting digital trust. Completing this concept, General Data Protection Regulation (GDPR) compliance ensures that AI tourism platforms follow strict data security laws, especially for users within the European Union. The major GDPR principles include valid and transparent data processing, data mineralization, user consent, the right to access and eradicate data, and the obligation to inform in the position of data violations (Mitrou, 2018). For tourism systems that collect and analyses large amounts of personal and practical data, GDPR compliance is not only a legal requirement but also a strategic commitment for data morality (Sharma, 2019). Integrating Celebrity-Dysine Principles with GDPR compliance enhances the user trust, legal accountability, and moral rule. Tourism platforms that prefer transparency and privacy from the design phase are better equipped to meet the user's expectations, regulatory standards, and global best practices—which are safe, inclusive, and coalition systems with the future of responsible AI in tourism (Domjan et al., 2021).

7. CASE STUDY / LANDSCAPE ANALYSIS

The AI in tourism has moved from theoretical promise to real-world application, showing practical benefits and revealing operational challenges. Since the future system is more advanced, it adds cyber threats, including data violations, adverse attacks, and manipulation risk. Effective response requires analysis of real-time danger, strong governance, and cooperation in areas. Major texts highlight the need for moral design, flexible cybersecurity infrastructure, and inclusive stakeholder engagement. Best practices now prefer transparency, user empowerment, and adaptive threat management. The underlining of the importance of balanced innovation with the development and practical application of the ongoing industry underlines the importance of balanced innovation with digital safety, eventually securing intelligent and guided development of tourism platforms with user traditions (Byelikova et al., 2024).

7.1 AI – Examples of Imagination or Real World

In tourism, Artificial Intelligence (AI) has long been conceived as a future innovation, which is often painted through the ideal concepts of robotic assistants, innocent privatization, and uninterrupted predictions (Abid, 2024). However, AI's contemporary deployment suggests a gradual change in reality from imagination, as real-world applications are rapidly integrated into tourism operations and passenger experiences. In the past, the role of AI in tourism was largely speculative, associated with science fiction or theoretical constructions, promising intelligent agents who were able to estimate the needs of every passenger. While this notion gave air to imagination and investment, it also created unrealistic expectations. Today, the AI system is actively affecting the travel plan, dynamic pricing, recommended engines, virtual assistants, facial identification for virtual assistants, and even the future-stating analysis for crisis management—assuming that AI is no longer a distant imagination but a functional reality. However, the practical implementation of AI reveals some limitations. Current systems depend a lot on data quality, reference relevance, and algorithm transparency, and they are often forced by infrastructure gaps, moral challenges, and user skepticism. For example, language barriers, cultural nuances, or biased training datasets can reduce the effectiveness of AI-based recommendations. These limitations highlight the difference between the ideological capacity of AI and its operational performance. Understanding AI in tourism thus requires a balanced perspective—recognizing its achievements and being important for its boundaries (Dredge & Gyimóthy, 2015). Technology is becoming real and advanced, but only when it is based on responsible design, where there is continued human monitoring and reference-incoleric use. Rather than a perfect fantasy, the AI is synonymous with a continued process of tourism—a process that is characterized by the progressive existence of innovative application, confidence building, and moral assimilation in determining its transformation capability within the actual.

7.2 Lessons and Best Exercises

Artificial Intelligence (AI) integration in the tourism system has provided priceless knowledge concerning the opportunities and drawbacks of digital transformation. The world tourism sector has adopted the AI-powered systems of privatisation, foresight, and automation; moreover, the lessons learned and the best practices are growing up to formalise the streamlined, secure, and customer-friendly travel universe of the future generation. Among the significant doctrines is the object that moral foresight needs to go hand in hand with technological innovation. Rapidly spreading AI can be used without compensation and put issues of data privacy, algorithm bias, and user neglect on the agenda (Kulveit et al., 2025). Moral-by-design theories, in such a way, should be incorporated into the development process itself, e.g., impartiality, accountability, and ability. This not only reduces risks but also promotes long-term user trust and system reliability. Another important lesson is the importance of flexible data infrastructure and cybersecurity readiness. The AI systems are only as strong as the data and network they work on. Many tourism organizations have learned, often through cyber phenomena, the requirement of strong data encryption and detecting the risk of real-time and casual planning. The best practices now include regular safety audits, penetration testing, employee training, and zero-trust security models. In addition, interdisciplinary cooperation has proved necessary. Effective AI implementation requires inputs from computer scientists, tourism professionals, moralists, legal experts, and user experience designers. Organizations promoting such cooperation are more likely to develop systems that are innovative and socially responsible. In the summary, the AI-tourism landscape provides significant lessons on balanced innovation with the AI-Parryn landscape responsibility. By institutionalizing these best practices, the tourism sector can manufacture secure, more inclusive, and forward-minded digital platforms.

8. NEW TRENDS IN SMART TOURISM SECURITY

The developed landscape of smart tourism is rapidly connected with advanced AI-operated technologies that increase the experiences of the future. However, pressure is required for a strong safety structure with increased dependence on data-intensive systems. Emerging trends recognize AI interpretation, ethical algorithmic design, and block-chain authentication to construct digital trusts. In addition, cross-sector cooperation between public institutions, private technical firms, and tourist organizations has been needed to address effectively the cybersecurity threats. Integrated prediction systems combining real-time crisis data, behavioral analysis, and travel preferences are setting new standards in passenger safety and service personalization. These trends collectively aim to balance innovation, moral rule, and future tourism among digital infrastructure.

8.1 AI-Explainable Depends on GUI is in Travel Applications

Artificial Intelligence has revolutionised the backend of future tourism applications, but its effectiveness also depends on whether users can interact with these systems through Graphical User Interfaces (GUIs). AI exploitation within the travel apps is a new trend to ensure that users can understand why some recommendations are made—the way to a travel route, hotel choice, or safety warning. By integrating the AI (XAI) model in the GUI design, these applications not only enhance the user trust but also meet the increasing regulatory demands for transparency in the decision-making algorithms (Reis et al., 2021). Explaining AI provides clarity on how inputs such as individual preferences, search history, environmental factors, or real-time geopolitical updates are weighed in providing personal recommendations. For example, flight booking users can be shown not only an alternative passage during the risk of an emerging season but also a visual justification—such as risk maps or predicted delays—generated by explanatory models. It adds a layer of cognitive belief and reduces dependence on opaque, black-box systems. In addition, inclusion of clear ability in the user interface helps address concerns related to algorithm bias, especially in diverse cultural contexts. In future tourism, where recommendations can affect safety and well-being, explain the capacity to empower users to make informed decisions and challenge flawed outputs. Importantly, GUI-Enhanced AI promotes the ability to promote inclusiveness by simplifying the complex AI output into spontaneous visual elements—charts, heatmaps, or traffic-light systems. From a cybersecurity point of view, transparency in AI-related suggestions discourages manipulation or misinformation, especially in adverse attacks where data can be spoiled to mislead the system. Developers are focused on integrating the human-in-loop system rapidly, where the user response also plays a role in withdrawing the model, making the ecosystem more flexible. In short, the A-explanation capacity in GUI design is no longer alternative; It is becoming a standard in moral, safe, and user-centric future tourism applications that prefer transparency and trust (Abid, 2024).

8.2 Cross-Sector Collaboration in the Cybersecurity Domain

AI—Cybersecurity challenges associated with the future tourism systems that run cannot be solved in isolation. Since the tourism ecosystem integrates data from various domains—transport, health, weather, finance, and law enforcement—cross-sector cooperation has emerged as an important trend to secure smart tourist platforms. Effective collaboration between public institutions, technology companies, tourism boards, cybersecurity experts, and international organizations can ensure that data protection and digital trusts are retained at every point of the travel price chain (Rashideh, 2020). Tourism platforms rely on rapid interconnected systems such as AI-competent booking engines, IOT-based smart housing, and real-time danger detection systems to process sensitive individual, biometric, and behavioral data. Any violation or manipulation can not only cause financial losses but can also cause risk to passenger safety and loss of reputation to destinations. A single weak link- Say, an unsafe third-party plugin or an irregular data-sharing—can compromise a compromised ecosystem. Therefore, cooperation between areas is necessary to ensure end-to-end data security. A successful model incorporates tourism authorities collaborating with national cybersecurity agencies to establish real-time danger intelligence sharing systems. This journey enables platforms to continuously respond to phishing, ransomware, or AI adverse attacks. Meanwhile, the International Tourism Organization can work with data protection bodies such as the GDPR task force or Asia-Pacific Privacy Officers so that data flows from across the border are both safe and obedient. Additionally, cross-sector partnership supports the development of a standardized ethical structure. For example, AI makers who are in collaboration with policy makers and tourism ethicists can develop open algorithms that will be culturally sensitive, non-profiling, and inclusive. Education also brings in AI ethics and trained cybersecurity experts, and hence the knowledge intervals get further increased. In summary, smart tourism safety is no longer the responsibility of a single actor. Its stability depends on coordinated, multi-field strategies that promote interoperability, rapid feedback capabilities, and a shared commitment for user privacy and digital trust.

8.3 Combining Systems for Prediction of Travel and Travel Crisis

In the modern era of future tourism, it has become necessary to fuse many intelligent systems to increase both travel planning and crisis reaction. Passengers now expect real-time, personal recommendations not only for destination and housing but also for safety, health, and dynamics (Obeng-Odoom, 2009). To meet this demand, the industry is rapidly connecting the AI model, geopolitical analysis, and crisis alert system to integrated travel intelligence platforms. These integrated systems attract different types of data sources—historical travel behavior, weather patterns, health alerts, social media spirit, and geopolitical development predict the disruption of travel or identify optimal travel routes. For example, the future models may estimate the airport congestion during the political unrest or flag routes exposed to climate-related hazards. By synthesizing input from health departments, meteorological agencies, and transport providers, these systems allow both users and providers to make adaptive travel decisions. Integration of such systems is particularly important in crisis conditions, including natural disasters, epidemics, or terrorist threats. AI-competent platforms can release passengers based on real-time travel advice, auto-reliable booking, and redirected risk profiles. Predictive Analytics not only ensures continuity of travel plans but can also reduce stress and nervousness among tourists by offering data-supported options and safety measures. From a cybersecurity angle, this interrelation demands rigorous protocol. As many platforms interact, it becomes important to ensure data encryption, authentication, and integrity. The blockchain-based verification system is being rapidly discovered to certify data inputs and preserve source reliability during crises. Additionally, federated learning systems are receiving traction, allowing the AI model to learn from user behavior without centralising sensitive data. The future of travel crisis management will be on this multi-script convergence of AI, cybersecurity, behavioral science, and disaster response. By combining future systems, the tourism industry not only enhances the features of the user but also makes flexibility against unexpected challenges, forcing a safe and more intelligent travel ecosystem.

9. CONCEPTUAL FRAMEWORK

Figure 1. AI-based travel intelligence systems for predictive tourism and cybersecurity solutions

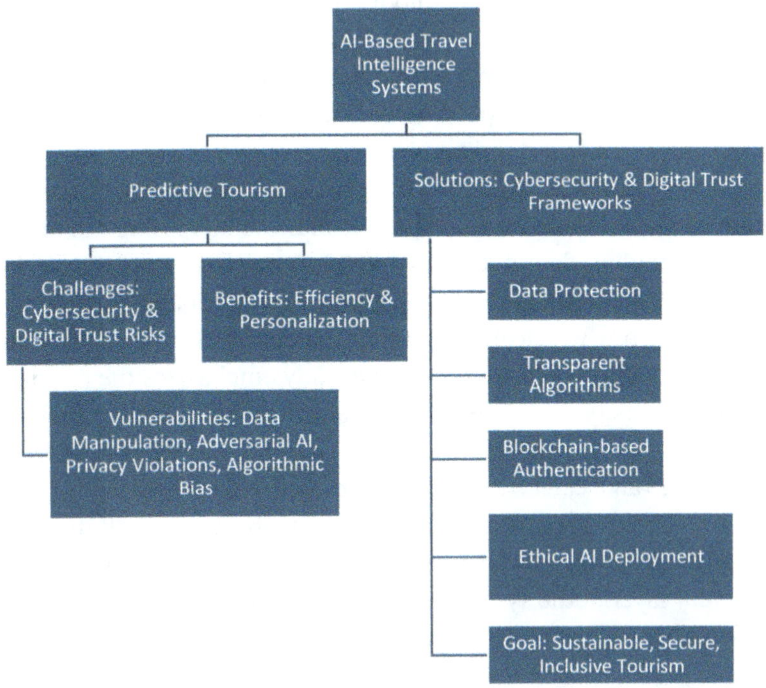

(Authors Compilation based on Reis et al., 2021)

The fig. 01 offers a clear ideological observation of the AI-based travel intelligence system, which is taken from our research on future tourism and cybersecurity. It emphasizes efficiency and privatization as a significant advantage by identifying future tourism as a main component. However, it also highlights real-world challenges, such as cybersecurity risk and digital trust risk, including data manipulation, unfavorable AI, privacy violations, and algorithm bias, which we discovered deeply. On the solution side, the diagram presents a cybersecurity and digital trust framework that focuses on data security, transparent algorithms, and blockchain-based certification. They are reinforced by moral AI fines, leading to durable, safe, and leading targets of inclusive tourism. As a final-year student engaged in AI and deeply engaged in tourism research, I find this model helpful to see how technological innovation should be combined with moral responsibility to ensure a safe and more reliable digital travel ecosystem in the future (Reis et al., 2021).

10. FINDINGS

Future tourism systems will integrate artificial intelligence. It becomes rapidly clear that AI-managed platforms—although exceptionally efficient—experience transformative possibilities and complex challenges. On the one hand, these intelligent systems are able to noticeably predict passenger behavior, accommodate the dynamic journey program, and personalize experiences based on real-time data such as places, weather, and political alerts. This level of accountability not only increases operating efficiency but also increases the satisfaction of the user to an unprecedented degree. However, findings also indicate increasing vulnerability for cyber hazards, including data poisoning, adverse attacks, and privacy violations, which can severely weaken the user's trust. Particularly related opaque, black-box algorithm is frequent use, which often lacks transparency and fairness, possibly except for marginalized user groups. In addition, the study emphasizes the requirement of pressure for moral safety measures—like clear AI models, consent-powered data governance, and inclusive system design. The chapter finds the role of blockchain, federated learning, and celebrity-by-design principles particularly promising in ensuring both technical strength and moral accountability. Overall, these findings suggest that while AI is a powerful promoter of smart tourism, its permanent future depends on every layer of the system, digital trust, human monitoring, and embedding moral integrity.

11. RECOMMENDATIONS

In the light of the developing digital landscape of future tourism, actionable recommendations are required to guide both tourism startups and cybersecurity physicians, which is towards the manufacture of flexible, reliable AI-based travel platforms (Sanjeev et al., 2024). For startups entering tourism technology locations, policy-oriented guidance is important. Governments and industry bodies should offer a regulatory sandbox where innovations can be tested in a controlled environment, which helps entrepreneurs to balance the balance with safety. Startups should be encouraged by moral AI principles—such as fairness, accountability, and transparency—in their design structure. Policies that encourage data minimalization, inclusive design, and open-source innovation can promote responsible development by protecting rights (Kibriya et al., 2024). In addition, cooperation with tourism boards and local governments must be formalized to ensure that digital products align with cultural, legal, and socio-economic standards. On the cybersecurity front, the best practices for AI-based tourist platforms should develop beyond standard firewall and encryption. These platforms handle the huge dataset associated with individual, biometric, and behavioral information, making them the major goals for adverse attacks, deepfakes, and algorithm manipulation. Thus, an active cybersecurity currency is required—one that includes multilevel safety architecture, continuous vulnerability assessment, and entry tests (Crawford, 2021). The AI clarification tool must be integrated into the user interface to demolish algorithm decisions to strengthen the user trust. In addition, zero-trust network frameworks, blockchain-based certification protocols, and federated learning techniques can greatly improve both data protection and system flexibility. Cybersecurity protocols should include a rapid event response system and clear privacy policies that educate users on data usage and their rights (Sargiotis, 2024). Tourism tech companies should promote a security culture by training developers and employees on the current danger landscape and compliance obligations. International cooperation is also important—cybersecurity norms across borders will ensure differences and collective defense against standard threats. Together, these policy and cybersecurity recommendations aim to balance innovation with moral governance and digital security, which is a more durable and reliable smart tourist ecosystem.

12. CONCLUSION

The discovery of the AI-based travel intelligence systems reveals an important intersection between innovation, cybersecurity, and digital trust in the rapidly developing domains of future tourism. One of the major points of this chapter is that artificial intelligence, while offering unprecedented efficiency in individual services, also introduces complex risks, including algorithms, data secrecy violations, and cyber vulnerability. Smart travel platforms, while offering a huge dataset and future-stolen model to estimate the passenger needs and customize experiences, yet without strong data security mechanisms and transparent governance, the user trust is easily compromised. This confirms the central argument of the chapter: innovation should go hand in hand, and digital trust is not optional—it is fundamental. Since tourism technologies are more predictive and connected, it becomes important to install a safe digital ecosystem that balances performance with moral responsibility.

This capacity to articulate the chapter on AI proves that the user-centered design and more inclusive policy frameworks that balance both tech advancement and the rights of the users are necessary. In addition, the next tourism relies on robust and flexible cybersecurity that is monitored, dynamic, and open. By implementing tools including blockchain, federated learning, and real-time Threat monitoring, the online travel platforms will not only advance their personalization applications but also be capable of achieving a higher level of safety of sensitive user information. Tourism technology startups should also have additional channels channelled by policy guiding policy, inter-sector collaboration, and constant security-related advancement. The government, schools, and companies should collaborate to establish worldwide standards, comply with cybersecurity training, and develop AI in an ethical way to cater to local and global travel requirements. Lastly, the future of tourist tourism is not merely a technological innovation, but it is a paradigm shift in how people order, experience, and feel about tourism. The future success of the region depends on cybersecurity and moral AI practices in tourism innovation, ensuring that the digital travel system remains safe, inclusive, and flexible for all stakeholders.

13. FUTURE STUDY

As the AI-operated tourist systems develop, future research must go beyond current technical applications to focus on systemic, moral, and regulatory dimensions that will shape the next stage of smart tourism. A major field for future studies is the development of a consistent AI (XAI) model, especially for tourism applications. While AI currently enhances privatization and prediction, the black-box nature of many algorithms limits the understanding of the user and increases the concerns of trust (Akhter, Jahan, et al., 2025; Akhter, Miah, et al., 2025). Researchers should check user-friendly interface designs that visually communicate how decisions are made, especially during important scenarios such as health emergencies or safety alerts (Yu et al., 2024). Additionally, interdisciplinary studies are required to find out how algorithm bias can be identified, measured, and reduced in tourism platforms, especially in multicultural and economically diverse contexts. Since tourism data flows rapidly across borders, future research should also check the international data governance model and propose integrated standards for data sharing, user consent, and platform accountability (Lomas, 2020). Emerging technologies such as federated learning—which allow the AI system to learn from the user behavior without centralizing the data—should be investigated more deeply for the promising routes for the protection-protection innovation. In addition, the travel in the infrastructure can increase the integration of the blockchain verification mechanism in the infrastructure, identity conservation, and transaction transparency, which is an important area for empirical research and pilot implementation. Cyber security will remain a significant concern; therefore, future studies should evaluate the effectiveness of multi-level security models against dynamic cyber hazards in real-time travel environments. Finally, as the AI is deeply inherent in the tourism scheme, scholars should find out the social and psychological effects of machine-based travel decisions on user autonomy, satisfaction, and cultural experiences (Hospitality *and Tourism Information Technology*, 2021). This includes long-term impact studies that assess how digital trust develops among passengers and how technical arbitration re-presents traditional assumptions of exploration and authenticity. In summary, future research should embrace a multidisciplinary attitude—teaching technology, morality, design, policy, and user psychology—to direct the development of safe, inclusive, and transparent AI-operated tourism systems. Finally, as the AI is deeply inherent in the tourism scheme, scholars should find out the social and psychological effects of machine-based travel decisions on user autonomy, satisfaction, and cultural experiences. This includes long-term impact studies that assess how digital trust develops among passengers and how technical arbitration re-presents traditional assumptions of exploration and authenticity. In summary, future research should embrace a multidisciplinary attitude—teaching technology, morality, design, policy, and user psychology—to direct the development of safe, inclusive, and transparent AI-operated tourism systems (Reis et al., 2021).

REFERENCES

Abid, H. Syed Far. (2024). *Utilizing AI and Smart Technology to Improve Sustainability in Entrepreneurship*. IGI Global.

Akhtar, M. A. K., Kumar, M., & Nayyar, A. (2024). The Role of Human-Centered Design in Developing Explainable AI. In Akhtar, M. A. K., Kumar, M., & Nayyar, A. (Eds.), *Towards Ethical and Socially Responsible Explainable AI: Challenges and Opportunities* (pp. 99–126). Springer Nature Switzerland., DOI: 10.1007/978-3-031-66489-2_4

Akhter, Md. S., Jahan, I., Tasnim, M., Miah, M. S., & Karim, A. J. M. S. (2025). AI-Driven Collaborative Robotics in Agriculture: Optimizing Soil and Crop Yield. In K. K. Reddy C., B. Saju, A. Hulus, T. Sibalija, & H. Nakouri (Eds.), *Advances in Computational Intelligence and Robotics* (pp. 57–88). IGI Global Scientific Publishing. DOI: 10.4018/979-8-3373-4207-8.ch003

Akhter, Md. S., Miah, M. S., Rahman, H., Rahman, S. M. M., Karim, A. J. M. S., Ratul, S. I., & Rahman, M. A. (2025). Agricultural Applications of Chalcogenide-Based Materials: Toward Sustainable, Smart, and Nutrient-Efficient Farming. In K. Kannan & V. Tari (Eds.), *Chalcogenide-Based Materials for Optoelectronics, Energy, and Sustainability* (pp. 409–438). IGI Global Scientific Publishing. DOI: 10.4018/979-8-3373-3962-7.ch016

Albattat, A., Azman, N., & Valeri, M. (Eds.). (2025). *Tracking tourism patterns and improving travel experiences with innovative technologies*. IGI Global.

Barboza, F., Kimura, H., & Altman, E. (2017). Machine learning models and bankruptcy prediction. *Expert Systems with Applications*, *83*, 405–417. DOI: 10.1016/j.eswa.2017.04.006

Brundage, M., Avin, S., Clark, J., Toner, H., Eckersley, P., Garfinkel, B., Dafoe, A., Scharre, P., Zeitzoff, T., Filar, B., Anderson, H., Roff, H., Allen, G. C., Steinhardt, J., & Flynn, C. hÉigeartaigh, S. Ó., Beard, S. J., Belfield, H., Farquhar, S., … Amodei, D. (2024). *The Malicious Use of Artificial Intelligence: Forecasting, Prevention, and Mitigation* (No. arXiv:1802.07228). arXiv. https://doi.org//arXiv.1802.07228DOI: 10.48550

Byelikova, M., Bezkhlibna, A., Polyezhayev, Y., Zaytseva, V., & Pukhalska, H. (2024). Informational and Digital Business Security in Tourism as a Component of the Coastal Region Competitiveness. In Semenov, A., Yepifanova, I., & Kajanová, J. (Eds.), *Data-Centric Business and Applications: Modern Trends in Financial and Innovation Data Processes 2023* (Vol. 1, pp. 117–145). Springer Nature Switzerland., DOI: 10.1007/978-3-031-54012-7_6

Chung, Y.-W., Khaki, B., Li, T., Chu, C., & Gadh, R. (2019). Ensemble machine learning-based algorithm for electric vehicle user behavior prediction. *Applied Energy, 254,* 113732. DOI: 10.1016/j.apenergy.2019.113732

Crawford, K. (2021). *The Atlas of AI: Power, Politics, and the Planetary Costs of Artificial Intelligence.* Yale University Press.

Degtyarevaa, K., Tynchenko, V., Tynchenko, V., Tynchenko, V., Panfilova, T., & Kukartseva, S. (2024). Automated System for Accounting of Customers and Orders. *2024 23rd International Symposium INFOTEH-JAHORINA (INFOTEH),* 1–4. DOI: 10.1109/INFOTEH60418.2024.10496048

Deldjoo, Y., Noia, T. D., & Merra, F. A. (2021). A Survey on Adversarial Recommender Systems: From Attack/Defense Strategies to Generative Adversarial Networks. *ACM Comput. Surv., 54*(2), 35:1-35:38. DOI: 10.1145/3439729

Domjan, P., Serkin, G., Thomas, B., & Toshack, J. (2021). *Chain Reaction: How Blockchain Will Transform the Developing World.* Springer Nature. DOI: 10.1007/978-3-030-51784-7

Dredge, D., & Gyimóthy, S. (2015). The collaborative economy and tourism: Critical perspectives, questionable claims and silenced voices. *Tourism Recreation Research, 40*(3), 286–302. DOI: 10.1080/02508281.2015.1086076

Favaretto, M., De Clercq, E., & Elger, B. S. (2019). Big Data and discrimination: Perils, promises and solutions. A systematic review. *Journal of Big Data, 6*(1), 12. DOI: 10.1186/s40537-019-0177-4

Gajdošík, T., & Marciš, M. (2019). Artificial Intelligence Tools for Smart Tourism Development. In Silhavy, R. (Ed.), *Artificial Intelligence Methods in Intelligent Algorithms* (pp. 392–402). Springer International Publishing., DOI: 10.1007/978-3-030-19810-7_39

Greaney, C. (2012). *Location Aware Apps for Tourism.* Lulu.com.

Gretzel, U., Sigala, M., Xiang, Z., & Koo, C. (2015). Smart tourism: Foundations and developments. *Electronic Markets, 25*(3), 179–188. DOI: 10.1007/s12525-015-0196-8

Guo, Q., Mu, L., & Lou, S. (2024). Revolutionizing travel experiences: An in-depth analysis of intelligent booking systems and behavioral patterns. *Intelligent Decision Technologies*, *18*(2), 1477–1494. DOI: 10.3233/IDT-230625

He, K., Kim, D. D., & Asghar, M. R. (2023). Adversarial Machine Learning for Network Intrusion Detection Systems: A Comprehensive Survey. *IEEE Communications Surveys and Tutorials*, *25*(1), 538–566. DOI: 10.1109/COMST.2022.3233793

Hemmati, A., Raoufi, P., & Rahmani, A. M. (2024). Edge artificial intelligence for big data: A systematic review. *Neural Computing & Applications*, *36*(19), 11461–11494. DOI: 10.1007/s00521-024-09723-w

Hesselman, C., Grosso, P., Holz, R., Kuipers, F., Xue, J. H., Jonker, M., de Ruiter, J., Sperotto, A., van Rijswijk-Deij, R., Moura, G. C. M., Pras, A., & de Laat, C. (2020). A Responsible Internet to Increase Trust in the Digital World. *Journal of Network and Systems Management*, *28*(4), 882–922. DOI: 10.1007/s10922-020-09564-7

Hospitality and Tourism Information Technology. (2021). USF M3 Publishing, LLC. DOI: 10.5038/9781732127593

Jeetesh, K., Manpreet, A., & Gül, E. B. (2024). *Exploring the Use of Metaverse in Business and Education*. IGI Global.

Kamyab, F., & Bahrami, S. (2016). Efficient operation of energy hubs in time-of-use and dynamic pricing electricity markets. *Energy*, *106*, 343–355. DOI: 10.1016/j.energy.2016.03.074

Khan, S. Z., Mohsin, M., & Iqbal, W. (2021). On GPS spoofing of aerial platforms: A review of threats, challenges, methodologies, and future research directions. *PeerJ. Computer Science*, *7*, e507. DOI: 10.7717/peerj-cs.507 PMID: 34013033

Khatwani, S., & Chandak, M. B. (2016). Building Personalized and Non Personalized recommendation systems. *2016 International Conference on Automatic Control and Dynamic Optimization Techniques (ICACDOT)*, 623–628. DOI: 10.1109/ICACDOT.2016.7877661

Kibriya, H., Khan, W. Z., Siddiqa, A., & Khan, M. K. (2024). Privacy issues in Large Language Models: A survey. *Computers & Electrical Engineering*, *120*, 109698. DOI: 10.1016/j.compeleceng.2024.109698

Knani, M., Echchakoui, S., & Ladhari, R. (2022). Artificial intelligence in tourism and hospitality: Bibliometric analysis and research agenda. *International Journal of Hospitality Management*, *107*, 103317. DOI: 10.1016/j.ijhm.2022.103317

Koo, I., Zaman, U., Ha, H., & Nawaz, S. (2025). Assessing the interplay of trust dynamics, personalization, ethical AI practices, and tourist behavior in the adoption of AI-driven smart tourism technologies. *Journal of Open Innovation, 11*(1), 100455. DOI: 10.1016/j.joitmc.2024.100455

Kulveit, J., Douglas, R., Ammann, N., Turan, D., Krueger, D., & Duvenaud, D. (2025). *Gradual Disempowerment: Systemic Existential Risks from Incremental AI Development* (No. arXiv:2501.16946). arXiv. https://doi.org//arXiv.2501.16946DOI: 10.48550

Larsson, S., Jensen-Urstad, A., & Heintz, F. (2021). Notified but Unaware: Third-Party Tracking Online. *Critical Analysis of Law: An International & Interdisciplinary Law Review*, *8*(1), 101–120. DOI: 10.33137/cal.v8i1.36282

Lomas, E. (2020). Information Governance and Cybersecurity: Framework for Securing and Managing Information Effectively and Ethically. In *Cybersecurity for Information Professionals*. Auerbach Publications. DOI: 10.1201/9781003042235-6

Malgieri, G. (2016). *Property and (Intellectual) Ownership of Consumers' Information: A New Taxonomy for Personal Data* (SSRN Scholarly Paper No. 2916058). Social Science Research Network. https://papers.ssrn.com/abstract=2916058 DOI: 10.37307/j.2196-9817.2016.04.05

McStay, A. (2020). Emotional AI, soft biometrics and the surveillance of emotional life: An unusual consensus on privacy. *Big Data & Society*, *7*(1), 2053951720904386. DOI: 10.1177/2053951720904386

Mitrou, L. (2018). *Data Protection, Artificial Intelligence and Cognitive Services: Is the General Data Protection Regulation (GDPR) 'Artificial Intelligence-Proof'?* (SSRN Scholarly Paper No. 3386914). Social Science Research Network. DOI: 10.2139/ssrn.3386914

Mrazovic, P., Larriba-Pey, J. L., & Matskin, M. (2017). Improving Mobility in Smart Cities with Intelligent Tourist Trip Planning. *2017 IEEE 41st Annual Computer Software and Applications Conference (COMPSAC), 1*, 897–907. DOI: 10.1109/COMPSAC.2017.144

Nguyen, T. T., Quoc Viet hung, N., Nguyen, T. T., Huynh, T. T., Nguyen, T. T., Weidlich, M., & Yin, H. (2024). Manipulating Recommender Systems: A Survey of Poisoning Attacks and Countermeasures. *ACM Comput. Surv., 57*(1), 3:1-3:39. DOI: 10.1145/3677328

Obeng-Odoom, F. (2009). The Future of our Cities. *Cities (London, England)*, *26*(1), 49–53. DOI: 10.1016/j.cities.2008.11.001

Pan, B., & Yang, Y. (2016). Monitoring and Forecasting Tourist Activities with Big Data. In *Management Science in Hospitality and Tourism*. Apple Academic Press.

Pencarelli, T. (2020). The digital revolution in the travel and tourism industry. *Information Technology & Tourism*, *22*(3), 455–476. DOI: 10.1007/s40558-019-00160-3

Raleigh, C., Kishi, R., & Linke, A. (2023). Political instability patterns are obscured by conflict dataset scope conditions, sources, and coding choices. *Humanities & Social Sciences Communications*, *10*(1), 74. DOI: 10.1057/s41599-023-01559-4

Rashideh, W. (2020). Blockchain technology framework: Current and future perspectives for the tourism industry. *Tourism Management*, *80*, 104125. DOI: 10.1016/j.tourman.2020.104125

Reis, T., Bornschlegl, M. X., & Hemmje, M. L. (2021). AI2VIS4BigData: A Reference Model for AI-Based Big Data Analysis and Visualization. In Reis, T., Bornschlegl, M. X., Angelini, M., & Hemmje, M. L. (Eds.), *Advanced Visual Interfaces. Supporting Artificial Intelligence and Big Data Applications* (pp. 1–18). Springer International Publishing., DOI: 10.1007/978-3-030-68007-7_1

Sanjeev, K., & Badruddoza, T. Mohammad, & Ana, P. (2024). *Utilizing Smart Technology and AI in Hybrid Tourism and Hospitality*. IGI Global.

Sargiotis, D. (2024). Data Security and Privacy: Protecting Sensitive Information. In Sargiotis, D. (Ed.), *Data Governance: A Guide* (pp. 217–245). Springer Nature Switzerland., DOI: 10.1007/978-3-031-67268-2_6

Serban, A. C., Ordéñez, P., Alkhaldi, A., & Lytras, M. D. (Eds.). (2025). *Innovation management for a resilient digital economy*. IGI Global., DOI: 10.4018/979-8-3693-8357-5

Sharma, S. (2019). *Data Privacy and GDPR Handbook*. John Wiley & Sons. DOI: 10.1002/9781119594307

Shrestha, L., Balogun, H., & Khan, S. (2025). AI-Driven Phishing: Techniques, Threats, and Defence Strategies. In Jahankhani, H., & Issac, B. (Eds.), *Cybersecurity and Human Capabilities Through Symbiotic Artificial Intelligence* (pp. 121–143). Springer Nature Switzerland., DOI: 10.1007/978-3-031-82031-1_7

Tripathi, M., & Mukhopadhyay, A. (2020). Financial Loss due to a Data Privacy Breach: An Empirical Analysis. *Journal of Organizational Computing and Electronic Commerce*, *30*(4), 381–400. DOI: 10.1080/10919392.2020.1818521

Wongchestha, N., Karim, F. B., & Wongmahesak, K. (Eds.). (2025). *Practical strategies and case studies for online marketing 6.0*. IGI Global Scientific Publishing., DOI: 10.4018/979-8-3373-2058-8

Yallop, A. C., Gică, O. A., Moisescu, O. I., Coro , M. M., & Séraphin, H. (2021). The digital traveller: Implications for data ethics and data governance in tourism and hospitality. *Journal of Consumer Marketing*, *40*(2), 155–170. DOI: 10.1108/JCM-12-2020-4278

Yang, Z., Yin, M., Xu, J., & Lin, W. (2019). Spatial evolution model of tourist destinations based on complex adaptive system theory: A case study of Southern Anhui, China. *Journal of Geographical Sciences*, *29*(8), 1411–1434. DOI: 10.1007/s11442-019-1669-z

Youssef, A. B., Dutta, P. K., Doshi, R., & Sajnani, M. (2024). *AI, Blockchain, and Metaverse in Hospitality and Tourism Industry 4.0: Case Studies and Analysis*. CRC Press. DOI: 10.1201/9781032706474

Yu, J., Shvetsov, A. V., & Hamood Alsamhi, S. (2024). Leveraging Machine Learning for Cybersecurity Resilience in Industry 4.0: Challenges and Future Directions. *IEEE Access : Practical Innovations, Open Solutions*, *12*, 159579–159596. DOI: 10.1109/ACCESS.2024.3482987

Chapter 2

Cyber Security and Sustainable Tourism Goals

Arif Rana
http://orcid.org/0000-0002-0602-1182
International University of Business Agriculture and Technology, Bangladesh

Md. Afzal Hossain
http://orcid.org/0000-0001-7902-0642
International University of Business Agriculture and Technology, Bangladesh

Wasef Rana
Xi'Jiaotong University, China

Shafiqul Islam
International University of Business Agriculture and Technology, Bangladesh

ABSTRACT

Cybersecurity and sustainable tourism are inseparable as they lead to the achievement of the United Nations Sustainable Development Goals (SDGs). In light of cyber threats that have been ramping up along with the digital transformation related risks of the tourism market. The chapter explores the concept of cybersecurity as a key element that can safeguard digital tourism infrastructure, enforce data privacy, and improve the level of stakeholder trust. It summarizes various theoretical voices, appraises the existing studies, and presents a framework that can balance cybersecurity and sustainable tourism objectives in terms of implementation. The major challenges like cyberattacks focused on tourism platforms, breaches in the data of the travelers, and incompetent regulations are examined. The paper provides

DOI: 10.4018/979-8-2600-1850-7.ch002

practical methods that can be employed to enhance cybersecurity resilience within tourism, in an effort to support SDGs such as decent work and economic growth (SDG 8), industry innovation (SDG 9) and sustainable urban development (SDG 11).

INTRODUCTION

Innovations of AI, Big Data Analytics, IoT and Blockchain in the tourism sector have transformed the experience of traveling tremendously and have brought the benefits of easy booking experiences, smart destinations and personalized services. This change can also be called Tourism 4.0, which is an extensive reconstruction of the traveling experience with the aim to ensure customized, transparent, and unforgettable services to tourists (Najlaoui & Ammari, 2024). The technological applications of smart technologies helped to introduce smart tourism ecosystems, improving resource management rates, competitiveness and sustainability. With such technologies, travelers can be provided with real-time availability and information, automated customer service and personalized itineraries, therefore, enhancing the degree of self-organization among tourists (Erdem & 5eker, 2022). Nevertheless, the digital transition can also create serious cybersecurity issues, where the entire tourism industry depends increasingly on digital mediums of making reservations, paying bills, and communicating with customers (Prajapat & R, 2024). The threat of data inflations, ransomware, phishing frauds, and identity thefts requires effective cybersecurity to achieve sustainability in the tourism development (Bekele & Raj, 2024). However, the platform of digital change still presents extraordinary opportunities of innovation and development in the sphere of tourism as the industry begins to adjust to the changing customer preferences and sustainability of the technology (Oppokkhonov, 2023).

The increase in cyber events in the tourism industry is an enormous risk to both the economy and consumer trust and this has been witnessed to a great extent with the 2018 breach of information involving the Marriott International guest database that collected information relating to almost 500 million visitors (Harit et al., 2024). Malware and phishing are only a few types of cyberattacks that result in financial losses to businesses and, in addition to that, disrupt operations and affect tourism-dependent economies in small jurisdiction (Tariq, 2024). The sustainable development goals (SDGs) of the United Nations highlight that the trend toward sustainable economic growth should be met by means of various sources, and tourism plays a significant role in the economy of the developing countries (Mairesse, 2022). Nevertheless, the growing exposure of the industry to the risk of cyber threats is a direct adversary of the SDG 8 (Decent Work and Economic Growth), and SDG 9 (Industry, innovation and Infrastructure) (Paraskevas, 2020). Tourism needs a holistic, risk-based approach to cybersecurity that will reduce these risks and make the tourism industry sustainable in the long run (Paraskevas, n.d.).

This chapter explores how secure infrastructures in cybersecurity are critical in enabling sustainable tourism based on some key areas. First, they secure digital assets through the protection of sensitive customer data and transactions in finances that are even more at risk given the use of recent technologies in the sphere (Paraskevas, 2020) (Mairesse, 2022). To prevent legal consequences and retain customer loyalty, compliance with data protection laws, including the GDPR and the CCPA is essential because the financial consequences of non-compliance can be serious (Talukder et al., 2024). Moreover, the implementation of secure innovation, such as the use of biometric authentication, supports organizational efficiency, reduces risks due to the procedures, and supports operation sustainability ("Strengthening sustainable tourism and ac...", 2023). Finally, to promote business resilience, it is necessary to address proactive threat monitoring and incident response procedures, as well as provide employees with cybersecurity training to reduce the number of encountered disruptions and increase the overall stability of the sector (Talukder et al., 2024).

Incorporating cybersecurity into tourism strategies is imperative to building the resilience of the operations and sustaining the growth amidst the changing digital threats. Increased interaction with information and communication technologies (ICT), alongside the convergence of disruptive technologies, has led to paradigm shifts in the tourism industry, which prompt the need to implement a comprehensive framework of cybersecurity to safeguard the stakeholders against vulnerabilities that come alongside such developments (Fennell, 2021) (Gössling & Gössling, 2021). Additionally, it is evident that sustainability and resilience are connected in tourism since it is mandatory to adopt a holistic strategy to encompass cybersecurity as an essential element of destination management, guaranteeing that the community can recover internships, without deteriorating economically and socially (Espiner et al., 2017). A holistic approach that evaluates the vulnerability and enhances resilience can help the stakeholders better handle the complexities concerning the cyber threat environment that eventually leads to the achievement of sustainable development goals in the tourism industry (Gössling, 2017) (Calgaro et al., 2014).

OBJECTIVES

This chapter seeks to discuss the nexus between sustainability and cybersecurity in the context of the Sustainable Development Goals (SDGs). Cybersecurity and sustainable tourism are two closely related topics due to the fast-paced process of digitalizing the tourist destination and industry, bringing them multiple efficiency-enhancing benefits and the necessity of implementing cyber security to protect the sustainability endeavors in the tourist industry and destination. Considering the active role of cybersecurity in sustainable tourism as an effective means of ensuring sustainability of tourism is in line with the Sustainable Development Goals (SDGs), which seek to promote environmentally friendly, economically viable and socially sustainable tourism by implementing a multidimensional solution to the challenges in the tourism system (Hall, 2019) (Boluk et al., 2017).

The specific objectives of this chapter are:

1. Examine the Relationship Between Cybersecurity and Sustainable Tourism in the Context of SDGs

With the growing awareness on the importance of cybersecurity in the achievement of sustainable tourism: interested not only by the United Nations Sustainable Development Goals (SDGs) of Goal 9, Goal 11 and Goal 16 that focus on resilient infrastructure and safe online and digital environments. Cyber threats threaten the operations of tourism through data breaches, ransomware, and other forms that can significantly deter tourism by compromising the trust of the tourists and moreover undermine the sustainability of touristic destinations, thus discouraging people to visit the destination (Lara-Morales & Clarke, 2022).

2. Analyze Existing Theoretical Perspectives on Cybersecurity in Tourism

The role of cybersecurity in tourism is becoming more relevant with digital transformation in the industry as it is probable that the level of certain types of cyber threats affecting tourism may have significant implications on the behavior of tourists and their trust. High-profile data breach events have alerted at the risks of the cyber ecosystems in tourism, and tourism requires a shift of the fragmented, compliance-based approaches to the comprehensive risk-based approaches with cybersecurity as the main business function (Mairesse, 2022) (Paraskevas, 2020.

3. Review Empirical Studies on Cyber Threats Affecting Tourism Sustainability

Tourism sector and the hospitality industry in specific are particularly at risk of cyber risks with examples such as the Marriott breach and other travel booking related scammers. Malware, phishing and insider threats are common problems and they expose sensitive information relating to customers and sensitive financial details (Tariq, 2024).

4. Propose Policy and Technological Solutions to Mitigate Cyber Risks in Tourism

In the backdrop of ever sophisticated cyber threats, tourism business and policymakers need to adopt multi-layered cybersecurity efforts, which include adoption of advanced technologies and hands on regulatory frameworks. It is also imperative to encrypt and use multi-factor authentication (MFA) as the primary security measures to prevent information leakages of sensitive data and achieve secure access to the systems to limit potential losses based on the financial transactions and customer data breach (Mairesse, 2022) (Paraskevas, 2020).

5. Develop a Conceptual Framework Integrating Cybersecurity with Tourism Sustainability

The suggested conceptual framework on how to bridge the gap between cybersecurity and sustainable tourism focuses on four aspects, including the protection of data and tourist privacy, cyber-resilient tourism infrastructure, consumer trust and digital ethics, and compliance and industry collaboration. With the travel industry progressively implementing emerging technologies, the industry is getting exposed to increased cyber risks, and this should not be approached with fragmented and compliance-centric strategies but rather a holistic risk-based approach where cybersecurity is central to a sustainable practice (Paraskevas, 2020).

THEORETICAL OVERVIEW

The theoretical foundation of this study integrates key concepts from sustainable tourism, cybersecurity, and digital trust to form a comprehensive analytical framework.

The UNWTO Sustainable Tourism Theory focuses more on the concepts of accepting environmental, social and economic factors when developing tourism and suggesting the smart usage of resources, which can reduce the effect of the environment degradation and improve the positive contribution to the construction of the local community (Sumariadhi, 2023). Digitalization in tourism should contribute to these sustainability aims to avoid contributing to the growth of overtourism, cultural commodification, etc. Both research demonstrates that moving toward low-carbon technologies and sustainable practices can dramatically decrease the tourism-induced carbon footprint and increase biodiversity with the possible rediction in carbon footprint by 40% and rise in the biodiversity indices by 25% (Wang, 2024). Beyond that, considerations of policy interventions and stakeholder cooperation are essential to achieve resilient tourism ecosystems because communities must play a key role in sustainable tourism development in places such as the island of Bali (Suta et al., 2021) (Streimikiene, 2023). Therefore, the convergence of digital technology and sustainability is essential in ensuring resilient tourism in the long run and community prosperity. To improve the cybersecurity framework of a digital tourism, integration of ISACA and NIST or ISO 27001 is critical in ensuring that digital tourism is enhanced and its systems more secure. The NIST framework takes a risk-based approach implying that it focuses on the security of sensitive traveler information given the vulnerability of newer technologies and the vastness of financial transactions in the tourism industry (Mairesse, 2022). On the other hand, ISO 27001 offers a well-organized approach to the management of information security, indicating best practices that can help reduce risk to a minimum (Roy, 2020). Research implies that numerous companies have already used a disjointed and checklist-oriented approach to cybersecurity, thus resulted in substantial breaches and the corruptions of images(Paraskevas, 2020). Incorporating these frameworks, the entities in the tourism industry will be able to apply the strong practices like data encryption, creating incident response plans, and partnering with other companies, thus strengthening their resiliency and enabling the sustainable growth in the highly digitalizing world (Ghaderi et al., 2024).

Digital Trust Theory, by Gefen et al. (2003), emphasizes the importance of perception of security, privacy and reliability in developing consumer responses within the digital environment, especially in the tourism industry. It is pointed out that aspects like navigation capabilities and perceived security can go a long way in increasing trustworthiness that boosts customer satisfaction and loyalty in tourism purchase online (Tia, 2014). Additionally, provided cybersecurity steps, such as encryption and multi-factor authentication have been demonstrated to build digital trust within the travel agencies, which strengthen customer engagement and customer satisfaction (El-Maksoud, 2024). The comparative loyalty to online booking systems explains that the effective security protocols and traditions of transparency are necessary among consumers to be able to build trust where gaps in security measures can jeopardize trust in the consumer (Himanshu et al., 2023). Therefore, it is essential to adopt transparent cybersecurity activities as a way of promoting trust and achieving a safe online landscape among tourists. Combined, these theories serve as the holistic framework of studying a sustainable, secure and trustworthy ecosystem in digital tourism. The study makes a contribution to the existing discourse as we find that there is an interrelation between the two considering their influence on the future of the industry.

LITERATURE REVIEW

Recent study highlights the serious interface of cyber security and tourism industry, discloses important vulnerabilities and regulatory issues and reiterates the circle of resilience. The increase in cyber threats including malware and phishing especially poses a risk to the tourism infrastructure as supported by researches on how the hospitality sector is highly dependent on digital systems that makes them own prime targets of cybercriminals (Harit et al., 2024). Moreover, even the regulatory framework is not the same everywhere, making the process of keeping up with the compliance and risk mitigation measures tedious, particularly in integrated industries, such as aviation and hospitality (Talukder et al., 2024). Strong signs of the new role of cybersecurity as an agent of destination resilience can be traced, with frameworks promoting robust incident response plans, encryption of data, and the involvement of stakeholders to boost resilience against cyber threats(Ghaderi et al., 2024). Such a holistic strategy is a necessary practice in relation to data security and subsequent confidence to the company of the customer in the tourism industry (Rivera-Lopez, 2023).

Table 1. Literature Review - Cybersecurity in Tourism

Author(s) & Year	Title of Study	Research Objective/ Purpose	Methodology	Key Findings
Harit et al. (2024)	Exploring the Growing Threat of Cyber Risks and Vulnerabilities in the Hospitality Industry.	Examine cybersecurity vulnerabilities in the hospitality sector due to digital reliance.	Case study (2021 ransomware attack on a major hotel chain).	Hospitality's heavy reliance on digital systems makes it a prime target for ransomware; lack of encryption/MFA increases risks.
Desai & R (2024)	Unveiling the Depths of Phishing: Understanding Tactics, Impacts, and Countermeasures.	Analyze phishing threats in online travel agencies (OTAs).	Quantitative (40%+ phishing incidents in OTAs; seasonal correlation).	Phishing attacks peak during booking seasons; fake confirmations and fraudulent emails are common.
Ghaderi et al. (2024)	Cybersecurity and smart tourist destinations resilience.	Assess cybersecurity as a pillar of destination resilience.	Qualitative (case studies: Iceland, Singapore, CTCI initiative).	Proactive audits, threat-sharing partnerships, and staff training enhance cyber-resilience in tourism.
Paraskevas (2020)	*Cybersecurity in Travel and Tourism: A Risk-Based Approach.*	Evaluate cybersecurity gaps in hospitality digital systems.	Literature review + case analysis.	Lag in adopting encryption/MFA; AI-driven scams (e.g., deepfakes) are emerging threats.
Talukder et al. (2024)	Impact of Cybersecurity in the Aviation, Tourism, and Hospitality Industries.	Examine regulatory inconsistencies in tourism cybersecuri- ty.	Comparative analysis (regional regulations, e.g., GDPR vs. ASEAN).	Fragmented regulations create vulnerabilities; GDPR influences Southeast Asia but disparities persist.
Rivera-López (2023)	Resilience in Tourism: A bibliometric analysis of trends and perspectives in research.	Propose adaptive security models for tourism ecosystems.	Conceptual framework + literature synthesis.	Overly strict security harms user experience; advocates for user-centric, adaptive models.
Chowbe & Bhosale (2024)	Addressing the Legal Quagmire of Jurisdiction in Cyberspace.	Analyze global cyberspace governance gaps in tourism.	Policy analysis + case studies (Latin America, Africa).	Unregulated cyberspace enables cross-border cybercrimes; proposes layered governance (global + regional).

continued on following page

Table 1. Continued

Author(s) & Year	Title of Study	Research Objective/ Purpose	Methodology	Key Findings
Masseno & Santos (2018)	Smart tourism destinations privacy risks on data protection.	Assess APEC Privacy Framework's applicability to hospitality.	Policy gap analysis.	Suggests extending APEC framework to cover hospitality for better international cooperation.
Lawal (2025)	Cybersecurity governance: Strengthening policy frameworks to address global cybercrime and data privacy challen ges.	Study cybersecurity compliance in SMEs in tourism-dependent regions.	Survey (SMEs in Africa/Latin America).	Cost and complexity hinder SME compliance; many lack basic cybersecurity measures.
Reda & M'Bark (2023)	Fostering Destination Resilience: A Conceptual Framework Linking Sustainable Tourism and Tourism Threats.	Explore trade-offs between security and user convenience in tourism.	Mixed-methods (interviews + surveys).	Overly stringent protocols deter tourists; balance needed for seamless experiences.

Key Observations from the Table

Research Gaps

The majority of them are concentrated on hospitality-related issues, thus not considering other tourism industries (e.g., aviation, attractions). Scarcity of empirical confirmation of resilience models (e.g., Ghaderi et al., 2024). Tourism-specific policy recommendation is lacking in the regulatory studies (Talukder et al., 2024).

Theoretical Contributions

On the rise, there is the Resilience Theory (Ghaderi et al.) and the Human-Centric Cybersecurity (Rivera-Lopez). International Relations (Chowbe& Bhosale) and Regulatory Governance (Talukder et al., 2024) are the most prominent topics concerning policy in China.

Practical Relevance

The dire necessity of SME-compliant cybersecurity solutions (Lawal, 2025). Phishing and ransomware need an effort with the collaboration of industries (Desai & R, 2024; Harit et al., 2024). This table summarizes the major lessons policymakers, tourism managers, and cybersecurity researchers can learn. Future research needs to look at the sector wide vulnerabilities, as well the resilience frameworks empirically.

FINDINGS AND DISCUSSIONS

The increased digitalization of the tourism sector has brought along a lot of efficiency and customer engagement opportunities. Nonetheless, it has also brought out serious cybersecurity risks that pose a danger to both the companies and the traveling population. The major implications of this study include the essential cybersecurity issues, the connection between cybersecurity and sustainable development, and the necessity of a better awareness of the stakeholders.

An Increasingly Serious Threat to Travel Application Security: Cyber Vulnerability

The high rate of poor authentication processes in facilities used in travels makes it vulnerable to several security risks that are inherent in weak password-based authentication, one of which is the brute-force and credential stuffing (Pelchen et al., 2019). Such vulnerabilities allow fraudsters to take over accounts and, as such, become the target of booking frauds and unwanted changes to reservations, costs of which may be recovered in the form of financial loss and even impersonation. Also, inadequate multi-factor authentication (MFA) factors heighten the weaknesses since traditional single-factor authentication protocols are proving to be insufficient as against the advanced cyber attacks ("Stronger Authentication", 2022). Although MFA is stronger overall, it can also be subject to design issues through which it can be hacked (Ang et al., 2024). Moreover, the lack of regard to encryption of data at payment gateways only increases the likelihood that important information will be stolen (Harris, 2014). This means that introducing security measures to protect travel applications, such as MFA and end-to-end encryptions, is a critical step towards protecting travel applications ("Stronger Authentication", 2022) (Su & Xi, 2024).

Cybersecurity plays an important role to achieve sustainable development, especially in the framework of SDG 9, concerning the resilient infrastructure, inclusive industrialization, and innovation. Cyberattacks like phishing, malware, and ransomware single out small and medium-sized travel enterprises (SMTEs) as their preferred victim as they are unable to allocate funds and resources to IT defense because of their smaller IT budget (Benjamin et al., 2024). Embedding AI-based cybersecurity platforms can greatly improve the resilience of such enterprises with cost-effective and scalable real-time threat detection capabilities that are specific to their needs (Fidel-Anyana et al., 2025). Besides, the implementation of holistic cybersecurity policies, frequent staff training, and high-tech solutions are critical mechanisms to reduce risks and ensure a safe digital landscape is reached (Braimah, 2024). Cybersecurity will restore not only the digital infrastructure but also ensure economic stability, as it will help get rid of the losses in the revenues caused by insider fraud and will promote innovation as it will be able to reassure the new systems like AI-based travel assistants and blockchain-based booking systems. Moreover, cybersecurity can help with the environmental sustainability by not requiring large amounts of energy in security patching and fraud mitigation strategies after a break, and proactive strategies like AI-based threat detection can streamline resources consumption (Ige et al., 2024). A synchronization of cybersecurity strategy with sustainable development goals is pertinent, as both cybersecurity strategies and sustainable development goals have the synergistic effect of creating a secure, resilient, and sustainably digital future, more likely to help the world achieve the SDGs (Ozkan& Spruit, 2020).

The Gap in Stakeholder Awareness and Preparedness

The lack of unity and focused-reactive approach to cybersecurity used in tourism industry is not making their industries vulnerable to the cyber attacks worse. Addressing this major cyber risk has required high profile organisations in the travel and tourist industry to switch to a more business-centered, risk-based and broader approach to cybersecurity (Paraskevas, 2020) (Mairesse, 2022) (Paraskevas, n.d.). In particular, small and medium-sized tourism businesses (SMTEs) are susceptible as they tend to underestimate their chances of becoming the target of a cyber-attack due to their small size, and lack formal cybersecurity policies, which render them open to data breaches (Paulsen, 2016). The lack of any mandatory cybersecurity certifications in the industry also contributes to the continued practice of substandard activities, and consumer behavior, which exposes them to more risk because they tend to reuse passwords and are relatively unable to recognize phishing attempts. In smart tourist destinations (STDs), the integration across systems and the dynamic/adaptable nature of the systems adds resilience to cyber attack, but the important elements here are data encryption, well developed incident response plans, and awareness programs. Cohabitation and engagement will also play a quality role in enhancing resilience by underscoring the importance that educational programs have on creating a culture of cybersecurity awareness among businesses and the consumers (Ghaderi et al., 2024).

SOLUTIONS AND RECOMMENDATIONS FOR CYBERSECURITY IN TOURISM

The growing digitization of the tourism industry has made cybersecurity a critical priority. To safeguard sensitive traveler data and maintain trust, businesses and governments must adopt comprehensive strategies. Below are expanded solutions to mitigate cyber risks effectively.

Table 2. Solutions and Recommendations for Cybersecurity in Tourism

Solution/Recommendation	Details	Key Benefits	Supporting References
1. Adopt Cybersecurity Standards (ISO 27001)	Implement an Information Security Management System (ISMS) to identify vulnerabilities and ensure compliance.	Enhances cybersecurity posture, improves incident response, and fosters security awareness.	Folorunso et al. (2024)
2. Enhance Data Encryption	Use advanced encryption methods (e.g., AES-256) for protecting personal and financial data during storage and transmission.	Reduces the risk of data breaches.	Folorunso et al. (2024)
3. Foster Public-Private Partnerships	Collaboration between tourism stakeholders, governments, and cybersecurity firms for threat intelligence sharing.	Improves collective resilience against emerging cyber threats.	Stoll (2019)
4. Conduct Employee Training	Regular training on phishing awareness, secure password management, and cybersecurity best practices.	Reduces human error, a major factor in breaches.	Zhong et al. (2021)
5. Harmonize Regulatory Standards	Align tourism cybersecurity regulations with frameworks like GDPR.	Streamlines compliance for multinational businesses and improves data handling accountability.	Demirel et al. (2021)
6. Develop Incident Response Plans	Establish clear protocols for containment, mitigation, and communication in case of cyberattacks.	Minimizes damage and ensures quick recovery.	Ertaş et al. (2021)
7. Leverage Blockchain for Secure Transactions	Implement blockchain for tamper-proof records and smart contracts in loyalty programs and transactions.	Reduces fraud risks and enhances transparency.	Treiblmaier et al. (2021)
8. Deploy AI-Driven Threat Detection	Use AI to analyze network traffic in real time and detect anomalies.	Improves threat detection efficiency and adapts to evolving attack patterns.	Richardson (2023)
9. Integration of AI with Other Technologies	Combine AI with blockchain, encryption, and regulatory policies for a holistic cybersecurity approach.	Strengthens defenses and aligns with SDG 9 (Industry Innovation) and SDG 17 (Partnerships).	Vorobeva et al. (2023), Wu et al. (2023), Shang & Luo (2023)

CONCEPTUAL FRAMEWORK

Figure 1. Conceptual framework - Connecting cybersecurity measures to sustainable tourism growth.

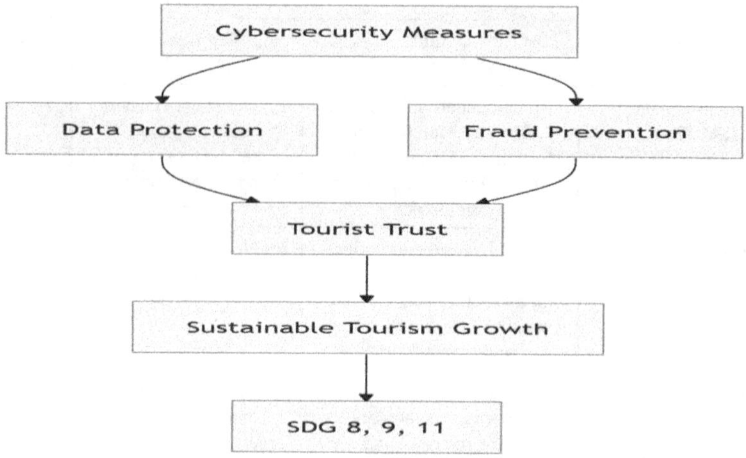

Source: Author Compilation

Cybersecurity Measures

This is fundamental component of the framework. It is a term used to denote the technologies, processes and practices intended to defend digital devices, networks as well as information. Cybersecurity in tourism is a priority because it involves technologies and processes that safeguard online systems and information against hackers, etc., thus securing the cybersecurity of online interactions and the safety of personal data (Gössling & Gössling, 2021).

Data Protection

The straightforward consequence of sound cybersecurity. Their adherence to regulations such as the GDPR is usually a sub-set of this element. The result of these measures is effective data protection that helps to secure sensitive data of the tourists, including their booking and payment data and informs about their adherence to such regulation regulations as GDPR (Gössling, 2021).

Fraud Prevention

Cybersecurity and data protection can assist in aiding against fraudulent sign-ins like phishing scams, identity theft, or fraudulent bookings. Capturing the digital platforms, businesses in tourism will eliminate threats to themselves and their customers. What matters more is that sound cybersecurity and data protection strategies are vital to prevent frauds, and should help contain the risk of phishing attacks and identity theft, which will negatively impact consumer confidence (Fennell, 2021).

Tourist Trust

The more tourists trust that their information will not be compromised and be at risks to become victims of fraud, the higher is their confidence in tourism websites, which is essential to make additional visits and recommend them positively to others, thus ensuring the sustainability of the industry (Roxas et al., 2020).

Sustainable Tourism Growth

The final objective of the framework of reliable and secure tourism practice is to comply with the United Nations Sustainable Development Goals (SDGs) by generating financial and societal stability in tourism industry. This is done by ensuring the inclusion of sustainable tourism indicators (STIs) which are crucial in effective tourism planning and management as they constitute a methodical linking of tourism practices to SDGs 8 which outlines a resilient way of tourism economy and focus on decent work and economic growth (Rasoolimanesh et al., 2020). The relevance of partnerships in tourism is emphasized as one of the ways to attain these objectives as was portrayed in the 2019 conference organized by Massey University on the role of tourism in achieving the SDGs (Scheyvens& Cheer, 2021). SDG 9 (Roxas et al., 2020) proposes a systems thinking approach to developing sustainable tourism and acknowledges the dynamic and complex nature of the tourism system and how sustainability considerations must be made to support the innovative and secure future digital infrastructure. Moreover, the bibliometric analysis demonstrates that sustainable tourism studies are increasingly becoming involved in the SDGs, meaning that the goals might be seen as a practical way of overcoming external threats, such as climate change, and ensuring long-term sustainable development of urban areas, in accordance with SDG 11(Moyle et al., 2021). Another area of focus is collaborative tourism design that works to increase the resilience of tourism practices towards sustainable development, a factor that further advances global priorities (Liburd et al., 2020).

FUTURE RESEARCH DIRECTIONS

The tourism sector needs to respond to the new cybersecurity issues presented by the shift in the digital environment to protect the companies and customers. The three areas such research should scrutinize are as follows: cross-border cyber polices, behavioral cybersecurity, and quantum computing risks.

Cross-Border Cyber Policies

Comparative analysis of cybersecurity policies reveals that there is a considerable gap that can be applied in real life in relation to cross-border tourism. General Data Protection Regulation (GDPR) passed by the European Union is an example of an excellent data protection standard that requires high standards of data collection, storage, data processing, and data consent. Such regulatory framework does not only boost consumer privacy but also creates trust within the international tourists that their personal and financial information will be treated with care when using European travel platforms, accommodation providers, and tour operators (Sarangan et al., 2022). On the contrary, most developing nations have been known to be governed by less detailed or irregularly applied laws in the field of cybersecurity and data protection. Such a regulatory gap can make tourists as well as tourism related businesses especially susceptible to cyber crimes. Some of the threats that tourists expose themselves to include phishing attacks, malware-infested online booking platforms, and data breaches related to poor payment gateways. Moreover, companies within these jurisdictions might be short of technical support or financial means to create sufficient cybersecurity to reduce the risk of future incidents, which can potentially damage reputations and discourage future visitors (Sarangan et al., 2022). The asymmetry in regulation also brings in the issue of compliance cost and consumer awareness. The legal environment in which tourism enterprises function in several jurisdictions is often in disjointed cans, resulting in high costs of complying to different standards, especially when the enterprise is catering to EU clients in GDPR. Concurrently, the traveler himself is often not aware of the varying degree of data protection provisions of different destinations. These knowledge gaps may undermine trust, particularly when the incidents can be observed in areas, which are interpreted as having a lax approach to cybersecurity (Femenia-Serra et al., 2021).

However, we can also learn some lessons based on regional blocks that have embarked on harmonisation of cybersecurity plans. As an example, the Association of Southeast Asian Nations (ASEAN) has undertaken the efforts to work on a common approach, including the ASEAN Agreement on Cybersecurity Cooperation and the Cybersecurity Framework. Even though the implementation process is still not evenly spread among the member states, the collaborative model ASEAN shows how the alignment of the region could further improve trust, simplify compliance among multinational tourism operators, and eventually increase the overall resilience of the entire sector to cyber threats (Anser et al., 2021). Thus, encouraging more regulatory convergence, following the example of the rigor of the GDPR and the collaborative tone of such systems as ASEAN, would be of great help in enhancing cybersecurity in global tourism. This would not only safeguard consumers and businesses but also help in the sustainable development of the cross-border travel in an ever digitalized and globalized world.

Behavioral Cybersecurity

Tourists should take caution on cyber attacks, especially as online technologies continue to form the basis of travel planning and experience. Fomenia-Serra et al. (2021) emphasize the urgency of researching the psychological factors influencing the cybersecurity behaviors of tourists, i.e. the perception of risk they have, the level of their trust to online service providers, and their overall digital literacy. This understanding of these psychological motivators is critical towards explaining why some travelers do not practice basic cyber hygiene on the boone of several awareness programs. Perception of risks, in particular, the level of seriousness with which people evaluate potential risks, often determines the decision to implement any protective measures. Similarly, the false sense of security in what these users are used to can lead to complacency, thus exposing them to phishing, malware, and data breaches. These issues should be addressed in specific empirical research through surveys and experimental designs in order to mitigate them effectively. These methodological strategies can demonstrate specific knowledge gaps and behavioural tendencies in different categories of tourists. The resultant findings would empower stakeholders, who are governments, tourism boards, and cybersecurity educators, to come up with specific awareness programmes that are psychologically engaging to the travelers. Such programmes can also include behaviorally informed interventions, e.g. nudges or scenario-based learning, to lead to increased engagement and retention. Finally, to overcome the gap between knowledge and behavior, it is important to have a subtle understanding of human behavior in the digital realm, which makes psychological knowledge an essential pillar in successful cybersecurity education in tourism (Femenia et al., 2021).

Quantum Computing Risks

Quantum computing poses a significant threat in the long term to the encryption algorithms already used in tourism software, particularly in terms of secure merchant gateways and personal data hubs that handle sensitive tourist data including payment and identities and itineraries. Since the tourism sector is becoming more and more reliant on web-based technologies to make booking transactions, handle customer relationships, and store data, the introduction of effective cybersecurity solutions cannot be avoided to maintain consumer confidence and business integrity. Without such protections, the industry can suffer significant economic and reputational harm in case the breaches on a large scale become a reality (Ram & Hill, 2022). The coming of quantum computers that have the capability of cracking popular cryptographic schemes like RSA and ECC might eliminate current security infrastructure. In order to reduce this upcoming threat, an active investment and deployment of post-quantum cryptography (PQC) is necessary. PQC consists of cryptographic algorithms which are resistant to classical and quantum computation attacks. According to the researchers, the shift to quantum-resistant solutions should be initiated long before quantum computers become reality, as it is a complicated and time-intensive process that will need qualitative changes in every component of the system (Ye et al., 2021). To the tourism industry, where the smooth and safe digital communications are essential, the adoption of PQC is not a technical improvement, but a strategic one that the industry must adopt to guarantee the ability to withstand over time and even to maintain the trust of travelers in a more quantum-prone digital environment.

CONCLUSION

The partnership between cybersecurity practitioners, policymakers, and the tourism sector is essential to creating quantum-safe frameworks to counter such threats before their effects can come to pass(Nam et al., 2021). Also, conducting periodic audits of the systems, training of employees, and employing high levels of encryption in systems can curb cyber threats and make the tourism sector more resilient to the threat of ICT risks in the future (Minca & Roelofsen, 2021).

The introduction of new technological advances including AI-powered threat detection mechanisms and the use of blockchain technology will add tremendous options to the security sphere in tourism thereby providing a much more safe and technologically advanced space in which travel is achieved. Such technologies as blockchain will provide decentralized assistance in securing sensitive information; it will also help conduct sustainable transactions, which are essential in establishing digital trust within the circles of eco-friendly travelers and their cooperation with responsible organizations (Nam et al., 2021) (Treiblmaier et al., 2021). In addition to the protection of assets, the incorporation of strong cybersecurity into sustainability plans also helps increase the resilience of even tourism destinations against crises, such as the COVID-19 pandemic (Pyke et al., 2021). By being concerned with digital safety assiduously, the tourism sector would be able to preserve its image and meet the sustainability goals on the global scale, where tourism will remain sustainable and sustainable throughout its existence (Soares et al., 2021) (Muharam et al., 2023).

REFERENCES

Ang, K. W., Chekole, E. G., & Zhou, J. (2024). *Excavating Vulnerabilities Lurking in Multi-Factor Authentication Protocols: A Systematic Security Analysis*. https://doi.org//arXiv.2407.20459DOI: 10.48550

Anser, M. K., Adeleye, B. N., Tabash, M. I., & Tiwari, A. K. (2021). Services trade–ICT–tourism nexus in selected Asian countries: New evidence from panel data techniques. *Current Issues in Tourism*, •••, 1–16. DOI: 10.1080/13683500.2021.1965554

Bekele, H., & Raj, S. (2024). Digitalization and digital transformation in the tourism industry: a bibliometric review and research agenda. *Revue de Tourisme*. DOI: 10.1108/TR-07-2023-0509

Benjamin, L. B., Adegbola, A. E., Amajuoyi, P., Adegbola, M. D., & Adeusi, K. B. (2024). Digital transformation in SMEs: Identifying cybersecurity risks and developing effective mitigation strategies. *Global Journal of Engineering and Technology Advances*, *19*(2), 134–153. DOI: 10.30574/gjeta.2024.19.2.0084

Boluk, K., Cavaliere, C. T., & Higgins-Desbiolles, F. (2017). Critical thinking to realize sustainability in tourism systems: Reflecting on the 2030 sustainable development goals. *Journal of Sustainable Tourism*, *25*(9), 1201–1204. DOI: 10.1080/09669582.2017.1333263

Braimah, S. (2024). *Innovative solutions for cybersecurity vulnerabilities in business operations: Scope and impact*. World Journal of Advanced Engineering Technology and Sciences., DOI: 10.30574/wjaets.2024.13.1.0427

Calgaro, E., Lloyd, K., & Dominey-Howes, D. (2014). From vulnerability to transformation: A framework for assessing the vulnerability and resilience of tourism destinations. *Journal of Sustainable Tourism*, *22*(3), 341–360. DOI: 10.1080/09669582.2013.826229

Chowbe, V. S., & Bhosale, S. S. (2024). *Beyond Borders: Addressing the Legal Quagmire of Jurisdiction in Cyberspace*. International Journal For Multidisciplinary Research., DOI: 10.36948/ijfmr.2024.v06i06.30051

Demirel, E., Zeren, S. K., & Hakan, K. (2021). Smart contracts in tourism industry: A model with blockchain integration for post pandemic economy. *Current Issues in Tourism*, •••, 1–15. DOI: 10.1080/13683500.2021.1960280

Desai, V., & R, K. (2024). Unveiling the Depths of Phishing: Understanding Tactics, Impacts, and Countermeasures. *International Journal of Innovative Research in Science, Engineering and Technology, 13*(5), 8596–8600. Advance online publication. DOI: 10.15680/IJIRSET.2024.1305331

El-Maksoud, R. A. (2024). *Exploring the Role of Cybersecurity in Enhancing Digital Trust of Egyptian Travel Agencies. Journal of Association of Arab Universities for Tourism and Hospitality (JAAUTH)*. Print., DOI: 10.21608/jaauth.2024.269299.1553

Erdem, A., & Şeker, F. (2022). *Tourist Experience and Digital Transformation.*, DOI: 10.4018/978-1-7998-8528-3.ch006

Ertaş, M., Sel, Z. G., Kırlar-Can, B., & Tütüncü, Ö. (2021). Effects of crisis on crisis management practices: A case from Turkish tourism enterprises. *Journal of Sustainable Tourism, 29*(9), 1490–1507. DOI: 10.1080/09669582.2021.1879818

Espiner, S., Orchiston, C., & Higham, J. (2017). Resilience and sustainability: A complementary relationship? Towards a practical conceptual model for the sustainability–resilience nexus in tourism. *Journal of Sustainable Tourism, 25*(10), 1385–1400. DOI: 10.1080/09669582.2017.1281929

Femenia-Serra, F., Ioannou, A., & Tussyadiah, I. P. (2021). Is smart scary? A mixed-methods study on privacy in smart tourism. *Current Issues in Tourism*, •••, 1–27. DOI: 10.1080/13683500.2021.1987399

Fennell, D. A. (2021). Technology and the sustainable tourist in the new age of disruption. *Journal of Sustainable Tourism, 29*(5), 767–773. DOI: 10.1080/09669582.2020.1769639

Fidel-Anyana, I., Onus, E. G., Mikel-Olisa, U., & Ayanbode, N. (2025). AI-Driven Cybersecurity Frameworks for SME Development: Mitigating Risks in a Digital Economy. *International Journal of Multidisciplinary Research and Growth Evaluation, 6*(1), 982–988. DOI: 10.54660/.IJMRGE.2025.6.1.982-988

Folorunso, A., Mohammed, V., Wada, I., & Samuel, B. J. (2024). The impact of ISO security standards on enhancing cybersecurity posture in organizations. *World Journal Of Advanced Research and Reviews, 24*(1), 2582–2595. DOI: 10.30574/wjarr.2024.24.1.3169

Gefen, D., Karahanna, E., & Straub, D. W. (2003). Trust and TAM in Online Shopping: An Integrated Model. *Management Information Systems Quarterly, 27*(1), 51–90. DOI: 10.2307/30036519

Ghaderi, Z., Béal, L., Hall, C. M., Zaman, M., Rather, R. A., & Som, A. P. M. (2024). Cybersecurity and smart tourist destinations resilience. *Tourism Recreation Research*, •••, 1–17. DOI: 10.1080/02508281.2024.2434791

Gössling, S. (2021). Technology, ICT and tourism: From big data to the big picture. *Journal of Sustainable Tourism*, *29*(5), 849–858. DOI: 10.1080/09669582.2020.1865387

Gössling, S., & Gössling, S. (2021). Tourism, technology and ICT: A critical review of affordances and concessions. *Journal of Sustainable Tourism*, *29*(5), 733–750. DOI: 10.1080/09669582.2021.1873353

Hall, C. M. (2019). Constructing sustainable tourism development: The 2030 agenda and the managerial ecology of sustainable tourism. *Journal of Sustainable Tourism*, *27*(7), 1044–1060. DOI: 10.1080/09669582.2018.1560456

Harit, P., Singh, A., Agrawal, K., Verma, D. N., Bathla, G., & Raina, A. (2024). Exploring the Growing Threat of Cyber Risks and Vulnerabilities in the Hospitality Industry. *Advances in Hospitality, Tourism and the Services Industry (AHTSI) Book Series*, 299–316. DOI: 10.4018/979-8-3693-6562-5.ch017

Harris, A. G. (2014). *The Weaknesses of Passwords and Alternative Authentication Technologies*.

Himanshu, V., & Vinita, H. (2023). *Security and Trust in Online Booking Systems: A Comparative Analysis Of Tour and Travel Websites. (2023)*. International Journal For Multidisciplinary Research., DOI: 10.36948/ijfmr.2023.v05i05.7334

Ige, A. B., Kupa, E., & Ilori, O. (2024). Aligning sustainable development goals with cybersecurity strategies: Ensuring a secure and sustainable future. *GSC Advanced Research and Reviews*, *19*(3), 344–360. DOI: 10.30574/gscarr.2024.19.3.0236

Lara-Morales, O., & Clarke, A. (2022). Sustainable tourism value chain analysis as a tool to evaluate tourism's contribution to the sustainable development goals and local Indigenous communities. *Journal of Ecotourism*, •••, 1–19. DOI: 10.1080/14724049.2022.2147189

Lawal, Q. (2025). Cybersecurity governance: Strengthening policy frameworks to address global cybercrime and data privacy challenges. *International Journal of Science and Research Archive*, *14*(1), 1146–1163. DOI: 10.30574/ijsra.2025.14.1.0225

Liburd, J. J., Duedahl, E., & Heape, C. (2020). Co-designing tourism for sustainable development. *Journal of Sustainable Tourism*, •••, 1–20. DOI: 10.1080/09669582.2020.1839473

Mairesse, F. (2022). *Cybersecurity in Travel and Tourism: A Risk-Based Approach* (pp. 1605–1628). Springer eBooks. DOI: 10.1007/978-3-030-48652-5_100

Masseno, M. D., & Santos, C. (2018). *Smart tourism destinations privacy risks on data protection. 1*(1).

Minca, C., &Roelofsen, M. (2021). Becoming Airbnbeings: on datafication and the quantified Self in tourism. *Tourism Geographies, 23*(4), 743–764. https://doi.org/. 2019.1686767DOI: 10.1080/14616688

Moyle, B. D., Moyle, C., Ruhanen, L., Weaver, D., & Hadinejad, A. (2021). Are we really progressing sustainable tourism research? A bibliometric analysis. *Journal of Sustainable Tourism, 29*(1), 1–17. DOI: 10.1080/09669582.2020.1817048

Moyle, B. D., Weaver, D., Gössling, S., McLennan, C., & Hadinejad, A. (2021). Are water-centric themes in sustainable tourism research congruent with the UN Sustainable Development Goals? *Journal of Sustainable Tourism*, •••, 1–16. DOI: 10.1080/09669582.2021.1993233

Muharam, I. N., Tussyadiah, I. P., & Kimbu, A. N. (2023). A theoretical model of user acceptance of blockchain-based peer-to-peer accommodation. *Current Issues in Tourism*, •••, 1–18. DOI: 10.1080/13683500.2022.2164485

Najlaoui, A. G., & Ammari, N. B. (2024). *Technological Revolution and Transformation of the Tourism Sector*. IGI Global., DOI: 10.4018/979-8-3693-2619-0.ch010

Nam, K., Dutt, C. S., Chathoth, P. K., & Khan, M. S. (2021). Blockchain technology for smart city and smart tourism: Latest trends and challenges. *Asia Pacific Journal of Tourism Research, 26*(4), 454–468. DOI: 10.1080/10941665.2019.1585376

Oppokkhonov, N. (2023). The Future of Smart Tourism: Transforming Travel Experiences. *YashilIqtisodiyotvaTaraqqiyot, 1*(mxs). DOI: 10.55439/GED/vol1_iss-maxsusson/a663

Ozkan, B. Y., & Spruit, M. (2020). Assessing and Improving Cybersecurity Maturity for SMEs: Standardization aspects. *arXiv: Cryptography and Security*. https://arxiv .org/pdf/2007.01751.pdf

Paraskevas, A. (2020). *Cybersecurity in Travel and Tourism: A Risk-Based Approach*. DOI: 10.1007/978-3-030-05324-6_100-1

Paraskevas, A. (n.d.). *Cybersecurity in Travel and Tourism: A Risk-Based Approach*. DOI: 10.1007/978-3-030-05324-6_100-1

Paulsen, C. (2016). Cybersecuring Small Businesses. *Computer, 49*(8), 92–97. DOI: 10.1109/MC.2016.223

Pelchen, C., Jaeger, D., Cheng, F., & Meinel, C. (2019). *The (Persistent) Threat of Weak Passwords: Implementation of a Semi-automatic Password-Cracking Algorithm*. Springer., DOI: 10.1007/978-3-030-34339-2_27

Prajapat, D. K., & R, D. (2024). Revolutionizing Tourism through Technology the Digital Transformation of Travel and Tourism. *International Journal of Research Publication and Reviews*. DOI: 10.55248/gengpi.5.0224.0626

Pyke, J., Lindsay-Smith, G., Gamage, A., Shaikh, S., Nguyen, V. K., De Lacy, T., & Porter, C. (2021). Building destination resilience to multiple crises to secure tourism's future. *Asia Pacific Journal of Tourism Research, 26*(11), 1225–1243. DOI: 10.1080/10941665.2021.1989000

Ram, Y., & Hill, C. (2022). The tourism industry and the risk of "the year 2038 problem": Long-term thinking and the illogical cycle of ICT risk management. *International Journal of Tourism Research, 24*(3), 501–514. Advance online publication. DOI: 10.1002/jtr.2517

Rasoolimanesh, S. M., Ramakrishna, S., Hall, C. M., Esfandiar, K., & Seyfi, S. (2020). A systematic scoping review of sustainable tourism indicators in relation to the sustainable development goals. *Journal of Sustainable Tourism, 32*, 1–21. DOI: 10.1080/09669582.2020.1775621

Reda, R., &M'Bark, M. (2023). *Fostering Destination Resilience: A Conceptual Framework Linking Sustainable Tourism and Tourism Threats*. DOI: 10.59285/rimec.390

Richardson, T. L. (2023). Artificial intelligence's impact on hospitality and tourism marketing: Exploring key themes and addressing challenges. *Current Issues in Tourism*, •••, 1–18. DOI: 10.1080/13683500.2023.2229480

Rivera-López, F. B. (2023). Resilience in Tourism: A bibliometric analysis of trends and perspectives in research. *The Journal of Economic History*, 37–48. Advance online publication. DOI: 10.35429/JEH.2023.13.7.37.48

Roxas, F., Rivera, J. P. R., & Gutierrez, E. L. M. (2020). Framework for creating sustainable tourism using systems thinking. *Current Issues in Tourism, 23*(3), 280–296. DOI: 10.1080/13683500.2018.1534805

Roy, P. P. (2020). *A High-Level Comparison between the NIST Cyber Security Framework and the ISO 27001 Information Security Standard*. DOI: 10.1109/NCETSTEA48365.2020.9119914

Sarangan, B., Hewege, C., & Perera, C. R. (2022). Fifty years of evolutionary trajectory of tourism industry regulations: A systematic literature review. *Asia Pacific Journal of Tourism Research, 27*(8), 781–806. DOI: 10.1080/10941665.2022.2119876

Scheyvens, R., & Cheer, J. M. (2021). Tourism, the SDGs and partnerships. *Journal of Sustainable Tourism*, ●●●, 1–11. DOI: 10.1080/09669582.2021.1982953

Shang, Z., & Luo, J. M. (2023). Topic modelling for wildlife tourism online reviews: Analysis of quality factors. *Current Issues in Tourism, 26*(14), 2317–2331. DOI: 10.1080/13683500.2022.2086107

Soares, J. C., Ruiz, T. C. D., & Ivars-Baidal, J. (2021). Smart destinations: A new planning and management approach? *Current Issues in Tourism*, ●●●, 1–16. DOI: 10.1080/13683500.2021.1991897

Stoll, M. (2019). *An Information Security Model for Implementing the New ISO 27001*. IGI Global., DOI: 10.4018/978-1-5225-7113-1.ch013

Streimikiene, D. (2023). Sustainability Assessment of Tourism Destinations from the Lens of Green Digital Transformations. *Journal of Tourism and Services*. DOI: 10.29036/jots.v14i27.651

Stronger Authentication (pp. 207–218). (2022). Apress eBooks. DOI: 10.1007/978-1-4842-8261-8_12

Su, Y., & Xi, M. (2024). Systematic Solutions to Login and Authentication Security: A Dual-Password Login-Authentication Mechanism. *arXiv.Org, abs/2404.01803*. https://doi.org//arXiv.2404.01803DOI: 10.48550

Sumariadhi, N. W.Ni Wayan Sumariadhi. (2023). Green Tourism. *Promoting Sustainable Practices for a Responsible Future., 1*(1), 19–25. DOI: 10.25078/ijoss.v1i1.2976

Suta, W. P., Abdi, N., & Astawa, I. P. M. (2021)... *Sustainable Tourism Development in Importance and Performance Perspective, 342–346*. Advance online publication. DOI: 10.2991/assehr.k.210424.066

Talukder, M. B., Hoque, M., & Kumar, S. (2024). *Impact of Cybersecurity in the Aviation*. Tourism, and Hospitality Industries., DOI: 10.4018/979-8-3693-2715-9.ch011

Tariq, M. U. (2024). Data Breach Incidents and Prevention in the Hospitality Industry. *Advances in Hospitality, Tourism and the Services Industry (AHTSI) Book Series*, 181–199. DOI: 10.4018/979-8-3693-2715-9.ch010

Tia, H. U. (2014). *A Study on Tourism Consumers' Trust,Satisfaction and Loyalty in Online Purchasing*. Tourism Science.

Treiblmaier, H., Leung, D. T., Kwok, A. O. J., & Tham, A. (2021). Cryptocurrency adoption in travel and tourism – an exploratory study of Asia Pacific travellers. *Current Issues in Tourism, 24*(22), 3165–3181. DOI: 10.1080/13683500.2020.1863928

Vorobeva, D., Costa Pinto, D., Antonio, N., & Mattila, A. S. (2023). The augmentation effect of artificial intelligence: Can AI framing shape customer acceptance of AI-based services? *Current Issues in Tourism*, •••, 1–21. DOI: 10.1080/13683500.2023.2214353

Wang, X. (2024). Sustainable tourism: Pathways to environmental preservation, economic growth, and social equity. *Applied and Computational Engineering*, *66*(1), 166–171. DOI: 10.54254/2755-2721/2024.20637

Wu, D., Li, H., Huang, Q., Li, C., & Liang, S. (2023). Measurement and determinants of smart destinations' sustainable performance: A two-stage analysis using DEA-Tobit model. *Current Issues in Tourism*, •••, 1–17. DOI: 10.1080/13683500.2023.2228977

Ye, H., Sun, S., & Law, R. (2021). An investigation of developing smart tourism from the perspective of stakeholders. *Asia Pacific Journal of Tourism Research, 26*(10), 1156–1170. DOI: 10.1080/10941665.2021.1953086

Zhong, L., Sun, S., Law, R., & Li, X. (2021). Tourism crisis management: evidence from COVID-19. *Current Issues in Tourism, 24*(19), 2671–2682. https://doi.org/. 1901866DOI: 10.1080/13683500.2021

Chapter 3
Smart Tourism Infrastructure and Security Challenges:
Toward a Cyber-Resilient Tourism Ecosystem

Piali Haldar
http://orcid.org/0000-0003-4729-6964
Brainware University, Kolkata, India

Dev Kumar Mandal
http://orcid.org/0009-0005-3740-6885
Brainware University, Kolkata, India

ABSTRACT

The digital era has transformed tourism into an intelligent ecosystem, driven by smart infrastructure and real-time services. These innovations enhance convenience and personalisation, but they also introduce significant cybersecurity vulnerabilities, including data breaches, phishing attacks, insecure IoT devices, partner-related risks, and operational disruptions from ransomware or denial-of-service attacks. Cybersecurity governance in tourism is largely generic, lacking sector-specific frameworks. This study emphasises the need for tailored and proposes a Cyber-Resilience Model built on four pillars: Technological layers, Organisational layers, Policy and Governance layers, and User-Centric layers. Practical implications will help policymakers, businesses, technology developers, academia, and tourists towards safer digital practices. As tourism advances digitally, building cyber resilience is essential for sustaining trust, operational continuity, and economic stability. By doing so, the sector can thrive in a globally interconnected and secure future.

DOI: 10.4018/979-8-2600-1850-7.ch003

1. INTRODUCTION

The beginning of the digital age has significantly transformed the travel sector, shifting from a manual and non-digital approach to a fully digital, automated, and data-centric system (Chon & Hao, 2025; Pencarelli, 2020; Xiang, 2018; Soava, 2015). This shift, which is commonly referred to as Smart Tourism, is the merging of Information and Communication Technologies (ICT), the Internet of Things (IoT), artificial intelligence (AI), and big data analytics, with the tourism infrastructure to ultimately create flexible and real-time environments that the traveler gets to enjoy and be serviced by providers more effectively and efficiently (Lee et al., 2020; Tsaih & Hsu, 2018; Bhuiyan et al., 2022; Buhalis & Amaranggana, 2014). It is not just about the utilization of new technologies, smart tourism is about the establishment of a tourism ecosystem in which the digitalization effect is manifested by the most-well-informed decision-making, the fastest service delivery and by the tourists being enabled through the most individually-tailored and context-aware of services (Buhalis & Amaranggana, 2014). The trio of digital devices, platforms, and intelligent services became almost a must in real-life travel situations (Talukder & Hoque, 2025; Yang & Wang, 2025; Ercan, 2020). Booking a hotel, mobile navigation application use, or even the use of augmented reality guides at heritage sites, in any case, one way or another digital incursion into the tourism industry has become an indispensable part of it. Today, smart tourism infrastructure is based on the premise of real-time data integration from various sources, such as tourist wearables, mobile apps, surveillance systems, and connected vehicles or IoT, to satisfy the unique needs and preferences through delivery of adjusted and automated services (Zhang et al., 2022).

On the other hand, significant cybersecurity risks are exposed as the integration of digital devices goes deeper and further (Möller, 2023; Jimmy, 2021). The tourism sector is a highly desirable target for cybercriminals when inter-tourism-related data flows, such as personally identifiable information (PII), financial transactions, biometric data, travel itineraries, and geolocation data, become more common, because tourist facilities are extensively interconnected and cybersecurity risks are all the more minimized (Nayak, 2016; Herke et al., 2025). Smart tourism has received support from the technological spine formed by cloud computing, being accessible by ADA compliance, IoT networks, mobile applications, and data-sharing hubs, thus also facilitating vulnerabilities to cyber-attacks (Shin & Kang, 2020). When the weak points reside in software systems then the systems can be the subject of malicious attacks, unencrypted data can be easily accessed, and ransomware and phishing attacks can be employed for the purpose of disrupting services or taking control of them, thereby not only endangering the economic side but also the trust and security of the user community (Aslan et al., 2023). The tourism industry has faced and publicized the very alarming risks due to the highlighted and highlighted the risks of cyber threats at several points prominently at different times that were also (PR) partly and deeply related and connected to (Shim et al., 2010). In such a situation, disasters are deemed to be mainly the result of not fully implementing security measures or awareness of cybersecurity threats. Cybersecurity attacks occurrence frequency has increased being a serious impact on direct and indirect international tourism revenue Chung et al., 2018 and thus becoming an issue that requires immediate responses and this research aimed at harnessing the most reluctant electronic travellers through an exhibition which was one of the most preferred methods provided that the support of the sector and the government will be sustained for the feasibility of the project at least for the following three years(Choi, 2022).

The implications of these vulnerabilities are huge. Visitors would want digital security services as well as any other service without the hassle of the process. The lack of trust in digital systems can result in tourists' rejection of smart services, thus leading to the erosion of the investments made in the place becoming "smart" (Xu & Lee, 2021). Therefore, cybersecurity should not be regarded as an isolated component or taken lightly in the process of smart tourism development. This chapter will dive into the topic of security and technical challenges in the smart tourism industry, focusing on the identification and examination of the tourist industry's main weaknesses. It will also assess the manner in which these weaknesses are being used and what legislation and technical frameworks can be employed to reduce them. Particularly, it will discuss the policy impact, both in the home country and internationally, and how the leisure industry authorities, service providers, and the government can, together, create a culture of cyber resilience.

Furthermore, the work examines not only the cybersecurity policies that the tourism sector exhibits but also the degree of trust in institutions and the level of digitalization among the different areas. This comprehensive view is essential due to the fact that, though the cybersecurity policies are very strong, they will still have no effect if the people and the private sector do not adhere to them or give no trust in them (Kshetri, 2017). Digital platforms are highly dependent on trust. Trust is even more critical for the diffusion of technologies when it comes to the use of biometric scanning, digital wallets, and cross-border data sharing. The author sums up this chapter with the assertion that a secure digital environment is the key criterion for fostering smart, sustainable tourism. This can be achieved through the implementation of governance models based on cooperation, the creation of strong legal frameworks such as the GDPR, the introduction of a proactive cybersecurity training program, and the regular conduction of system audits to have a closer look at and remove any breaches of security present in the system. Security is definitely the main thing to reckon with while going along the path of smart tourism.

1.1 Research Gap

Even with the growing attention and research given to the topic of smart tourism and cybersecurity, there are still wide gaps where they meet. Of primary concern, the research done could not identify the issue of systemic vulnerabilities, governance mechanisms, and the dynamics of user trust within the digitally transformed tourism ecosystems. Whereas the earlier research works (Buhalis & Amaranggana, 2014; Tsaih & Hsu, 2018) mostly explored the technological side of smart tourism, the case of tourism-specific cybersecurity frameworks is still one that is not well-handled, but other routes taken in the study are completely different. The majority of the extant works are focused on only one side—operational, regulatory, or behavioral—even though the industry of tourism is diverse in terms of data flows, user profiles, and service architectures. Trust has been acknowledged as a major factor in technology adoption (Xu et al., 2023), although how smart tourists perceive and react to cybersecurity breaches has not yet been extensively studied, especially when it comes to the restoration of digital trust after such incidents.

Even with the variances in digital maturity, legal regimes, and trust in institutions, there is still rather little cross-border or cross-regional comparative research in the digital fields of study. Also, tourism is mainly supported by small and medium enterprises (SMEs), the team leaders of which do not have enough resources and experts' knowledge to implement robust security, an area that has not been critically discussed in the literature so far. The most common methodology is to use only a few case studies with no or very limited ongoing investigation of the long-term effects on tourist behaviour or the image of the destination. A good example of this proponents of the view (e.g., Herke et al., 2025) argue that cybersecurity, the phenomenon that is not yet entirely understood, is somehow related to governance. Because more coordinated and harmonized governance has been suggested, our societies could be more cyber-secure if it were the case. Moreover, in system architecture, interoperability, or privacy-by-design in smart tourism technologies, the issue has become so acute that policy-makers and industrial actors have to give it a high priority. The cybersecurity aspect still is not sufficiently addressed by the research and might even endanger the future of smart and safe tourism, i.e., the guiding principle for the development of tourism.

1.2 Research Objectives

The main purposes of this study are:

1. To investigate the evolution and components of smart tourism in the digital age.

2. To identify the main cybersecurity threats and vulnerabilities in electronic tourism systems, platforms, and devices.
3. To evaluate the worldwide and regional policy and governance arrangements presently in effect that pertain to cybersecurity within the tourism sector.
4. To propose a comprehensive, fully inclusive model of cyber resilience that blends technical, organizational, and regulatory approaches.
5. To assess the effect of the implications on interested parties, for example, the policymakers, service providers, IT developers, and the tourists themselves, who have a stake in them.

2. LITERATURE REVIEW

2.1 Smart Tourism

Smart tourism is the application of smart technologies and digital innovations in the tourism industry to enhance service quality, improve resource utilisation, and enrich tourist experiences (Gretzel et al., 2015). The basis of "smart" cities extends into the area of "smart" tourism, which makes heavy use of Information/Communication Technologies (ICT), the Internet of Things (IoT), cloud computing, big data analytics, and artificial intelligence (AI) to turn tourism destinations into environments that actually "talk" to the tourists and vice versa (Buhalis & Amaranggana, 2014).

2.2 Smart Tourism Infrastructure

The backbone of the digital transformation of the tourism industry is smart tourism infrastructure. This is a matter of cooperation among the elements of the select technologies, platforms, and systems within the establishment of a responsive, effective, and personalized tourist experience set. However, there is an odd thing about all of these. If someone is or is going to be interested in creating a smart tourism infrastructure, then he/she must know of two principles and one technology (Buhalis & Amaranggana, 2014; Gretzel et al., 2015). This infrastructure is not only about the digitization of tourism services. It is a blend of many adjoined technologies, e.g., Information and Communications Technologies (ICTs), the Internet of Things (IoT), Artificial Intelligence (AI), cloud computing, augmented reality (AR), and, of course, big data analytics along with numerous other integrated technologies, all of which are meant to work hand in hand towards a shared objective and a better tourist experience, besides, for the resource management and operations of the tourism service.

2.3 Components of Smart Tourism Infrastructure

The smart tourism infrastructure is made up of physical and digital systems that enable data collection, transmission, analysis, and the delivery of services. It contains:

- Sensor networks and IoT-enabled devices for monitoring visitor flow and environmental conditions (Zhang et al., 2022).
- According to Lee et al. (2020), real-time travel information, booking services, and augmented reality experiences can be accessed with mobile apps and digital kiosks
- According to Shin & Kang (2020), cloud platforms are used to ensure that there is enough data storage and electronic storage that will meet the increasing demand.
- AI and machine learning algorithms for personalisation, forecasting, and recommendation systems (Bhuiyan et al., 2022).

These infrastructure components are the key contributors that keep the tourism system in both natural and agile ways. They provide services that are context-driven, personalised, and efficient. Moreover, some of the services are context-aware.

One can divide the layers of wise tourism technological infrastructures in multiple ways.

- Perception Layer: Includes sensors, RFID tags, GPS devices, and other tools for data acquisition (Buhalis & Amaranggana, 2014).
- Network Layer: Facilitates communication through wireless, 5G, or broadband technologies (Talukder & Hoque, 2025).
- Data Processing Layer: Leverages big data and cloud computing for storage, processing, and analysis (Ercan, 2020).
- Application Layer: Encompasses end-user platforms, mobile apps, and digital assistants for service delivery (Yang & Wang, 2025).

Every layer plays an essential role in ensuring the real-time, user-centric services that are the key to smart tourism.

2.4 Smart Destinations and Urban Integration

Smart tourism is a topic that is closely tied to smart cities; it is necessary to have a broad comprehension of it. The smart city context, as one of the components, sees the sites that are paved with information and communication technologies (ICT) not only limited to those that tourism is related to, but to other sectors such as city transport, energy, and security. The aim is to offer a disturbance-free experience to all the destination visitors (Gretzel et al., 2015; Pencarelli, 2020). In four cities, the plans for tourism were already a part of the comprehensive urban smart infrastructure. Barcelona, Amsterdam, Seoul, and Singapore have smart cities, narrowed down to destinations being a good fit for the public that travels and does other activities with the help of technology (Buhalis & Amaranggana, 2014).

2.4.1 User Experience and Service Personalisation

One very meticulous study of the territory with SMART Tourism is the automation of the services by making use of real-time data. The said thing has been made feasible with smart infrastructure that the studies have indicated to involve the service customisation in real time based on the user preferences, the user behaviour understanding through data analytics, and the optimization of the service delivery through artificial intelligence and machine learning.

- Predictive service offerings based on user behaviour and preferences (Xiang, 2018).
- Augmented reality and virtual guides for enhanced heritage site experiences (Soava, 2015).
- Adaptive pricing, promotions, and real-time feedback systems to improve satisfaction (Talukder & Hoque, 2025).

The improvements described earlier address the issue of tourist capability and the power to decide for oneself, which are at the core of the smart tourism value proposition (Buhalis & Foerste, 2015).

Even though smart tourism infrastructure appears to hold some advantages, some issues call for attention:

- The vast amount of personal and biometric data being collected creates a privacy breach and cybersecurity risk (Kshetri, 2014; Möller, 2023).
- A widening gap between technological haves and have-nots results in exclusion of elderly tourists and low-tech SMEs that do not participate in or cannot afford smart infrastructure (Herke et al., 2025).
- The fact that the use of technology is given too much emphasis may lead to fewer human interactions, and the experience of cultural events may become less authentic (Ercan, 2020).

Even though the smart infrastructure is very reliable and rapid, the chance of the unexpected, which plays a major part in the travel experience, might be eliminated in the process.

2.5 Smart Tourism and Sustainability

Current literature is probing the role of intelligent infrastructure in making sustainable tourism a reality. Smart tools can help achieve this by doing such things as optimising energy use, reducing "people" congestion, and monitoring (and even controlling) real-time environmental impact. Intelligent infrastructure is the answer to achieving (or at least working toward) the sustainability of tourism (Lee et al., 2020). Sustainable Smart Tourism integrates digital innovation with eco-friendly and socially responsible practices (Pencarelli, 2020).

- Edge Computing and 6G: To reduce latency and dependency on central servers.
- Digital Twins of Destinations: For real-time simulation and planning of visitor flows.
- Blockchain: For secure, decentralised data storage and smart contracts in tourism transactions (Aslan et al., 2023).
- Emotion-aware AI: To enhance human-computer interaction in tourism experiences.

Critics say that a smart infrastructure can do more harm than good if there is no proper governance in place a natural thing, such as surveillance or profit maximization, might be involved. There is quite a rapid progress observed in published work on smart tourism infrastructure, with a rise in the latest reports. However, it remains somewhat of a mystery what the exact activities in the field are. Companies in the travel and accommodation business fields have made quite a lot of progress in the integration of digital systems into their service lines. The academic paper trail, especially in the sciences and social sciences, shows no denial of the insufficiency of ominous predictions regarding the end of smart tourism. I tend to believe that the reality is a mix of both the proof and the opposing views.

3. DISCUSSION

3.1 The Digital Age in Tourism: The Rise of Smart Infrastructure

The revolution led by digital technology across the tourism sector involves abandoning the old, stagnant way of providing services in favour of the new, dynamic, responsive systems empowered mainly by artificial intelligence. Nowadays, intelligent infrastructure allows for the real-time synchronization and collaboration of the various elements of city tourism ecosystems, going beyond the usual stopping points like hotels and tourist guides to even the new digital technologies that are already part and parcel of the city's structure (Buhalis & Amaranggana, 2014; Xiang & Fesenmaier, 2018). A common denominator of this change is the idea of the smart destination, which is heavily relying on the use of coexisting and interoperable technologies such as IoT sensors, geospatial tools, cloud platforms, multilingual systems, augmented reality, and AI-driven chatbots to provide the visitor with personalised and captivating experiences (Lee et al., 2020). Boosting productivity, efficiency, and market position are similar reasons these steps were taken; nevertheless, they entirely depend on seamless data exchange through numerous platforms and machines. Thus, the network of connections gives the tourist industry an easy time of becoming the victim of significant cyber threats, such as, but not limited to, data breaches, ransomware, identity theft, and phishing attacks (Gretzel et al., 2015; Talukder & Hoque, 2025; Kshetri, 2014; Möller, 2023). The problem is that sensitive data like travel itineraries, location information, and biometric identifiers, as well as payment credentials, fall prey to cybercriminals. Security for data protection is a must for smart tourism development, as tourists are increasingly looking for personalized services and good data protection measures. Thus, the future of smart tourism lies in sustainable and legal means, such as the development of solid, credible, and culture-specific cybersecurity approaches with the involvement of the authorities, service providers, and users (Xu et al., 2023).

3.2 Cybersecurity Challenges in Smart Tourism

As we rely more on digital infrastructure, the perils tied to cybersecurity grow sharper, more intricate, and more impactful. For the tourism industry, this is especially so because, despite the benefits tied to technological advancements, cloud computing, for example, artificial intelligence (AI), the smart ecosystem tied to tourism has expanded its surface area for grand cyber schemes and threats. The top-most impressive smart tourism systems threats are mentioned in Figure 1.

Figure 1.

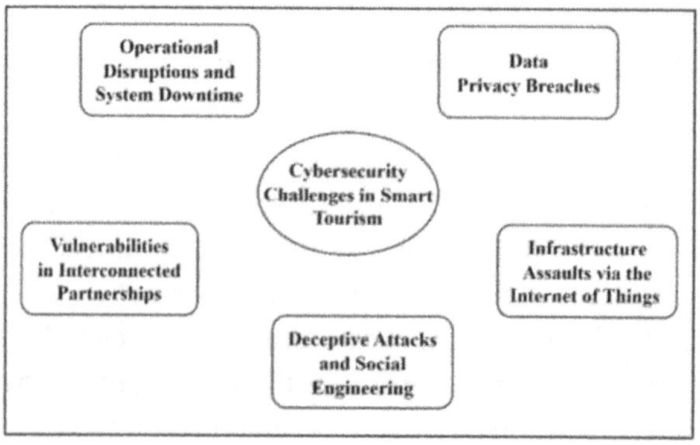

Source: Author's Work

3.2.1 Data Privacy Breaches

The most urgent problem facing smart tourism today is the exposure of "Personal Identifiable Information" (PII). "Tourists routinely submit highly sensitive information to digital tourism platforms, including passport and visa data, flight and health insurance details, and payment info." Mismanaged PII, resulting from inadequate encryption, improper storage, and poor access controls, can and does lead to data theft and identity fraud. Smart tourism nodes may handle PII in ways that not only compromise the security of the travellers involved but also national security, especially when cross-border travellers are involved (Kshetri, 2017; Herke et al., 2025).

3.2.2 Infrastructure Assaults via the Internet of Things (IoT)

The complex web of networked devices that forms the IoT-based infrastructure, from smart room controls, facial recognition gates, and connected transport hubs to digital kiosks, that we have come to rely upon, is becoming a hacker's paradise. These networked devices are often mindlessly obedient. They are the smart way in for bad guys who want to get to the things (or the people) that a smart system is supposed to protect. Endpoint security, the physical and digital smarts that secure a device and a networked relationship between an IoT device and the smart system, is the only way to make an IoT-based system worthwhile (Shin & Kang, 2020).

3.2.3 Deceptive Attacks and Social Engineering

Phishing and social engineering attacks often target tourists, who are usually not well-acquainted with the digital systems of the places they are visiting. Such attacks might be carried out by:

- Phony reservation internet sites that resemble real platforms.
- Travel apps that collect personal data under the guise of being legitimate are, in fact, fraudulent. These apps use various methods to obtain your sensitive information.
- Promotional offers that trick you into believing they are legitimate, sent by email or through messaging services.

These assaults take advantage of the trust and urgency that are often part of travel planning. Social engineering, of which this is one kind, works on human psychology, making folks nice and vulnerable to the ploys of bad guys. It's true that a VPN wins over all those annoying devices set up by the techs to safeguard us. Because of the fact that the mode of transportation is more mobile and less permanent compared to other human behaviours, it is a hacker's paradise for the tourists (Aslan et al., 2023).

3.2.4 Vulnerabilities in Interconnected Partnerships

Tourism is based on a web of interconnectivity among digital entities like hotels, online travel agencies (OTAs), transport providers, third-party review platforms, and fintech services, and this collaborative network extends its hands to IT. They share connections through application programming interfaces (APIs), databases, or partner portals. They build up a trust chain. But in case one of them is not secure, it may offer a keyhole to the whole system for the attackers, even when the other safe platforms have strong cybersecurity policies. Being an industry that extensively uses partners and that is a key factor in their relationships apart from data keeping the same, tourism proves to be a particularly soft target in this kind of inherited insecurity scenario (Nayak, 2016).

3.2.5 Operational Disruptions and System Downtime

Conventional attacks that disrupt the operations are not only a threat to the online services being provided by a smart tourism system. In fact, they are also a risk for the offline services. The smart tourism system is designed to be compatible with both types of services. In the case that the smart tourism system is out of service or an opportunity is provided for the attack of certain types, the tourism sector is affecteAttacks by ransomware that encrypt the systems used to make hotel and airline reservations.

- Denial-of-Service (DoS) attacks that inundate servers and stop people from accessing certain websites.
- Software maliciously designed to interrupt internal communication or staff scheduling systems.

The inconveniences of this sort may bring up a large number of cancellations, upset the routine, cause financial damage, and severely stain the reputation of a company. Cyberspace battles on the main systems can lead to the lowering of tourists' trust and even to the moral damage of tourism in general, particularly during busy travel seasons (Möller, 2023). The newer technology used in tourism, the greater the need for a piercing and multilayered cybersecurity approach to be able to secure that all the systems work perfectly, the data is not stolen, and no one's rights are violated.

3.3 Cybersecurity Governance and Policies for Improving Tourism Ecosystem

The governance of cybersecurity is undergoing digitalisation. Yet the big problem in this area is that there are no tailor-made governance frameworks available to the tourism sector, frameworks that could guide the sector in cybersecurity decisions. The available governance models, which have been conceived in the e-commerce, finance, or smart city domain, are either too broad to be useful for the tourism sector or too nebulous to address the kind of complex real-time data flow, as well as the stakeholder fragmentation, that is a hallmark of the tourism sector. This chapter argues for the establishment of a governance framework at the behest of the tourism sector. Thus, the chapter's authors provide a go-it-alone framework model that can be put to work by the tourism sector. Three aspects of this governance model are key. The model that has been proposed includes five components that fit together like a jigsaw puzzle, and each one of them covers a critical shortcoming in the current cybersecurity arrangements of the tourism sector, as given in Figure 2.

Figure 2.

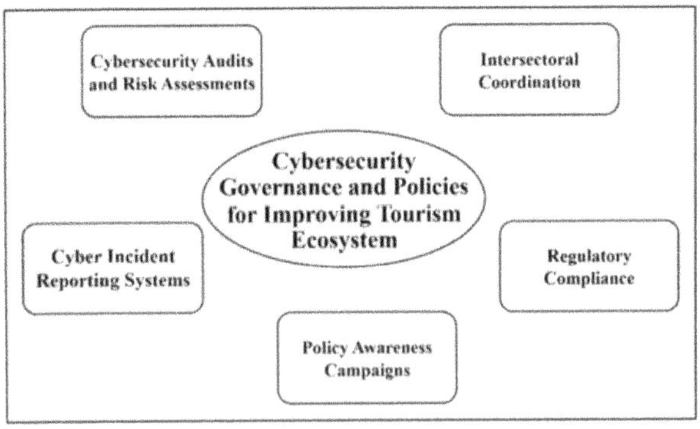

Source: Author's Work

3.3.1 Regulatory Compliance

Entities involved in tourism must be instructed to follow regional and global cybersecurity standards that are in place to ensure the confidentiality, integrity, and availability of data and systems associated with tourists. These standards consist of:

- General Data Protection Regulation (GDPR): Regulates and protects the personal data of citizens of the EU and acts as a global benchmark for the kind of privacy regulations that the citizens of other countries can expect.
- ISO/IEC 27001: Gives a framework for setting up, putting into operation, maintaining, and continuously improving an Information Security Management System (ISMS).
- PCI-DSS (Payment Card Industry Data Security Standard): Ensures the safe handling of credit card information in hospitality and travel-related transactions.

These standards should not only be adopted but also contextualised for the tourism environment. This guarantees that the particularities of a platform, such as booking engines, digital concierge services, and biometric immigration processing, are dealt with appropriately considering the case of tourism.

3.3.2 Intersectoral Coordination

The lack of current tourism stakeholders' siloed operations shows a major weakness in the cybersecurity governance. Reducing this distance is a principal part of what the framework is dealing with. Creating multi-stakeholder cybersecurity councils or working groups at the national and regional levels is what this movement is all about. The following are the necessary working groups:

- Government entities (for instance, ministries of tourism and digital affairs)
- Providers of critical infrastructure (telecom, airport, transport authorities), like Cybersecurity companies, and Ethical hacking corporations
- Associations in the hospitality and travel sectors
- Digital rights advocates in civil society

These committees would be given the job of setting policy benchmarks, steering the coordination of incident response drills, and whipping up shared standards for such things as data protection and breach notification protocols. It is possible to change the configurations for the audience that belongs in the security domain.

3.3.3 Cybersecurity Audits and Risk Assessments

The essential structure of an effective routine audit is shown in this graphic. However, keeping regularly scheduled audits as a component of the network security policy and using them, in a way, to "check the pulse" of the organization is the critical thing.

- E-commerce of travel and event tickets
- Online reservation and ticketing systems
- Intelligent hotels and Internet of Things-enabled devices
- Systems for cross-border travel that utilize blockchain technology
- Service platforms for AR and real-time directions
- Service platforms that use geolocation for enhanced service
- Real-time user engagement and augmented intelligence platforms

These inspections must be obligatory during peak travel seasons, like summer vacations, religious festivals, or major events such as the Olympics or World Expos, and they should:

- Levels of system vulnerability
- Encryption of the data

The coordination of the outfit is not merely the task of a single team but of all employees.

- The network's exposure to penetration

- Policies dealing with data from third parties
- Prevention of insider threats

Tourism regulatory authorities may partner with certified cybersecurity auditors to guarantee compliance and cybersecurity toughness.

3.3.4 Cyber Incident Reporting Systems

The travel and tourism industry is one of the most technologically connected sectors in the world, with a lot of e-Commerce operations. Thousands of companies offer more or less the same services; on top of that, the e-tourism sector is among the most frequently targeted business segments, so the business continuity plan must be well elaborated and include real-time backup procedures for the databases. Meanwhile, the industry is inevitably moving towards the IoT, but what would actually give it an advantage is if it could quickly adapt to the development of the botnet and separate itself from the burden of looking after the road warriors, ubiquitous computing, and AI algorithms governing the chatbots of the digital assistants.

- Monitor and log cyber threats (e.g., phishing, ransomware, DoS, breaches of data security), which can be processed into useful intelligence.
- Track impacts and responses
- Distribute immediate notifications to tourism sector stakeholders.
- Provide technical support for containment and recovery.

Indeed, the national Computer Emergency Response Team (CERT) could be the place where this solution is put. However, it ought to have a special sector interface in the tourism sector, thus making the service available for hotels, OTAs, tour operators, and airports to report cyber incidents in a very short and confidential period from the time of the incident.

3.3.5 Policy Awareness Campaigns

Even the most sophisticated technological defences are useless without the watchful eyes of human beings. Tourists and tourism professionals are often unaware of fundamental cybersecurity practices, and because of that, they are easy prey for phishers and con artists who operate online. The proposed framework comprises:

- Training workers in the tourism sector regarding good cyber hygiene, such as staff at the front desk, guides in the field, and digital marketers.

- Incorporate cybersecurity awareness modules in the curricula of tourism and hospitality higher education.
- Campaigns in airports and hotels for public awareness using the internet and sharing personal data.
- Toolkits for digital literacy are provided in a variety of languages for the use of both international and domestic travelers.

The above text indicates that the whole tourism ecosystem will become more responsible and knowledgeable if a cybersecurity culture is built. The idea is to establish cybersecurity governance at all levels of the tourism value chain, i.e., regulatory, operational, and cultural, to foster a resilient and reliable tourism ecosystem in touch with the digital step. Smart governance by sectoral means is a reactive and limited way, only up to a certain level of impact and scope, and may be the way.

4. RESEARCH MODEL

4.1 Building a Cyber-Resilient Tourism Ecosystem

Smart tourism has been associated with applications connected to space, exchange of on-time data, or even advanced technology in tourists' experiences. Even though this use of technology is for a better and more personal visitor experience, the other side of the story is that it is putting the tourism industry at the very heart of cyber-attacks. Considering that, the tourism industry needs to invest in building strong cyber resilience to provide secure, reliable, and private transactions between tourists and service providers. Cyber resilience is not equivalent to traditional cybersecurity since it is based not only on the prevention but also on the capacity of a system to respond to incidents, keep operational continuity, recover quickly, and learn from the interruptions. The capability of a system to achieve a rapid and efficient reconciliation with minimal impact on the operating system will, on one hand, enable the service providers to continue business operations after an attack, and on the other hand, it will reduce the probability of recurrence of similar incidents.

4.1.1 Strategic Pillars of a Cyber-Resilient Tourism Ecosystem

Development of a tourism ecosystem that is robust to cyber-attacks requires a coordinated effort through the use of technology, market, and policy, as well as through the human dimension. The first pillar is about the creation of an infrastructure that is inherently secured, which includes the use of AI-based threat intelligence systems for round-the-clock monitoring and risk mitigation, the use of zero-trust architectures and blockchain that guarantee the security of data and also to have periodical penetration testing done on the tourism platforms.

The second pillar is about the role of cyber-aware companies and human resources through the use of training programs, creating cybersecurity units within the tourism organizations, and imposing certification and compliance requirements on third-party vendors.

The third pillar of governance and policy integration is composed of developing policies on cybersecurity, which are unique to tourism but are at the same time in conformity with recognized international practices such as GDPR, NIST, and ISO 27001, and including breach reporting, encryption, and cyber insurance in the mandatory requirements for tourism.

On top of that, smart cities should be both cyber-safe and well-suited for tourism at the same time by protecting the infrastructure of IoT and by fostering the relationships among civic authorities, tech companies, and tourism businesses. Besides, the tourists who are supplied with the necessary means are also becoming a very important factor by means of providing the awareness of the importance of cyber hygiene, adopting a code of safety that can be easily understood through all languages, and sharing their data with companies only if they comply with the required global regulations.

4.1.2 Challenges to Implementation

Despite the growing recognition of cybersecurity's importance in tourism, several barriers persist, as given in Figure 3.

Figure 3.

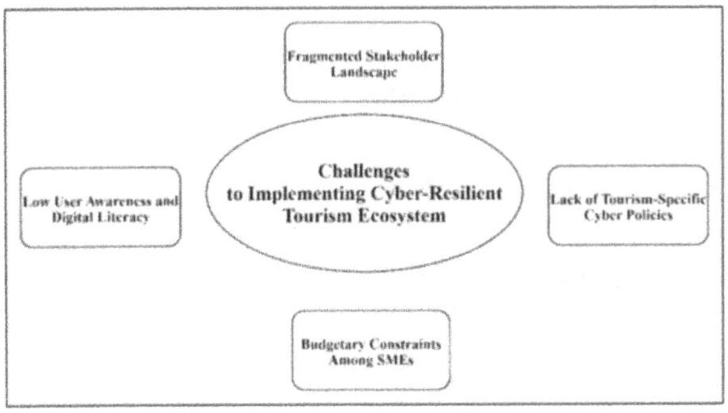

Source: Author's Work

Fragmented Stakeholder Landscape

The inherent nature of the tourism industry being multi-stakeholder means it brings together many different players: public sector bodies (such as tourism ministries, municipal governments); private enterprises (like hotels, airlines, and booking platforms); tech and service providers (ranging from app developers to cloud services); and consumers.

This brings many different players to the table. And this makes:

- It is hard to put into practice the policies that coordinate cybersecurity.
- Passing on information is inefficient or incomplete.
- Accountability weakened, most notably in responses to incidents or data breaches.

Lacking definite structures for agency-to-agency partnership and confidence in the governing of shared information, we seem unable to coordinate our efforts at stimulating pre-reaction resilience in our systems.

Lack of Tourism-Specific Cyber Policies

Most current cybersecurity laws are either comprehensive (like the GDPR or ISO standards) or tailored to specific sectors (like our banking and healthcare regulations). There's nothing comparable for tourism. And the cybersecurity industry isn't going to fill that vacuum. The result: a huge and unregulated target for cybercriminals.

- Businesses in the tourism sector tend to use one-size-fits-all security measures that don't take into account the unique cybersecurity challenges tourism enterprises face—such as being overly dependent on customer-generated data.
- Regulatory oversight frequently does not apply to the digital tourism infrastructure (such as AR kiosks, smart hotel systems) that is often constructed by the private sector in public spaces.
- Inconsistent protections exist for international tourists across different countries, resulting in a range of legal and ethical grey areas.

Budgetary Constraints Among SMEs

Several Small and Medium-sized Enterprises (SMEs) in the tourism sector operate with restricted budgets and limited technical know-how, which yields the following outcomes:

- Unpatched systems and software that are outdated are at risk of being attacked.

- Lacking the funds to pay for top-notch cybersecurity solutions, insurance, or IT staff.
- Insufficient preparedness for cyber events, most small and medium-sized enterprises do not even have rudimentary response strategies.

Since SMEs are central to providing tourist experiences (particularly in local, cultural, or rural tourism), their cybersecurity problems are a systemic risk.

Low User Awareness and Digital Literacy

The tourists, particularly the first-time travellers, seniors, and individuals with less experience in digital communication, often are short on:

- Knowledge of phishing assaults, counterfeit websites, and fraudulent travel offers.
- Ability to assess the reliability of applications, networks, and booking platforms.
- Knowing all about the rights of data privacy and the methods to safeguard it, i.e., by using multi-factor authentication and VPNs.

The tourism sector is rushing into a digital transformation where cyberattack is a common target of critical and financially rewarding assets. For sure, the multidimensional cyberattack may occur, but this challenge is more or less unseen because of its invisibility in cyberspace. It is a fact very few of these initiatives have made any progress.

Figure 4.

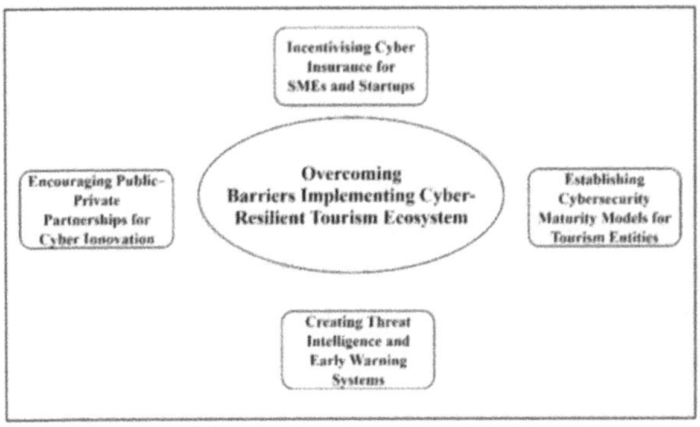

Source: Author's Work

4.2 Establishing Cyber Resilience in Smart Tourism

Creation of cyber maturity models just for tourism with a clear purpose is a must in order to boost security practices in the field as a whole. There will be a group of directed tools that would help stakeholders to enhance performance, which at the same time would enable them to be ready to identify weaknesses, and to be proactive as well as prioritize their corrective actions. It is equally necessary to guarantee that the new models are expandable and can fit in a wide range of tourism entities; further, but not limited to, multinational corporations in the hotel and airline industry and, the smallest corner travel shops found at the grass root by with- the governance, technical, sharing, and responding to incidents as part of the spectrum. The formation of joint threat intelligence and warning systems is equally significant. As a consequence of it, the international data exchange and country-level cooperation are what will give the fastest and most valuable intelligence about criminal acts where ransomware, phishing, and major data breaches are occurrences. If such systems are made the essential parts of tourism platforms or national digital infrastructures, the industry will not only be able to react faster but also reduce the systemic risk.

Public–private partnerships, in addition, are also essential elements in the process of cyber innovation. The trio of government, academic institutions, and cybersecurity businesses must work together to cost-effectively produce solutions that are specific to the sectors. Among these are the protection of digital-only enabled smart hotels, the safeguarding of biometric data utilized in the electronic visas and border systems, and the increasing of the level of fraud detection within online booking platforms. The situation of financially weak small and medium-sized firms makes it necessary to introduce incentives, for example, for taking out cyber insurance that is specific to the sector. Besides, these insurance products can defray the cost of direct financial losses, reputational harm, penalties for non-compliance, and recovery services, and hence they contribute to the enhancement of organizational resilience as well as building trust in the long run in the smart tourism system. On the other hand, the World Economic Forum predicts the approaching dangers by mentioning the convergence of smart technologies and the administration of the tourism sector as one of the causes for the easy access of cybercriminals. Cybercriminals threaten not only the online infrastructures but also the trust, competitiveness, and attractiveness of a location as a tourism destination, and thus, would-be visitors might decide to go to another place.

5. PROPOSED CYBER-RESILIENCE MODEL FOR SMART TOURISM

The proposed Cyber-Resilience Model for Smart Tourism addresses these challenges by embedding resilience across four interrelated levels: technological systems, organisational processes, sectoral governance, and user engagement. Developed by researchers at the University of Denver, the model emphasises prevention, response, recovery, and adaptive learning, enabling tourism ecosystems to withstand cyberattacks while maintaining service continuity and safeguarding traveller trust, as given in Figure 5.

Figure 5.

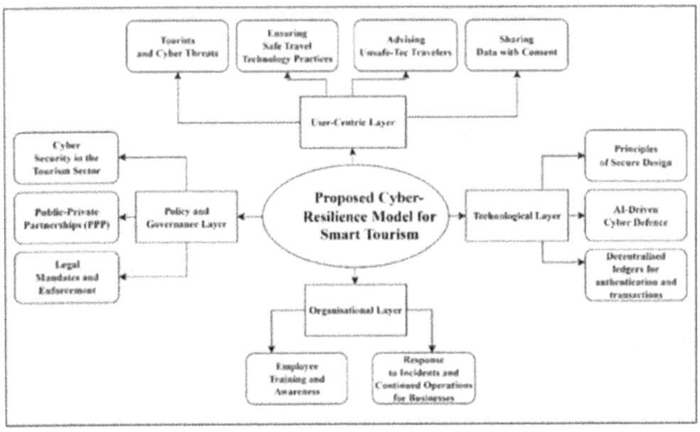

Source: Author's Work

5.1 Technological Layer

Embedding security directly into system architecture, the technological layer acts as the ground of cyber resilience in smart tourism. It is the main technological layer that offers secure, reliable, and responsive digital tourism ecosystems. This layer is the key focus of the latest technologies for stopping vulnerabilities as well as supporting real-time threat detection and response. One of the main aims for this is the use of a secure-by-design strategy, i.e., the adoption of secure coding practices, such as input validation, sandboxing, encrypted Application Programming Interfaces (APIs), and strict access control mechanisms, for the incorporation of security in the software development process. These measures significantly lessen the chances of being hacked across a variety of platforms, including booking systems, mobile apps, and service portals. Along with that, AI and machine-learning-driven cyber defence has become the core part of the ecosystem. The goal is that these technologies will observe the network traffic and the user, take note of the anomalies, and automatically respond in real time to protect the network from threats. They are intelligent enough to allow the security systems to cope properly with the constantly changing cyber risks. Eventually, decentralised ledger technologies, for instance, blockchain can be used to considerably protect authentication, transactions, and data integrity. Moreover, in the case of tourism, blockchain-enabled smart contracts are able to automate processes such as hotel check-ins and guest payments, thereby improving transparency, trust, and operational security.

5.2 Organizational Layer

Strengthening the internal readiness and resilience of tourism entities, including hotels, tour operators, travel agencies, and digital service providers, is the main goal of the organisational layer. The integration of cybersecurity with the daily workflow, organizational culture, and strategic decision-making is indeed more preferable than treating it as a mere technical function. The core component of this is employee training and awareness. It is necessary for all employees to have a sound grasp of the most basic cyber hygiene, phishing attacks, and safe data handling, while some frontline staffers should be the ones to go through training on how they can identify and report breaches affecting customer data or company systems. Another key is having a well-informed IT governance team that takes a proactive approach to the IT requirements of the company. Regular cybersecurity audits, penetration testing, and constant monitoring of the cloud infrastructure are some of the activities that contribute to the very early identification of threats and vulnerabilities. The use of a zero-trust architecture model is one of the methods wherein no user or system is automatically trusted. Lastly, the existence of a strong incident response and business continuity planning is a basic requirement. The setup of Digital Infrastructure Response Teams (DIRTs) that follow NIST incident response guidelines enables companies to be in control of the threat and, at the same time, minimize service disruption and financial losses.

5.3 Policy and Governance Layer

In this section, stress was laid on the significance of governance throughout the sector, and regulation from the top down to have a reliable and efficient cybersecurity across the tourism ecosystem. Governance with a firm hand leads to the harmonization of activities among the involved parties, the application of standards throughout, and the belief that the threats from cyber will be defeated all the time; it is also possible that these will escalate. One of the main aspects is the formulation of cybersecurity policies for tourism. The existing national and regional cybersecurity frameworks are very often general and do not take into account the specific characteristics of tourism that make it more vulnerable to cyber threats, such as the high mobility of the tourist data, spikes in demand for services by customers during the busy months of the year, and the sector's reliance on third-party platforms. Hence, it is necessary to have adapted policies to mirror the operational conditions of the sector. The third pillar, which is formed through Public-Private Partnerships (PPPs), is also of utmost importance. Cooperation among the government, tourism authorities, and private enterprises helps in the sharing of information, the creation of a secure infrastructure by means of a joint investment, and the establishment of the model of joint responsibility by engaging businesses in the process. The last action of adopting the model is very important in the course of the practical implementation. Then, legal requirements combined with sanctions are the means through which compliance is to be ensured. The laws related to the sector are set up to be compliant with the global ones, such as the GDPR, ISO/IEC 27001, and PCI-DSS, to be parallel to them and enforce the industry's ethics and professionalism.

5.4 User-Centric Layer

Tourists are an integral part of the cyber-resilience ecosystem because their digital behaviours, choices, and level of awareness have a direct impact on the security of the tourism platforms. The smarter the tourism industry gets, the more both the digital and physical parts of the tourist experiences will depend on having knowledgeable and responsible tourists in the participation equation. One of the paramount conditions is to make tourists conscious of the cyber threats. One of the problem areas is that the tourists are frequently naive in terms of the risks when they are in the digital unknown realm, like the use of public Wi-Fi, downloading fake booking apps, and even clicking the phishing links given in the emails. The responsible thing to do is for the tourism platforms to equip the travellers with the necessary information and to help them through their journey by issuing warning alerts in different languages, providing guidance through the app, and notifying the users in real-time when they engage in safe online activities. An important part of it is also making sure that travel technology is used safely. It is the official tourism platforms that should recommend the users to only use a verified digital channel for gaining information and, at the same time, to restrict unauthorized services and the fraudulent peer-to-peer transactions. In some environments, the risk is so high that tourists should be advised that, in case they need to, it is better to use low-tech alternatives. Finally, data sharing must follow a strict consent-first rule. This is where the platforms' major role lies in granting the public access to the personal data they collect in a transparent and user-centric manner, in line with the designated law, i.e., the GDPR.

6. PRACTICAL IMPLICATIONS

This chapter provides key insights that are highly needed and issues that might be difficult for all players in a tourism ecosystem, which is now data-driven and digitally connected more than ever. Thus, every stakeholder from the government to the traveler is solely responsible for securing their digital presence while, at the same time, contributing to the enhancement of the full sector's cybersecurity resilience.

One bright example is the policymakers who need to take action on this matter without any delay. They must create and implement laws and regulations for cybersecurity that are specific to tourism. This includes the setting up of cybersecurity units that are solely responsible for this sector within the tourism ministries, mandating the embedding of security-related requirements in the national tourism development strategies, and making the legal frameworks comply with international standards like GDPR and ISO/IEC 27001. Along with that, effective and powerful institutional mechanisms are necessary to make sure that everyone complies with the new rules, to monitor potential dangers, and to give the opportunity for networking among the sectors during cyber incidents.

Cybersecurity is becoming a must-have instead of just being a good idea for travel-oriented enterprises, as this area critically exposes the revenue, customer confidence, and daily work delivery. Consequently, to keep the trade running and the paychecks coming, many hotels, travel companies, tour organizers, and web-based businesses shall be made to spend the money on strong, secure, and robust payment systems, as well as to know who has access to what.

Smart tourism, for the tech industry, becomes the ultimate mode to use their potential in the areas of safety, fast, and compliant digital solutions. They range from secure travel applications, AI-based fraud detection systems, privacy-enhancing biometric systems, and efficient, blockchain-powered transaction setups.

In the context of academic and research institutions, interdisciplinary cooperation is crucial. Standardized curricula, practical research, and cooperation with industry can do wonders for closing the knowledge gap between cybersecurity and tourism management, hospitality education, and digital ethics.

Security matters should be a first-item consideration for tourists at all times. Alongside Governments, the travel industry should use all available means to increase the alertness among tourists concerning identity theft, scamming, ransomware, and the use of Wi-Fi through the issuance of travel advisories and the consistent use of digital platforms. All these activities combine to lay the groundwork for an innovative, resilient, and secure smart tourism ecosystem.

7. CONCLUSION

In the present era of digital technology, the travel and tourism sector at a global level resembles a different face in terms of its nature and operation, mainly because the digital technological advancement requires the modernization of the long-term tourism traditional systems. Artificial intelligence (AI), the Internet of Things (IoT), and other technologies are in charge of the production of smart tourism infrastructure, and as a result, the old ways of tourism planning, booking, and experiencing have changed. They use a plethora of different devices and applications, working in harmony, to be able to give such fast, personalized, and context-dependent experiences. Smart tourism is therefore a new travel paradigm whose very structure is based on the idea of mobility without limits, thanks to the use of multilingual services, augmented reality, easy payments, and intelligent recommendations. Geospatial mapping, digital ticketing, and cloud services are key attributes of a smart city, one aspect of which is the integration of smart tourism. In fact, smart tourism has the ability to transform the city into a more sustainable place, along with other technological advancements such as environmental monitoring and sensor-based crowd management. These technologies- individually or together- influence, directly or indirectly, the three major issues of the city: efficiency, accessibility, and sustainability. Yet, the vulnerability exposed by the digital makeover is the ascendancy of potential cybersecurity threats that come hand in hand with the augmenting streams of real-time data, the evolving dependence on the cloud, and the pervasive application of mobile communication technologies, all of which have provided new ways for cyber attackers to pose as tourism sector for data breaches, identity theft, and social engineering. In this way, cybersecurity in tourism would imply the guarding of the overall security of the system, making sure that the functionality was secured, and no unwanted access to significant data was allowed.

Dealing with the above-mentioned issues would require an interdisciplinary, cooperative approach that is not limited by the traditional or separate cybersecurity models. The future-focused tourism cybersecurity strategies will call for a couple of integrated pillars. For the sake of the above operational differences of tourism bodies, it is very much needed that these governance structures should sharply define the various responsibilities, duties, and cooperation mechanisms by being at the very least a replica of international standards such as GDPR and ISO/IEC 27001. Among the many key actions taken by special industries to prevent and neutralize their cyberthreats would be to adopt their long-term security policies. Smart hotels, digital places, and transport in smart cities are seen as the most common targets of cyberattacks hence the need for special industry-specific policies as well. The partners from the public and private sectors may together not only take full responsibility but also allow for the introduction of a new technology and be the source of the information that is shared among the different stakeholders. The need to educate and make the digital protection of tourism the subject of public awareness is utmost since it will not only decrease the risks but also make the staff and tourists more careful in using the technology. Moreover, following the security-by-design principles and the ability to recover quickly and effectively from incidents will be the main elements to have resilient systems in place. It is a matter that policymakers, businesses, technology developers, and even tourists need to work together in a coordinated fashion to guarantee that smart tourism is also secure.

8. FUTURE RESEARCH DIRECTIONS

Tourism and digital technology are merging that is creating one of the fastest-growing and most appealing fields for academic research. It is essential to narrow down the research focus and conduct qualitative research as smart tourism infrastructure becomes an inseparable part of the global travel market, not only for the sake of developing the theory but also through the provision of practical tools and policies that establish secure and sustainable digital tourism systems. One of the major pathways for the research is the work on tourism-specific cybersecurity frameworks. While the business sector is becoming more reliant on the digital infrastructure, there is still no single model that covers all aspects of the risk it has, such as crime, terror, and the points of being the heaviest assets and visitors' flow. Nearly as much as that, it is also significant to develop the cyber risk assessment models to fit the small and medium-sized enterprises (SMEs), which are the backbone companies of the tourism industry, but still have a limited budget for investment in IT. Another aspect of the problem of travel is cybersecurity, as the situation would be worth investigating further in the case of tourists. It is really the best way for us to know the whole story about the situation if we can ask the traveller how and where he/she feels a cyberthreat and how, through everyday security measures, the vulnerability can be eliminated. At the same time, separate fields of high-level interdisciplinary research are pointed to when it comes to AI and blockchain, and specifically so in the case of the applications of the same to the tourism industry. One such sector of high-level research is that of ethical technology and data protection. The recent evolution in the category of digital technology is the greater amount of tourism data being shared across borders. By this, it is very important for scholars to investigate the issue of informed consent, privacy, and legal accountability with a specific reference to marketing practices and data-sharing. Moreover, the effect of the new husband technologies, such as augmented reality (AR), digital twins, and 5G infrastructure, on the rise of cybersecurity threats necessitates a clean analysis. The last point is the education and capacity building that should be given strict notice. The methods of evaluating the digital literacy programmes, the cybersecurity training, and certification initiatives for tourism players (professionals, developers, and tourists) should also be one of the essential topics. Thus, the development of smart tourism innovation that is be developed in a safe, moral, and institutionally equipped ecosystem can be guaranteed through research work of all these areas.

REFERENCES

Aslan, Ö., Aktuğ, S. S., Ozkan-Okay, M., Yilmaz, A. A., & Akin, E. (2023). A comprehensive review of cyber security vulnerabilities, threats, attacks, and solutions. *Electronics (Basel), 12*(6), 1333. DOI: 10.3390/electronics12061333

Bhuiyan, K. H., Jahan, I., Zayed, N. M., Islam, K. M. A., Suyaiya, S., Tkachenko, O., & Nitsenko, V. (2022). Smart tourism ecosystem: A new dimension toward sustainable value co-creation. *Sustainability (Basel), 14*(22), 15043. DOI: 10.3390/su142215043

Buhalis, D., & Amaranggana, A. (2014, December). Smart tourism destinations enhancing tourism experience through personalisation of services. In *Information and communication technologies in tourism 2015: Proceedings of the international conference in Lugano, Switzerland, February 3-6, 2015* (pp. 377-389). Cham: Springer International Publishing.

Chon, K. K. S., & Hao, F. (2025). Technological evolution in tourism: A Horizon 2050 perspective. *Tourism Review, 80*(1), 313–325. DOI: 10.1108/TR-10-2023-0753

Ercan, F. (2020). An examination on the use of immersive reality technologies in the travel and tourism industry. *Business & Management Studies: An International Journal, 8*(2), 2348–2383. DOI: 10.15295/bmij.v8i2.1510

Gretzel, U., Sigala, M., Xiang, Z., & Koo, C. (2015). Smart tourism: Foundations and developments. *Electronic Markets, 25*(3), 179–188. DOI: 10.1007/s12525-015-0196-8

Herke, C., Tóth, D., & Perkumienė, D. (2025). The Role of Artificial Intelligence in Cybercrime in the Tourism Sector. In *Tourism and Heritage: Shaping Sustainable and Innovative Futures* (pp. 415–433). Springer Nature Switzerland. DOI: 10.1007/978-3-031-81485-3_17

Jimmy, F. (2021). Emerging threats: The latest cybersecurity risks and the role of artificial intelligence in enhancing cybersecurity defenses. *Valley International Journal Digital Library, 1*(2), 564–574. DOI: 10.18535/ijsrm/v9i2.ec01

Kshetri, N. (2014). The emerging role of Big Data in key development issues: Opportunities, challenges, and concerns. *Big Data & Society, 1*(2), 2053951714564227. DOI: 10.1177/2053951714564227

Lee, P., Hunter, W. C., & Chung, N. (2020). Smart tourism city: Developments and transformations. *Sustainability (Basel), 12*(10), 3958. DOI: 10.3390/su12103958

Möller, D. P. (2023). Cybersecurity in digital transformation. In *Guide to cybersecurity in digital transformation: Trends, methods, technologies, applications and best practices* (pp. 1–70). Springer Nature Switzerland. DOI: 10.1007/978-3-031-26845-8_1

Nayak, H. (2016). Impact of cybercrime on tourism industry. *International Journal of Management and Social Sciences*, *4*(4), 160–174.

Pencarelli, T. (2020). The digital revolution in the travel and tourism industry. *Information Technology & Tourism*, *22*(3), 455–476. DOI: 10.1007/s40558-019-00160-3

Soava, G. (2015). Development prospects of the tourism industry in the digital age. *Revista tinerilor economişti*, (25), 101-116.

Talukder, M. B., & Hoque, M. (2025). Navigating the Digital Horizon: Transforming Travel Agencies in the Digital Era. In *Perspectives on Digital Transformation in Contemporary Business* (pp. 383-410). IGI Global Scientific Publishing.

Tsaih, R. H., & Hsu, C. C. (2018). Artificial intelligence in smart tourism: A conceptual framework.

Xiang, Z. (2018). From digitization to the age of acceleration: On information technology and tourism. *Tourism Management Perspectives*, *25*, 147–150. DOI: 10.1016/j.tmp.2017.11.023

Xu, Y., Shi, Y., & Qin, T. (2023). Challenges in smart tourism: A media content analysis of digital barriers for senior tourists in China. *Information Technology & Tourism*, *25*(4), 665–682. DOI: 10.1007/s40558-023-00270-z

Yang, F. X., & Wang, Y. (2025). Rethinking metaverse tourism: A taxonomy and an agenda for future research. *Journal of Hospitality & Tourism Research (Washington, D.C.)*, *49*(1), 3–12. DOI: 10.1177/10963480231163509

Zhang, Y., Sotiriadis, M., & Shen, S. (2022). Investigating the impact of smart tourism technologies on tourists' experiences. *Sustainability (Basel)*, *14*(5), 3048. DOI: 10.3390/su14053048

Chapter 4
Cybersecurity Nexus for Achieving Sustainable Development Goals (SDGs) in Tourism:
A Digital Resilience and Governance Perspective

Md. Saddam Hossain
http://orcid.org/0009-0001-9996-4963
Khulna University, Bangladesh

ABSTRACT

The chapter discusses the role of cybersecurity in realization of the United Nations Sustainable Development Goals (SDGs) in tourism sector. With time, tourism is becoming a digital industry, so powerful cybersecurity is necessary to make data resilient, foster trust, and prevent malicious attacks. This chapter proposes a new term, Cyber-Sustainability Nexus, demonstrating the interface between cybersecurity and four SDGs (SDG 8, SDG 9, SDG 11, and SDG 16). Using Resilience and Institutional theories, it explains cybersecurity as a flexible approach to respond to digital menace as well as a demand of governance. Case studies and best practices focus on emerging technologies like blockchain and AI along with major digital issues (e.g., inequality and poor regulation). The chapter concludes with recommendations for policy, capacity building, and inclusive digital development to promote secure and sustainable tourism systems.

DOI: 10.4018/979-8-2600-1850-7.ch004

INTRODUCTION

Tourism has become a predominant source of economic growth. In addition to this, it has been a field of sustainable development in recent years. With the implementation of the most recent digitally-enabled AI-based travel services, smart destination management systems, and contactless payment systems, the given industry is currently making sure that it offers a seamless and radically new experience. Nevertheless, this advancement comes with a secondary risk of cybersecurity vulnerabilities and, this is why the gender aspect of the cybersecurity and sustainable tourism agendas around the SDGs is a high interest area. The privacy of travelers, the stability of the infrastructures of tourists and the electronic infrastructure pose such a risk when the state of cybersecurity is underdeveloped.

Sustainable tourism cybersecurity can be a significant contributor to achievement of the SDGs. One of the basic elements of it is the necessity of a strong digital infrastructure that will support tourism activities, economic growth and the sustainability of services (Ige et al., 2024; Odumesi & Sanusi, 2023). Cybersecurity secures personal and functional information, builds online trust, and accessibility to tourism technologies will span geographical and demographic boundaries.

It is possible to enhance the security systems using such technologies as blockchain and artificial intelligence since they enhance transparency, data integrity, and minimize fraud in tourist purchases (Ige et al., 2024; Achuthan et al., 2024). However, with these developments new aspects of challenges exist. Without such intervention, new cyber threats, including ransomware, fraud, and system intrusion, can jeopardize the sustainability initiatives (Mohamed & Abuobied, 2024). Identification of these risks and creation of countermeasures strategies, such as global cooperation, awareness of cybersecurity challenges, and broad-based online policy, are the way to the stability of the industry (Ige et al., 2024). Additionally, incorporation of cybersecurity into the Environmental, Social and Governance (ESG) disclosure may lead to the alignment of tourism organizations with SDG indicators, support the credibility of stakeholders, and foster a positive sustainable governance. Nevertheless, the eco-impact of cybersecurity technologies cannot be neglected either. Such solutions, as cryptographic protocols or real-time threat detection systems are of solutions that are resource intensive and inconsistent with the greater ecological goals. Sustainable tourism can therefore only be guaranteed by a balance between sustainability, security and environmental sustainability (Achuthan et al., 2024).

As the tourism industry conforms to the SDGs of the United Nations, cybersecurity must be viewed as a flattener of not only the undesirable features of globalization, but also a part of the resilient, inclusive and tourism-ready processes. This chapter introduces the concept of the 'Cyber-Sustainability Nexus' which suggests the incorporation of cybersecurity into the sustainable tourist development.

OBJECTIVES

- To examine how cybersecurity enables sustainable tourism aligned with SDGs;
- To introduce the concept of a Cyber-Sustainability Nexus;
- To explore the application of Resilience and Institutional theories in tourism cybersecurity;
- To recommend policy-level solutions for secure digital tourism governance;

THEORETICAL FRAMEWORK

This chapter uses two complementary theories so that the sustainable tourism promoted by cybersecurity in line with the UN Sustainable Development Goals (SDGs) can be analyzed properly:

Resilience Theory: It is necessary that cybersecurity should be conceptualized as a means of creating adaptive, and resilient tourism systems, being capable of withstanding and recovering from disruptions.

Institutional Theory: This theory describes how adoption of cybersecurity practices are influenced by formal organizational structure types and norms, as well as control in the tourism industry.

The combination of the two theories provides the multi-dimensional insight into the necessity of cybersecurity within the tourism sustainability, and motivations that are pushing towards its adoption.

Resilience Theory

The manner in which a system is resistant to breaking, how systems achieve adaptation to stresses, and how systems continue on functioning in the face of shocks is the Resilience Theory, an ecological and systems science (Holling, 1973). In the context of digital tourism systems, the theories of resilience provide a generalization of the role of cybersecurity to protect the stability and functionality of the tourism infrastructure in the face of the increasing cyber-attacks.

Logical Justification

Tourism, on its part, is highly dependent on digital networks because it is one of the industries that bundle technologies and unveil smart solutions, such as an IoT-based hotel, a digital guest experience, and online booking services. Ransomware and distributed denial-of-service (DDoS) attacks can make the entire tourism operation inactive that may result in financial loss. To mitigate this problem, cybersecurity measures, including intrusion protection, data encryption and disaster recovery plan should be implemented to enhance the ability of a tourism system to withstand such incidences.

Links to SDGs

Sustainable Cities and Communities (SDG 11): To be inclusive, safe and resilient, smart tourist destinations require safe digital infrastructure that can cope with *SDG 11*.

Industry, Innovation and Infrastructure (SDG 9): Cyber resilience, innovative and digitized tourism services are feasible, as they are stable and continuous.

In this way, the sphere of cybersecurity can be discussed as one of the drivers of long-term sustainability since it strengthens the robustness of a system in terms of its digital vulnerability.

Institutional Theory

Institutional Theory (Meyer & Rowan, 1977; DiMaggio & Powell, 1983) outlines that the organizational behavior is influenced by the institutional rules, expectations, and norms that play an important role in determining how the organizations behave. This theory plays a pertinent role in the context of the tourism industry where the relationship is marked by mixed jurisdiction and borders, interconnectedness, and multifarious stakeholders, in addition to individual stakeholders who visit or contiguously visit more than one region.

Logical Justification

Tourism companies do not implement cybersecurity because of the technical reasons only, in most cases, they do it because of regulatory pressure, normative influence, and mimetic behavior.

Regulatory Pressure: It indicates adherence to national or international regulation (e.g. GDPR, ISO27001).

Normative Influence: It refers to the expectations by industry bodies, certification agencies and professional association.

Mimetic Behavior: It depicts the adaptation of the best practices adopted by leading companies in an aim to add legitimacy and earn trust.

This institutional environment promotes the process of normalizing cybersecurity as an organizational rule and strategic necessity, specifically around the agenda of sustainability.

Links to SDGs

Peace, Justice and Strong Institutions (SDG 16): This SDG consists of transparency, accountability and governance-all of which are straight impacts of institutionalized practices of cybersecurity.

Decent Work and Economic Growth (SDG 8): When the institutions are able to adopt cybersecurity as a new norm, they can easily ensure the trustworthiness of digital tourism ecosystems. Thus the development of entrepreneurship, employment, and responsible innovation can be promoted in a smooth way.

In this respect, the institutional theory helps explain how cybersecurity can be integrated into the governance of tourism systems and compatible with the sustainable development agenda.

Integrating the Two: A Coherent Lens for Cyber-Sustainable Tourism

The Resilience Theory helps explain that the perpetuity of the tourism systems can be ensured under threats by cybersecurity where the Institutional Theory explains how to adopt and shape the cybersecurity practices and their legitimation in the system.

Table 1. Comparison of Resilience and Institutional Theories

Dimension	Resilience Theory	Institutional Theory
Focus	System adaptability and recovery	Organizational behavior and conformity
Core Contribution	Explains role of cybersecurity in sustaining operations	Explains diffusion and adoption of cybersecurity norms
Relation to SDGs	Sustainable Cities and Communities (SDG 11), Industry, Innovation and Infrastructure (SDG 9)	Peace, Justice and Strong Institutions (SDG 16), The Decent Work and Economic Growth (SDG 8)

These theories describe a framework that discusses cybersecurity as a technical infrastructure and a governance instrument on how to achieve the said SDGs. In such a way, systems in tourism must remain adaptive (resilient) and compliant (institutionalized) by making cybersecurity an inevitable component of creating a safe, inclusive, and future-ready tourism ecosystem.

Conceptual Framework: Cyber-Sustainability Nexus

Framework Components

1. *Cybersecurity Enablers*
    - o Digital infrastructure (IoT, platforms)
    - o Emerging technologies (AI, Blockchain)
    - o Human resources (awareness, skills)
2. Theoretical Drivers
    - o System resilience
    - o Institutional compliance and norms
3. Governance Mechanisms
    - o Policy integration
    - o Crisis response protocols
    - o ESG alignment
4. Outcomes
    - o Achieving SDGs 8, 9, 11, 16
    - o Inclusive access and stakeholder trust
    - o Sustainable digital transformation

Visual Summary

```
[Cybersecurity Enablers]
↓
[Theoretical Drivers: Resilience Theory + Institutional Theory]
↓
[Governance & Strategic Integration]
↓
[Tourism SDG Outcomes (8, 9, 11, 16)]
```

The above mentioned framework hints cybersecurity as a technical fix and a holistic approach. But governance, education, and institutional support are urgently needed for sustainable tourism.

LITERATURE REVIEW

Cybersecurity Tools and Innovations in Tourism

Cybersecurity-enhanced technologies are treated as blessings to the modern tourism systems because they are very crucial in protecting sensitive information and improving efficiency in the operations. Besides, they are able to create resilience to the increasing cyber-threats. Since the industry continues to rely heavily on AI, IoT, cloud-based services, and customer-related applications, effective cybersecurity is no longer an option because it can guarantee safe transactions and sustain the long-term trust among stakeholders. It is especially important in an industry with lots of personal and monetary deals being conducted. Without proper security measures, customer information, which includes identity papers and payment details, is prone to malicious cyberattacks (Mairesse, 2022). Furthermore, tourists are also at a high risk of a cyber-threat because they are least familiar with the local legal framework and system and it is easy to trick them using cybercrimes based on language barriers (Kovacic et al., 2022). Cybersecurity practices in tourism are being altered by innovative technologies. In cloud computing and enhanced data analytics, they are capable of monitoring in real-time, the ability to detect threats, as well as the provision of scalable protection infrastructure (Bazazo et al., 2019; Bazazo & Rami, n.d.). Moreover, the inclusion of cybersecurity guidelines in apps like customer relationship management (CRM) software and online reservation systems provides the data security of the information, the encryption of the data transfer, and effective authentication patterns (Kuzman et al., 2024). These tools are reactive as well as predictive where the tourism organizations are enabled to look ahead and prevent the possible risks before they escalate. There is a paradigm shift in moving compliance-based cybersecurity to risk-based cybersecurity strategies. Integrated scheme that incorporates cybersecurity in the overall tourism business strategies is currently being implemented (Mairesse, 2022). Such a strategy highlights cybersecurity not only as the set of items to make sure the laws are followed but also the course of action that should be undoubtedly dynamic and the one that is embedded into the business needs, partners, and customer expectations of an individual tourism organization. Although the tourism industry has still made major strides, the industry still suffers a shortage of all-purpose research, industry-related guidelines as well as sensitization on the best cybersecurity measures. Various small and medium companies are still not well prepared in terms of technical infrastructure, as well as policy arrangement. This highlights the necessity of further investment into the education, industry, and knowledge transfer regarding cybersecurity on a global level that is adapted to the needs of the branch. The development of cybersecurity solutions, and strategies in tourism have improved greatly with the emergence of cloud solutions, risk-based approaches, and combined booking systems.

Smart Tourism Infrastructure

Smart tourism infrastructure is a complex notion. It basically is structured through the integration of modern technologies and environmental friendly activities to support the tourism experiences, economic development, and environmental sustainability. With digitalization of world travel, destinations are implementing intelligent solutions to offer seamless, personal and sustainable services to travelers. This change is associated with integration of digital platforms, real-time data analysis, and greener modes of transport solutions, the goal of which is to establish a resilient and diverse tourism ecosystem.

The digital infrastructure and connectivity are one of the most pivotal infrastructures of smart tourism. The technologies base the creation of real-time communication, data processing system, and delivery of service include digital platforms, mobile apps, and IoT. Such tools enable tourists to obtain information in real-time, create itineraries, obtain safety-related information, and telecommute with services during the travel, increasing convenience and safety (Khandelwal, 2024; Diaz-Parra et al., 2023). Smart connectivity also enables tourism operators to know the behavior of the visitors, how to better their services and how to respond to them with a very supportive manner.

The other important aspect is sustainable transportation that looks into the environmental effect caused by the tourism practices. For ensuring smart tourism infrastructure optimization, people in the smart tourism industry will have to use of electric vehicles, green public transportation, and an interconnected mobility system to minimize carbon pollution and traffic. Such sustainable transport systems do not only contribute to the SDGs but also make destinations more appealing because cleaner and easier transportation is offered through this approach (Orbelyan, 2024; Tee, 2024). The maintenance of both cultural and natural heritages is also very crucial in the establishment of smart tourism systems. Cultural experience is being made personal through digital tools that ensure minimal intrusion into the sensitive areas. Smart data about destinations allows the control of the number of visitors, avoid overcrowding, and save historical places (Tee, 2024). Tourism when combined with technology can result in long term socio-cultural sustainability because it involves protecting the heritage systematically.

The involvement of technology is also another method of advancing tourism industry. Virtual reality (VR) and augmented reality (AR) technologies produce rich and engaging interactions Generally, people can experience a cultural or natural tourist attraction as they move and look around through VR and AR. Technologies that provide contactless services, e.g. mobile payments and digital ticketing, are also more efficient and contactless that the whole world experienced especially during the post-pandemic period (Khandelwal, 2024).

The consequences of smart tourism infrastructure on the urban ecosystems are wide-ranged. On the economic issue, smart tourism systems create jobs opportunities and pave the way of making investment in the local economy. Thus the systems can appeal to new-fangled tourists who want creative travel encounters and bring more income to destinations (Tee, 2024). The Smart systems are greener when it comes to the promotion of the responsible use of assets and reduction of the ecological footprint by means of green mobility and power services (Mishra et al., 2023).

Social inclusiveness is another of such significance. Through the assistance of smart technologies, accessible touristic services can be created to people with disabilities, senior citizens, and the impoverished and less privileged members of society. Digital platforms might also offer real-time support and multilingual assistance or even specific navigation tools that would be more equal in tourism (Orbelyan, 2024).

Digital Forensics and Incident Response

The more tourism is intertwined using digital tools and internet services, the more it is exposed to cyber threats. The hacker attacks, information leakages, and the ransomware attacks are not exceptional anymore. These threats may bring about great issues to tourism businesses. They are able to stop services, reveal customer data, and taint the profile of destinations. Such problems need to be prevented and managed, and therefore require digital forensics and incident response (DFIR) systems.

Digital forensics is the process of gathering and examining information that happens following a cyberattack. It assists the tourism organizations on what went wrong, who was responsible of the problem, and how it can be prevented in future. Incident response can be described as response time when there is occurrence of a cyberattack. In combination, the tools enable companies to respond quickly and limit out damage as well as develop safer systems in the future. They are particularly crucial in the case of tourism as the processes of the industry depend on the digital arrangements of booking and payment, which falls under communication and customer control.

According to Mohamed & Abuobied (2024), this is because cyber threats are advancing and getting difficult to handle. The situation with various types of cybersecurity laws in different countries complicates the adequate response of the global industry such as tourism. The capacity to promptly explore and react to a cyberattack is significant to retain trust when it occurs. Tourists exchange such sensitive information as passport numbers, credit card numbers, and travel programs. The company and the travelers will be harmed in case this data is stolen. With digital forensics, organizations are able to monitor the route with which the attack occurred and by whom. This is also useful in the litigation issue and enhances the confidence of the populace on the tourism sector.

Here digital forensics and incident response is also related with the sustainability goals. Dede et al. (2024), expressly note that including cybersecurity initiatives, such as DFIR, in the Environmental, Social, and Governance (ESG) reports can utilize this opportunity to demonstrate that the companies are responsible and progressive. ESG reporting is the manner of companies to demonstrate their intentions related to global initiatives in the areas like clean industry, fair work conditions, and powerful institutions. DFIR ensures that one demonstrates that a company can manage risks and safeguard both information and individuals.

This is backed up by Ige et al. (2024) who opined that connecting with sustainable development goals (SDGs) to cybersecurity strategies makes businesses in the tourism industry more resilient. This is to say that companies which are ready to avoid cyber dangers have a greater chance to survive even amidst the problems. This aligns with the SDG 8 (Decent Work and Economic Growth), SDG 9 (Industry, Innovation, and Infrastructure) and SDG 16 (Peace, Justice, and Strong Institutions).

Cyber systems are very vital in smart tourism destinations. To illustrate, people tend to utilize their mobile apps to book hotels, purchase tickets, or refer to maps and guides as tourists. Such services must be secure. Ghaderi et al. (2024) hold the position that such destinations must contain a powerful incident response strategy, data security regulations, and the interaction of stakeholders. In case of some malfunction, DFIR will be able to resolve the problem fast and restart services.

This methodology also has theory to back it. The Resilience Theory states that systems must change and recoup aftershocks. The DFIR can also assist tourism companies in dealing with cyberattacks and returning to work in this case without any substantial delays. It safeguards digital processes so that they are not unstable and that this helps long term success of the tour industry.

Companies can do this due to the presence of legal regulations, the norms of the sector or to imitate practices of successful firms (Meyer & Rowan, 1977; DiMaggio & Powell, 1983). According to Odumesi & Sanusi (2023), the strengths found in institutional support cybersecurity such as DFIR are that it enhances governance, transparency, and justice that are some of the elements of SDG 16.

Although other researchers fail to directly address digital forensics, their research nevertheless endorses high cybersecurity. Barik et al. (2024) concentrate on the necessity of cyber resilience as the key to SDGs. This involves constructing systems which are capable of sustaining an attack and also recovering swiftly. Kosnikov et al. (2024) provide the information on how the national cybersecurity plans can aid in the overall digitalization, as well as tourism. They call for the necessity of having DFIR in policy and planning.

Nevertheless, it has its handicaps. Andreyeva et al. (2020) caution that having our eyes too wide on digital issues might make us overlook other key sustainability objectives, including nature and becoming more fair. We should also find an equilibrium among cybersecurity, environmental, and social agendas. Digital forensics and incident response are the main points in establishing a safe, secure and sustainable tourism industry. They assist in the management of cyber risks, the safekeeping of customer information and furthering the agenda of development in the world. In the age of the digital tourism industry, DFIR needs to be at the center of planning, governance, and routine operations.

Blockchain and AI for Transparency

The development of Digital tourism has increased the significance of protecting data and establishing confidence between users. Many of the issues that the tourism sector is struggling with today can be resolved with the help of two potent forms of technology. These are fraud issues in online reservation, there is a lack of openness in the financial transactions, and the incapability to verify services. Blockchain and artificial intelligence have the potential to develop safer, transparent, and trustworthy systems when used in coexistence. The combination is vital towards the realization of Sustainable Development Goals (SDGs), in particular, economic growth, strong institutions, and digital resilience.

Why Blockchain and AI Matter in Tourism

When it comes to tourism, numerous services are actively ordered on websites or app on mobile phones. These are hotels, air tickets, organized tours, and transports. These digital platforms can also become targets of fraud. Individuals might also get trapped in phony sites or even pay money on services that are not there. Blockchain and AI collaborate in order to address these problems.

Blockchain offers a method of transaction documenting in a secure and immutable way. All the bookings, payments, or reviews of customers are kept in a decentralized ledger that is not easily tamperable. This is tamper-proof and will engender trust. AI, instead, facilitates the process of analysis of large amounts of information in real-time. It is able to identify abnormal behavior, identify trend towards fraud, and can initiate action quicker than a human being.

By the information presented by Gajjar et al. (2025) and Priyadarshana et al. (2024), it is stated that the possibility of fraud due to blockchain is limited because the records cannot be edited by any means after being stocked. This can be utilized in the tourism industry whereby most trade is carried out between citizens of various nations. AI will provide a further circle of security in detecting suspicious activity in real-time. As an example, provided a person attempts to use the same credit card on various accounts, the AI systems will highlight it instantly (Martinez et al., 2024).

Improving Transparency Through Smart Tools

It is also blockchain which makes smart contracts a possibility: pre-programmed contracts automatically fulfilling transactions once the prerequisite is achieved. These cut down on the contact of middlemen and lower the possibility of a human error. According to Sankar & David (2024) and Narwal et al. (2024), the use of smart contracts can facilitate automating bookings and payments in the sphere of tourism, and the whole process is easier and more clean.

In combination, AI and blockchain allow traceability. It implies that every booking/check can be traced and confirmed at every stage. When a tourist needs to ensure that his or her payment has arrived in the correct hotel or tour company, he or she can view transactions history of the payment. This traceability enables the development of trust between the customer and the tourism providers besides accountability (Gajjar et al., 2025; Sankar & David, 2024).

Supporting the Sustainable Development Goals

The combination of the blockchain and AI contributes to the advancement of more extensive prospects. As an example, it contributes to the development of a secure digital economy, thereby encouraging of decent work and economic growth (SDG 8). Tourism will be in a better position to create employment while the businesses will be confident and they will reduce fraud as well as increase trust. The technologies are also helpful in achieving strong institutions and justice (SDG 16) because these facilitate transparency and minimize corruption (Martinez et al, 2024). The opportunity to improve the digital governance and fraud avoided by using blockchain and AI is mentioned (Kontogianni & Alepis, 2023). This integration assists in developing a tourism in a safer, more harbouring and SDGs based system. It indicates the practical development in the application of these technologies to develop smarter and sustainable destinations.

All the studies do not, however, exhaust the integration between blockchain and AI. Walmsley (2023) and Treiblmaier (n.d.) address the role of blockchain in increasing the transparency of the tourism industry due to the secure and traceable transactions. However, they never dwell upon the working principles of blockchain in collaboration with AI and the role that this collaboration plays in sustainable development. On a similar note, Mo (2023) acknowledges the contribution of blockchain to sustaining and promoting transparency but does not associate it with AI or cybersecurity. The current research demonstrates the potential of blockchain but proposes that additional investigation should be conducted on how their integration would bring more advantages.

The other study by Xiubo et al. (2018) explains the effect of a blockchain-based tourism anti-fraud system on ensuring security. They employ blockchain to help control their account system, digital footprints and verify fraud instances. This enhances the level of trust between tourists and tourism providers and compliments the target of enhancing better governance and cybersecurity aspects of tourism.

Despite a number of benefits of blockchain and the use of AI in the tourism industry, there exist a number of challenges. It is a complex and bulky technology, and could be prohibitively expensive to some businesses. The other complications include non-specificity of the data privacy rules or regulations and transnational collaboration. Adoption barriers may comprise a technical barrier, and regulatory issues that act to delay it as discussed by Priyadarshana et al. (2024). This is the reason why there must be more work, training, and cross-boundary work to bring out maximum potential of these tools in the tourism sector.

Blockchain and AI are really potent methods to make tourism a much safer, efficient and trustworthy industry. Blockchain makes sure that any record cannot be altered. AI identifies fraud in real-time and assists in making quick smart decisions. Coupled with one another, the technologies enhance transparency, boost the confidence in the online systems, and make the tourism sector consistent with the Sustainable Development Goals. As far as there is yet some need to clear, the current developments are quite promising. The further investment in these technologies and improved global policies will provide the key to unlock the full potential that these technologies may have in making tourism future smarter, safer, and more sustainable.

Cyber-Secure SDG Reporting Systems

Countries and organizations need to keep monitoring their progress with regards to achieving the Sustainable Development Goals (SDGs), which means using large quantities of data. This involves the environment related information, economical and wellbeing of people. Data tend to be sensitive in most cases, more so when data concerns the identity of the stakeholders, the outcomes of the community, or the state of the environment. Thus, it is important to secure this data. In the absence of robust cybersecurity, the SDG-related information might be altered, stolen, and misused, which may harm communities and destroy confidence in the reporting process. Cybersecurity prevents cyber-attack to data thus making it reliable and safe. This enables the decision makers to know what needs improvement or what is working in sustainable development programs.

Cybersecurity: The Foundation of Reliable Sustainability Reporting

Cybersecurity has become a consideration of sustainability. According to Sargsyan (2024), the issue of safeguarding digital systems is as important as protection of natural resources. In case cyberattack happens on SDG data systems such as pollution monitoring, emissions, or availability of clean water, it may result in improper decisions or slow reaction. This is why it is necessary to ensure safety of the systems on which this data is stored and processed.

Incorporation of cybersecurity in Environmental, Social, and Governance (ESG) report also aids the companies to remain resilient. By cybersecurity factor being a part of the ESG plan of businesses, it can lead to reaching the sustainability objectives of companies and preventing crises. This demonstrates that substantive digital security is not only a technical necessity but the duty that contributes to the overall SDG improvement.

The Role of New Technologies

SDG reporting systems can be enhanced in terms of cybersecurity because emerging technologies often reinforce the idea, and blockchain and artificial intelligence (AI), in particular, have the potential to make SDG reporting systems stronger than ever. These are intelligent and secure methods of data security. As an instance, the information stored on a blockchain is such that reforming it is almost impossible without being noticed. This makes sure that the information on environmental impact or on social programs in a system cannot be lost once enrolled in system.

Both Ige et al. (2024) and Obasi et al. (2024) point to the fact that these technologies could assist organizations in their response to the increased cyber-risks. AI has the potential of detecting anomalies or suspicious trends in data access, prior to their occurrence, thereby preventing an attack. These tools provide the sustainability professionals with a wall stouter against the hacking threats that might compromise the development initiative.

Achuthan et al. (2024) express the same views as well by promoting the notion that advanced cybersecurity systems such as AI and blockchain should be used to secure the sustainability data as it relates to tourism. A major focus of their work underlines the need to have secure reporting systems not only by governments but also by businesses and other sectors such as tourism that are relevant to the delivery of SDGs.

Strategic Actions for Cyber-Resilient SDG Reporting

In an attempt to ensure the SDG reporting is more secure, a few strategic measures are suggested:

- International Cooperation: Nations must collaborate by sharing experience, norms and methods of response. Threats on cyberspace are not national, and thus a multinational solution towards curbing them should be provided.
- Training on Cybersecurity: This education will make the users, and most importantly those who will be using SDG data, harder to fall prey to cyber-criminals, as well as more resistant to mistakes.
- Inclusive Practices: The attempt to enhance cybersecurity should be open to the inclusion of all types of users (particularly those residing in disadvantaged and remote regions) to be equally insured and provided with the same level of access.

Ige et al. (2024) and Obasi et al. (2024) support these suggestions and introduce the concept of such comprehensive and holistic cybersecurity approaches that involve training, policymaking, and mitigation plans.

The frameworks also assist organizations to learn and manage the intricate threats that come in digital and still remain on the streak of achieving their SDG goals.

Vachheta et al. (2024) present a systematic plan to help SDG data by balancing the risk-based management with the user awareness of the problem and mitigated threats, as well as response in real-time. Their model emphasizes the need to have a transparent system developed in order to manage the cyber risks during sustainability reporting.

The same is echoed by Weng & Wu (n.d.), which indicate the necessity of more laws and systems protecting data on a country-to-country level. They are keen to underline the fact that safe SDG reporting would not only guard sensitive information but also facilitate the development of confidence among the population in sustainability initiatives.

Challenges and the Need for Continuous Improvement

However, there are challenges and the necessity of the constant improvement. On the one hand, cybersecurity is a crucial factor, but, on the other hand, it is dynamic. New online threats are coming up continuously. Reporting systems can also be easy targets once they are not updated on a regular basis. Mohamed & Abuobied (2024) stress that cybersecurity systems must be enhanced on a regular basis. Otherwise, they will not even be able to monitor emerging risks with the help of the most effective SDG dashboards.

The success of the sustainable development initiatives takes place under secure SDG reporting systems. Cybersecurity protects sensitive information and makes the reporting honest, complete, and timely. Organizations can develop more robust systems by means of employing highly efficient tools such as blockchain, AI, promoting global collaboration, and increasing user education. These activities endorse the spirit of transparency, reliance, and glassy eyes towards the global development commitment. The future of sustainable development remains to be guarded with the never'ceasing innovation and cooperation as digital threats will keep evolving.

Barriers and Opportunities in Cybersecurity Implementation

Some of the challenges affecting the adoption of cybersecurity by tourism business include several operational and organizational hurdles despite the presence of tools.

Lack of Cyber Awareness in Tourism SMEs

The tourism industry is made up of the small and medium-sized enterprises (SMEs). All of these enterprises including guesthouses restaurants and travel agencies tour operators and local attractions are responsible in providing cultural rich and personalized experiences. Low awareness and knowledge on cybersecurity issues are however a challenge that faces most of these SMEs. This paves the way to cyber awareness, which presents some glaring vulnerability and they are easy prey to cybercriminals. As the tourism sector goes digital, the need to close this gap is even more urgent.

Understanding the Awareness Gap

Quite a number of tourism SMEs fail to recognize the threats of cyber-attacks. As stated by Junior et al. (2023), this is among the greatest causes of such businesses not installing effective security measures. Not having a proper idea about dangers like phishing, malware, or ransomware, these companies tend to neglect simple security measures like software updating, data encryptions, or staff education.

According to Renaud & Ophoff (2021) situational awareness is relevant to enhance cybersecurity in small businesses. What this implies is that SMEs should be cognizant about the nature of their digital environment, the kind of attacks that they are exposed to, and how these attacks would impact on their workings. Unluckily, most tourism SMEs do not enjoy this kind of awareness and this makes them vulnerable even against trivial assaults.

Limited Resources and Support

Inadequate cybersecurity investments in the financial and human resources to be invested around SMEs in the tourism industry is one of the greatest challenges that the industry has been exploited with. Assistance in terms of cybersecurity tools, training and expertise might turn out costly and in the case of small businesses that have thin margins in their operations, this element might be viewed as an optional extra but not a necessity. Junior et al. (2023) point out that a lack of finance is one of the widely recognized causes of bad cybersecurity wear among SMEs.

In the developing nations, the issue is particularly acute since fewer people have access to technologies and training and have a steady internet connection. The lack of an effective infrastructure and a lower digital literacy level exposes tourism SMEs in these locations even further to the threats of cyber risks.

Gaps in Research and Guidance

Although cybersecurity is increasingly becoming an issue in the tourism industry, it has been observed that limited studies are dedicated to the smaller firms in this business segment. Chaudhary et al. (2023) also note that special research is required that can examine the niche requirements of SMEs in the tourism sector in relation to cybersecurity awareness. In the absence of this knowledge, there is no easy way to come up with the training programs/training facilities that will work with the particular needs of these businesses.

This inability to do focused research is not novel. Bougaardt & Kyobe (2011) conducted a study more than 10 years ago and discovered that a majority of SMEs do not realize or calculate their losses induced by cybercrime, which makes them more exposed. However, most recently, Valli et al. (2021) supported this argument by stating that, to date, efforts made to provide tailored assessments of the cybersecurity stances of SMEs were slow to improve.

Many SMEs are not able to make informed decisions even in situations in which there is some form of awareness. According to Renaud & Weir (2016), this is because cyber threats that SMEs are knowledgeable about are confused with mixed messages, and even contradictory advice that the SMEs receive. Such misunderstanding, as well as the assumption that cybersecurity is very costly or complex, does not allow many SMEs to act.

The Specific Case of Tourism

Cybersecurity in the tourism industry has special issues. According to Kovacic et al. (2022), tourism is particularly prone to cyber-attacks due to their exposure to unknown digital spaces, and in that regard, it is even more crucial to have secured service providers. However, according to the same study, there is actually a deficiency in cybersecurity research in relation to tourism and possibly because of that the SME in this sector are not equipped similarly to others.

Al Aamer & Hamdan (2023) outline in particular that tourism SMEs may experience severe losses (profit loss or reputation loss) due to the low level of cybersecurity awareness. This necessitates the need to embrace improved practices by such businesses.

In addition, Paraskevas (2020) notes that a technology-centric fragmented approach to cybersecurity is followed by a great number of tourism businesses. This implies that it is a piecemeal approach and not an approach that is risk-based. This creates construction holes in their systems and threat to privacy of information, particularly their systems dealing with customer information, and containing sensitive personal and financial data.

Indicators of Progress and Possibility of Expansion

Cyprus has made some encouraging signs in spite of all these. There are also tourism SMEs trying to seek new solutions to enhancing their cybersecurity. These can be the collaboration with technological companies, connecting to local or regional networks to share cyber resources, or adopting something as basic yet efficient as secure payment gateways and two-factor authentication.

This indicates that tourism SMEs can be better when there is the necessary support. This can only be achieved by a concerted initiative which comprises of specific trainings, policy backing and additional funds sources. International organizations, governments and tourism boards ought to invest in awareness which will be simple to understand and can be accessible to both small and large businesses.

The lack of cybersecurity awareness in the tourism SMEs is a problem that endangers both the businesses and the customers. Poor education, economic, and lack of research within an industry are some of the factors, which makes such business challenges to confront the rising digital menace. Nevertheless, tourism SMEs can enhance their defense by obtaining a better situational awareness, encouraging focused research, and providing them with the means to develop them and education. Sustainable development, economic sustainability, and security over a long period of time of delivering digital tourism services require construction of cyber supportive tourism industry.

Digital Inequality Across Destinations

Digital inequality is one of the main impediments to the development of the global tourism industry. Most of the developing and rural tourist areas do not have the essential digital resources and infrastructures to cope with the online world. These regions tend to lack internet connectivity, poor connectivity, obsolete gadgets, and not enough trained hands to control cyber systems. It implies that these destinations are falling behind in terms of adoption of cybersecurity practices and digital innovations. Not only does this lower their economic potential but also exposes them to increased cyber risks and increasing the disparity between tourism development in urban and rural settings.

Gaps in Digital Infrastructure

This lack of consistent internet and online infrastructure in places of residence in locations like rural and isolated areas has been mentioned as one of the factors that remain one of the causes contributing to digital inequity. According to Duggi et al. (2025), many destinations are not connected and have limited access to the devices, which means that new technologies are not available in the tourism industry. Online booking systems, intelligent payment methods and online promotional models need good internet infrastructure most of the time lacking in rural areas.

According to Rydzewski, (2025), absence of proper infrastructure ends up denying tourism destinations the capacity to participate effectively in the digital markets. They are unable to capture the market of the tech-savvy tourist who uses websites to organize tours, search services and book them. This disorganization decreases visibility and restricts traffic and profits to visitors.

Sekhar (2024) goes further to state how there is lack of good electricity supply coupled with unphysical coverage of internet based areas in the rural areas causing it to be challenging to support basic cybersecurity systems. Without having secure digital networks, the realization of safe transactions or the data protection is almost never possible.

The unequal access to the information infrastructure (what is called the first-level digital divide) may be expanded to widen the differences in the economy between urban and rural areas (Fu et al., 2024). This applies especially to tourism which has been facing the need to be ready or prepared to meet the digital world in case they need to manage and prevent cyber threats on themselves.

Shortage of Skills and Training

The infrastructure is not sufficient. Inhabitants of such areas also require the digital tools usage skills. According to Carlisle et al. (2021), most potential and present tourism employees have problems accessing digital education. The obstacles render it difficult to develop the capabilities of practicing cybersecurity, online communications, and data systems.

The article by Bhatia (2023) demonstrates that this gap may be solved with the assistance of community-based training. By training local people in information and communication technology (ICT) option, locals in the area can find it easier to market and organize tourism services through the internet. This enhances the digital literacy as well as economic activity at the local level.

Equipping the locals with digital knowledge makes them more apt to use technology and keep it safe. They will be able to care about websites that they manage, use customer data safely and access the world of tourism economy with new confidence with proper training.

According to Yang et al. (2010), age, income, level of education as well as geographic location are some of the factors that are largely associated with digital inequality. Farther into the rural regions, those inhabiting the areas might find it harder to use the digital devices, and the poor might not be able to afford them. One should take such social factors into account when planning inclusive digital solutions.

Economic Consequences

The effects of digital inequality are economic in nature. Khosravi et al. (2025) state that the readier destinations are digital, the more they receive tourists and investors. Those areas which are not in advance in relation to digital progress are considered less competitive and reliable, particularly in those cases when they are not able to ensure its safety as regards services and arranging reservations online.

Further, Rydzewski (2025) mentions that digital technologies increase service quality and efficiency that are the main factors of attracting and retaining tourists. Without such tools, rural destinations would soon become the losers of tourism development, missing the revenues and employment to cover the local needs.

Toward Inclusive Digital Tourism

It is necessary to pay attention to digital infrastructure, and, on the other hand, specialists warn that one should not overlook other types of sustainability. The short-sighted orientation with technology can neglect cultural, environmental and social avenues that are important as well. Sustainable tourism should find the balance between digitalization and heritage, nature, and identities of the local people.

The issue of digital inequality should be handled with a balanced approach and may refer to investment in the infrastructural layer, training, and policy support. They should also have digital inclusion as part of their national tourism strategies particularly in the underserved rural zones. Infrastructure gap can be closed with financing of broadband expansion, local technology centers as well as public Wi-Fi initiatives.

A training program must be set around people of different ages and education levels, in the local languages, and involving culturally oriented content. University, NGO, and privately owned tech business collaborations can help in the provision of tools and resources which can be used to fast track digital learning.

It is also crucial that the authorities, transnational organizations, or the boards of tourism realize that cybersecurity is a necessary component of digital inclusion. Although communities can be offered access to internet, there should also be a protection against any cyber threat, which may affect their reputation, finances, or trust of their visitors.

It is possible, though, with specific investments in the infrastructure and education, to enhance the digital capacity of rural destinations. An inclusive, resilient, and cyber-secure development of tourism will be realized through holistic approach, which holds both technological and cultural assets in high regard. The digital inequality problem is not a technology dilemma, it is a question of equity, sustainability and opportunity.

Regulatory Gaps and Global Coordination

At the current stage or tourism economy, personal and operational data is moving fast globally with booking engines, travel products, and online services. Nevertheless, there is a serious threat caused by the absence of global cybersecurity regulation. A mix of rules at the national level means that cross boundary sharing of sensitive tourism data is full of confusion, inconsistency, and loopholes in global protection of vital tourism data. Such regulatory lapses impede proper realization of cybersecurity and impossible to govern data protection legislation alongside the tours and travels webs of countries.

Inconsistent Legal Frameworks Across Countries

Diversity of regulatory standards is one of the greatest issues that transnational cybersecurity might face. The European Union is one of the examples of a strict approach to the protection of personal data since the General Data Protection Regulation (GDPR) has the reputation of a vigilant watchdog over the data. It demands laborious approvals, data security as well as effective enforces. But, in other parts, such equivalent policies are not followed in large numbers. Eshbaev (2024) explains that Asian, African, and even North-American countries do not hold as strong data protection policies. This discrepancy causes the global scene to be very fragmented with the extent of the protection being largely dependent on the geography.

Malabo Convention which is an African Union Convention on Cyber Security and Personal Data Protection was brought on board to deal with cybersecurity among African countries. However, Bouke et al. (2023) also emphasize that the existence of different legal frameworks in Africa and the poor implementation rates of member states have hampered the process. In the absence of such harmonization, the countries will continue working in silos in their approaches to cybersecurity, therefore, lowering the resilience of the African continent to various global cyber-attacks.

The Urgency of International Cooperation

The international cooperation is necessary since cybercrime has no boundaries. Tourism systems that are attacked by hacking are usually done by countries other than the country involved and may affect almost all destinations and service provider globally. According to Qudus (2025), the only way to address this issue is to collaborate globally that is, when it comes to intelligence exchange, collective approaches to cyber-defense, and development of similar policies.

Tourism being an industry that is too interconnected needs infrastructure and services that are shared among different jurisdictions. As an example, a booking of a tour in Southeast Asia by a European vendor takes place on the European platform but can be paid out via the U.S. with its data stored on a cloud in another country. Uniting cybersecurity policies is highly challenging without which it is excruciatingly hard to protect data on this journey.

Kong (2010) pays attention to the role that bilateral, regional, and multilateral cooperation can play to develop standards of secure trans-border data flows. Such alliances make sure that the countries maintain similar legal protection and observance of privacy rights despite the location of data. The United Nations, World Tourism Organization, International Telecommunication Union are a few multilateral institutions the efforts could be pushed ahead and can be the course of action.

Conflicting Data Transfer Policies

The other obstacle to harmonization is the incompatibility in national rules on transfer of data. Various regions apply various models by which the data may get transmitted or transmitted across the borders. For instance:

- The GDPR of EU permits transferring data only to those countries that are deemed to have adequate protections.
- United Kingdom is governed by its National Security and Investment Act that grants to the government the ability to examine data-sharing agreements on security reasons.
- In North America, cross-border data transfer mechanisms are provided in the United States-Mexico-Canada Agreement (USMCA) which has some profound differences compared with those of Europe.

Pohl (2023) states that, due to these differing approaches, it is difficult to know what can be defined as an acceptable or non-acceptable restriction. This disparity in consistency makes the tourism business to be uncertain in the countries where it operates. It also makes it hard to construct smooth, safe processes around receiving and data storing customer information, and travel as well as payment transactions.

Moving Toward Interoperable Global Frameworks

Although the GDPR is regarded as a golden standard of data protection, the model cannot be universal as it is practically impossible due to legal, political, and cultural variety among states. Nevertheless, according to some of the scholars, interoperable frameworks, or frameworks that are in agreement on their principles and technology protocols, but do not ground each other in complete legal equivalence, may appear as a solution.

Differences may be crossed via multilateral agreements which are backed by international organizations and standard-setting bodies. Such efforts may involve common understanding of sensitive data, acknowledgment of levels of protection and synchronization of incident response plans. The enhanced cybersecurity of the world can be achieved without violating the sovereignty of nations as long as the latter follows compatibility as opposed to uniformity.

The digital divide can also be bridged with such frameworks where global tourism can be accessed by the developing countries safely and with confidence. The majority of these countries would continue to fall behind in the digital economy unless solutions are offered to harmonize the regulations.

The lack of uniform privacy laws in every corner of the world is a real menace to such operations which entail transporting tourists across borders. It is continuously crossing borders, and in lack of proper organization of standards, there is space in which errors occur, violations, and invasions of privacy. This division is further complicated by political differences, disparities in the degree of digital development, and even conflicting national interests.

This, however, could be improved. Gaps in regulation can be addressed through strengthening international cooperation, interoperability, and multilateral cooperation. To attain sustainable, inclusive, and secure tourism, the global community must stop perceiving cybersecurity to be the issue of domestic policy; instead, it is the issue of the common responsibilities and borders.

Strategic Opportunities

The increasing digitalization of tourism industry is a threat, and does not only pose risks to the industry, but also there is good opportunity to increase cybersecurity practices and align them to sustainable development goals (SDGs). Due to the high level of digital threats, it is advised in the literature that forward-thinking strategy is put in place: the maturity at sector-wide level should be established through cooperation, training specificity, quality managed. Such strategic opportunities can allow the tourism stakeholders to be heading to a more secure, inclusive, and sustainable digital future.

Partnership-Based Resilience Programs

Partnerships are one of the most useful resilience building tools. It does not lend itself to being sorted out. The pillar of tourism is based on several players, such as the input of hotels, tour operators, transport agencies, tech-driven platforms, and government agencies to the overall extent of a digital environment. Feedback loops are defined by Tabansky & Lichterman (2024) as the type of exchange that can be established by the partnership to share information in real-time, recognize threats with enough accuracy and timeliness, and synchronize in response to cyber incidents. This teaming approach strengthens rather than strengthens systems in general.

It is also emphasized by Ige et al. (2024) that the collaboration on the international level is an essential issue. International collaboration assists with the revolution of cybersecurity in the framework of the sustainable development agenda and makes sure that every nation, particularly developing nations, is included in the creation of a secure digital infrastructure. This will entail the exchange of tools, knowledge, and standards over the borders, and as a consequence, even smaller destinations in tourism will enjoy global experience and assistance.

Collaborations are also resource efficient since they give organizations the chance to unite resources thus lessening the individual responsibility to invest in cybersecurity. There are multi-stakeholder efforts that will include regional networks, industry-led partnerships, or even the partnership of governments and the private sector that can help to establish collective resilience in the support of SDGs.

Targeted Cybersecurity Training

Education and training is its other major opportunity. Effective cybersecurity strategy should have a well trained workforce as its solid foundation. The most sophisticated systems can go wrong without individuals who can assess dangers, equipment, and procedures. Ige et al. (2024) state that it is a high priority to spend money on cybersecurity education, notably in tourism because most employees in the tourism sector lack extensive technical experience.

There should be focused training. As an illustration, Yulianto et al. (2023) discuss the importance of red teaming threats: a simulated cyberattack that allows exploring how a given organization can respond to an attack. Such training is not an awareness training alone, but it is a training that would develop capabilities to improve real-world application and maturity in IT governance with the intent such organizations will be in a position to identify their weakness before they turn into threats.

The information security education must be approached in line with different target groups such as the bottom of the pyramid tourism employees, those professionals in the information technology department, and management. The hierarchical structure ensures that every individual, including the customer service agents and system administrator, is allowed to contribute his/her share so as to ensure safety in an electronic world.

Governance Models Aligned with SDGs

Cybersecurity governance is also subject to strategic opportunities to deal with. The reason is that organizations may devise well thought-out governance frameworks that threaten the digital systems, yet may facilitate sustainability agendas. Maleh & Sahid noted (2024) that these frameworks will assist in evaluating and increasing maturity of information security governance being able to be sure that the information security measures are integrated with the rest of the organizational practices.

This form of governance is not about policies and rule adherence; it is the establishment of a culture of security. When cybersecurity is regarded as a strategic priority combining it with planning and operation, it assists in transparency, accountability and responsible decision-making.

Corporate resilience may also be increased by connecting cybersecurity governance to Environmental, Social, and Governance (ESG) reporting. Incorporating ESG reporting practices into organizations, companies are eager to portray their efforts towards sustainability and adding cybersecurity to them proves that they are willing to preserve not only the environment and community but their cyberspace integrity as well. The integration can be used to align corporate actions and business practices with the SDGs and win the trust of stakeholders.

Addressing Implementation Challenges

These strategies come with great opportunities, but they do not come without challenges. One of the biggest problems is the resource limitation especially to small businesses or destinations in developing regions. Investment training programs, developing partnerships and using governance models all cost money and this cannot be appreciated easily without outside help.

Moreover, integration of various systems and stakeholders may be slow at the implementation phase. It is not an easy task to harmonize the activities of both public and private participants, in various jurisdictions and on various platforms technology. It involves open communication, common mission and usually a third party coordinator.

The following challenges will need specific policy support, incentives on investment, as well as leadership, both in the public and private sector. With these barriers put straight in front of the tourism industry, it will be able to use cybersecurity to its full potential to ensure sustainable growth of the industry.

Cybersecurity helps enhance tourism opportunities which are quite achievable. The presence of partnership-based resilience programs, specific training, and governance models focused on SDGs will help to increase the digital maturity of the sector in general. These methods can not only enhance the security of systems, but also enhance economic activities, openness, and social contribution. However, funding and co-ordination are some of the practices that will be subjected to the harnessing of this potential. As soon as these are evaded, cybersecurity may turn out to be a powerful tool of developing a secure, inclusive, and sustainable tourism variant.

Table 2. Comparative Academic Contributions in Cybersecurity and SDGs

Author(s)	Area of Focus	Main Contribution
Ige et al. (2024)	Cybersecurity & SDGs	Developed a model linking cybersecurity strategies to sustainable development goals.
Achuthan et al. (2024)	Digital Infrastructure	Proposed a framework for assessing blockchain risks in sustainable digital systems.
Mohamed & Abuobied (2024)	Global Cyber Threats	Highlighted issues in global cybersecurity due to regulatory fragmentation.
Odumesi & Sanusi (2023)	Policy and Governance	Advocated for inclusive cybersecurity policies aligned with national sustainability.

Summary of the Comparative Framework

- Ige et al. highlight the fusion of cybersecurity and SDGs, which provide them with an effective way to propose a systematic model of safe and sustainable development.
- Achuthan et al. explore the technological risk, especially regarding blockchain, and the issue of risk assessment in critical infrastructures.
- Mohamed & Abuobied pay attention to the presence of global discrepancies in cybersecurity legislation and their effects on cross-border digital risks management.
- Odumesi and Sanusi shed light on the policy coherence and urge to adopt inclusive policies in order to strike a balance between cybersecurity and development requirements.

This table correlates with the conceptual focus of the chapter on a Cyber-Sustainability Nexus, a connection between technical innovational and institutional frameworks to achieve SDG targets in tourism and other areas.

FINDINGS AND DISCUSSIONS

The novelties of cybersecurity applications

The future of cybersecurity in smart tourism is developed through a number of technological advances which aim at increasing the level of security, transparency and sensitivity. Cybersecurity is a major issue that should be ensured with heightened digital acceleration within some sectors including tourism where much data is being utilized. Some of the key developments that can facilitate cybersecurity Agendas but also align with Sustainable Development Goals (SDGs) are described in this section.

Smart Tourism infrastructure

Possession of smart infrastructure in tourism systems has its risks as well as opportunities. The more the services become digitalized, namely, with the use of smart hotels and digital check-in process and connected transport mode, the more important is the security of user data.

- *Encrypted Systems*: These systems are crucial on protecting the flow of personal and financial data. Special encryption algorithms prevent unauthorized users, and information exchange between users and online resources remains secret and intact.
- *Privacy-Respecting Solutions*: The agreement with the global data protection laws, like GDPR, is not an option. Kumar & Pham (2024) point out that the new ethics of using data in smart tourism implies giving prime priority to the ethical treatment of data, where privacy-by-design solutions are used to restrict non-essential data acquisition, with secure user consent nature.

Integration of AI and Blockchain

The pair of modern technologies, Artificial Intelligence (AI) and blockchain, is changing cybersecurity and allows anticipating risks and unrestricted transactions of information. Together, these technologies will provide a strong basis of secure, verifiable, and trusted tourism services.

- *Increased Transparency*: Blockchain uses a decentralized ledger that does not tamper with a recording of the transactions. This is especially useful in tourism bookings and payments as in this case, it never encourages fraud. According to Gajjar et al. (2025) and Muheidat & Tawalbeh (2021), blockchain can guarantee the integrity of the digital transactions as it enhances transparency to the service providers and consumers.

- *Fraud Mitigation*: AI based analytics can identify anomaly in real time and anticipate a fraudulent pattern. With the help of learning big data, AI systems are able to identify irregular booking patterns, fraudulent reviews or bad actors trying to illegally access payment systems. This complements the entire cybersecurity as well as increases operational efficiency.

Digital Forensics

With the associated increase in cyber threats, digital forensics has come to be a major constituent of incident response and resilience in organizations.

Reputation recovery: When a threat to data breach or cyber-attack occurs, forensic investigation is employed to trace the origin, vulnerability, and avert occurrence of any further eventualities. According to Muheidat & Tawalbeh (2021), the sense of accountability and transparency that digital forensics enables is crucial in restoring confidence in the harmed tourism brands. Evidence-based explanations also contribute to improving legal and image status after the incidence of incidents.

Institutional Accountability: The institutional learning can also be assisted with help of forensics so that organizations understand how and why failure occurred. This kind of knowledge is important in improving cybersecurity framework and excellent governance.

SDG Dashboards and Secure Data Protocols

Proper and reliable data is also required to track to the SDGs. The foundations on which the performance indicators gathered and shown on dashboards are built must have solid security foundations because it may not be altered and ensure the privacy and confidence of its stakeholders.

- *Secure Data Protocols*: These are data validation, access control and encryption controls that should ensure that only authorized parties change sensitive indicators and that they access them. Muheidat & Tawalbeh (2021) also claim that the role of cybersecurity systems that ensure SDG reporting accuracy cannot be overestimated.
- *Transparency in Development Reporting*: Good dashboards will assure governments, Non-Government Organizations and corporations to access the dashboards to monitor and report on the progress in a transparent manner. This openness not only makes the peoples liable, it acts to motivate citizen participation as well as donor confidence.

Emerging Perspectives and Future Research

Outside of the technical capacity of these innovations, lies an increased amount of research that demands additional investigation with a view of conforming with global development goals. According to Kontogianni & Alepis (2022), the integration of AI, blockchain and cyber tourism in the existing research agendas provides a wider perspective of the smart tourism ecosystems. They attribute these areas to play a central role in transforming next generation of secure, personalized, and sustainable tourism services.

Despite the mentioned positive outcomes of the mentioned innovations, there are problems. New technology presents new weaknesses and excessive automation might leave a blind spot in system management. There is also the necessity of regular revisions to encryption codes, AI algorithms and forensic methods, the only way to keep up with more complicated threats.

Emerging Challenges

Since cybersecurity is rapidly emerging as a high priority in the era of digitalization not just in the tourism industry but also in respect of small and medium-sized enterprises (SMEs), various structural and strategic barriers still complicate the process. Among them, cyber illiteracy, digital inequality and lack of regulations are of special concern. These concerns lower the potentiality of SMEs integration of effective cybersecurity policies thus posing such institutions to face exposure to data and image and financial vulnerability. These issues have to be taken into account and addressed so that it became possible to construct a safe and welcoming digital space in accordance with Sustainable Development Goals (SDGs).

SMEs Cyber Illiterate

Lack of awareness and knowledge about cybersecurity is arguably one of the biggest problems that surround SMEs and make it difficult to gain success in the industry. This issue known as cyber illiteracy is caused by the lack of knowledge and limited resources.

- *Ignorance and Fallacies*: As Junior et al. (2023) have said, most SMEs hold a misconception that they are not appealing prospects to cybercriminals because of their size. This notion usually leads to poor or inexistent cybersecurity measures. Simple measures of maintaining passwords, updating software and safe handling of data are ignored most of the time.
- *Unavailability of Resources and Prioritization*: In most instances, SMEs prioritize their present business operations such as customer service or invento-

ry management at the expense of making available resources towards investing in cybersecurity. As Kandpal et al. (2023) emphasize, such a responsive attitude results in these businesses being unready to combat smart hackers.

- *Training and Culture Change*: There is a necessity to change culture to a proactive form of cybersecurity. According to Mkhulisi et al., (2024), training programs should be friendly to the availability of the program, its feasibility and sustainability. One of the many goals that such programs can attain is developing not just technical aptitude but also a particular mindset willing to place cybersecurity in the context of an extension of usual operations.

Through cyber literacy, SMEs are able to minimize vulnerability and become resistant to cyber-attacks. Government, industry bodies and large companies can extend training, mentoring, and scalable security to the needs of the SMEs.

Inequality in the digital world

Digital inequality is also a major challenge on the way to cybersecurity maturity, especially in developing countries or even rural locations and SMEs. Small firms cannot even consider the simplest cyber protection due to unequal access to, in particular, stable internet, the digital instruments, and qualified staff.

- *Infrastructural Inequalities*: As it is also noted by Kang (2024), a lack of basic infrastructure (access to broadband or steady supply of electricity) presents a major challenge. Such gaps restrict the usage of digital services, and SMEs do not have the access to modern cybersecurity options through the cloud-based threat detection or encrypted communications.
- *Financial Limits*: In addition to infrastructure, Kang (2024) also speaks of financial constraints, which do not allow to invest in even the most basic cybersecurity tools. As an example, small and medium-sized firms (SMEs) might not be able to spend money on antivirus software, firewalls, or IT consulting services, particularly in the case where their margin is rather low.
- *Policy Support, Incentives*: The platform to bridge this gap lies on the crafting of policies that encourage inclusiveness in the expansion of digital platforms. Tax breaks, grants or low interest loans targeted at SMEs in an attempt to strengthen digital infrastructure and cybersecurity capabilities should be considered by governments. According to Kang (2024), these actions may make the underserved regions more competitive in terms of their digital status.

The subject of digital inequality is not only a matter of fairness but also a condition of creating well-structured, highly resilient world tourism on which every stakeholder can operate safely.

Regulatory Gaps

The third issue refers to the absence of consistent regulatory systems, especially as regards to cross-border data flows and SMEs-related cybersecurity standards.

- *Unharmonization*: As pointed out by Ozkan & Spruit (2019), the cybersecurity environment is not harmonized in the world. Diversity makes SMEs which have international clients or work on global platforms perplexed about what rules to follow and how to adhere to them. This poses uncertainty to the law and a greater risk to operations.

    Lack of Personalized Standards: The majority of global cybersecurity standards are elaborated with large companies being targeted. Based on this, Ozkan & Spruit (2019) advocate the creation of practical SME-specific guidelines. They should offer straightforward structures which assist small companies to evaluate risks, apply some protection mechanisms, and bring reports without much complication.
- *The need of International Coordination*: A stronger coordination between the governments, international organizations and industry segments to bridge these gaps is required. Global cyber resilience might be enhanced through common minimum standards and mutual recognition agreements that would ease compliance.

Unless there exists good, clear, and widespread regulation, the SMEs will still be missing the mark overregulating in fear or under regulating due to ignorance and expense.

Cyber illiteracy, digital inequality, and regulatory gaps are complex and structural problems standing on their way to building cybersecurity resilience in the SMEs in the tourism sector. Not only do these challenges make small businesses susceptible to growing dangers, but also exacerbate the chances of achieving greater security, inclusiveness, and sustainability in the digital ecosystems.

Though these concerns are considerable, they are also preceded by the increasing awareness of cyber threats among SMEs that could be used as the starting point of the positive change. The threat of concerted action exists as various stakeholders, including governments, industry leaders, and the civil society increasingly come to realize the urgency of these problems.

SOLUTIONS AND RECOMMENDATIONS

Develop SDG-Aligned Cybersecurity Standards

The tourism business should have clear and user-friendly cybersecurity regulations. The standards developed by the national tourism agencies and international groups must correspond to SDG indicators, particularly SDG 8 (Decent Work and Economic Growth), SDG 9 (Industry, Innovation and Infrastructure) as well as SDG 16 (Peace, Justice and Strong Institutions). The regulations should be applicable in both high tech cities as well as poor rural areas.

Promote Infrastructure in Underserved Destinations

Digital disparities damage resilience, particularly in the developing and rural tourist destinations. In order to bridge this gap, governments and donor agencies need to develop simple infrastructure, including broadband internet, consistent power supply, and helpful ICTs. This allows tourist activity in the region to have access to cybersecurity, address online markets, and compete on equal terms in the global arena.

Train Stakeholders in Cyber Risk and Privacy

Building skills is crucial. Special cybersecurity education of tourism individuals, including tour operators, hotel managers, guides, local governments and transport authorities can create awareness and establish security culture preparedness. Specialize in practicable abilities such as securing data, corruption identification, secure payment and crisis management.

Integrate Cyber Risk in Disaster Response

The cyber threats should be included in general disaster and crisis plans. Emergency procedures in tourism must involve digital forensics, threat info and backup plans. It increases preparedness and maintains business operations in cases of discharge in the digital or physical disruption.

Encourage International Cyber Tourism Agreements

Tourism does not respect national borders, and thus cross-border collaboration is crucial to safeguard the travel information and bring privacy regulations into balance. Secure visa procedure, encrypted booking systems, data exchange on threats, and common data security requirements ought to be forwarded with bilateral and multilateral transactions.

Support Secure, Inclusive Data Governance for SDG Reporting

Effective sustainability dashboards identifying the contribution of tourism to SDGs have to be based on precise and secure data. The stakeholders should apply inclusive data regulations that safeguard privacy and introduce transparency and incorporates the voices of women, indigenous groups, and small operators. These reporting tools should include cybersecurity to maintain trust and quality of data.

Launch Innovation Grants for Cyber Initiatives

Local and regional tourist tourism-related cybersecurity projects should be supported by funding schemes such as innovation grants or schemes of public institutional investments. To expand their solutions, the startups, NGOs, and small business, which develop fraud prevention tools, secure online shopping, or risk detection, should receive the reward.

Align ESG Metrics with Cybersecurity Protocols

Tourism is becoming more of an ESG reporter. Having cybersecurity policies in the ESG metrics improves their transparency, resilience, and endorsing sustainability commitments. This too appeals to the investors of safe and ethical online operations.

Establish Local Cyber Governance Bodies

Cybersecurity task forces or cybersecurity advisory groups should be established at the local tourism boards and destination managers. Such groups would be able to research local risks, conduct training, and assemble cyber preparedness plans with the national agencies. Local control causes the solutions to be localized.

Foster Multi-Stakeholder Partnerships

Tourism cybersecurity cannot be undertaken by a group alone. Government-to-government (and other) flexibility, business, academic, and civil society partnerships are necessary. Collaboration allows groups to share facilities, develop tools, and write policies that can satisfy the interests of the tourism players.

CONCLUSION

The issue of cybersecurity is no longer a mere technological requirement in the context of the expanding field of digital and connected tourism, but it stands as a key principle of sustainable growth. This segment has demonstrated how cybersecurity is connected to the SDGs in the tourism sector, identifying the emerging tools that increase the resilience as well as the current issues that damage digital equity and trust.

Activities of new technologies, AI, blockchain, digital forensics, provide opportunities to implement a greater level of transparency, trust, and safety in the tourism sector. The technologies not only preserve data security, but also contribute to a larger number of SDG targets, such as decent work, strong institutions, and inclusive growth. Likewise, smart tourism infrastructure, AI-based fraud prevention systems, and blockchain monitoring are no longer hypothetical or proposed concepts in the future to enable a safe and inclusive travel economy.

Nevertheless, there are still the challenges. Small and mid-size businesses being cyber-illiterate, digital disparities between rural and developing locations across the globe hinder full digital transformation. Unless a coordination is in place, these gaps remain and restrict the growth of tourism and digital sustainability.

This section presents a list of solutions and policy proposals: make SDG-compatible cyber rules, invest in underserved locations digital infrastructure, train and educate the stakeholders on the cyber threat, and pioneer multi-stakeholder partnerships. The recommendation in particular emphasizes the implementation of cybersecurity into the ESG metrics and SDG reports since governance needs to cross the lines between tech, institutional, and ethical.

To conclude, cybersecurity plays one of the primary roles of safe, fair, and sustainable tourism. It must not be viewed as a cost, a compliance product, but instead as a long-term resilience and trust-creating strategic investment. A combination between cyber rules and sustainability is why the tourism stakeholders can build a connected, secure, inclusive, and just future.

REFERENCES

Achuthan, K., Raman, R., Sankaran, S., & Roy, S. (2024). Sustainable Cybersecurity Practices: Past Trends and Future Directions. https://doi.org/DOI: 10.2139/ssrn.4826820

Al Aamer, A. K., & Hamdan, A. (2023). *Cyber Security Awareness and SMEs' Profitability and Continuity: Literature Review*. Springer Nature., DOI: 10.1007/978-981-99-6101-6_43

Andreyeva, D., Bogolyubova, S., Bogolyubov, V., & Malinin, A. (2020). *Digital solutions as a key element in improvement of levels of economic security and attractiveness of tourist destinations*. https://doi.org/DOI: 10.1145/3444465.3444470

Barik, K., Misra, S., Mishra, B., Maathuis, C., & Chockalingama, S. (2024). *Cyber Resilience for SDG Towards the Digitization: An Imperial Study*. Springer International Publishing., DOI: 10.1007/978-3-031-53433-1_18

Bazazo, I. K., Al-Orainat, L. M., Abuizhery, F., & Al-Dhoun, R. A. (2019). Cyber Security Applications in the Modern Tourism Industry. *Journal of Tourism, Hospitality and Sports, 43*, 46–55. https://www.iiste.org/Journals/index.php/JTHS/article/view/49618

Bougaardt, G., & Kyobe, M. (2011). Investigating the Factors Inhibiting SMEs from Recognizing and Measuring Losses from Cyber Crime in South Africa. *Electronic Journal of Information Systems Evaluation, 14*(2). https://academic-publishing.org/index.php/ejise/article/view/258

Bouke, M. A. ALshatebi, S. H., Abdullah, A., Cengiz, K., & Atigh, H. E. (2023). African Union Convention on Cyber Security and Personal Data Protection: Challenges and Future Directions. *arXiv.Org, abs/2307.01966*. https://doi.org/DOI: 10.48550/arXiv.2307.01966

Carlisle, S., Ivanov, S. H., & Dijkmans, C. (2021). *The digital skills divide: evidence from the European tourism industry*. https://doi.org/DOI: 10.1108/JTF-07-2020-0114

Chaudhary, S., Gkioulos, V., & Katsikas, S. K. (2023). A quest for research and knowledge gaps in cybersecurity awareness for small and medium-sized enterprises. *Computer Science Review, 50*, 100592. Advance online publication. DOI: 10.1016/j.cosrev.2023.100592

Dede, G., Petsa, A. M., Kavalaris, S., Serrelis, E., Evangelatos, S., & Oikonomidis, I. (2024). *Cybersecurity as a contributor to United Nations SDGs towards enhancing the ESG reporting*., DOI: 10.1109/EEITE61750.2024.10654435

Díaz-Parra, A., Rodríguez-Lara, B. M., Salgado Ramírez, J. C., Trejo-Macotela, F. R., & Aguilar-Ortiz, J. (2023). *Smart Tourism*. IGI Global., DOI: 10.4018/979-8-3693-0373-3.ch005

DiMaggio, P. J., & Powell, W. W. (1983). The iron cage revisited: Institutional isomorphism and collective rationality in organizational fields. *American Sociological Review*, *48*(2), 147–160. DOI: 10.2307/2095101

Duggi, N., Bhadri, S., & Varala, C. R. (2025). *Gaps in the Grid: Access and the Digital Inequality Crisis*. 152–162. https://doi.org/DOI: 10.9734/bpi/mono/978-93-48859-10-5/CH13

Eshbaev, G. (2024). GDPR vs. Weakly Protected Parties in Other Countries. *Uzbek Journal of Law and Digital Policy.*, *2*(6), 55–65. DOI: 10.59022/ujldp.254

Fu, H., Guan, J., Wang, R., Kong, L., & Dai, Q. (2024). How does digitalization affect the urban-rural disparity at different disparity levels: A Bayesian Quantile Regression approach. *Technology in Society*, *78*, 102633. DOI: 10.1016/j.techsoc.2024.102633

Gajjar, T., Parikh, S., & Shekokar, K. (2025). Integrating Blockchain Technology with AI to Enhance Security Measure. *Indian Scientific Journal Of Research In Engineering And Management*, *09*(01), 1–9. DOI: 10.55041/IJSREM40423

Ghaderi, Z., Beal, L., Hall, C. M., Zaman, M., Rather, R. A., & Som, A. P. (2024). Cybersecurity and smart tourist destinations resilience. *Tourism Recreation Research*, •••, 1–17. DOI: 10.1080/02508281.2024.2434791

Holling, C. S. (1973). Resilience and stability of ecological systems. *Annual Review of Ecology and Systematics*, *4*(1), 1–23. DOI: 10.1146/annurev.es.04.110173.000245

Ige, A. B., Kupa, E., & Ilori, O. (2024). Aligning sustainable development goals with cybersecurity strategies: Ensuring a secure and sustainable future. *GSC Advanced Research and Reviews*, *19*(3), 344–360. DOI: 10.30574/gscarr.2024.19.3.0236

Kandpal, S., Bhatt, S., Mohan, L., Patwal, A., & Kumar, P. (2023). Cyber security implementation issues in small to medium-sized enterprises (SMEs) and their potential solutions: A comprehensive analysis. In *Proceedings of the 14th International Conference on Computing Communication and Networking Technologies (ICCCNT)* (pp. 1–5). IEEE. https://doi.org/DOI: 10.1109/ICCCNT56998.2023.10307363

Kang, W. (2024). *A Systematic Review: Bridging the Digital Divide in SME Digitalization. 2024*(2). https://doi.org/DOI: 10.62594/atom0002

Khandelwal, J. (2024). Enhancing Journeys in the Digital Age of Tourism Through the Implementation of Smart Tourism Framework. *Advances in Hospitality, Tourism and the Services Industry (AHTSI) Book Series*, 149–164. https://doi.org/DOI: 10.4018/979-8-3693-3715-8.ch008

Kong, L. (2010). Data Protection and Transborder Data Flow in the European and Global Context. *European Journal of International Law*, *21*(2), 441–456. DOI: 10.1093/ejil/chq025

Kontogianni, A., & Alepis, E. (2022). AI, Blockchain & Cyber tourism joining the Smart Tourism realm. *International Conference on Information, Intelligence, Systems and Applications*, 1–6. https://doi.org/DOI: 10.1109/IISA56318.2022.9904393

Kontogianni, A., & Alepis, E. (2023). Tourism embraces blockchain towards the smart tourism era. *Intelligent Decision Technologies*, *17*(3), 811–838. DOI: 10.3233/IDT-230073

Kosnikov, S. N., Zolkin, A. L., Artemyev, N. V., & Lepshokova, A. N. (2024). Cybersecurity as a factor of sustainable development of the digital economy. *Èkonomika i Upravlenie: Problemy. Rešeniâ*, *12/15*(153), 221–229. DOI: 10.36871/ek.up.p.r.2024.12.15.026

Kovacic, M., Cicin-Sain, M., & Milojica, V. (2022). Cyber security and tourism: Bibliometric analysis. *Journal of Process Management. Nuclear Technology*, *10*(3–4), 75–92. DOI: 10.5937/jpmnt10-41205

Kumar, N., & Pham, H. T. (2024). Smart Tourism. *Advances in Hospitality, Tourism and the Services Industry (AHTSI) Book Series*, 351–372. https://doi.org/DOI: 10.4018/979-8-3693-3715-8.ch019

Kuzman, B., Petković, B., & Milovančević, M. (2024). *Information and communication technology in tourism*. https://doi.org/DOI: 10.52370/TISC2475BK

Mairesse, F. (2022). *Cybersecurity in Travel and Tourism: A Risk-Based Approach* (pp. 1605–1628). Springer eBooks. https://doi.org/DOI: 10.1007/978-3-030-48652-5_100

Maleh, Y., & Sahid, A. (2024). *A Case Study on Cyber-Governance for Resilient Organizations*. IGI Global Scientific Publishing., DOI: 10.4018/979-8-3693-3431-7.ch007

Martínez, D. E., Magdalena, L., & Savitri, A. N. (2024). AI and Blockchain Integration: Enhancing Security and Transparency in Financial Transactions. *International Transactions on Artificial Intelligence*, *3*(1), 11–20. DOI: 10.33050/italic.v3i1.651

Meyer, J. W., & Rowan, B. (1977). Institutionalized organizations: Formal structure as myth and ceremony. *AJS; American Journal of Sociology, 83*(2), 340–363. DOI: 10.1086/226550

Mishra, S., Bhatt, V. D., & Singh, A. (2023). *Smart Infrastructure in Smart Cities Scope and Implications for Sustainable Tourism Development.* IGI Global., DOI: 10.4018/979-8-3693-0650-5.ch010

Mkhulisi, N., Dube, S., & Radebe, F. (2024). *Towards a Conceptual Framework for Cybersecurity Skill Requirements in Small and Medium-Sized Enterprises.* https://doi.org/DOI: 10.1109/IMITEC60221.2024.10851058

Mo, L. (2023). *Blockchain and Sustainable Tourism: Unlocking the Opportunities for a Greener Future.* https://doi.org/DOI: 10.20944/preprints202306.1517.v1

Mohamed, N. N., & Abuobied, B. H. H. (2024). Cybersecurity challenges across sustainable development goals: A comprehensive review. *Sustainable Engineering and Innovation, 6*(1), 57–86. DOI: 10.37868/sei.v6i1.id207

Narwal, R., Gupta, A., Gupta, A., & Kukreja, A. (2024). AI and Blockchain: Transforming Digital Transactions. *International Journal of Advanced Research in Science. Tongxin Jishu*, 542–545. Advance online publication. DOI: 10.48175/IJARSCT-17669

Obasi, C., Solomon, N. O., Adenekan, O. A., & Simpa, P. (2024). *Cybersecurity's Role in Environmental Protection and Sustainable Development: Bridging Technology and Sustainability Goals.* https://doi.org/DOI: 10.51594/csitrj.v5i5.1140

Odumesi, J. O., & Sanusi, B. S. (2023). *Achieving Sustainable Development Goals from a Cybersecurity Perspective.* Advances in Multidisciplinary and Scientific Research Journal., DOI: 10.22624/AIMS/CSEAN-SMART2023P3

Orbelyan, G. (2024). Socio-Economic Challenges for the Urban Ecosystem: Complex Model of Smart Tourism and Infrastructure. *Socioeconomic Challenges, 8*(4), 146–160. DOI: 10.61093/sec.8(4).146-160.2024

Ozkan, B. Y., & Spruit, M. (2019). Cybersecurity Standardisation for SMEs: The Stakeholders'. *International Journal of Standardization Research, 17*(2), 41–72. DOI: 10.4018/IJSR.20190701.oa1

Paraskevas, A. (2020). *Cybersecurity in travel and tourism: a risk-based approach.* Springer Nature., DOI: 10.1007/978-3-030-05324-6

Pohl, J. H. (2023). *International Data Transfers and Cybersecurity.* Cambridge University Press., DOI: 10.1017/9781009374576.006

Priyadarshana, D., Ramachandra Rao, T., & Sambasiva Rao, M. (2024). AI and blockchain technology for secure and transparent financial transactions. *International Journal of Science and Research Archive, 13*(1), 2013–2019. DOI: 10.30574/ijsra.2024.13.1.1845

Qudus, L. (2025). Cybersecurity governance: Strengthening policy frameworks to address global cybercrime and data privacy challenges. *International Journal of Science and Research Archive, 14*(1), 1146–1163. DOI: 10.30574/ijsra.2025.14.1.0225

Renaud, K., & Ophoff, J. (2021). *A cyber situational awareness model to predict the implementation of cyber security controls and precautions by SMEs. 1*(1), 24–46. https://doi.org/DOI: 10.1108/OCJ-03-2021-0004

Renaud, K., & Weir, G. R. S. (2016). Cybersecurity and the Unbearability of Uncertainty. *Conference on Computational Complexity*, 137–143. https://doi.org/DOI: 10.1109/CCC.2016.29

Rydzewski, P. (2025). Digital Inequality and Sustainable Development. *Problemy Ekorozwoju, 20*(1), 96–108. DOI: 10.35784/preko.6691

Sankar, J. G., & David, A. (2024). *Transforming the Travel Landscape*. IGI Global., DOI: 10.4018/979-8-3693-1532-3.ch012

Sargsyan, G. (2024).. . *Cybersecurity as a Backbone for Sustainability, 526–530*, 526–530. Advance online publication. DOI: 10.1109/CSR61664.2024.10679426

Sekhar, K. S. V. (2024). Digital Infrastructure Challenges for Techno-Entrepreneurs in Rural Areas. *Advances in Electronic Commerce Series*, 127–156. https://doi.org/DOI: 10.4018/979-8-3373-0086-3.ch007

Tabansky, L., & Lichterman, E. (2024). PROGRESS: The sectoral approach to cyber resilience. *International Journal of Information Security, 24*(1), 18. Advance online publication. DOI: 10.1007/s10207-024-00910-3

Tee, M. K. (2024). *Malaysia's Smart Tourism Framework*. IGI Global., DOI: 10.4018/979-8-3693-1978-9.ch003

Treiblmaier, H. (n.d.). *Blockchain and Tourism*. https://doi.org/DOI: 10.1007/978-3-030-05324-6_28-2

Vachheta, H. C., Pawar, I., Hukare, K. G., & Jadhav, S. B. (2024). Cybersecurity in the Digital Era: A Comprehensive Framework for Safeguarding Data Integrity, Privacy and Critical Infrastructures Against Evolving Threats. *International Journal of Advanced Research in Science. Tongxin Jishu*, •••, 471–486. DOI: 10.48175/IJARSCT-22665

Valli, C., Martinus, I. C., Stanley, J., & Kirby, M. (2021). *CyberCheck.me: A Review of a Small to Medium Enterprise Cyber Security Awareness Program*. Springer., DOI: 10.1007/978-3-030-71017-0_17

Walmsley, B. (2023). A Blockchain-Based Tourism Industry. *Advances in Electronic Government, Digital Divide, and Regional Development Book Series*, 27–50. https://doi.org/DOI: 10.4018/978-1-6684-4153-4.ch002

Weng, Y., & Wu, J. (n.d.). Fortifying the Global Data Fortress: A Multidimensional Examination of Cyber Security Indexes and Data Protection Measures across 193 Nations. *International Journal of Frontiers in Engineering Technology*. https://doi.org/DOI: 10.25236/IJFET.2024.060203

Xiubo, L., Keting, Y., Wei, L., Qilei, L., & Weiwei, Q. (2018). *A tourism anti-fraud system based on a block chain*.

Yang, K. H., Park, S. K., Yoon, S. N., & Kim, J. (2010). Measurement of the digital inequality in remote rural areas: Case of South Korea. *International Journal of Information Technology and Management*, *9*(2), 142–161. DOI: 10.1504/IJITM.2010.030458

Yulianto, S., Lumban Gaol, F., Supangkat, S. H., & Ranti, B. (2023). *A Comprehensive Model for Enhancing Cybersecurity Resilience and IT Governance Through Red Teaming Exercises*. 1–7. https://doi.org/DOI: 10.1109/ICT60153.2023.10374068

Chapter 5
Cybersecurity in Vietnam's Sustainable Tourism Practices

Hanh Thi Pham
http://orcid.org/0000-0001-7527-5154
Vietnam Women's Academy, Vietnam

Abdul Jamal
http://orcid.org/0000-0001-8752-7507
The New College, University of Madras, India

Thang Duc Nguyen
East Asia University of Technology, Vietnam

Anh Lan Nguyen
http://orcid.org/0009-0007-5380-2743
Academy of Policy and Development, Vietnam

Loi Duc Vu
http://orcid.org/0009-0001-6270-4797
Hanoi School of Business and Management, Vietnam National University, Hanoi, Vietnam

ABSTRACT

This chapter explores a paradox in Vietnam's tourism strategy: digital technologies promote sustainability but also increase cybersecurity risks. It argues that cyber resilience is essential for achieving Sustainable Development Goals (SDGs), particularly SDG 11 (heritage protection) and SDG 12 (responsible consumption). Using qualitative interviews with policymakers, industry, and tech leaders, the

DOI: 10.4018/979-8-2600-1850-7.ch005

study highlights the dependency of smart infrastructure-such as IoT and AI-on cybersecurity. Through the Technology-Organization-Environment (TOE) framework, it analyzes major threats like ransomware and data breaches. Case studies of attacks on InterContinental Hotels and Vietnamese airports reveal evolving motives, including geopolitical disruption. The chapter introduces a conceptual model linking cyber incidents to SDG indicators and applies Protection Motivation Theory (PMT) to explain stakeholder behavior. It concludes by urging a multi-stakeholder approach, viewing cybersecurity as a strategic investment in sustainable tourism and national resilience.

1. INTRODUCTION

1.1. Background of the Study

Vietnam's tourism sector is at a critical juncture, defined by a powerful post-pandemic recovery, a national strategic commitment to sustainable development, and a government-driven agenda for comprehensive digital transformation. The industry has not only rebounded but is positioned as a key economic driver, with ambitious goals to attract up to 28 million international visitors by 2025. Central to this vision is the dual imperative of sustainability and digitalization. Sustainable tourism has been legalized and prioritized as essential for long-term competitiveness, aligning with modern traveler preferences.

This sustainability agenda is being operationalized primarily through the creation of a "smart tourism" ecosystem, which leverages advanced technologies like the Internet of Things (IoT), Artificial Intelligence (AI), and big data analytics. This digital infrastructure is the engine for achieving sustainability goals-from optimizing resource consumption in smart hotels to managing tourist flows at sensitive heritage sites to prevent over-tourism. However, this profound dependency on digital systems simultaneously creates a vast and complex attack surface, exposing the entire tourism value chain to an escalating array of cyber threats.

1.2. Problem Statement

The rapid deployment of smart tourism infrastructure, utilizing technologies like the Internet of Things (IoT), Artificial Intelligence (AI), and big data analytics, is central to Vietnam's national strategy for achieving its Sustainable Development Goals (SDGs), particularly those related to responsible consumption (SDG 12) and sustainable cities and communities (SDG 11). This digital infrastructure is the primary mechanism for implementing sustainability practices, such as optimizing energy and water usage, managing tourist flows to prevent over-tourism, and protecting cultural heritage. However, this deep integration of operational technology with digital networks creates a vast and complex cyberattack surface. A successful cyberattack on these systems-for instance, a ransomware attack on a smart building's management system or the manipulation of data from environmental sensors-is no longer just a technical or data privacy issue; it represents a direct threat to the very sustainability outcomes these technologies are designed to achieve. The core problem is the significant lack of research and validated frameworks that systematically assess and quantify the direct impact of these cybersecurity vulnerabilities on the progress toward specific SDGs within the tourism sector. This leaves a critical blind spot in national development and security strategies, where the infrastructure intended to drive sustainable progress could become its greatest liability.

1.3. Research Questions

1.3.1. Primary Research Question

To what extent do cybersecurity vulnerabilities within Vietnam's smart tourism infrastructure directly impede or reverse progress toward the nation's key environmental and economic Sustainable Development Goals?

1.3.2. Secondary Research Questions

(1) Which specific smart tourism technologies (e.g., IoT sensors for resource management, AI for visitor flow analytics, centralized data platforms) are most critical for achieving targeted SDGs in Vietnam's tourism sector, and what are the precise mechanisms of this dependency?
(2) What are the most significant cybersecurity threats and vulnerabilities (e.g., IoT device exploitation, data integrity attacks, ransomware on operational technology) associated with this critical smart tourism infrastructure?
(3) How can the impact of specific cyberattack scenarios on smart tourism infrastructure be modeled and measured in terms of their direct consequences on SDG indicators (e.g., measurable increases in energy consumption, failure to manage visitor density at protected sites, disruption to local economies)?

1.4. Research Objectives

(1) **To Identify and Map:** To systematically identify and map the critical dependencies between smart tourism infrastructure components and the key performance indicators of relevant SDGs within the Vietnamese context.

(2) **To Assess:** To conduct a comprehensive threat assessment of this infrastructure, analyzing the most probable and high-impact cybersecurity vulnerabilities and attack vectors that could disrupt sustainability-oriented operations.
(3) **To Develop:** To develop a novel conceptual framework for evaluating the direct impact of cybersecurity incidents on SDG attainment, allowing for a quantifiable risk analysis that connects technical vulnerabilities to sustainability outcomes.
(4) **To Recommend:** To formulate evidence-based policy and governance recommendations for integrating cybersecurity resilience into Vietnam's national sustainable tourism strategy, ensuring that digital transformation securely and effectively contributes to its SDG commitments.

1.5. Scope and Delimitations

This study will focus specifically on the tourism sector within Vietnam. The scope is centered on the cybersecurity vulnerabilities inherent in the *smart infrastructure* (IoT, AI, Big Data) being deployed to achieve national *sustainable development goals*. The research is delimited to a qualitative exploration aimed at building a foundational understanding and a conceptual framework. It will not conduct a quantitative measurement of all cyber risks across the entire industry but will instead focus on the perceived impacts of key threats on SDG attainment.

1.6. Significance of the Study

This research is significant for three key stakeholder groups:

(1) **For Policymakers:** It will provide an evidence-based framework to inform the integration of cybersecurity into national sustainable tourism and digital transformation strategies, highlighting security as a core pillar of sustainable development.
(2) **For the Tourism Industry:** It will offer practitioners a clearer understanding of critical cyber vulnerabilities within their operational technologies and demonstrate the tangible link between cybersecurity investment and the achievement of sustainability targets, which are increasingly important for brand reputation and competitiveness.
(3) **For Academia:** It will address a critical and underexplored gap at the intersection of cybersecurity, smart tourism, and sustainable development. By proposing a novel analytical framework, it will provide a foundation for future empirical research in this emerging field.

2. LITERATURE REVIEW

2.1. Chronological Review of Literature

The literature on cybersecurity in sustainable tourism practices in Vietnam reflects a progression from foundational ICT development and initial cybersecurity strategies to more advanced integration of artificial intelligence, big data, and smart technologies. Early works focus on national cybersecurity policies and ICT growth, setting the stage for addressing cyber threats in tourism. Recent scholarship emphasizes the adoption of AI, IoT, and blockchain to enhance data protection, network security, and sustainable tourism experiences while considering economic impacts and ethical challenges. Emerging research also highlights the importance of risk management, governance, and the implications of AI-driven cybersecurity solutions for enhancing resilience in Vietnam's tourism sector.

Table 1. Chronological review of literature

Year Range	Research Direction	Description
2013–2015	Foundations of ICT and Cybersecurity Strategy in Vietnam	Initial research focused on the development of ICT infrastructure and the formulation of national cybersecurity strategies addressing vulnerabilities and policy frameworks. Studies explored the role of information technologies in sustainable tourism, emphasizing environmental and socio-cultural impacts, setting a baseline for integrating cybersecurity with tourism sustainability.
2018–2021	Early Big Data and AI Adoption in Tourism	Research during this period examined the application of big data and artificial intelligence to enhance tourism management and customer experiences. Studies highlighted the potential of AI and data analytics to optimize resource allocation, personalize services, and improve operational efficiency, while acknowledging the challenges in adoption and data governance.
2022–2023	Smart Tourism and Cybersecurity Risk Management	Focus shifted to smart tourism paradigms influenced by Industry 4.0 technologies, with emphasis on risk-based cybersecurity approaches. Literature addressed the integration of IoT, AI, and digital platforms for improving safety, communication, and sustainable tourism practices, alongside identifying cybersecurity risks and the need for comprehensive frameworks.
2024	Advanced AI-Driven Cybersecurity and Sustainable Tourism Practices	Recent literature concentrates on leveraging AI, machine learning, and blockchain to enhance cybersecurity, data protection, and network resilience in tourism. Research also explores emerging cyber threats, ethical considerations, and economic impacts of cybersecurity investments. Studies emphasize interdisciplinary collaboration, governance, and the role of advanced technologies in fostering secure, sustainable, and economically viable tourism ecosystems.

Source: Author's compilation

2.2. Agreement and Divergence Across Studies

The reviewed studies collectively recognize the critical role of cybersecurity frameworks, AI, IoT, and big data in enhancing sustainable tourism practices, particularly in protecting data and improving network resilience. There is broad consensus on the integration of advanced technologies like AI for threat detection, personalized tourist experiences, and operational efficiency. However, divergences appear regarding the maturity and implementation of cybersecurity measures in Vietnam's tourism sector and the extent to which economic impacts have been empirically assessed. Differences are also evident in perspectives on challenges such as ethical concerns and governance, reflecting variation in study focus, methodology, and regional context. Overall, the literature underscores the need for interdisciplinary approaches and adaptive strategies to address evolving cyber threats within sustainable tourism.

Table 2. Agreement and Divergence Across Studies

Comparison Criterion	Studies in Agreement	Studies in Divergence	Potential Explanations
Cybersecurity Framework Effectiveness	Multiple studies emphasize the necessity of comprehensive, risk-based, and adaptive cybersecurity frameworks to protect tourism data and infrastructure effectively, highlighting the use of AI and ML for enhanced threat detection and response (Alonso-Almeida & Giglio, 2024) (Paraskevas, n.d.) (Kumari, 2024) (Raji et al., n.d.). The importance of integrating cybersecurity within sustainable tourism and environmental protection frameworks is also stressed (Obasi et al., 2024) (Sargsyan, 2024).	Some works point to the embryonic stage of cybersecurity policy implementation in Vietnam, noting challenges in achieving strategic cybersecurity goals despite governmental initiatives (Dai, 2015) (Dai, n.d.). A few studies highlight fragmented or compliance-oriented approaches in tourism cybersecurity that undermine effectiveness (Paraskevas, n.d.).	Agreement arises from shared recognition of cybersecurity's importance for sustainability; divergence stems from contextual differences—Vietnam's emerging cybersecurity landscape versus more developed or theoretical frameworks elsewhere. Methodological variation (empirical vs. conceptual) also explains discrepancies.
Network Security Resilience	Scholars agree that robust network security is vital for ensuring tourism safety and operational continuity, supported by smart infrastructure and IoT integration (Rudenko et al., 2024) (Halim et al., 2023) (Sankar & Ilangovan, 2024). AI-driven analytics and automation are seen as key to enhancing infrastructure resilience against cyber threats (Traversa, 2024) (Akinloye. et al., 2024). The application of multilayered protective measures across information lifecycles is widely advocated (Rudenko et al., 2024).	Some studies reveal gaps in real-time threat monitoring and challenges in implementing effective resilience strategies in tourism-specific digital ecosystems, particularly in developing contexts (Dai, 2015) (Paraskevas, n.d.). Differences arise regarding readiness for integrating advanced IoT and AI tools in tourism infrastructure (Nguyen, 2021) (Chakraborty, 2024).	Consensus is supported by technological advances and industry trends; divergence is influenced by varying levels of digital infrastructure maturity, resource availability, and policy enforcement in different regions, especially contrasting Vietnam's developing context with global perspectives.
Economic Impact Analysis	There is agreement that cybersecurity investments can positively influence tourism safety, business continuity, and competitiveness, with AI and big data improving operational efficiency and customer satisfaction, indirectly supporting economic gains (Khalid, 2024) (Stroumpoulis et al., 2022) (Dar & Dar, 2024) (Traversa, 2024). Some studies recognize the economic benefits of personalized tourism services enabled by AI and technology integration (Doğan & Niyet, 2024) (Bešić et al., n.d.).	Few studies provide direct empirical evaluations of the economic impacts of cybersecurity in Vietnam's tourism sector, with some indicating limited research on cost-benefit analysis and long-term economic outcomes (Dai, 2015) (Paraskevas, n.d.). Divergence also exists in the level of emphasis placed on economic versus technological/security aspects (Singh & Hassan, 2024) (Chakraborty, 2024).	Agreement reflects general understanding of technology's economic benefits; divergence arises from scarcity of localized empirical data in Vietnam and different disciplinary foci (technology vs. economics), as well as the nascent stage of economic impact studies in this specific sector/context.

continued on following page

Table 2. Continued

Comparison Criterion	Studies in Agreement	Studies in Divergence	Potential Explanations
Cyber Threat Typology	The literature generally identifies phishing, social engineering, fraud, and AI-driven sophisticated attacks as prevalent cyber threats impacting tourism and digital ecosystems (Alonso-Almeida & Giglio, 2024) (Paraskevas, n.d.) (Familoni, 2024) (George, 2024). AI-powered threats and zero-day attacks are highlighted as emerging challenges requiring adaptive defense measures (Kumari, 2024) (Yarali et al., 2023) (Raji et al., n.d.). The need for human security education and awareness is also emphasized (Alonso-Almeida & Giglio, 2024).	Variability exists in detailed threat categorizations and their relative frequency in different tourism contexts; some studies focus more on general cybersecurity challenges rather than tourism-specific threats (Dai, 2015) (Paraskevas, n.d.). The scale and sophistication of threats perceived differ between developed and emerging digital tourism markets (Obasi et al., 2024) (Sargsyan, 2024).	Differences may stem from regional cyber threat environments, the scope of the studies (broad vs. tourism-specific), and temporal factors with rapidly evolving threat landscapes. Variations in methodological depth also contribute to discrepancies in threat typologies.
Technology Integration Level	There is widespread consensus that AI, IoT, big data analytics, blockchain, and related technologies are transforming sustainable tourism by enhancing cybersecurity, resource management, personalized experiences, and operational efficiency (Alonso-Almeida & Giglio, 2024) (Khalid, 2024) (Das, 2024) (Chakraborty, 2024) (Doğan & Niyet, 2024) (Sandhya & Varghese, 2024) (Stroumpoulis et al., 2022) (Traversa, 2024). Numerous studies advocate leveraging these technologies to optimize environmental sustainability and economic viability (Obasi et al., 2024) (Sankar & Ilangovan, 2024) (Eswaran et al., 2024) (Topsakal, 2024). The role of AI in predictive analytics and threat mitigation is especially noted (Kumari, 2024) (Kashyap, 2024) (Raji et al., n.d.).	Divergence appears in the extent and maturity of technology adoption reported, with some studies indicating early-stage or limited implementation in Vietnam compared to broader global or theoretical trends (Dai, 2015) (Nguyen, 2021). Ethical and governance challenges related to technology use, including data privacy and algorithmic bias, are highlighted differently across studies (Familoni, 2024) (Raji et al., n.d.) (Spalevic et al., 2024). The speed of technological change also creates variance in findings.	Agreements reflect global recognition of technology's transformative power; divergence is due to developmental stages, regulatory environments, regional infrastructure differences, and the scope of ethical considerations emphasized. This is aggravated by the rapid evolution of AI and IoT technologies, making some findings quickly outdated.

Source: Author's compilation

3. RESEARCH METHODOLOGY

3.1. Research Approach

This study will adopt a qualitative research approach. This methodology is chosen because the research questions are fundamentally exploratory, aiming to uncover the complex, context-dependent relationships between cybersecurity, smart infrastructure, and sustainability outcomes. A qualitative approach is best suited for developing the novel conceptual framework sought by the research objectives, as it allows for in-depth data collection that can capture the nuanced perspectives of key stakeholders and build theory from the ground up.

3.2. Data Collection Method

The primary data collection method will be *semi-structured interviews.* This method offers a balance of consistency and flexibility, allowing the researcher to use a pre-defined interview guide to cover all research questions while also providing the freedom to probe deeper into emergent themes and unexpected insights shared by participants.

3.3. Target Population and Sampling

The target population consists of senior professionals and experts with knowledge spanning tourism strategy, technology/cybersecurity, and sustainable development policy in Vietnam. A purposive sampling strategy will be used to deliberately select participants based on their specific roles and expertise. This will be supplemented by snowball sampling, where initial interviewees will be asked to recommend other relevant experts in their network. The target sample size is 15-20 interviews, or until data saturation is reached.

The population will be drawn from three key groups:

(1) **Policymakers and Regulators:** Senior officials from the Vietnam National Authority of Tourism (VNAT), the Ministry of Public Security, and the Ministry of Culture, Sports and Tourism.

(2) **Industry Leaders:** C-level executives (CISOs, CTOs, Directors of Sustainability) from major hotel chains, tour operators, and OTAs operating in Vietnam.

(3) **Technology and Security Experts:** Senior consultants from cybersecurity firms and smart technology providers with direct experience in Vietnam's tourism sector.

3.4. Data Analysis Plan

The data collected from the interviews will be analyzed using Thematic Analysis. This rigorous qualitative method involves a systematic process:

(1) **Transcription:** All interview recordings will be transcribed verbatim.
(2) **Familiarization:** The researcher will read and re-read the transcripts to become deeply familiar with the data.
(3) **Initial Coding:** The data will be systematically coded to identify interesting features and patterns relevant to the research questions.
(4) **Theme Development:** Codes will be collated into potential themes, and all relevant coded data extracts will be gathered within these identified themes.
(5) **Reviewing and Refining Themes:** The themes will be reviewed and refined to ensure they accurately represent the data and are coherent and distinct.
(6) **and Naming Themes:** Each final theme will be clearly defined and named, and a detailed analysis will be written, supported by direct quotations from the transcripts.

This methodology will provide a rich, nuanced understanding of how cybersecurity challenges in Vietnam's tourism sector can impact the country's sustainable development goals (SDGs), particularly in the areas of resource management, cultural preservation, and tourism growth.

4. FINDINGS AND ANALYSIS

4.1. Anatomy of a Crisis: Lessons From Cyber Incidents in and Around Vietnam

Theoretical discussions of cyber threats become starkly real when examined through the lens of actual incidents. The attacks that have struck the tourism and hospitality sector in Vietnam and the wider Southeast Asian region offer invaluable, albeit harsh, lessons. They reveal the attackers' evolving tactics, expose common organizational weaknesses, and underscore the devastating potential for operational, financial, and reputational damage.

4.1.1. Case Study: The 2022 InterContinental Hotels Group (IHG) Attack - A Paradigm Shift

The cyberattack on IHG, a global hospitality giant with a significant presence in Vietnam, represents a critical case study for the entire industry. Its simplicity of execution and destructive outcome serve as a chilling warning.

- **Attack Deconstruction:** The incident was not the work of a sophisticated state actor but a young couple from Vietnam (NDTV, 2022). They gained initial access through a classic social engineering tactic: a phishing email with a malicious attachment sent to an employee. This allowed them to bypass the company's two-factor authentication (2FA) security (Infosecurity Magazine, n.d). Once inside the network, their path to widespread compromise was shockingly straightforward. They discovered the login credentials for the company's internal password vault, which was protected by the notoriously weak and common password (NDTV, 2022).

- **The "For Fun" Motive:** The attackers' initial goal was financial: they attempted to deploy ransomware. However, IHG's IT team responded quickly, isolating servers and thwarting the ransomware deployment. Frustrated, the attackers pivoted to a purely malicious motive. As they told the BBC, they decided to "have some fun" and launched a "wiper attack" instead, a form of malware designed solely to permanently erase data (NDTV, 2022). This shift from a financial to a nihilistic motive is a crucial development in the threat landscape.

- **Repercussions:** The impact was severe. The wiper attack caused massive disruption to IHG's central booking systems, mobile app, and other applications, leaving customers unable to make reservations and hotels unable to manage them efficiently (NDTV, 2022). The operational paralysis led to significant direct financial losses and prompted a class-action lawsuit from franchisees in the United States, who claimed millions in lost revenue due to the company's alleged "inadequate data security measures" (Sangfor, n.d). Beyond the financial cost, the incident inflicted severe reputational damage, exposing fundamental failures in basic cyber hygiene at one of the world's largest hotel companies.

4.1.2. Case Study: The 2016 Vietnamese Airports Hack - When Tourism Becomes a Geopolitical Target

This incident illustrates how critical tourism infrastructure can be weaponized for political purposes, turning a travel hub into a propaganda platform.

- **Incident Overview:** On July 29, 2016, the flight information screens at Vietnam's two largest airports-Noi Bai International Airport in Hanoi and Tan Son Nhat International Airport in Ho Chi Minh City-were hijacked. Instead of flight details, they displayed derogatory messages critical of Vietnam and the Philippines regarding their territorial claims in the South China Sea. The public address systems were also compromised to broadcast similar political messages. Simultaneously, the official website of Vietnam Airlines was defaced, and, most damagingly, the personal data of approximately 411,000 members of its Golden Lotus frequent flier program was stolen and leaked online.

- Strategic Implications: This coordinated attack demonstrates that tourism infrastructure is considered a legitimate target for geopolitical signaling. The hackers, allegedly the Chinese group 1937CN, exploited the high visibility of airports to maximize the impact of their message. The incident highlighted the vulnerability of interconnected systems; the attack on the airport displays was linked to a breach of the airline, causing cascading failures. The immediate result was chaos and operational disruption, with over 100 flights delayed and thousands of passengers affected as airport staff reverted to manual check-in procedures. The long-term implication is that risk assessments for critical tourism infrastructure must now account for state-sponsored or politically motivated actors whose goal is not financial gain but public disruption and national embarrassment.

Figure 1. Anatomy of a Crisis: Timeline and Impact of Major Tourism Cyber Incidents

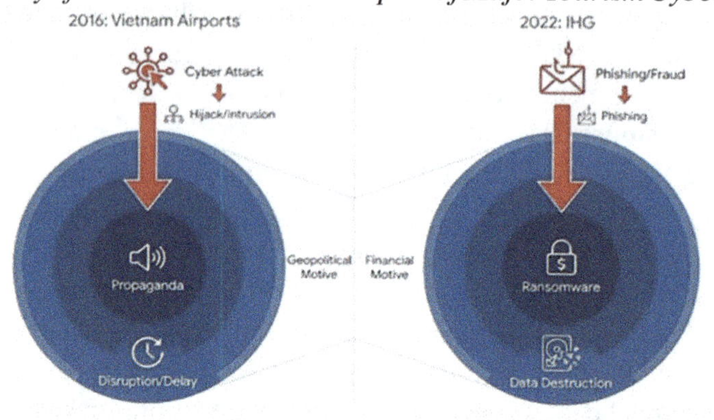

This figure contrasts the 2016 Vietnamese Airports Hack (Geopolitical Motive) with the 2022 IHG Attack (Nihilistic/Financial Motive), detailing the attack vectors and the cascading operational consequences.

Source: Author's compilation

4.1.3. Regional Context: A Shared Vulnerability

The challenges faced by Vietnam are not unique but are part of a broader regional pattern of vulnerability in the tourism sector.

- Thailand (2021): A massive data leak exposed the personal details of over 106 million travelers to Thailand, with records dating back to 2011. A security researcher discovered the unsecured database, which contained names, passport numbers, and residency status (SecurityWeek, 2021). While authorities secured the data quickly after being notified, the incident highlights the immense systemic risk posed by large-scale government data aggregation projects when they are not adequately protected.

- **Singapore (2023):** Even Singapore, a nation renowned for its sophisticated cybersecurity posture, is not immune. The high-profile Marina Bay Sands integrated resort suffered a data breach that exposed the personal information of 665,000 of its loyalty program customers (Asia Pacific Foundation of Canada, 2024). This incident proves that even the most prominent and well-resourced tourism brands are constant targets and that a strong national security framework does not guarantee security for individual enterprises.

These cases reveal a critical shift in the nature of cyber risk. The motivations driving attacks on the tourism sector are diversifying beyond pure financial gain. They now include nihilistic destruction, as seen with the IHG attack, and geopolitical signaling, as demonstrated by the Vietnamese airports hack. This evolution demands a fundamental change in how tourism organizations conduct risk assessments. A model based solely on the monetary value of data is no longer sufficient. The traditional approach asks, "What is our data worth?" This is a necessary question, but it is incomplete. The new risk calculus must also address questions like, "What is the reputational and operational cost if our systems are simply destroyed?" and "Could our brand or infrastructure be used as a pawn in a larger conflict?" This has direct and urgent implications for crisis management and incident response planning, which must now prepare for scenarios of pure data destruction and public defacement, not just data theft or encryption for ransom.

The following table provides a comparative analysis of these incidents, highlighting key patterns and strategic takeaways for tourism stakeholders.

Table 3. Comparative Analysis of Major Cyber Incidents in Southeast Asian Tourism

Incident/ Year	Target	Attack Vector	Primary Impact	Key Strategic Takeaway
IHG Attack/2022	Global Hotel Chain	Phishing & Weak Password	Data Destruction & Operational Disruption	Basic cyber hygiene (password security, user training) is a critical, top-tier defense (Sangfor, n.d)
Vietnamese Airports Hack/2016	National Airports & Airline	System Hijack & Defacement	Data Theft & Geopolitical Propaganda	Critical tourism infrastructure is a viable target for politically motivated actors.
Thailand Visitor Data Leak/2021	Government Database	Unsecured Database	Mass PII Exposure	Large-scale data aggregation by government entities creates a single point of failure with systemic risk (SecurityWeek, 2021).
Marina Bay Sands Breach/2023	Integrated Resort	Unknown	Customer Loyalty Data Exposure	High-profile, iconic brands are perpetual targets, regardless of the host country's security posture (Asia Pacific Foundation of Canada, 2024).

Source: Author's compilation

4.2. Qualitative Research Results

This chapter presents the findings derived from the semi-structured interviews conducted with key stakeholders across Vietnam's tourism, technology, and policy sectors. The analysis is structured around the core themes of the research, aiming to deconstruct the complex relationships between smart tourism infrastructure, cybersecurity vulnerabilities, and the attainment of Sustainable Development Goals (SDGs). Thematic analysis of the interview data is employed to answer the secondary research questions, culminating in the development of a conceptual framework that models the impact of cyber incidents on sustainability outcomes. The insights presented herein are supported by direct quotations and synthesized perspectives from the expert participants.

4.2.1. Theme 1: The Critical Role of Smart Infrastructure in Vietnam's Sustainable Tourism Vision

This section addresses the first secondary research question by identifying the specific smart technologies deemed most critical for achieving sustainability targets and detailing the mechanisms through which these dependencies operate. The findings reveal a strong consensus among policymakers and industry leaders that digital transformation is not merely an adjunct to sustainability but its primary implementation engine (OpenGov Asia, 2025).

4.2.1.1. Identifying Key Technologies for SDG Attainment

Analysis of the interview data highlights three categories of smart technologies as foundational to Vietnam's sustainable tourism strategy:

(1) Internet of Things (IoT) for Resource Management: Participants consistently identified IoT sensors and connected devices as critical for advancing SDG 12 (Responsible Consumption and Production). Experts pointed to the deployment of smart meters in hotels to monitor and optimize energy and water consumption, smart waste management systems in tourist complexes, and environmental sensors at natural heritage sites to monitor air and water quality (CYFIRMA, 2024). As one industry leader stated, *"We cannot manage what we do not measure. IoT gives us the real-time data to make our operations visibly greener and more efficient, which is no longer a 'nice-to-have' but a core competitive requirement."*

(2) Big Data and AI for Visitor Flow Management: Interviewees emphasized the use of big data analytics and AI-powered predictive modeling as essential tools for mitigating the negative impacts of over-tourism, directly contributing to SDG 11 (Sustainable Cities and Communities) (Travel and Tour World, 2025). The national tourism database, combined with real-time data from mobile apps and public transport, is envisioned as a mechanism to manage crowd density at sensitive cultural sites, predict traffic congestion, and dynamically adjust pricing or access to encourage a more even distribution of tourists (JETT Business Technology, 2025).

(3) Centralized Digital Platforms for Inclusive Growth: Stakeholders from government agencies highlighted the role of national digital platforms, such as the "Vietnam Travel" app and the national tourism database, in promoting more inclusive and sustainable economic growth (SDG 8: Decent Work and Economic Growth).[9] These platforms are intended to provide small and medium-sized enterprises (SMEs) in rural areas with access to a national market, enabling them to participate more equitably in the tourism value chain and promoting community-based tourism initiatives (Lázaro Florido-Benítez, 2024).

4.2.1.2. Mechanisms of Dependency: How Technology Translates to Sustainability

The interviews revealed that the link between these technologies and SDGs is not abstract but operates through specific, tangible mechanisms. For instance, the data from IoT energy sensors in a hotel doesn't just provide a report; it feeds directly into an automated building management system that adjusts HVAC and lighting in real-time, creating a direct, measurable reduction in the hotel's carbon footprint. Similarly,

AI-driven visitor flow analytics are not just for observation; they are designed to integrate with e-ticketing and dynamic pricing systems to actively manage visitor numbers, thus directly preserving the physical integrity of heritage sites. This deep, functional integration means that the reliability and integrity of the technology are synonymous with the reliability and integrity of the sustainability outcome.

4.2.2. Theme 2. The Anatomy of Vulnerability in Smart Tourism Infrastructure

This section addresses the second secondary research question by analyzing the most significant cybersecurity threats and vulnerabilities associated with the critical smart infrastructure identified above. The findings, interpreted through the Technology-Organization-Environment (TOE) framework, show that vulnerabilities are a product of the technology itself, the organizations deploying it, and the external threat environment (CYFIRMA, 2023).

4.2.2.1. Perceived Threats: From Ransomware on OT to Data Integrity Attacks

Security experts and CTOs interviewed for this study identified a consistent set of high-impact threats:

(1) Ransomware on Operational Technology (OT): The most frequently cited fear was a ransomware attack that moves beyond traditional IT systems (like booking databases) to cripple the OT that manages physical infrastructure. As one cybersecurity consultant explained, *"A ransomware attack that encrypts guest data is bad. A ransomware attack that shuts down the air conditioning, smart locks, and water systems for a 500-room resort during peak season is a catastrophe. It's a direct threat to physical safety and business continuity."* (VnExpress International, n.d).

(2) IoT Device Exploitation: A major concern is the vulnerability of the vast network of IoT devices. Experts noted that many of these devices lack robust, built-in security features and are often deployed without being properly configured or patched, making them easy entry points for attackers to pivot into the core network (Center for Strategic and International Studies, 2024).

(3) Data Integrity Attacks: A more subtle but equally damaging threat identified was the malicious manipulation of data from sustainability-focused sensors. An expert described a scenario where an attacker could subtly alter the data from environmental sensors to mask pollution levels or manipulate visitor-counting sensors to create artificial overcrowding or under-utilization, thereby sabotaging data-driven management efforts and directly undermining sustainability reporting and operations (Infosecurity Magazine, n.d.).

4.2.2.2. *An Analysis Through the TOE Framework*

The persistence of these vulnerabilities can be understood through the three contexts of the TOE framework:

Technological Context: The inherent complexity of integrating diverse IoT, OT, and IT systems creates unforeseen security gaps (IBM, n.d.). The lack of security standards for many consumer-grade IoT devices used in hospitality further exacerbates this issue (Travelers Insurance, n.d.).

Organizational Context: Participants overwhelmingly pointed to a lack of organizational readiness. This is driven by a severe shortage of skilled cybersecurity professionals with hybrid expertise in both IT and OT systems, and a lack of top management support that often views cybersecurity as a cost center rather than a strategic enabler of sustainability (Business Queensland, n.d.).

Environmental Context: The external environment is characterized by increasingly sophisticated threat actors, including ransomware-as-a-service gangs and potentially state-sponsored groups, who are constantly evolving their tactics.[29] Furthermore, while new data protection laws like the PDPL create regulatory pressure, many SMEs lack the resources to achieve compliance, leaving them exposed (PwC, n.d.).

4.2.3. Theme 3: A Conceptual Framework for Linking Cyber Incidents to SDG Impacts

This section synthesizes the findings from the preceding themes to address the third secondary research question, proposing a model for measuring the impact of cyberattacks on SDG indicators. The framework is built by tracing the cascading effects of specific attack scenarios and incorporating the human behavioral response as understood through Protection Motivation Theory (PMT).

4.2.3.1. *Scenario Analysis: Tracing the Ripple Effects of Cyberattacks*

Based on the interview data, two illustrative scenarios demonstrate the causal chain from a cyber incident to a negative SDG impact:

(1) Scenario A: Data Integrity Attack on a Smart Heritage Site. An attacker compromises the IoT sensors that monitor visitor numbers at a UNESCO site like Hoi An Ancient Town. The manipulated data falsely indicates low visitor density, causing the AI-driven management system to continue selling tickets and allowing entry. The direct result is severe overcrowding, leading to physical degradation of ancient structures and a negative visitor experience. This directly reverses progress on SDG 11.4 (strengthen efforts to protect and safeguard the world's cultural and natural heritage).

(2) Scenario B: Ransomware Attack on a Smart Resort's OT Network. A phishing attack on an employee allows attackers to deploy ransomware that encrypts and disables the resort's Building Management System (BMS). This cripples control over HVAC, lighting, and water recycling systems, causing them to run at maximum capacity for 72 hours until the system can be restored. This leads to a massive, measurable spike in energy and water consumption and waste generation. This directly impedes progress toward SDG 12.2 (achieve the sustainable management and efficient use of natural resources) and SDG 7.3 (double the global rate of improvement in energy efficiency).

4.2.3.2. The Human Factor: Applying Protection Motivation Theory (PMT)

The impact of these scenarios is amplified by the human response, which can be explained by PMT. In Scenario B, the resort manager's response is critical.

(1) Threat Appraisal: The manager perceives the threat as severe (high perceived severity) and recognizes their resort is a target (high perceived vulnerability).

(2) Coping Appraisal: However, due to the cybersecurity skills gap, the manager has no trained staff and feels technically unqualified to handle the incident (low self-efficacy). They may also believe that paying the ransom is the only effective way to restore the system (low response efficacy for internal solutions). PMT predicts that this combination of high threat appraisal and low coping appraisal will lead to maladaptive responses, such as delaying action, making panicked decisions, or paying the ransom, all of which extend the system downtime and magnify the negative impact on the SDG indicators.

4.2.3.3. Proposed Impact Model

Based on this analysis, a conceptual model is proposed. It is a matrix that maps specific cyber threats (e.g., Ransomware, DDoS, Data Integrity Attack) against critical smart infrastructure components (e.g., BMS, Visitor Sensors, Central Database). Each intersection in the matrix details the potential cascading failures and links them to specific, measurable SDG indicators (e.g., kWh of energy wasted, tons of CO2 emitted, number of hours a heritage site is closed). This framework provides a novel, structured method for translating abstract cyber risks into tangible impacts on internationally recognized sustainability metrics.

The findings from the qualitative interviews confirm that Vietnam's sustainable tourism ambitions are inextricably linked to the security of its smart infrastructure. The analysis identified the key technologies driving this agenda, the specific and significant cyber threats they face, and the organizational and environmental factors that perpetuate these vulnerabilities. By synthesizing these findings, this chapter has proposed a novel conceptual framework that traces the pathway from a cyberattack, through the technological and human response, to a direct and measurable impact on Sustainable Development Goals. This framework provides the foundation for the discussion and policy recommendations that will be presented in the final chapter.

Table 4. Operational Framework for Assessing Cyber-Attack Impacts on SDG Attainment in Smart Tourism

Cyber-Attack Scenario	Targeted Smart Infrastructure	Cascading Operational Failures	Direct Impact on SDG Indicator(s)	Illustrative Mitigation Strategy
Ransomware on Operational Technology (OT)	Smart Building Management System (BMS) in a resort complex.	Loss of control over HVAC, lighting, smart locks, and water recycling systems. Physical safety risks. Business continuity halt.	**SDG 7.3:** Massive, unmanaged energy consumption reverses energy efficiency gains. **SDG 12.2:** Inefficient use of water resources. **SDG 8.9:** Direct economic losses and reputational damage harm sustainable tourism promotion.	**Technical:** Network segmentation to isolate OT from IT networks. **Procedural:** Robust, air-gapped, and regularly tested backup and recovery plans for OT systems.
Data Integrity Attack	IoT visitor-counting sensors and AI-driven flow management platform at a UNESCO heritage site.	Falsified data masks overcrowding, leading to the failure of dynamic access controls.	**SDG 11.4:** Physical degradation of cultural heritage due to unmanaged visitor density. Negative visitor experience erodes the site's value.	**Technical:** Use of data anomaly detection algorithms and cryptographic signatures to ensure data integrity from sensor to platform. **Procedural:** Manual spot-checks and human oversight to validate automated system outputs.
Mass Data Breach via Phishing	Centralized customer database of a national OTA or hotel chain.	Theft and public leak of millions of tourist Personal Identifiable Information (PII), including passport and payment details.	**SDG 16.4 / 16.10:** Erosion of public access to information and fundamental freedoms due to loss of privacy. **SDG 8.9:** Severe damage to national tourism brand trust, impacting future visitor numbers.	**Organizational:** Continuous, engaging security awareness training with realistic phishing simulations for all staff. **Technical:** Mandatory multi-factor authentication (MFA) on all critical systems.

Source: Author's compilation

4.3. A Proposed Multi-Layered Conceptual Model of Cyber-Sustainability Impact

4.3.1. Detailed Breakdown of Model Layers

The model will consist of five distinct but interconnected layers:

Layer 1: The Threat Environment (TOE-E): This initial layer serves as the input stage of the model. It will be represented by text boxes or icons that define the external catalysts, including "Threat Actors" (e.g., Ransomware-as-a-Service Gangs, State-Sponsored Groups, Malicious Insiders) and their corresponding "Attack Motives" (e.g., Financial Gain, Geopolitical Signaling, Nihilistic Destruction), drawing directly from the analysis of the IHG and Vietnamese airports incidents.

Layer 2: The Vulnerable Ecosystem (TOE-T & TOE-O): This layer represents the target of the attack. A central box labeled "Smart Tourism Infrastructure" will contain specific examples identified as critical in the findings, such as IoT Environmental Sensors, AI Visitor Flow Management Platforms, Operational Technology (OT) / Building Management Systems (BMS), and Centralized Customer Databases. This entire layer will be framed by an outer box representing the "Techno-Organizational Context," which lists the underlying vulnerabilities that enable an attack, such as "System Complexity," "Lack of Standards," "Skills Shortages," and "Low Management Support".

Layer 3: The Incident & Cascading Failures: An arrow originating from Layer 1 and piercing the vulnerable frame of Layer 2 will trigger this layer. It will consist of a box labeled "Cyber Incident" (e.g., Ransomware Deployment, Data Manipulation) which then leads to a sequence of boxes detailing the "Cascading Operational Failures." These will contain concrete examples drawn directly from Table 4, such as "Loss of control over HVAC & water systems" or "Falsified data masks overcrowding at heritage site".

Layer 4: The Human Response Junction (PMT): This is the crucial micro-level, mediating layer, depicted as a decision diamond. The inputs flowing into this junction will be the core constructs of Protection Motivation Theory: "Threat Appraisal (Severity, Vulnerability)" and "Coping Appraisal (Self-Efficacy, Response Efficacy)." Two distinct causal paths will emerge from this junction, visually representing the argument from Section 4.2.3.2:

- **Path A (Adaptive Response):** This upward or positive path will be labeled with the conditions "High Self-Efficacy & High Response Efficacy." It leads to a box of actions such as "Activate Incident Response Plan," "Isolate Systems," and "Utilize Backups." An arrow from this box, labeled "Mitigated Impact," proceeds to the final layer.

- **Path B (Maladaptive Response):** This downward or negative path will be labeled with the conditions "Low Self-Efficacy & Low Response Efficacy." It leads to a box of actions such as "Delayed Action," "Panicked Decisions," or "Pay Ransom." An arrow from this box, labeled "Magnified Impact," proceeds to the final layer.

Layer 5: Quantifiable SDG Degradation: This is the final output layer, representing the return to the macro-level impact. The "Mitigated Impact" and "Magnified Impact" arrows from Layer 4 will point to a final box labeled "Direct Impact on SDG Attainment." This box will list the specific, measurable SDG indicators identified as being at risk in the chapter's analysis, including "SDG 11.4: Degradation of Cultural Heritage," "SDG 12.2: Inefficient Use of Natural Resources," "SDG 7.3: Reversal of Energy Efficiency Gains," and "SDG 8.9: Damage to Sustainable Tourism Promotion".

4.3.2. Proposed Table: Model Component Glossary

To ensure academic rigor and prevent misinterpretation of the visual model, it is recommended to introduce a new table immediately following the figure. This table will serve as a glossary, explicitly defining each major component of the model and linking it back to the theoretical foundations and textual evidence within the chapter.

Figure 2. A Conceptual Model of Cyber-Attack Impacts on SDG Attainment

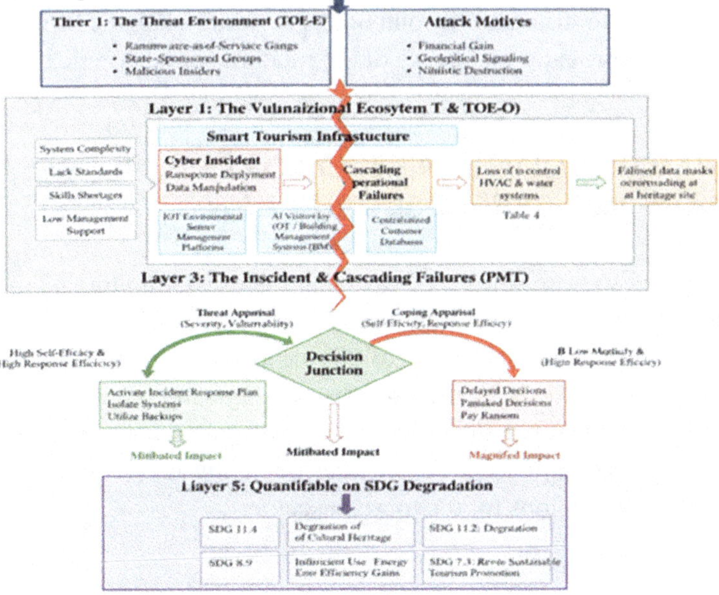

Source: Author

Table 5. Glossary of Conceptual Model Components

Model Component	Definition	Theoretical Basis	Chapter Reference
Threat Environment	The external context of malicious actors and their motivations that catalyze cyber incidents.	Technology-Organization-Environment (TOE) Framework	Section 4.1
Vulnerable Ecosystem	The specific smart tourism infrastructure and the inherent technological and organizational weaknesses that make it susceptible to attack.	Technology-Organization-Environment (TOE) Framework	Section 4.2.1, 4.2.2
Human Response Junction	The critical stakeholder decision-making process during a crisis, which mediates the severity of the outcome based on cognitive appraisals.	Protection Motivation Theory (PMT)	Section 4.2.3.2
SDG Degradation	The measurable negative impact of a cyber incident on internationally recognized targets for sustainable development.	UN Sustainable Development Goals (SDGs)	Section 4.2.3.1, Table 4

Source: Author's compilation

"To synthesize the complex interplay of these technological, organizational, and human factors, the following conceptual model is proposed. Figure 1 visually represents the causal pathway from an external cyber threat, through the vulnerable smart tourism ecosystem, to a direct and measurable impact on Sustainable Development Goals. Crucially, the model integrates Protection Motivation Theory to illustrate how stakeholder responses at the human level can either mitigate or magnify the ultimate sustainability outcome, providing a holistic framework for risk analysis. Table X provides a glossary of the model's core theoretical components."

5. VIETNAM'S EVOLVING REGULATORY RESPONSE: THE DRAFT 2025 CYBERSECURITY LAW

The Vietnamese government, recognizing the escalating threats in cyberspace and the complexities of its existing legal framework, is undertaking a significant legislative overhaul. The centerpiece of this effort is the draft consolidated Law on Cybersecurity, slated for 2025, which aims to merge and modernize the country's primary cybersecurity regulations. This new law is poised to fundamentally reshape the compliance landscape for all businesses operating in Vietnam's digital space, with profound implications for the tourism sector.

5.1. The Existing Legal Quilt

To appreciate the significance of the new draft, one must understand the current regulatory environment. It is a patchwork of several key laws and decrees, including the 2018 Law on Cybersecurity (LOCS), the 2015 Law on Network Information Security (LOCIS), and the landmark 2023 Decree on Personal Data Protection (PDPD) (DLA Piper, (n.d.). This fragmented structure has created overlaps, inconsistencies, and shared responsibilities between different government bodies, primarily the Ministry of Public Security and the Ministry of Information and Communications, leading to challenges in enforcement and compliance (Tilleke & Gibbins, 2025). The draft 2025 law seeks to remedy this by consolidating these frameworks under the sole authority of the Ministry of Public Security (Tilleke & Gibbins, 2025).

5.2. The Draft 2025 Consolidated Law: A Paradigm Shift

The draft 2025 Cybersecurity Law introduces several pivotal changes that will directly impact tourism operators.

- **Expanded Scope of "Service Providers":** The new law dramatically broadens the definition of entities subject to its regulations. The scope now explicitly covers a wide range of businesses integral to the tourism supply chain, including internet service providers, social networks, financial institutions, e-commerce platforms, and logistics providers (Tilleke & Gibbins, 2025). This means that virtually any tourism business with an online presence-from large Online Travel Agencies (OTAs) and hotel chains to smaller operators that use online booking or payment systems-will fall under its purview.

- **Removal of Data Localization and Local Presence Requirements:** Perhaps the most significant change for international operators is the removal of the controversial data localization provisions from the 2018 LOCS. The previous law required certain foreign and domestic companies to store specific types of user data within Vietnam and, under certain conditions, establish a local branch or representative office (Tilleke & Gibbins, 2018). The removal of these requirements in the new draft signals a more pragmatic regulatory approach that balances national security with the realities of global digital business (Tilleke & Gibbins, 2025). This move is likely to encourage foreign investment in Vietnam's digital economy and better aligns the country with international data transfer norms and trade commitments.

- **New Obligations for Combating High-Tech Cybercrime:** Reflecting growing concern over sophisticated cybercrime, the draft law introduces a new chapter dedicated to its prevention and handling. It imposes direct obligations on service providers to actively assist authorities. These include requirements to verify user identities upon registration, report cyberattacks to the authorities within 24 hours, and cooperate fully with official investigations, which may involve freezing accounts or suspending transactions (Rouse, 2025). These mandates place a significant new operational and compliance burden on businesses, requiring them to have robust identity verification and 24/7 incident reporting mechanisms in place.

- **Strengthened Content Controls:** The draft law reinforces the government's authority to manage online content. It requires service providers to implement mechanisms to block or remove content deemed illegal or harmful within 24 hours of receiving a formal request from a competent authority (Tilleke & Gibbins, 2025). This tightens the rules around unsolicited communications and prohibited content, compelling businesses to have either active content monitoring systems or a rapid-response capability to handle takedown requests.

5.3. Implications for Sustainable Tourism Operators

The draft 2025 Cybersecurity Law presents a dual reality for tourism businesses in Vietnam. On one hand, it offers greater regulatory clarity and removes a major barrier to entry for foreign companies by eliminating the data localization mandate. On the other hand, it imposes stricter, more resource-intensive compliance obligations, particularly regarding cooperation with law enforcement and content management. For sustainable tourism operators, who must already balance economic, social, and environmental considerations, navigating this new legal landscape will be a critical challenge. The law effectively raises the baseline for digital governance, demanding a more mature and proactive approach to cybersecurity from all players in the industry.

The following table summarizes the key legal shifts and their direct operational implications for tourism businesses.

Table 6. Key Provisions of Vietnam's Draft 2025 Cybersecurity Law for Tourism Operators

Provision Area	Old Rule (2018 Law / 2015 Law)	New Rule (Draft 2025 Law)	Operational Implication for Tourism Business
Scope of Application	Ambiguous scope, primarily focused on telecom and internet services (Tilleke & Gibbins, 2018).	Broadly defined to explicitly include e-commerce, logistics, finance, etc(Tilleke & Gibbins, 2025).	Most tourism businesses, including online tour operators and hotels with booking sites, are now clearly covered.
Data Localization	Mandatory data storage in Vietnam and local presence required for certain services under specific conditions (Tilleke & Gibbins, 2018).	Data localization and local presence requirements are removed (Tilleke & Gibbins, 2025).	Foreign OTAs and hotel chains can operate more freely without the cost and complexity of establishing local servers.
Cybercrime Cooperation	General duties to cooperate with authorities (Tilleke & Gibbins, 2018).	Specific obligations to verify user identities, report attacks within 24 hours, and facilitate investigations (Rouse, 2025).	Requires a formal, 24/7 incident reporting process and potentially costly user verification systems.
Content Management	General requirements to prevent prohibited content (Tilleke & Gibbins, 2018).	Mandate to block or remove illegal content within 24 hours of a formal request from authorities (Vietnam Law & Legal Forum, 2025).	Necessitates active content monitoring or a rapid-response capability to comply with takedown orders.

Source: Author's compilation

6. DISCUSSION, RECOMMENDATIONS, AND CONCLUSION

This final chapter synthesizes the findings presented in Chapter 4, interpreting their significance in the context of the existing literature and the overarching research questions. The study set out to explore the extent to which cybersecurity vulnerabilities within Vietnam's smart tourism infrastructure impede progress toward its Sustainable Development Goals (SDGs). The qualitative findings have confirmed this link, revealing the critical dependencies, significant threats, and systemic challenges that define this complex relationship. This chapter will first discuss the key findings, connecting them to the theoretical frameworks employed. It will then translate these insights into a series of actionable, multi-stakeholder recommendations. Finally, the chapter will acknowledge the limitations of the study, propose directions for future research, and offer a concluding statement on the imperative of integrating cybersecurity into Vietnam's sustainable tourism strategy.

6.1. Discussion of Key Findings

The research has produced several key findings that contribute to a deeper understanding of the cybersecurity-sustainability nexus in Vietnamese tourism.

First, the study confirms that smart tourism infrastructure is the primary vehicle for achieving sustainability goals, creating a "double-edged sword" scenario. The very technologies-IoT, AI, and Big Data-that are essential for optimizing resource use (SDG 12) and managing visitor flows (SDG 11) simultaneously introduce critical vulnerabilities that can directly reverse this progress. This finding moves beyond the conventional view of cybersecurity as a data protection issue, reframing it as a core component of environmental and cultural preservation policy. A ransomware attack on a smart hotel's operational technology is not just an IT incident; it is an environmental one, leading to measurable waste and undermining the "green" brand Vietnam seeks to cultivate.

Second, the development of the conceptual framework for linking cyber incidents to SDG impacts, as visually articulated in Figure 1, represents a significant contribution. The literature on cyber incident costs has traditionally focused on direct financial losses, regulatory fines, and reputational damage. The proposed model (Figure 1) provides a novel lens for analysis, translating technical vulnerabilities into tangible impacts on internationally recognized sustainability metrics...". The literature on cyber incident costs has traditionally focused on direct financial losses, regulatory fines, and reputational damage. The proposed model provides a novel lens for analysis, translating technical vulnerabilities into tangible impacts on internationally recognized sustainability metrics. This allows for a more holistic risk assessment where the consequences of a data integrity attack, for example, are measured not just in compromised records but in the potential degradation of a UNESCO heritage site, a direct setback to SDG 11.4.

Third, the application of the TOE and PMT frameworks effectively explains *why* these vulnerabilities persist despite high awareness of threats. The TOE analysis confirms that for tourism SMEs, the technological context (high cost and complexity of solutions) and organizational context (lack of resources and expertise) are significant barriers to adoption. The PMT analysis explains the "awareness-to-action" gap at the individual level, where managers may have a high threat appraisal but a low coping appraisal due to a lack of confidence and skills (low self-efficacy), leading to inaction or maladaptive responses. This underscores that the problem is deeply socio-technical and cannot be solved by technology alone. The concept of the "human firewall," currently applied only to employees (OpenGov Asia, 2025), should be extended to include the tourist as a key actor whose trust is a prerequisite for system efficacy.

6.2. Recommendations

Based on the findings, the following multi-layered recommendations are proposed to build a more cyber-resilient and sustainable tourism sector in Vietnam.

6.2.1. For National and Regional Policymakers (e.g., Ministry of Culture, Sports and Tourism; Ministry of Public Security)

(1) Integrate Cybersecurity into National Tourism Strategy: Formally recognize cybersecurity as a core pillar of sustainable tourism in all national development plans. It should be treated with the same strategic importance as environmental protection and cultural preservation, ensuring that security is a foundational element of the "green, sustainable, attractive global destination" brand.

(2) Develop Sector-Specific Guidance for PDPL Compliance: The Ministry of Public Security, which enforces data protection laws, must issue clear, practical, and tourism-specific guidelines for the new Personal Data Protection Law (PDPL) effective January 1, 2026. These guidelines should clarify how hotels, tour operators, and OTAs can use data for personalization and smart management while complying with the PDPL's stringent consent and cross-border transfer requirements, thus preventing the law from inadvertently stifling innovation.

(3) Establish a National Tourism-ISAC: Create a Tourism Information Sharing and Analysis Center (ISAC) as a public-private partnership. This center would facilitate the trusted, anonymized sharing of threat intelligence, incident reports, and best practices among all stakeholders, enabling a coordinated, sector-wide response to major incidents like the ransomware and phishing campaigns currently targeting the industry.

(4) Subsidize and Standardize SME Security: Address the critical vulnerability of SMEs by creating a government-backed program that provides access to vetted, affordable cybersecurity solutions. Prioritizing locally developed "Make in Vietnam" products, which are noted for their cost-effectiveness, could make this program more accessible. Mandating a baseline security standard for SMEs wishing to participate in national tourism platforms would elevate the security posture of the entire ecosystem.

Tier 1 (Micro-enterprises): Policy should focus on government-funded awareness campaigns and free, easily implementable tools. This could include providing simple guides on strong password policies, offering free access to government-vetted phishing simulation tools, and promoting basic cyber hygiene through industry associations.

Tier 2 (Small Enterprises): The government could develop a subsidized "Cybersecurity Starter Kit." This kit would feature vetted, low-cost "Make in Vietnam" solutions for essential protections like endpoint security, automated cloud backups, and basic network firewalls, addressing the cost-effectiveness point raised in the chapter.

Tier 3 (Medium Enterprises): For larger SMEs, policy could establish co-funded programs for more advanced security assessments, penetration testing, and direct support for achieving compliance with complex regulations like the Personal Data Protection Law (PDPL). This tiered approach provides more practical and credible policy guidance tailored to the diverse needs of the sector.

6.2.2. For Tourism Enterprises and Associations (e.g., Vietnam Tourism Association)

(1) Cultivate a Cybersecurity Culture: Leadership must champion a shift from viewing cybersecurity as a compliance burden to embedding it as a core business value. This requires securing buy-in from top management, establishing clear security policies, and transforming employees from the "weakest link" into a robust "human firewall".

(2) Adopt a Risk-Based Approach: Businesses, especially SMEs, must prioritize the protection of their most critical assets, such as guest databases, payment systems, and operational technology. This includes implementing fundamental controls like multi-factor authentication, network segmentation, and, most critically, robust and regularly tested data backup and recovery systems to ensure resilience against ransomware.

(3) Invest in Continuous and Engaging Training: Implement regular, practical, and engaging cybersecurity training for all staff. This should include realistic phishing simulations and clear incident response drills to ensure employees know their roles during a crisis and can help mitigate the 95% of breaches attributed to human error.

6.2.3. For Technology Developers and Innovators

(1) Embrace "Security and Privacy by Design": Embed security and privacy considerations into the earliest stages of the product development lifecycle for all new smart tourism applications, IoT devices, and platforms. This proactive approach is far more effective and less costly than attempting to patch vulnerabilities after deployment.

(2) Focus on Usable Security: Design security features with the end-user in mind. Overly complex or inconvenient security controls are often bypassed by tourists and employees alike. The goal should be to create security that is as seamless and intuitive as possible, enhancing trust without creating unnecessary friction.

6.3. Limitations of the Study

This research, while providing valuable foundational insights, is subject to several limitations. First, its qualitative nature and reliance on purposive sampling mean the findings are contextually rich but not statistically generalizable to the entire Vietnamese tourism industry. Second, the study's geographic focus on Vietnam means its conclusions may not be directly transferable to other nations without considering their unique regulatory, cultural, and technological landscapes. Finally, the dynamic threat landscape of cybersecurity means that the specific threats identified represent a snapshot in time; new vulnerabilities and attack vectors will inevitably emerge.

6.4. Directions for Future Research

This study opens several avenues for future scholarly inquiry:

(1) Quantitative Validation: Future research should aim to quantitatively test the conceptual framework developed here. This could involve creating a survey instrument to measure the relationships between specific cyber incidents and SDG indicators across a large sample of tourism enterprises.

(2) Longitudinal Studies: A longitudinal study tracking the evolution of cybersecurity posture and SDG attainment over several years would provide invaluable insights into the long-term impacts of policies like the 2026 PDPL and the adoption of new technologies.

(3) The Tourist Perspective (TAM): An empirical study using an extended Technology Acceptance Model (TAM) is needed to investigate how Vietnamese and international tourists' perceptions of cybersecurity and data privacy influence their trust in and adoption of Vietnam's smart tourism applications and services.

(4) Comparative Analysis: A comparative study of cybersecurity integration in the sustainable tourism strategies of different ASEAN countries could identify regional best practices and areas for cross-border collaboration.

6.5. Conclusion

The digital transformation of Vietnam's tourism sector holds immense promise for achieving the nation's ambitious economic and sustainable development goals. However, this research concludes that this promise is fundamentally jeopardized by a failure to treat cybersecurity as a strategic imperative. The findings demonstrate that the smart infrastructure intended to build a green, sustainable, and resilient tourism industry is itself fragile and exposed. A cyberattack is no longer a peripheral IT risk;

it is a direct threat to sustainability outcomes, capable of causing environmental damage, degrading cultural heritage, and eroding the trust of global travelers.

Moving forward requires a paradigm shift. Cybersecurity must be woven into the fabric of national tourism policy, industry practice, and technological innovation. This demands a collaborative, multi-stakeholder effort grounded in a shared understanding that in the digital age, a truly sustainable tourism ecosystem must first be a secure one. By embracing the recommendations outlined in this study, Vietnam can move beyond a reactive security posture and proactively forge a tourism future that is not only smart and sustainable but also safe and resilient.

REFERENCES

Akinloye., A., Anwansedo, S., & Akinwande, O. T. (2024).*AI-Driven Threat Detection and Response Systems for Secure National Infrastructure Networks: A Comprehensive Review*. DOI: 10.51583/IJLTEMAS.2024.130710

Alonso-Almeida, M. del M., & Giglio, C. (2024). Cybersecurity in tourism and hospitality management research: Current issues, trends, and an agenda for future research. *Cuadernos de Turismo*, (53), 243–260. Advance online publication. DOI: 10.6018/turismo.616471

Asia Pacific Foundation of Canada. (2024). *Southeast Asia, cyber threats, and opportunities for Canadian cooperation*. Retrieved August 5, 2025, from https://www.asiapacific.ca/publication/southeast-asia-cyber-threats-and-opportunities-canadian-co

Bešić, C., Bogetić, S., Bakator, M., & Petrevska, I. (n.d.).*The impact of sustainability, digital technologies, and employee knowledge on the competitiveness of personalized tourist offer*. DOI: 10.5937/menhottur2400010B

Business Technology, J. E. T. T. (2025). *Cybersecurity in hospitality industry: Top tips & threats*. Retrieved August 5, 2025, from https://jettbt.com/news/essential-guide-on-cybersecurity-for-the-hospitality-industry-top-tips-and-threats/

Center for Strategic and International Studies. (2024). *Cyber scamming goes global: Unveiling Southeast Asia's high-tech fraud factories*. Retrieved August 5, 2025, from https://www.csis.org/analysis/cyber-scamming-goes-global-unveiling-southeast-asias-high-tech-fraud-factories

Chakraborty, P. P. (2024a). *The Role of Technology in Enhancing Sustainable Tourism Practices.Advances in Hospitality, Tourism and the Services Industry (AHTSI)*. Book Series., DOI: 10.4018/979-8-3693-5903-7.ch011

Chakraborty, P. P. (2024b). *Tourism in Transition in Sustainable World.Advances in Hospitality, Tourism and the Services Industry (AHTSI)*. Book Series., DOI: 10.4018/979-8-3693-5903-7.ch017

CYFIRMA. (2023). *The changing cyber threat landscape Southeast Asia*. Retrieved August 5, 2025, from https://www.cyfirma.com/research/the-changing-cyber-threat-landscape-southeast-asia/

CYFIRMA. (2024). *The changing cyber threat landscape Southeast Asia*. Retrieved August 5, 2025, from https://www.cyfirma.com/research/the-changing-cyber-threat-landscape-southeast-asia-2/

Dai, C. T. (2015). Cybersecurity in Vietnam: Formulation and Implementation of a New Strategy. *Herodote, 157*(2), 126–140.

Dai, C. T. (n.d.).*La cybersécurité au Viêt Nam: formulation et mise en œuvre d'une nouvelle stratégie*. DOI: 10.3917/her.157.0126

Dar, H., & Dar, M. A. (2024). *Redefining Success of the Tourism Sector Through Technological Advancements.Advances in Hospitality, Tourism and the Services Industry (AHTSI)*. Book Series., DOI: 10.4018/979-8-3693-5678-4.ch008

Das, S. (2024). *Application of AI Technology for the Development of Destination Tourism towards an Intelligent Information System*. Eonomic Affairs., DOI: 10.46852/0424-2513.3.2024.31

Doğan, S., & Niyet, İ. Z. (2024).*Artificial Intelligence (AI) in Tourism*. DOI: 10.1108/978-1-83753-970-320241001

Eswaran, U., Eswaran, V., & Eswaran, V. (2024). *AI Technologies for Personalised and Sustainable Tourism.Advances in Hospitality, Tourism and the Services Industry (AHTSI)*. Book Series., DOI: 10.4018/979-8-3693-5678-4.ch001

Familoni, B. T. (2024).*Cybersecurity challenges in the age of ai: theoretical approaches and practical solutions*. DOI: 10.51594/csitrj.v5i3.930

Florido-Benítez, L. (2024). The cybersecurity applied by online travel agencies and hotels to protect users' private data in smart cities. *Smart Cities*, *7*(1), 19. https://www.mdpi.com/2624-6511/7/1/19. DOI: 10.3390/smartcities7010019

George, S. (2024). *Artificial Intelligence-Powered Cybersecurity*. Advances in Information Security, Privacy, and Ethics Book Series., DOI: 10.4018/979-8-3373-1102-9.ch008

Halim, N. A., Norizan, N. S., & Thirumoorthi, T. (2023).*A digital safe-zone tourism network*. DOI: 10.4324/9781003291763-41

IBM. (n.d.). *What is Digital Forensics and Incident Response (DFIR)?* Retrieved August 5, 2025, from https://www.ibm.com/think/topics/dfir

Insurance, T. (n.d.). *How digital forensics detectives investigate a data breach*. Travelers. Retrieved August 5, 2025, from https://www.travelers.com/resources/business-topics/cyber-security/digital-forensics-detectives-investigate-data-breach

Kashyap, S. (2024). The Influence of Artificial Intelligence on Cybersecurity. *International Journal of Innovative Research in Computer and Communication Engineering*. DOI: 10.15680/IJIRCCE.2024.1203503

Khalid, Md. (2024). *S*. Sustainable Tourism's Tomorrow., DOI: 10.4018/979-8-3693-3390-7.ch008

Kumari, A. (2024). The role of artificial intelligence and machine learning in enhancing cybersecurity in the digital economy.*International Journal of Research in Management*. DOI: 10.33545/26648792.2024.v6.i1c.140

Magazine, I. (n.d.). *Hackers admit destroying InterContinental Hotels Group's data 'for fun'*. Retrieved August 5, 2025, from https://www.infosecurity-magazine.com/news/hackers-destroying-ihgs-data-for/

NDTV. (2022.). *Vietnamese couple deletes British hotel chain data for fun: Report*. Retrieved August 5, 2025, from https://www.ndtv.com/world-news/vietnamese-couple-deletes-british-hotel-chains-data-for-fun-report-3355116

Nguyen, T. T. (2021). *Developing Smart Tourism in 4.0 Industrial Age: The Case of Vietnam*. DOI: 10.5220/0010592804890493

Obasi, S. C., Solomon, N. O., Adenekan, O. A., & Simpa, P. (2024). *Cybersecurity's Role in Environmental Protection and Sustainable Development: Bridging Technology and Sustainability Goals*. DOI: 10.51594/csitrj.v5i5.1140

OpenGov Asia. (2025). *Vietnam: Digital transformation to bolster economic ambitions*. Retrieved August 5, 2025, from https://opengovasia.com/vietnam-digital-transformation-to-bolster-economic-ambitions/

Paraskevas, A. (n.d.).*Cybersecurity in Travel and Tourism: A Risk-Based Approach*. DOI: 10.1007/978-3-030-05324-6_100-1

Piper, D. L. A. (n.d.). *Data protection laws in Vietnam*. Retrieved August 5, 2025, from https://www.dlapiperdataprotection.com/?t=law&c=VN

PwC. (n.d.). *Forensics*. Retrieved August 5, 2025, from https://www.pwc.com/vn/en/services/deals/forensic-services.html

Queensland, B. (n.d.). *IT threat response for tourism organisations*. Retrieved August 5, 2025, from https://www.business.qld.gov.au/industries/hospitality-tourism-sport/tourism/crisis-support/it-threat

Raji, A. N., Olawore, A. O., Ayodeji, A., & Joseph, J. (n.d.).*Integrating Artificial Intelligence, Machine Learning, and Data Analytics in Cybersecurity: A Holistic Approach to Advanced Threat Detection and Response*. DOI: 10.30574/wjarr.2023.20.3.2741

Rouse. (2025). *Vietnam's draft cybersecurity law 2025 – Key changes businesses need to know*. Retrieved August 5, 2025, from https://rouse.com/insights/news/2025/vietnam-s-draft-cybersecurity-law-2025-key-changes-businesses-need-to-know

Rudenko, M., Кочума, І., Кравченко, О., & Tretiak, N. (2024). Information security in smart tourism: risk management, marketing strategies, perspectives. *Вісник Хмельницького Національного Університету*. DOI: 10.31891/2307-5740-2024-328-42

Sandhya, H., & Varghese, B. (2024).*Smart Tourism Narratives*. DOI: 10.4018/979-8-3693-1058-8.ch010

Sangfor. (n.d.). *IHG hack claimed by vindictive couple using wiper malware*. Retrieved August 5, 2025, from https://www.sangfor.com/blog/cybersecurity/ihg-hack-claimed-by-vindictive-couple-using-wiper-malware

Sankar, J. G., & Ilangovan, K. (2024). *The Role of Smart Technology in Enhancing Sustainable Tourism Experiences.Advances in Hospitality, Tourism and the Services Industry (AHTSI)*. Book Series., DOI: 10.4018/979-8-3693-7388-0.ch014

Sargsyan, G. (2024).*Cybersecurity as a Backbone for Sustainability*. DOI: 10.1109/CSR61664.2024.10679426

SecurityWeek. (2021). *Details of 100M visitors to Thailand exposed online: Research firm*. Retrieved August 5, 2025, from https://www.securityweek.com/details-100m-visitors-thailand-exposed-online-research-firm/

Singh, P., & Hassan, V. (2024).*Application of Artificial Intelligence-Based Technologies for Promoting Sustainable Tourism Practices*. DOI: 10.4018/979-8-3693-6260-0.ch015

SiteMinder. (n.d.). *Cyber security in the hospitality industry*. Retrieved August 5, 2025, from https://www.siteminder.com/r/cyber-security-hospitality-industry/

Spalevic, Z., Milosavljević, B., & Marković, S. (2024). Legal Basis of Educational Processes of Artificial Intelligence Algorithms in E-tourism.*International Journal of Cognitive Research in Science, Engineering and Education*. DOI: 10.23947/2334-8496-2024-12-1-209-217

Stroumpoulis, A., Kopanaki, E., & Varelas, S. (2022). Role of artificial intelligence and big data analytics in smart tourism: A resource-based view approach. *WIT Transactions on Ecology and the Environment*, 99–108. Advance online publication. DOI: 10.2495/ST220091

Tilleke & Gibbins. (2018). *Vietnam's controversial new cybersecurity law raises questions*. Retrieved August 5, 2025, from https://www.tilleke.com/insights/vietnams-controversial-new-cybersecurity-law-raises-questions/19/

Tilleke & Gibbins. (2025). *Draft of Vietnam's consolidated 2025 cybersecurity law released.* Retrieved August 5, 2025, from https://www.tilleke.com/insights/draft-of-vietnams-consolidated-2025-cybersecurity-law-released/

Topsakal, Y. (2024). *Artificial Intelligence-Based Sustainable Tourism Planning. Advances in Hospitality, Tourism and the Services Industry (AHTSI).* Book Series., DOI: 10.4018/979-8-3693-3715-8.ch004

Travel and Tour World. (2025). *Vietnam sparks summer travel frenzy while cybercrime shadows the season.* Retrieved August 5, 2025, from https://www.travelandtourworld.com/news/article/vietnam-sparks-summer-travel-frenzy-while-cybercrime-shadows-the-season/

Traversa, F. (2024).*Artificial Intelligence in Tourism.* DOI: 10.1016/B978-0-443-13701-3.00344-3

Vietnam Law & Legal Forum. (2025). *New cybersecurity law drafted to regulate information security, cybersecurity.* Retrieved August 5, 2025, from https://vietnamlawmagazine.vn/new-cybersecurity-law-drafted-to-regulate-information-security-cybersecurity-74800.html

Yarali, A., Rodocker, E., & Gora, C. (2023).*Artificial Intelligence in Cybersecurity: A Dual-Nature Technology.* https://doi.org/DOI: 10.1109/CSCI62032.2023.00042

Chapter 6

Forensic Intelligence and Cyber Resilience for Smart Tourism Ecosystems:

Integrating AI and Blockchain for Trustworthy Digital Transformation

Bekzod Madaminov
Mamun University, Khiva, Uzbekistan

R. N. Ravikumar
http://orcid.org/0009-0009-3705-1681
Marwadi University, Rajkot, India

S. Aarthi
http://orcid.org/0009-0006-9064-2091
Marwadi University, Rajkot, India

ABSTRACT

This chapter presents a Cyber Resilient Smart Tourism Framework that combines digital forensics, Artificial Intelligence (AI), and blockchain to improve security, transparency, and trust in online tourism systems. The framework is structured into four layers preventive, detective, responsive, and adaptive each designed to detect, analyze, and mitigate cyber threats efficiently. It shows how AI helps with predicting trends and spotting potential threats, while blockchain keeps evidence safe from tampering and makes everything clear and open. Case studies, including

DOI: 10.4018/979-8-2600-1850-7.ch006

the Collins Aerospace cyberattack and the Italy hotel data breach, demonstrate the framework's real-world applicability. The integration of forensic intelligence with AI and blockchain strengthens data protection, incident response, and cross-domain collaboration among tourism stakeholders. The chapter points out the need for proactive resilience, forensic readiness, and adaptive learning to secure the next generation of smart tourism infrastructures.

1. INTRODUCTION

The immense level of digitalization in the tourism and hospitality sector has changed the manner in which the destinations receive, sell and interact with their customers. Innovative technologies, which have been offered through smart tourism ecosystems, have also led to a seamless connectivity (Iot, AI, Blockchain, and Cloud Computing) and custom service delivery and data-driven decision-making. However, the specified technological advancement also entails new cyber security challenges that threaten privacy of the data, financial and consumer confidence. With the ongoing growth of the software-based environment, devices and platforms are growing more interconnected making cyberattacks, ransomware, phishing, and identity theft an even greater threat (Gretzel et al., 2023a). This chapter gives importance of digital forensics and cyber resilience in mitigating such threats. It highlights on integration of the frameworks of forensic investigation and methods of cybersecurity to offer continuity, accountability, and transparency to the tourism systems. This section preconditions the discussion of what smart tourism stakeholders can do in order to secure their activities and establish cyber-sound systems which will be able to resist and recover in case of digital disturbances.

1.1 Evolution of Smart Tourism Ecosystems

The integration between digital technologies and data analytics has developed smart tourism ecosystems to improve the tourist experience. At first, the tourism industry used to be dependent on the fixed information system and handbook reservations. Real-time personalization of the provided services and optimization of available resources are now possible through the integration of cloud computing, IoT sensors, and mobile applications (Gretzel et al., 2023b). The current tourism ecosystems are smart systems that bridge the gap between destinations, service providers and tourists by predicting user preferences, tracking the flow of tourists and offering safety. The governments and businesses have invested in the infrastructure of smart cities that facilitate the process of tourism in terms of digitalized kiosks, virtual tours, and chatbots powered by AI. The extension of digital attack surface is also enhanced due to this evolution. The interconnection between devices and systems is so large that smart tourism is susceptible to breaches of information, unauthorized surveillance, and cyber sabotage (Litavniece et al., 2023). Therefore, it is necessary to learn about this evolution to create complete cybersecurity and forensic strategies that ensure the safety of digital resources and tourist confidence. The figure 1 demonstrates how the traditional digital platforms have evolved to smart tourism ecosystem, where IoT, AI and big data increase the user experience, yet the cyber risks are growing and cybersecurity and digital forensics are required.

Figure 1. Evolution of Smart Tourism Ecosystems

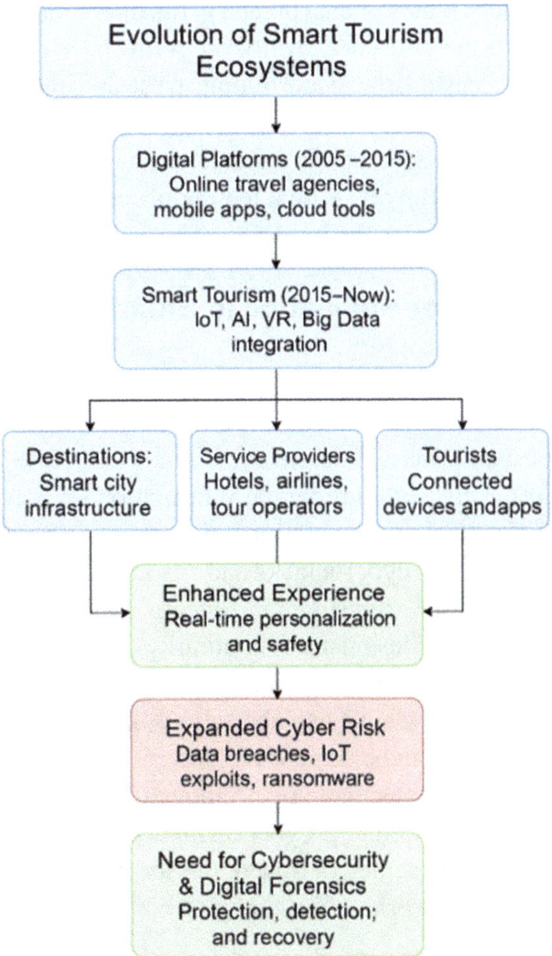

1.2 Cyber Threat Landscape in Digital Tourism

The tourism industry has been experiencing an increasing number of cyber threats that undermine the operations of the business as well as the integrity of customer data. Hotel booking portals, online travel agencies and airline systems contain huge amounts of sensitive personal and financial data, therefore, they are an attractive target to cybercriminals. There are the common ransomware attacks that interrupt the functioning, the phishing attacks that defraud the travelers, and the DDoS attacks that cripple the online services (Arbatskaya & Khoreva, 2021). Additionally, the use of IoT systems in smart destinations, including surveillance systems, the digital payment system, and smart transportation creates exploitable vulnerabilities that can be accessed remotely. Cases of data breach in the international hotel chains, and unauthorized access to the customer loyalty programs have compromised several millions of records of customers, undermining trust and reputation (Solanke & Biasiotti, 2022). The complexity of the Internet tourism sites is not only a problem in cybersecurity, but also a problem of forensic tools to investigate, allocate, and respond to the intrusion effectively with a feeling of responsibility and complying with regulations and laws across the borders.

1.3 The Need for Cyber Resilience in Smart Tourism

The significant levels of digitization of tourism services have contributed significantly to high dependency on the interdependent nature and the sector is highly vulnerable to cyber disruptions. A single cyberattack can close the activities of a hotel, disrupt flight tickets and confidential information on behalf of traveling to cause considerable financial and reputational damages. As a result, the ability to predict, maintain, and recycle cyber-attacks and ensure their capability is known as cyber resilience, which is now the strategic concern of smart tourism ecosystems (Katiyar et al., 2024). It provides business continuity on the most advanced threats like ransomware, data breach, and use of the IoT. Digital forensics and cybersecurity enhance the capability of identifying aberrations, keeping digital evidence, and producing intelligence that can be acted on to prevent future attacks. It also has to adaptively learn, align policy-technological innovation to establish good tourism infrastructures and resiliency. Finally, cyber resilience is the security of the online resources, the increase in the degree of trust of the stakeholders, and the stability of the tourism networks in the world in the changing environment of threats.

2. BACKGROUND TO THE STUDY

The current study is interdependent with the past in regard to cybersecurity of tourism systems and digital innovation. As tourism organizations are confronted with the danger of cyber exploitation as internet-based infrastructure and service provision enabled by an IoT is on the rise. Digital forensics has been discussed as one of the major areas that may be implemented to respond to such dangers by facilitating the process of finding, preserving and examining of digital evidence after a cyber-attack (Mitchell, 2014). This area describes the dual importance of cybersecurity and digital forensics as the component to ensure a stable operation of smart tourism systems and their reliability. It puts in place the context within which forensic investigation is a reactive defense mechanism proactive. In addition, it looks into how cyber resilience can assist organizations to deal with the issue by making sure that they are able to recuperate fast after being disrupted without financial and reputational losses. Sustainable and technology-based tourism governance is a product of a mixture of cybersecurity and digital forensics. (Jarrett & Choo, 2021).

2.1 Significance of Cybersecurity in Tourism and Hospitality

Security of digital tourism services is rudimentary in the determination of confidentiality, integrity and availability of the services. The tourism and hospitality industry deals with high volume of data including payment credentials, travel itineraries, and identity documents something that would prove to be enticing to bad actors. Such a phenomenon may result in financial, legal, and wasted customer loyalty (Arcuri et al., 2020). It is on this basis that it is important to set multi-layered defensive infrastructure i.e. firewalls, intrusion detection systems, and encryption protocols. The frames of cybersecurity in this field are not based on technical security only; organizational awareness, training of employees, and compliance with such international requirements as ISO/IEC 27001 are also related to this concept. The digital concierge services, IoT devices, and smart operations of hotels represent another field of smart technology protection against their exploitation with the help of cybersecurity (Yallop et al., 2023). In addition, the regulatory systems such as the General Data Protection Regulation (GDPR) and Payment Card Industry Data Security Standard (PCI-DSS) lay a lot of emphasis on accountability of the data processing. An excellent cybersecurity, thus, might be a competitive advantage, and a strategic driver of sustainable tourism development.

2.2 Role of Digital Forensics in Securing Smart Destinations

Digital forensics field provides investigational assistance to the smart tourism context by providing a guideline on how to analyze cyber incidences. It refers to the process of collective collection, storage, and generalization of electronic data to identify how, when, and the effects of security breaches. Forensic tools are used in order to trace the path of unauthorized access and recreate attack chronology in smart destinations where sensors, cameras, and digital kiosks constantly create data (Micah et al., 2023). Such methods as log file analysis, malware reverse engineering, and blockchain-based validation of evidence improve the accuracy of the investigation. Furthermore, digital forensics helps to maintain the legal and ethical principles because evidence presented in the court can be accepted. In addition to investigation, forensic preparedness helps tourism organizations to predict the occurrence and decrease the recovery period (Abdel-Basset et al., 2022). Smart destinations can enhance their resilience, protect the traveler data, and continue running digital operations without interruption even in the face of changing cyber threats by combining forensic intelligence with real-time monitoring systems. The figure 2 shows that digital forensics activities enhance the security of smart tourism by making it possible to collect evidence, analyse it, validate it, and reconstruct an incident to become resilient and protect the data of travellers.

Figure 2. Role of Digital Forensics in Securing Smart Destinations

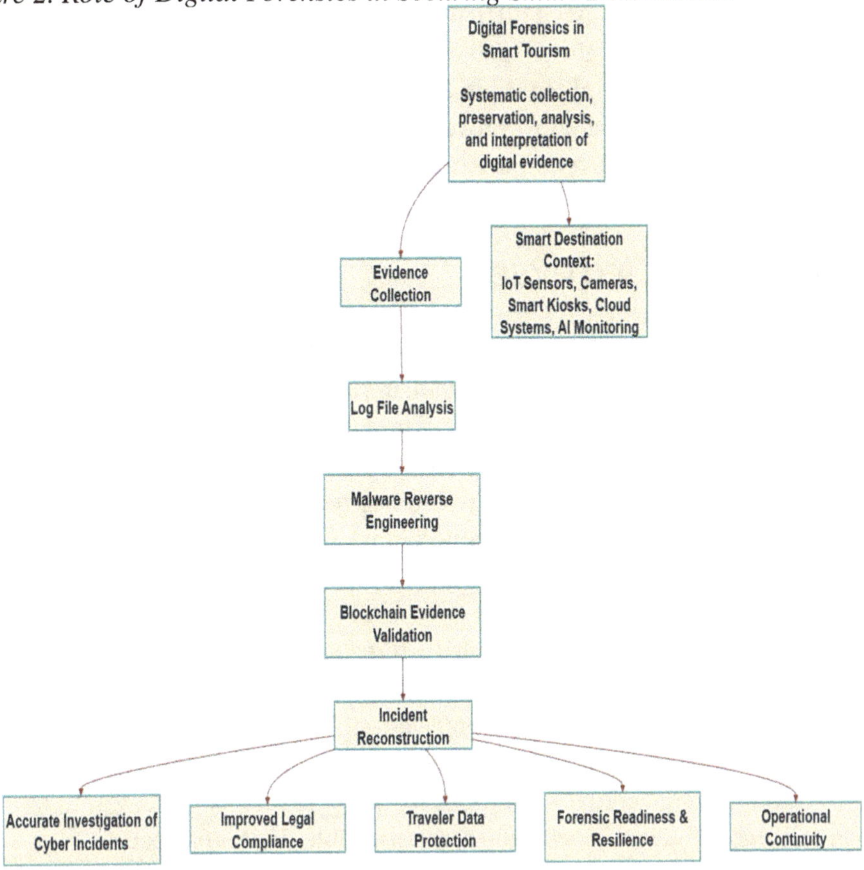

2.3 Emerging Challenges in Tourism Cybersecurity

The digital revolution that is occurring in the tourism industry has brought about both opportunities and threats because the rate of adopting technology is increasing at a very high rate than the rate of implementing the appropriate security measures. The integrated IoT-based devices, artificial intelligence customisation systems, and reservation-based systems on the cloud have made the area of attack digital, and delicate traveler and financial data could be used. Cybercriminals target hotel management systems, online travel agencies and airline networks with phishing, ransomware, and insider manipulations quite often(Perrett & Wilson, 2023). Many small to medium tourism enterprises lack solid cybersecurity foundation and are thus easy prey in the global tourism system. Also, the reliance of the industry to third party interlinked vendors introduces additional risks since when a threat is executed on one platform, the lives of many stakeholders could be at stake. Foreign legal and jurisdictional issues also make it difficult to undertake a forensic investigation and data recovery. It is in the light of such challenges that, a series of elaborate cyber-security architecture touching on digital forensics, congruency in policy and even staff training must be initiated to provide resilience, trust, and long-term digital tourism operation in the current tourism ecosystem.

3. RESEARCH OBJECTIVES

The overall objective of this chapter is to identify how digital forensics and cyber resilience approaches can be used to establish security and trust in the framework of smart tourism. As the industry of tourism system becomes increasingly more digital, the necessity to identify, probe, and eliminate cyber threats is structured and evidence-based. The research questions outlined below will inform the study as per the attainment of knowledge on the technological, operation, and governance issues within the area of cybersecurity in the tourism and hospitality sector.

- To analyze the major cybersecurity threats affecting digital tourism platforms, including hotels, travel agencies, and smart destinations.
- To examine the role of digital forensic tools and techniques in investigating and mitigating cyber incidents in tourism infrastructures.
- To develop a conceptual framework for cyber resilience, integrating forensic intelligence, AI, and blockchain for sustainable digital protection.
- To evaluate legal, ethical, and regulatory frameworks that influence digital evidence handling and cross-border investigations in tourism.
- To propose strategic recommendations for enhancing forensic readiness, incident response, and organizational resilience within smart tourism ecosystems.

4. CONCEPTUAL MODEL

The framework of the chapter provides a theoretical framework and a functional workflow of a smart tourism ecosystem resistant to a cyber-attack. It also stresses the focus on the inclusion of digital forensics, cybersecurity and resilience engineering, which is what establishes the assurance of the resilience of the tourism infrastructures to withstand, identify and recover cyber-attacks. The model is assumed to be a multi-layered model that consists of prevention, detection, response, and recovery phases. Primarily, it promotes initiative-driven model to vulnerability detection, real-time tracking and forensic intelligence to examine the incident (Bs et al., 2023).

The other key aspect of the framework is the interconnection of the stakeholders, such as tourism enterprises, technology providers, and law enforcement agencies to maintain the forensic preparedness and adherence to regulations. The conceptual framework is likely to create a flexible ecosystem that will balance technology-led processes and human control with continuity of operation, data integrity and customer confidence of the system in the wake of new cyber threats to digital tourism platform and smart destinations. (Xu, 2023a).

4.1 Cyber Resilient Smart Tourism Framework

The intended Cyber Resilient Smart Tourism Framework represents a combination of cybersecurity and forensic intelligence, which can be used to improve the digital safety of the whole systems of tourism. It consists of four major layers such as Preventive, Detective, Responsive and Adaptive. The Preventive layer consists of the actions in the form of policies and blocking and encrypting the vulnerabilities (Xu, 2023b). Detective layer concentrates on the threats monitoring, intrusion detection, and anomaly analytics. Digital forensics is part of the Responsive layer to acquire, store and examine digital evidence right after an incident. And lastly is the Adaptive layer that applies machine learning and blockchain forecasting of resilience and blockchain monitoring of cyber events. All these layers are joined together and form a warning and a provision of forensic information in real-time using centralized dashboards (Savchenko et al., 2020). Other than this, the structure enables interoperability of tourism platforms that promotes cross-domain exchange of evidences among the hotels, airlines and travel agencies. This progressive resolution will guarantee that, the ecosystems that are attached to tourism are not only restored within a very short period after the attacks but are restored smart so that any other mode of disturbance will not be experienced, a move that will improve sustainability and ultra confidence related to the cyber world. The figure 3 illustrates the 4-level system of Preventive, Detective, Responsive and Adaptive that integrates cybersecurity and digital forensics to establish a strong and safe smart tourism system.

Figure 3. Cyber Resilient Smart Tourism Framework

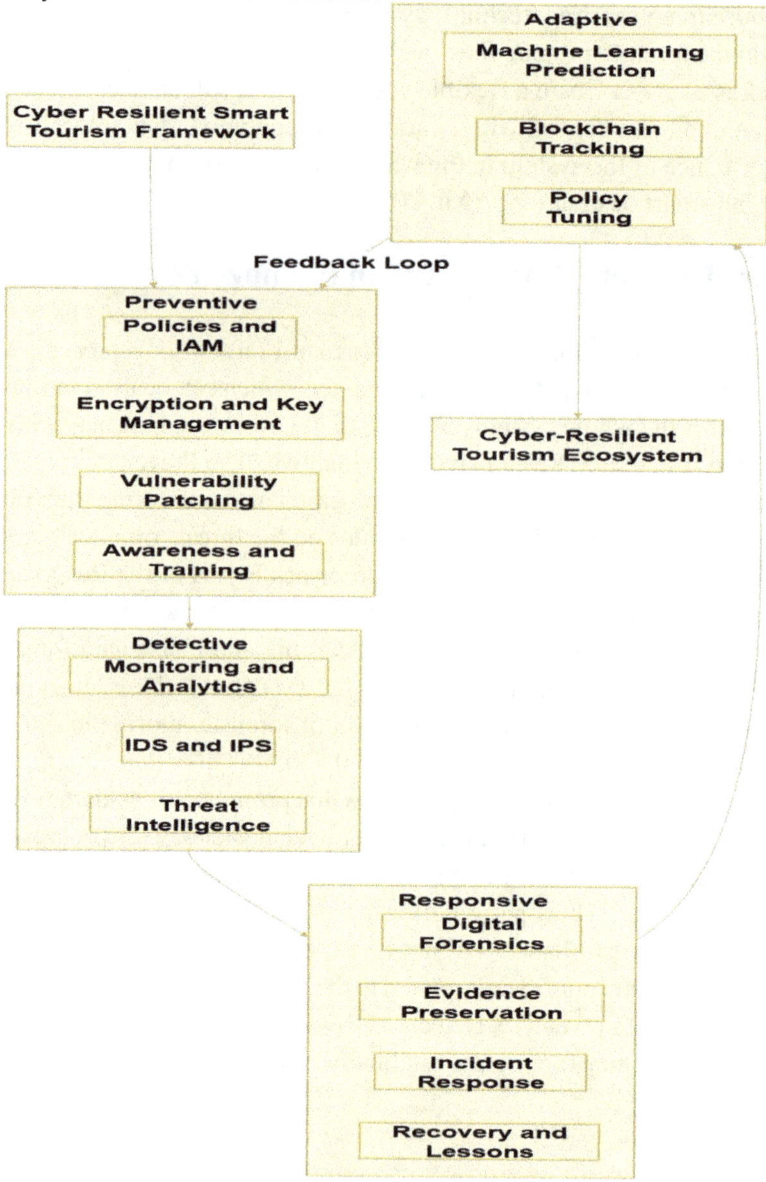

4.2 Integration of Forensics, AI, and Blockchain in the Model

The implementation of forensics, artificial intelligence (AI), and blockchain in the framework of smart tourism ecosystems can help tourists perform their tasks in a more efficient and reliable manner. Threat and behavioral analytics detection can be performed in a more automated manner with the help of the AI algorithms, as the irregularities in the patterns of transactions, user behavior, and system logs are identified (Tham & Sigala, 2020). These models help in reducing the response time by a huge margin and the accuracy of the forensic explanations. Rather, blockchain technology can offer data integrity and the possibility of evidence alterations in order to enable the investigators to follow the digital footprints safely and prove the authenticity of evidence with the help of distributed ledgers. Combined with AI-based surveillance to generate validated evidence, AI-based detection systems commit the evidence to blockchain repositories, which establish a transparent and uncompromising forensic chain of custody (Wani et al., 2021). The integration facilitates collaboration between the stakeholders such as the law enforcers, the cybersecurity, as well as the tourism businesses. In addition, smart contract-based blockchain networks can be used to automate incident alerts and forensic reporting, creating a well-established and trustworthy framework that may oversee a sense of responsibility, transparency and information security in digital tourism infrastructure. One can comprehend the figure 4 that artificial intelligence, digital forensics, and blockchain combined can positively transform the smart tourism ecosystems, as well as increase the threat detection, evidence integrity, and system transparency.

Figure 4. Integration of Forensics, AI, and Blockchain in the Model

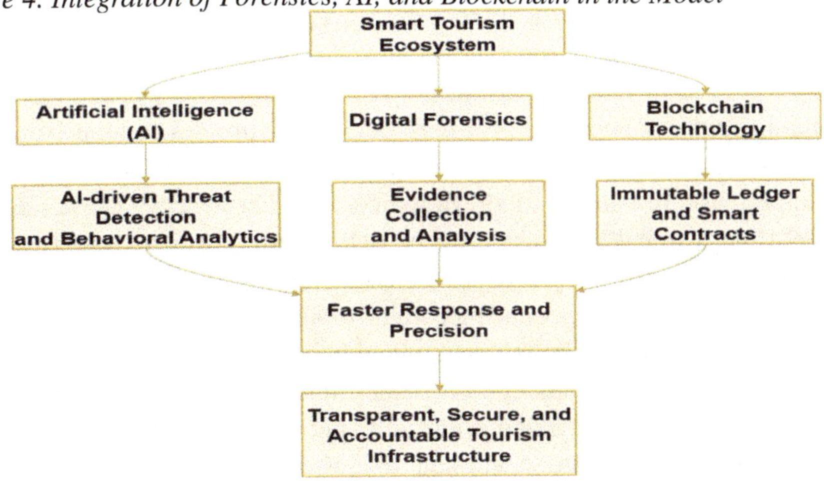

5. RESEARCH METHODOLOGY

This study will have a research design of qualitative and exploratory-based research that focuses on the analysis of digital forensics and cyber resilience implementation in smart tourism. It is an amalgamation of theoretical data and case study of practical implementations to uncover the most appropriate practices and issues of the implementation (Deng et al., 2022). The secondary data will be gathered with the help of academic articles, cybersecurity reports, and industry whitepapers and will be supported with case studies of cyber-attacks in tourism and hospitality. The research procedure involves three stages namely, data collection, analysis and framework check. The data are analyzed by thematic coding to discover the general patterns and emergent trends of forensic preparedness and resilience. The triangulation of the various sources of data is sound since it is historical and it is extensive in interpretation. The latter are observed ethics that include confidentiality and authenticity of data. The selected research approach is a powerful basis that could be exploited in the development of a conceptual framework that would be applied in connecting the forensic investigation possibilities and resiliency-enhancing mechanisms within the tourism ecosystems. (Shin et al., 2024a).

5.1 Research Design and Data Sources

The qualitative study will assume a multi-method design that will entail the literature review, analysis of the case study, and expert validation. The design of the study will be such that the study is able to evoke both empirical and theoretical information. They will consist of peer-reviewed journal articles that touch upon the problem of cybersecurity and tourism management, databases on the subject matter, reports on forensic research, and global indices of cybersecurity (Schwendicke et al., 2020). International hotel chain cases, online travel agencies and smart city tourism platforms can be analyzed by case studies. It picks cases based on relevancy, accessibility to digital evidence and their value to Resilience in operations. Content analysis and comparative synthesis are applied in data analysis to find out the pattern in cyber incidents and strategies used in forensic responses. The observance of ethics is maintained by making use of only publicly available sources or ones that are authorised. The strategy will help to close the chasm between theoretical frameworks and practice, generating practical contributions to improving forensic preparedness and cyber resilience in smart tourism systems (Ercan, 2023a). tool

5.2 Analytical Tools and Forensic Techniques Used

The paper utilizes a collection of digital forensic tools and methods of analysis to examine cyber-attacks on tourism infrastructure. To examine, retrieve, and investigate the evidence, files and memory, the most vital ones are EnCase, Autopsy, FTK (Forensic Toolkit) and Volatility. Wireshark and Splunk are applicable in the monitoring network traffic and in the correlation of logs, which will assist in determining the pattern of unauthorized access and data exfiltration (Shin et al., 2024b). Machine learning tools are useful in classifying malware behavior and identify frauds during communication between users. Further, blockchain audit systems are examined under the context of safe evidence and integrity check. The analytical techniques that are employed to monitor attack chains and verify the digital artifacts include timeline reconstruction, hash verification and pattern clustering. These integration tools help in the overall investigation which is consistent with the international forensic standards. The paper presents the application of technological-based forensic methods as the means of enhancing the situational awareness and accelerating recovery in the smart tourism ecosystems (Kovačić et al., 2022). Some of the most commonly used digital forensic tools and their capabilities in the tourism systems investigation are listed in the table 1.

Table 1. Comparative Analysis of Digital Forensic Tools Used in Tourism Cyber Investigations

Tool Name	Primary Function	Application in Tourism Sector	Advantages	Limitations
EnCase	Disk imaging and evidence recovery.	Analyzing compromised hotel servers.	Reliable evidence preservation.	High cost; complex interface.
Autopsy	Open-source digital investigation.	Examining user data from travel agency systems.	Free and customizable.	Limited cloud data support.
FTK (Forensic Toolkit)	File recovery, indexing, and hashing.	Investigating email leaks and credential theft.	Efficient keyword searching and indexing.	Requires high system resources.
Wireshark	Network packet analysis.	Monitoring malicious traffic on IoT-enabled destinations.	Real-time packet capture and filtering.	Steep learning curve.
Volatility	Memory forensics and malware detection.	Detecting RAM-based threats in hotel systems.	Excellent for live system analysis.	Command-line dependent.

6. LITERATURE REVIEW

Such digitalization of the tourism and hospitality industry has entirely transformed the industry regarding the application of modern technologies, such as artificial intelligence, the Internet of Things (IoT), blockchain, and cloud computing, to enhance the efficiency and experience of a customer. The same digital advancement has also come with assurances that it has exposed the industry to the array of cyber threats hence the need to have digital forensics and cyber resiliency (Shoetan et al., 2024). The literature review is a compilation of some of the most topical studies and models that will be consistent with the purpose of the present research- the state of digital forensic practices, the cybersecurity models, and resilience strategies in tourism ecosystems. Literature shows that digital forensics has now matured to leave the traditional reactive-based investigation techniques and focus on proactive preparations in forensics (Shahana et al., 2024). Initial studies made digital forensics a formal procedure that includes finding evidence, keeping it, examining it, and presenting it. These processes play a crucial role in tourism and hospitality stages of investigating data breaches, identity theft, and online payment fraud. The growth of online platforms including online booking systems, smart hotel infrastructure and travel applications have also complicated the collection of evidence digitally (Chen et al., 2024). Forensic readiness framework has been suggested to help tourism organizations to prepare in advance to the occurrence of incidents in order to be ready to retrieve data timely and maintain chain of custody during investigations.

Digital forensics is a crucial part in the field of securing IoT-based systems in the framework of smart tourism. Guest management, energy management, and facial recognition are all devices installed in hotels and airports that are interconnected. Vulnerable IoT sensors or improperly set APIs may become loopholes to cyber-attacks (Klopper & Eloff, 2023). The forensic approaches should thus be applied to these embedded systems, which should include the log analysis, network traffic tracking and anomaly detection in order to track illegal activities. Smart environments have been modified to use advanced forensic tools including EnCase, Volatility and Autopsy in the analysis of volatile memory and encrypted data. Another aspect brought to light by researchers is the use of blockchain in securing digital evidence, making it impossible to alter and traceable over a distributed platform (Ercan, 2023b). Similar to the development of digital forensics, the idea of cyber resilience has recently become prominent because organizations have acknowledged that it is not realistic to eliminate cyber incidents entirely. Resilience is a change in emphasis of pure defense to flexibility and restoration. In tourism ecosystems, resilience refers to the capacity of digital infrastructures to survive during disruptions and recover their state of normalcy after cyberattack very quickly. Some of the frameworks combine principles of resilience including anticipation, monitoring, response, and learning

(Krishnappa, 2023). The models of incident management, which have been widely referred to include the National Institute of Standards and Technology (NIST) and ISO 27035 models, focus on continuous improvement cycles.

Studies have found out that successful tourism systems must be synchronized about cybersecurity, digital forensics, and risk management. Artificial intelligence and big data analysis have been addressed by the hospitality cyber resilience models in predicting the vulnerabilities and automatic response. The machine learning tools compare the behavioral patterns and identify the insider threats or phishing attacks before they happen and arousal. Besides, the digital forensic analysis of an incident post-factum could serve to derive helpful data to strengthen defensive architectures and policy controls (Pendey, 2023). Blockchain and AI-based forensic integration is one of the similar areas of concern. In its turn, blockchain ensures that the evidence provided by a forensic is authentic and unalterable, but AI is applied when dealing with large volumes of data, which will be generated in the course of the investigation. The smart contracts can be used to perform evidence validation, and deep learning models with multifaceted datasets can detect malware signatures. The effectiveness and reliability of investigations in case of forensic investigations in tourism and hospitality industries are increased by this technological convergence.

Besides, the anthropocentric and regulatory facets of digital forensics and resilience are highlighted in the literature. The management of cyber attacks should be supported by the services of qualified individuals who will be professionally trained in the technical forensics and law. Policies on legislations like the General Data Protection Regulation (GDPR) and domestic cybersecurity policies ensure that organizations are forensically fit and can present evidence before a court of justice. The lack of international frameworks, however, turns out to be an issue in investigating across the borders especially where the international tourism activities are taking place (Kumar et al., 2023). The other theme which has been reiterated is the overlap between forensics intelligence and organizational governance. Instead of viewing the concept of digital forensics as an after-factum, proactive models propose to add the concept of digital forensics to the cybersecurity policy and standard operating procedures. The rest of them involve the application of continuous log auditing and AI-driven anomaly detection software which would assist in setting up a proactive forensic environment. Similarly, resilience models that have real-time data visualization, incident dashboards, and sharing of threat intelligence enable decision-makers to respond to cyber crises within a shorter time (Kim and Shon, 2023). Overall, the literature review reveals that the relationship between digital forensics and cyber resiliency plays a critical role in the development of reliable and secure smart tourism systems. Even though technology has increased the range of attack, it gives new opportunities at detecting, analyzing, and recoveries. By balancing between forensic preparedness and dynamic cybersecurity, it is possible to guarantee sensitive information security, continuity of operations, and confidence of tourists. All outcomes of the previous studies led to the development of a complex system the interrelation of forensic intelligence and resilience engineering with governance- to identify the varying digital threats in the tourism sector. (Thapaliya & Bokani, 2024). The table 2 is a brief overview of significant areas of focus in the existing literature on the topics of digital forensics and cyber resiliency in smart tourism ecosystems.

Table 2. Summary of Literature on Digital Forensics and Cyber Resilience in Smart Tourism

Focus Area	Key Insights	Implications for Smart Tourism
Digital Forensics Practices	Transition from reactive investigation to proactive forensic readiness; use of advanced tools (FTK, EnCase, Autopsy).	Enables efficient evidence preservation, early threat identification, and regulatory compliance.
IoT and Smart Infrastructure	Forensics extended to IoT devices and cloud-based systems; need for device-level evidence extraction.	Protects smart hotels, transport systems, and destination management platforms from exploitation.
Blockchain-Based Forensics	Blockchain ensures tamper-proof evidence storage and transparency.	Strengthens data integrity and inter-organizational trust during cyber investigations.
AI-Powered Forensic Analytics	Machine learning models used for anomaly detection, threat prediction, and automated evidence classification.	Enhances real-time monitoring and accelerates investigation of cyber incidents.
Cyber Resilience Frameworks	Emphasis on adaptability, continuous improvement, and rapid recovery from cyber incidents.	Builds sustainable and secure digital tourism operations capable of withstanding disruptions.
Legal and Ethical Governance	Regulatory frameworks (GDPR, ISO 27035) guide forensic admissibility and data protection.	Ensures accountability, cross-border collaboration, and stakeholder confidence.
Human Capacity and Training	Need for multidisciplinary expertise in forensic investigation and policy compliance.	Improves forensic readiness and crisis management capabilities in tourism organizations.

The literature notes that to achieve the cyber resilience of smart tourism, the digital forensics, artificial intelligence, and blockchain technology should meet, along with the comprehensive human capacity building and a legal framework. Collectively, these studies suggest a passive-aggressive stance of cybersecurity to an active resilience model that is forensically induced and ensures sustainability, trust, and innovation in the digital tourist era.

7. RESULTS AND DISCUSSION

The findings demonstrate that smart tourism systems are extremely susceptible to cyber-attacks because of their reliance on digital connected services, IoT services, and the exchange of data with the Internet. It is revealed that ransomware, phishing, DDoS, and data breach of hotel booking systems, payment gateway, and customer databases are the most popular attacks. The forensic investigations revealed that it possessed poor encryption and patch controls and laxity by insiders. The digital forensics influence on the work of the tourism cybersecurity positively impacted the accuracy of the threat detection process, quality of the evidence, and the success of the recovery. Besides, the evidence tracking on blockchain also made it possible to improve the level of data transparency and minimize the possibility of manipulation. The results result in the fact that the process of resilience-building should go further than the technological protection into the sphere of governance, training and activating the forensic preparedness. This discussion goes further to discuss the integration of both forensic intelligence and resilience systems in ensuring that the organizations will minimize threats, offer stability in operations and give the stakeholders increased confidence in world tourism systems.

7.1 Analysis of Cyber Threats and Forensic Findings

The forensic evaluation of the cases that were chosen showed that there were common trends in the occurrence of cyber vulnerabilities in tourism infrastructures. The breach of data in hotel chains and travel agencies was usually initiated via phishing or the stolen employee credentials. Smart systems like digital locks, sensors and guest networks that can be operated using IoT were identified to be the most vulnerable because they were deployed using default settings and unpatched software (I. Alghamdi, 2021). Wireshark and Autopsy were the forensic tools that were used to identify traffic explosion caused by unauthorized access, malware code, and exfiltration of credentials. Verification mechanisms that were based on blockchain provided authenticity in evidence management, which minimized the chances of manipulation. Also, log correlation and memory analysis revealed consistent threats and sideways motion amongst cloud-based systems. The general results support that the traditional security tools are not enough to be used without the digital forensic integration (Camacho, 2024). Through integration of real-time surveillance, forensic analytics with blockchain integrity checks, tourism organizations can have a more efficient detection, evidence preservation, and mitigation of the changing cyberattacks in smart environments. The following table 3 enumerates the significant cyber threats to smart tourism systems and the potential consequences to the systems operations.

Table 3. Common Cyber Threats and Their Implications in Smart Tourism Ecosystems

Type of Threat	Description	Targeted System	Impact on Tourism Operations	Forensic Response Technique
Phishing Attacks	Fraudulent emails or messages used to steal credentials or financial data.	Hotel booking systems, OTAs	Unauthorized access to user accounts; financial fraud.	Log analysis, email header examination.
Ransomware	Malware encrypting data and demanding payment for decryption.	Smart city servers, IoT systems	Service disruption, data loss, reputational damage.	Malware reverse engineering, memory dump analysis.
DDoS Attacks	Overloading servers to disrupt website or network availability.	Airline booking platforms, tourism portals	Website downtime and financial losses.	Network traffic correlation, IP tracing.
Insider Threats	Employees leaking or mishandling sensitive data.	Hotel chains, travel agencies	Data theft, privacy breaches.	Access log auditing, digital fingerprinting.
IoT Exploits	Compromise of connected devices or sensors.	Smart hotels, digital kiosks	Unauthorized surveillance or control.	Device log inspection, firmware forensics.

7.2 Discussion on Cyber Resilience and Strategic Implications

The discussion points out that ensuring cyber resilience in tourism will embrace a holistic approach in technology, governance and human intelligence. The organizational approach to forensic preparedness must be included in the organizational strategy and it will allow responding objectively and timely to an incident. NIST and ISO 27035 principles permit the application of resilience frameworks, which help in proactive planning, real-time threats analysis, and post-event learning. The AI-based systems can enhance the situational awareness by predicting the attack vectors, but the blockchain can deliver the integrity of evidence and clear audit trails. (Abrahams et al., 2024). Tactically, resiliency requires the partnership between the government and business entities as well as forensic team to exchange intelligence and align data protection guidelines. Companies that embrace the use of continuous monitoring, access controls based on risks and training of employees have quicker recovery periods and minimized the damage to their reputations. In the end, the idea of incorporating digital forensics into the resilience methodology will convert the reactive form of cybersecurity into an adaptive, intelligent defense model- which ensures sustainable trust, continuity of operations, and digital safety of global smart tourism ecosystems.

8. CASE STUDY: DIGITAL FORENSICS IN TOURISM CYBER INCIDENTS

To demonstrate how digital forensics are applied in practice, this section takes a closer look at the world tourism and hospitality sector and considers recent and major cyber-attacks that happen in this sector. Case studies can help to reveal how the forensic methods, e.g., the analysis of logs, tracking of malware, the use of blockchain-based evidence preservation, etc., can be applied to help the investigation, and resilience construction after an incident. The examples selected are the violations and ransomware attack which disrupted the tourism processes, compromised the data of its customers and the process of digital governance that was in question (dos Santos et al., 2025). In both instances, investigative processes, technology applications, and appraisals regarding the ways to proceed in the area of cyber preparedness are shown. With those analyses, the section has identified the importance of forensic preparedness, surveillance using artificial intelligence, and evidence safeguarding on tourism buildings. Finally, the case studies indicate the significance of digital forensics that could be utilized to convert the reactive approach to the incidents into the proactive model of providing cyber continuity and resilience in the operations in the context of the smart tourism ecosystem.

8.1 Case Example 1: Cyberattack on Collins Aerospace / Airport Systems (2025)

This was after Collins Aerospace, a major provider of software to the airports and airlines, was attacked in September 2025 in a colossal cyberattack that impacted the check-in and boarding systems in several European airports, such as Dublin, Heathrow and Zurich. This was directed at the vMUSE platform of the company and ARINC AviNet communications systems that play a critical role in passenger processing, baggage handling and flight coordination. The forensic evidence revealed that the network authentication layer had a weakness of ransomware attack (Agrawal et al., 2023). This caused catastrophic delays in the name of airlines who grounded their flights on hundreds resulting in the impact of thousands of passengers. The digital forensic teams performed log correlation, memory analysis, and reverse engineering of malware so that they could trace the source of intrusion. The evidence of lateral movement was identified to be the subsequent interrelated aviation subsystem and unauthorized credential escalation. Block chain audit trails were introduced and they were aimed at preserving integrity of records associated with investigations. The attack highlighted the interdependency of the aviation and tourism digital ecosystems in terms of the need to have coordinated systems of forensics, zero-trust access controls and strong communication systems within common airline-tourism webs to prevent the breakdown of the system due to the collapse of the system further down the line in the future. The number 5 depicts the sequence of the 2025 Collins Aerospace cyberattack, such as the application of ransomware, the course of forensics and the role of the cyber resilience in coordinating.

Figure 5. Cyberattack on Collins Aerospace (2025)

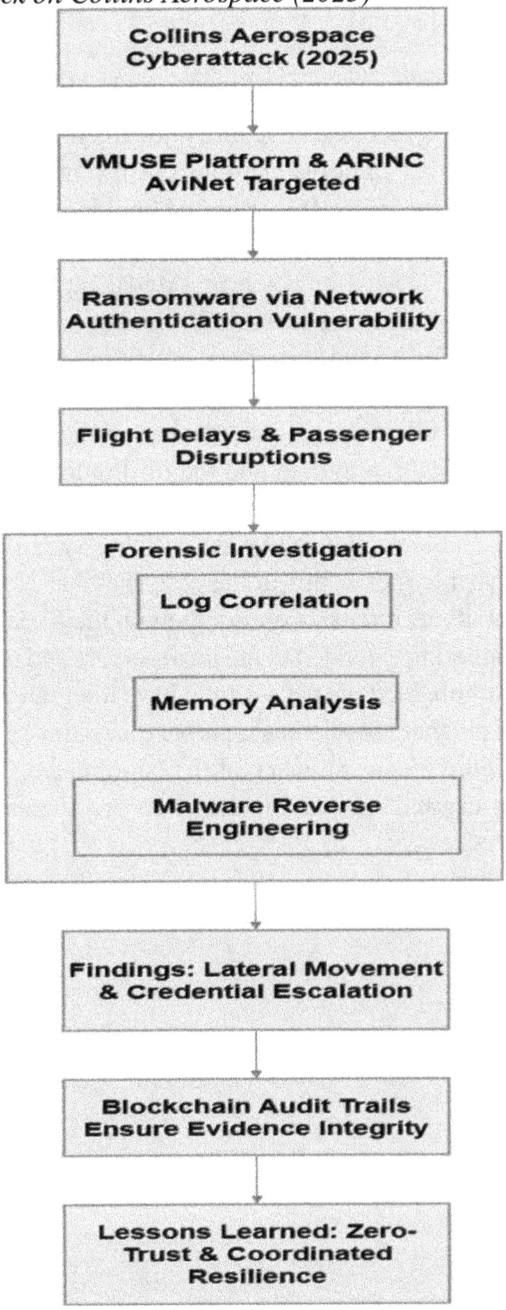

8.2 Case Example 2: Wide-Scale Hotel Data Attack in Italy (2025)

A cyberattack in mid-2025 was coordinated to attack various hotels in Italy and affected thousands of guest records and identity documents. The going by the name mydocs, the hacker group has come out claiming the responsibility in which they had leaked samples of stolen passports, ID cards, and booking information purportedly obtained through centralized guest record systems. The Agenzia per l'Italia Digitale (AGID) in Italy states that at least ten hotels reported unauthorized access of data of almost 100,000 documents (Karimipour et al., 2019). The hack used the old version of property management software and poor remote desktop settings that enabled lateral movements of similar hotel systems connected to each other. Forensic investigators did log correlation, network mapping, data reconstruction by time so that they can trace the attacker data exfiltration path and the infiltration path. To confirm files that have been compromised, metadata verification and digital watermarking were used. The small and mid-sized hotels that do not have specific IT security teams depicted immense cyber hygiene gaps in the case (Fakiha, 2023). Furthermore, it highlighted the necessity of forensic coordination on the basis of the jurisdictions since the evidence gathering extended to the local servers and cloud-based booking systems. This event highlighted the necessity to have integrated security measures, round-the-clock surveillance, and forensic preparedness in the decentralised tourism facilities. The figure 6 is a summary of the coordinated 2025 cyberattack on Italian hotels and its causes, forensic investigation process and major lessons on cybersecurity preparedness.

Figure 6. Wide-Scale Hotel Data Attack in Italy (2025)

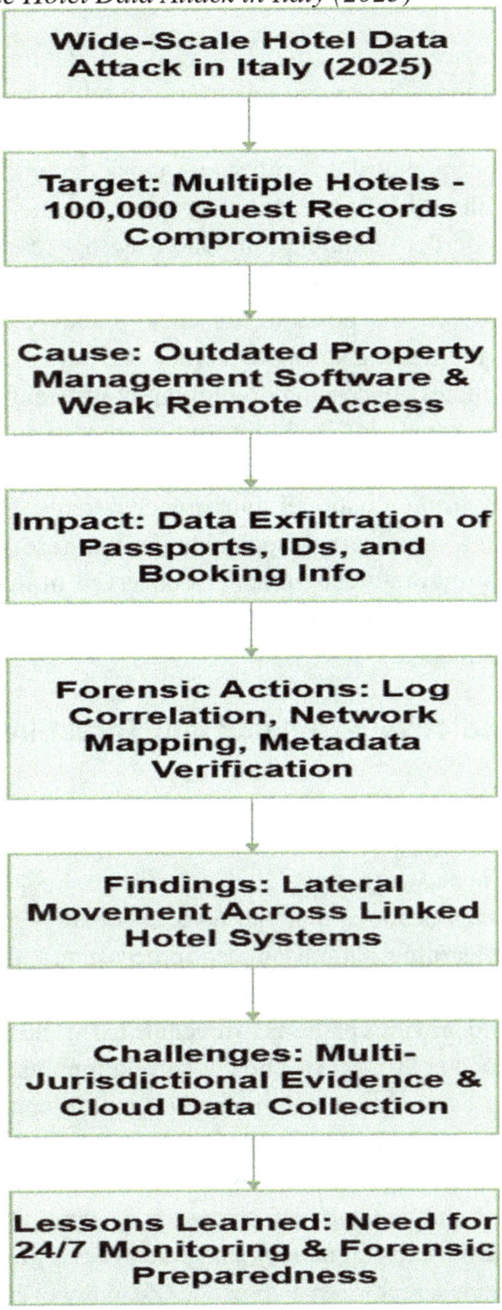

9. FUTURE RESEARCH

The future of cybersecurity and digital forensics in the tourism industry is using the current technologies to enhance predictive intelligence, evidence security, and international cooperation. Cyber threats continue to develop in terms of their complexity, which means that the traditional forensic techniques will need to be complemented with the AI-infused analytics, quantum-safe encryption, and the frameworks of cross-border collaboration. One way that research can be done is how artificial intelligence can be used to automate the process of digital evidence identification and forecast the possible breaches of the system before they are breached. Likewise, there are also opportunities and threats related to quantum computing, and the studies concerning cryptography-resistant to quantum decryption are needed (Djenna et al., 2023). More studies are also required on integration of legal and regulation frameworks of exchanging digital evidence across national boundaries especially in multinational tourism ecosystems. Digital forensics can be proactive, scalable and ethically responsible through research making the new creative technologies relevant to the practices observed in the world with global standards, which are capable of making the system resilient to cyber attack in the smart tourism environment.

9.1 AI-Driven Predictive Forensics and Threat Intelligence

The Artificial Intelligence (AI) concept is changing the digital forensics because it suggests the proactive and self-driven roles in identifying, analyzing and reacting to the cyber threats. The project to be studied in the future should be the development of AI-based forensic applications that can detect anomalies in real-time with the assistance of machine learning, natural language processing, and pattern recognition. The predictive forensics enables a preemptive strike on an attacker in accordance to behavioral patterns and previous patterns to preclude harm and avert the cyberattack happening (Vila-Blanco et al., 2023). The log correlation, malware categorization and threat attribution can be done automatically through application of artificial intelligence-based programs and save a lot of time spent on investigations. Moreover, integrating threat intelligence systems and AI will enable one to become able to learn in continuous and develop self-protection systems. All of these barriers, including algorithmic bias, explainability, and data privacy are to be considered to achieve ethical and transparent forensic practice (Zeadally et al., 2020). The development of AI-based forensics will not only promote the development of situational awareness but also make tourism cybersecurity a smart and active defense system.

9.2 Quantum-Safe Cryptography and Cross-Border Forensic Cooperation

Another large threat posed by the introduction of quantum computers is the existing encryption-related standards, as newer studies of quantum-resistant cryptography will be needed. Future studies should take into consideration post-quantum cryptography such as lattice-based cryptography and multi-variate polygons in order to safeguard forensic data against the capability of quantum algorithms of decrypting forensic data. This is particularly imperative when it comes to the security of delicate tourism intelligence stored within blockchain and cloud computing systems. Meanwhile, the global nature of the tourism sector dictates the need to establish strong cross-border collaboration in the aspect of forensic operations, which will enable nations to share digital evidence according to the law (Iqbal and Abed Alharbi, 2020). The issues of compatibility with the evidence preservation and the compatibility of data protection laws and mutual recognition of digital evidence between international treaties are to be researched. International cooperation will be enhanced by creating a single digital forensic governance framework and supporting it with blockchain to ensure tracing evidence and managing information transfer. Quantum-safe cryptography and coordinated forensic networks will go hand in hand to provide sustainable and resilient global tourism cybersecurity. The table 4 indicates the support of AI and blockchain technologies to the digital forensic in the context of tourism cybersecurity.

Table 4. Integration of AI and Blockchain in Digital Forensic Investigations

Technology	Function in Digital Forensics	Tourism Application Example	Key Advantages	Future Research Focus
Artificial Intelligence (AI)	Automates threat detection and pattern analysis.	AI-based anomaly detection in hotel network logs.	Accelerates incident detection and classification.	Developing explainable AI forensic models.
Machine Learning (ML)	Predictive forensics through trend and anomaly prediction.	Predicting phishing campaigns in travel portals.	Reduces investigation time, enhances accuracy.	Real-time integration with cloud forensics.
Blockchain Technology	Ensures integrity and immutability of forensic evidence.	Blockchain ledger for storing investigation logs.	Guarantees tamper-proof evidence and transparency.	Cross-border blockchain interoperability.
Quantum-Safe Cryptography	Protects evidence from quantum-based attacks.	Securing digital evidence in global travel databases.	Long-term confidentiality assurance.	Developing post-quantum forensic encryption protocols.

9.3 Human-Centered Cyber Awareness and Capacity Building

The next generation of studies should entail humanizing the cyber awareness and capacity building measures which are specific to tourism and hospitality sectors. Although technological breakthroughs, including AI, blockchain, and quantum-safe cryptography, can be used to increase the level of security, the human factor is the most critical vulnerability of cyber resilience. Often, employees are the first point and line of defense against phishing, social engineering, and insider threats; thus, it is essential to provide employees with the knowledge and behavioral practices they can use. Studies on adaptive learning systems and gamified training platforms to simulate real-world situations of an attack to improve employee engagement and retention of cybersecurity concepts should be conducted (Khan et al., 2021). In addition to that, cross-cultural research is required to know differences in awareness of cyber among global tourism workforce and development of context-specific training strategies. It will also be needed to implement uniform certifications and lifelong learning courses on the digital forensics and cybersecurity of the tourism professionals. The smart tourism ecosystem will have human capacity building as an addition to technological defenses, creation of a culture of vigilance, accountability and resilience.

10. MANAGERIAL IMPLICATIONS

As a manager, it is a strategic requirement of cyber resilience and forensic preparedness in safeguarding the tourism operations and making sure that it does not lose the faith of its customers. Managers should recognize cybersecurity as an investment and not a technical expense towards the sustainability of the organization. The transparency and accountability will be enhanced with the introduction of the layered defense systems, the AI-based surveillance, and the utilization of the blockchain-based audit trails. Staff training, planning incident response, and auditing forensic preparedness should be the top concerns of leadership in order to prepare against potential breaches (University & Kulakhmetova, 2025). Moreover, by means of forensic intelligence as a part of decision-making, managers can estimate the risks, make the resource allocation process efficient, and adhere to global rules of data protection. Industry stakeholders, policymakers, and experts in digital forensics should work together to have resilient tourism infrastructures. In general, the managerial foresight and active governance are needed to incorporate cybersecurity and digital forensics in the DNA of the current tourism businesses.

10.1 Strategic Recommendations for Tourism Enterprises

Digital forensics should be implemented as an investigative and preventive measure in a multi-layered approach to cybersecurity that tourists enterprises should employ. Cyber incidents can be dealt with by setting up forensic preparedness structures to quickly gather and analyze evidence. Companies are advised to use AI-based surveillance tools to identify anomalies in the real-time and install blockchain-based evidence management in order to provide audit trails that are difficult to alter. Consistent vulnerability testing, penetration testing and data encryption requirements should be implemented in order to maintain system integrity (Iyer & Babu, 2025). Furthermore, the companies are expected to instill the culture of cyber awareness by educating the workforce about phishing, handling of data securely and reporting of incidents. Cooperation with cybersecurity bodies and managed security service providers can help to increase the detection and recovery. Lastly, the data governance policies shall be periodically reviewed per the GDPR and ISO 27001 so as to guarantee the compliance as well as the stakeholder interest. All these proactive actions would increase the resilience and credibility of the tourism businesses in a more digitalized world.

10.2 Policy, Legal, and Governance Recommendations

A unified strategy of policy arrangements is required by sound cybersecurity policy, where both national and international laws are harmonized. Their governments are expected to possess their cyber forensics facilities to make the investigations easy and to align the process of evidence processing across the borders. It should have policies that will encourage the use of quantum safe cryptography, data anonymization, and blockchain-based audit systems to the extent of ensuring privacy and integrity (Villar Miguelez et al., 2023). The government agencies should insist that those tourism companies that handle confidential traveler information be certified on forensic preparedness. The law ought to evolve to enable the admissibility of digital evidence and according to the privacy laws across boundaries. Besides, the international tourism organizations such as UNWTO and WTTC can be utilised to standardise the data-sharing processes and collaborative response mechanisms in the event of transnational cyber-attacks. The coordinated response to the cyber threats and situation awareness will be improved due to the governmental structures that include the public- private cooperation (Trim & Lee, 2022). Such measures driven by policy create a middle-ground digital security platform, accountability, resiliency and ethical digital transformation are ensured within the global tourism industry.

11. CONCLUSION

The advent of digitization of tourism and hospitality industry has introduced unparalleled challenges of effective operations, customer individualization and data-driven innovation. The rapid process of digitalization has exposed the industry to the threat of growing scope of cyber threats as well and as such, digital forensics and cyber resilience have become the unavoidable component of sustainable tourism management. The chapter has tackled the complex association between technological development, information security and business sustainability and there is need to act that involves an initiative that incorporates forensic intelligence, management and innovation. The chapter discussed evidence-based investigation, blockchain integrity, and AI-assisted analytics as a tool of making the tourism ecosystem resistant to the emerging cyber threats, and all of them will help in securing the ecosystem. The results prove the importance of the fact that cybersecurity in tourism is not only a technical requirement, but also a strategic source of confidence and sustainable development. The reviewed case studies presuppose that the data breach of the most famous hotel brands, as well as the ransomware attack on smart tourism networks, had estimated that the use of the forensic procedures including the analysis of logs, traces of malware, and evidence verification, may lead to the successful identification of attack vectors, evidence preservation, and recovery procedures.

Also, predictive forensics that will be applied by AI and transparency that will be provided by blockchains will make sure that the threats will be tracked all the time, anomalies will be identified in real-time, and the evidence will be modified with massive effort. The existence of such type of technological convergence denotes the transition of the responsive approach of incident management to proactive cyber protection. Forensic preparedness and cyber resilience models that should be in place in the managerial and policy facet should guarantee the continuity of services and safeguard the trust of stakeholders. Managers will need to spend money on education of their employees, in flexible security infrastructure, and in the global requirements of data security, including GDPR and ISO 27035. Conversely, policy makers are prompted to support the collaborative system of cross-border sharing of digital evidence and to embrace quantum safe encryption to address the threats emerging. Lastly, paradigm change of the approach to security governance based on collaborative, transparent and intelligence-driven should be made to allow the construction of meaningful and sustainable systems of cyber-resilience tourism. Policy and education convergence Technology: this will assist the tourism organizations to mitigate, in addition to evolving into strong digital ecosystems that will survive the upcoming cyber disruptions. As tourism embraces the use of smart technologies, safe, trusted, and sustainable digital tourism will be defined as convergence of digital forensics and AI and resilient governance.

REFERENCES

Abdel-Basset, M., Moustafa, N., Hawash, H., & Ding, W. (2022). Introduction conceptualization of security, forensics, and privacy of internet of things: An artificial intelligence perspective. In *Deep Learning Techniques for IoT Security and Privacy* (pp. 1–35). Springer International Publishing., DOI: 10.1007/978-3-030-89025-4_1

Abrahams, T. O., Ewuga, S. K., Dawodu, S. O., Adegbite, A. O., & Hassan, A. O.Temitayo Oluwaseun AbrahamsSarah Kuzankah EwugaSamuel Onimisi Dawodu-Abimbola Oluwatoyin AdegbiteAzeez Olanipekun Hassan. (2024). A review of cybersecurity strategies in modern organizations: Examining the evolution and effectiveness of cybersecurity measures for data protection. *Computer Science & IT Research Journal*, *5*(1), 1–25. DOI: 10.51594/csitrj.v5i1.699

Agrawal, J., Kalra, S. S., & Gidwani, H. (2023). AI in cyber security. *International Journal of Communication and Information Technology*, *4*(1), 46–53. DOI: 10.33545/2707661X.2023.v4.i1a.59

Alghamdi, I. M. (2021). Digital forensics in cyber security—recent trends, threats, and opportunities. In Cybersecurity Threats with New Perspectives. IntechOpen. DOI: 10.5772/intechopen.94452

Arbatskaya, E., & Khoreva, L. (2021). Blockchain as an innovative digitalization achievement in logistics of eco-tourism. E3S Web of Conferences, 258, 02016. DOI: 10.1051/e3sconf/202125802016

Arcuri, M. C., Gai, L., Ielasi, F., & Ventisette, E. (2020). Cyber attacks on hospitality sector: Stock market reaction. *Journal of Hospitality and Tourism Technology*, *11*(2), 277–290. DOI: 10.1108/JHTT-05-2019-0080

Bs, G. P., Gm, D. K., & Ha, D. D. (2023). AI-Driven cyber security: Security intelligence modelling. *International Journal of Multidisciplinary Research and Growth Evaluation*, *4*(6), 961–965. DOI: 10.54660/.IJMRGE.2023.4.6.961-965

Camacho, N. G. (2024). The role of AI in cybersecurity: Addressing threats in the digital age. Journal of Artificial Intelligence General Science (JAIGS) ISSN:3006-4023, 3(1), 143–154. DOI: 10.60087/jaigs.v3i1.75

Chen, Y., Zhang, N., & Cheng, X. (2024). The spillover effects of online tourism platforms on sustainable development. *Information Systems Journal*, *34*(3), 788–827. DOI: 10.1111/isj.12448

Deng, L., Wan, L., & Guo, J. (2022). Research on security anomaly detection for Big Data platforms based on quantum optimization clustering. *Mathematical Problems in Engineering*, *2022*, 1–10. DOI: 10.1155/2022/4805035

Djenna, A., Barka, E., Benchikh, A., & Khadir, K. (2023). Unmasking cybercrime with artificial-intelligence-driven cybersecurity analytics. *Sensors (Basel)*, *23*(14), 6302. DOI: 10.3390/s23146302 PMID: 37514596

dos Santos, R. M., Boente, A. N. P., Ferreira, V. M. da S., Boente, R. M. P., da Luz, D. O., Duarte, L. M. E., Dos Santos, A. J. B., & Vasconcelos, G. C. K. (2025). Artificial intelligence and cybersecurity: A study of Artificial intelligence in cybernetic defense. *ARACÊ*, *7*(5), 23155–23178. DOI: 10.56238/arev7n5-133

Ercan, F. (2023a). Smart tourism destination: A bibliometric review. *European Journal of Tourism Research*, *34*, 3409. DOI: 10.54055/ejtr.v34i.2788

Ercan, F. (2023b). Smart tourism destination: A bibliometric review. *European Journal of Tourism Research*, *34*, 3409. DOI: 10.54055/ejtr.v34i.2788

Fakiha, B. (2023). Enhancing cyber forensics with AI and machine learning: A study on automated threat analysis and classification. *International Journal of Safety and Security Engineering*, *13*(4), 701–707. DOI: 10.18280/ijsse.130412

Gretzel, U., Lee, H., Lee, E., Chung, N., & Koo, C. (2023a). Enhanced smart tourism and its role in reshaping the tourism industry. *Journal of Smart Tourism*, *3*(4), 23–31. DOI: 10.52255/smarttourism.2023.3.4.4

Gretzel, U., Lee, H., Lee, E., Chung, N., & Koo, C. (2023b). Enhanced smart tourism and its role in reshaping the tourism industry. *Journal of Smart Tourism*, *3*(4), 23–31. DOI: 10.52255/smarttourism.2023.3.4.4

Iqbal, S., & Abed Alharbi, S. (2020). Advancing automation in digital forensic investigations using machine learning forensics. In *Digital Forensic Science*. IntechOpen., DOI: 10.5772/intechopen.90233

Iyer, V. R., & Babu, K. (2025). Resilience at the core: Enhancing cyber-resilience and cybersecurity practices in healthcare sector. *Journal of Contingencies and Crisis Management*, *33*(3), e70061. Advance online publication. DOI: 10.1111/1468-5973.70061

Jarrett, A., & Choo, K.-K. R. (2021). The impact of automation and artificial intelligence on digital forensics. *WIREs Forensic Science*, *3*(6), e1418. Advance online publication. DOI: 10.1002/wfs2.1418

Karimipour, H., Dehghantanha, A., Parizi, R. M., Choo, K.-K. R., & Leung, H. (2019). A deep and scalable unsupervised machine learning system for cyber-attack detection in large-scale smart grids. *IEEE Access : Practical Innovations, Open Solutions*, *7*, 80778–80788. DOI: 10.1109/ACCESS.2019.2920326

Katiyar, D. N., Tripathi, M. S., Kumar, M. P., Verma, M. S., Sahu, D. A. K., & Saxena, D. S. (2024). *AI and Cyber-Security: Enhancing threat detection and response with machine learning*. Educational Administration Theory and Practices., DOI: 10.53555/kuey.v30i4.2377

Khan, A. A., Uddin, M., Shaikh, A. A., Laghari, A. A., & Rajput, A. E. (2021). MF-ledger: Blockchain hyperledger sawtooth-enabled novel and secure multimedia chain of custody forensic investigation architecture. *IEEE Access : Practical Innovations, Open Solutions*, *9*, 103637–103650. DOI: 10.1109/ACCESS.2021.3099037

Kim, M., & Shon, T. (2023). Digital forensics for E-IoT devices in smart cities. *Electronics (Basel)*, *12*(15), 3233. DOI: 10.3390/electronics12153233

Klopper, C., & Eloff, J. (2023). Fingerprinting network sessions for the discovery of cyber threats. *International Conference on Cyber Warfare and Security*, 18(1), 171–180. DOI: 10.34190/iccws.18.1.1027

Kovačić, M., Čičin-Šain, M., & Milojica, V. (2022). Cyber security and tourism: Bibliometric analysis. *Journal of Process Management New Technologies*, *10*(3–4), 75–92. DOI: 10.5937/jouproman2203075K

Krishnappa, T.London Metropolitan University. (2023). A review on artificial intelligence techniques in preventing cyber threats. *International Journal of Engineering Applied Sciences and Technology*, *8*(1), 185–189. DOI: 10.33564/IJEAST.2023.v08i01.029

Kumar, S., Gupta, U., Singh, A. K., & Singh, A. K. (2023). Artificial Intelligence. Journal of Computers. *Mechanical and Management*, *2*(3), 31–42. DOI: 10.57159/gadl.jcmm.2.3.23064

Litavniece, L., Lonska, J., Zvaigzne, A., Wieda, N., & Adamoniene, R. (2023). Smart tourism in the Baltic states: Current developments and trends. *Worldwide Hospitality and Tourism Themes*, *15*(5), 486–496. DOI: 10.1108/WHATT-06-2023-0073

Micah, E. E. M., Saidu, I. H., Ibitomi, T., & Sanusi, B. S. (2023). Digital forensics in the era of cybercrime: Emerging trends and challenges for forensic accountants in Nigeria. European Journal of Accounting. *Auditing and Finance Research*, *11*(9), 85–100. DOI: 10.37745/ejaafr.2013/vol11n985100

Mitchell, F. (2014). The use of Artificial Intelligence in digital forensics: An introduction. *Digital Evidence and Electronic Signature Law Review*, *7*(0). Advance online publication. DOI: 10.14296/deeslr.v7i0.1922

Pendey, B. (2023). Artificial Intelligence And Cyber Security. *Journal Transnational Universal Studies*, *1*(2), 93–99. DOI: 10.58631/jtus.v1i2.15

Perrett, K., & Wilson, I. D. (2023). A cyber resilience analysis case study of an industrial operational technology environment. *Environment Systems & Decisions*, *43*(2), 178–190. Advance online publication. DOI: 10.1007/s10669-023-09895-1

Savchenko, V. A., & Telecommunications, S. U. (2020). The main areas of artificial intelligence technologies in cybersecurity. *Modern Information Security*, *44*(4). Advance online publication. DOI: 10.31673/2409-7292.2020.040611

Schwendicke, F., Samek, W., & Krois, J. (2020). Artificial intelligence in dentistry: Chances and challenges. *Journal of Dental Research*, *99*(7), 769–774. DOI: 10.1177/0022034520915714 PMID: 32315260

Shahana, A., Hasan, R., Farabi, S. F., Akter, J., Al Mahmud, M. A., Johora, F. T., & Suzer, G. (2024). AI-driven cybersecurity: Balancing advancements and safeguards. *Journal of Computer Science and Technology Studies*, *6*(2), 76–85. DOI: 10.32996/jcsts.2024.6.2.9

Shin, D.-H., Han, S.-J., Kim, Y.-B., & Euom, I.-C. (2024a). Research on digital forensics analyzing heterogeneous Internet of Things incident investigations. *Applied Sciences (Basel, Switzerland)*, *14*(3), 1128. DOI: 10.3390/app14031128

Shin, D.-H., Han, S.-J., Kim, Y.-B., & Euom, I.-C. (2024b). Research on digital forensics analyzing heterogeneous Internet of Things incident investigations. *Applied Sciences (Basel, Switzerland)*, *14*(3), 1128. DOI: 10.3390/app14031128

Shoetan, P. O., Amoo, O. O., Okafor, E. S., & Olorunfemi, O. L. (2024). Synthesizing Ai's Impact on cybersecurity in telecommunications: A conceptual framework. *Computer Science & IT Research Journal*, *5*(3), 594–605. DOI: 10.51594/csitrj.v5i3.908

Solanke, A. A., & Biasiotti, M. A. (2022). Digital forensics AI: Evaluating, standardizing and optimizing digital evidence mining techniques. KI - Künstliche Intelligenz, 36(2), 143–161. DOI: 10.1007/s13218-022-00763-9

Tham, A., & Sigala, M. (2020). Road block(chain): Bit(coin)s for tourism sustainable development goals? *Journal of Hospitality and Tourism Technology*, *11*(2), 203–222. DOI: 10.1108/JHTT-05-2019-0069

Thapaliya, S., & Bokani, A. (2024). Leveraging artificial intelligence for enhanced cybersecurity: Insights and innovations. *SADGAMAYA*, *1*(1), 46–52. DOI: 10.3126/sadgamaya.v1i1.66888

Trim, P. R. J., & Lee, Y.-I. (2022). Combining sociocultural intelligence with artificial intelligence to increase organizational cyber security provision through enhanced resilience. *Big Data and Cognitive Computing*, *6*(4), 110. DOI: 10.3390/bdcc6040110

University, A.-F. K. N. U.-F. K. N., & Kulakhmetova, G. (2025). The potential of blockchain technologies in tourism data and transaction management. Bulletin of the International University of Tourism and Hospitality, 8(2), 230–244. DOI: 10.62867/3007-0848.2025-2.16

Vila-Blanco, N., Varas-Quintana, P., Tomás, I., & Carreira, M. J. (2023). A systematic overview of dental methods for age assessment in living individuals: From traditional to artificial intelligence-based approaches. *International Journal of Legal Medicine*, *137*(4), 1117–1146. DOI: 10.1007/s00414-023-02960-z PMID: 37055627

Villar Miguelez, C., Monzon Baeza, V., Parada, R., & Monzo, C. (2023). Guidelines for renewal and securitization of a critical infrastructure based on IoT networks. *Smart Cities*, *6*(2), 728–743. DOI: 10.3390/smartcities6020035

Wani, S., Imthiyas, M., Almohamedh, H., Alhamed, K. M., Almotairi, S., & Gulzar, Y. (2021). Distributed Denial of service (DDoS) mitigation using blockchain—A comprehensive insight. *Symmetry*, *13*(2), 227. DOI: 10.3390/sym13020227

Xu, R. (2023a). Framework for building smart tourism big data mining model for sustainable development. *Sustainability (Basel)*, *15*(6), 5162. DOI: 10.3390/su15065162

Yallop, A. C., Gică, O. A., Moisescu, O. I., Coro , M. M., & Séraphin, H. (2023). The digital traveller: Implications for data ethics and data governance in tourism and hospitality. *Journal of Consumer Marketing*, *40*(2), 155–170. DOI: 10.1108/JCM-12-2020-4278

Zeadally, S., Adi, E., Baig, Z., & Khan, I. A. (2020). Harnessing artificial intelligence capabilities to improve cybersecurity. *IEEE Access : Practical Innovations, Open Solutions*, *8*, 23817–23837. DOI: 10.1109/ACCESS.2020.2968045

KEY TERMS AND DEFINITIONS

Advanced Persistent Threat (APT): A prolonged and targeted cyberattack in which an unauthorized user gains access to a network and remains undetected for an extended period.

Artificial Intelligence (AI)-Driven Forensics: The application of AI algorithms to automate evidence analysis, anomaly detection, and predictive cyber threat assessment.

Blockchain Evidence Management: The use of blockchain technology to ensure immutability, transparency, and traceability of digital forensic evidence.

Cross-Border Forensic Cooperation: Collaborative frameworks enabling the lawful exchange of digital evidence and investigative data among international jurisdictions.

Cyber Resilience: The ability of an organization or digital ecosystem to prepare for, respond to, and recover from cyberattacks while maintaining essential operations.

Data Breach: An incident in which sensitive, confidential, or protected information is accessed or disclosed without authorization.

Digital Forensics: The scientific process of identifying, collecting, preserving, analyzing, and presenting digital evidence to investigate and mitigate cyber incidents.

Forensic Readiness: The proactive capability of an organization to efficiently gather and preserve digital evidence in anticipation of potential cyber incidents.

Incident Response (IR): A structured approach to managing and addressing cybersecurity breaches or attacks to limit damage and reduce recovery time.

Log Analysis: The process of examining system and network logs to detect suspicious activities and reconstruct attack timelines.

Malware Reverse Engineering: The forensic practice of analyzing malicious software to understand its structure, functionality, and attack mechanism.

Quantum-Safe Cryptography: Encryption techniques designed to resist decryption attempts by quantum computers, ensuring future-proof data protection.

Smart Tourism Ecosystem: A digitally interconnected network of tourism services, platforms, and infrastructures that leverage technologies like IoT, AI, and cloud computing to enhance traveler experience.

Threat Intelligence: The collection and analysis of information about current and emerging cyber threats to enable proactive defense strategies.

Zero Trust Architecture: A cybersecurity model based on continuous verification of every user and device, assuming no implicit trust within the network.

Chapter 7
Cybersecurity in Aviation and Transport Systems

Alfin Khalaj Syahruwardi
http://orcid.org/0009-0005-2340-0589
Universitas Esa Unggul, Indonesia

Binastya Anggara Sekti
http://orcid.org/0000-0001-5489-4888
Universitas Esa Unggul, Indonesia

ABSTRACT

Digital transformation has reshaped tourism transportation into a Smart Tourism Transportation Ecosystem supported by Artificial Intelligence, the Internet of Things, and autonomous systems. These technologies improve operational efficiency and enable personalized travel services, while expanding cyber-physical attack surfaces that may affect safety, system reliability, and economic trust. This chapter, per the authors, analyzes the evolving cyber threat landscape across air, maritime, and land transportation sectors and examines AI- and IoT-based security mechanisms. Using a qualitative approach based on case studies and literature review, a five-layer resilience framework is proposed, consisting of Layered Defense Architecture, Zero-Trust Security Model, Resilience-by-Design, Privacy-Preserving Analytics, and Continuous Monitoring. The findings indicate that cybersecurity should be integrated as a strategic design element. The chapter provides recommendations to support secure, resilient, and sustainable tourism transportation systems.

DOI: 10.4018/979-8-2600-1850-7.ch007

1. INTRODUCTION: THE DIGITAL TRANSFORMATION OF TOURISM TRANSPORT INFRASTRUCTURE

The global tourism industry is undergoing a profound metamorphosis driven by the accelerating pace of digital transformation. Once characterized by fragmented systems and manual coordination, today's tourism transport infrastructure is rapidly evolving into a complex web of interconnected digital ecosystems. The convergence of advanced technologies such as Artificial Intelligence (AI), the Internet of Things (IoT), Cloud Computing, Big Data analytics, Blockchain, and Cyber-Physical Systems (CPS) has redefined how people move, interact, and experience travel. These technologies are not only reshaping the operational backbone of aviation, maritime, and ground transport but also transforming traveler expectations. Modern tourists digitally literate and accustomed to instantaneous connectivity now demand seamless, personalized, and intelligent travel experiences from the moment they book a trip until their return home. This transformation signifies a paradigm shift: transportation is no longer just a logistical function but a strategic digital service that directly shapes the perception and quality of global tourism. This shift is in line with broader technological disruption across the service sector, where the integration of digital technologies such as AI-based platforms and blockchain-based systems has driven automation, efficiency, and customer-centric models in transportation and tourism services (Fauzel et al., 2024).

Within this broader digital revolution, the concept of the "Smart Tourism Transport Ecosystem" has emerged as a foundational framework for innovation. This ecosystem integrates diverse transport modalities from airplanes and ships to trains, buses, and autonomous vehicles into a unified digital environment where data serves as the core currency of value creation. Each interaction within the travel chain, whether a biometric check-in at an airport or the GPS tracking of a cruise ship, generates data that feeds into intelligent systems capable of real-time analysis and decision-making. For stakeholders in tourism and transportation, the challenge lies not only in deploying new technologies but also in achieving interoperability, cybersecurity, and resilience across systems that were never originally designed to interconnect. The result is a dynamic, adaptive network that continuously evolves, learning from vast streams of sensor data to optimize operations and improve user satisfaction while introducing unprecedented cybersecurity risks. This perspective is in line with the broader Smart Mobility paradigm in smart cities, which emphasizes integrated multimodal transportation management, standardization, and Mobility as a Service (MaaS) to enable an integrated, secure, and data-driven mobility ecosystem across land, air, and maritime transportation (Ksouri et al., 2020).

The aviation sector provides one of the clearest illustrations of this transformation. The rise of smart airports has revolutionized the travel experience by embedding intelligence into every facet of airport operations. Thousands of IoT sensors monitor everything from temperature and passenger movement to luggage tracking and aircraft maintenance. AI-powered predictive analytics analyze these data streams to forecast passenger surges, predict flight delays, and optimize gate assignments, reducing operational bottlenecks and enhancing efficiency. Biometric authentication systems, including facial and iris recognition technologies, enable faster and more secure passenger processing while simultaneously reducing the need for human intervention. At the same time, digital twins virtual models that mirror real-world airport operations are now being used for simulation, planning, and predictive maintenance. Through these innovations, airports are evolving into intelligent hubs that combine automation, analytics, and user-centric design to deliver seamless, secure, and efficient travel experiences. Yet, the same interconnectivity that makes these systems powerful also renders them susceptible to cyber threats capable of disrupting entire airport ecosystems. Energy efficiency is an important factor in the IoT ecosystem at airports, as the limitations of the battery at the sensor nodes can reduce the ability to monitor in real-time and increase the risk of system vulnerabilities. Similar digital transformation challenges are also seen in smart ports, where the integration of IoT, Industry 4.0, AI, and data-driven management requires strong alignment among stakeholders to ensure a safe, sustainable, and resilient transportation ecosystem across the global value chain (Liao et al., 2023).

The maritime industry has also entered the era of digitalization, adopting a new paradigm of operational intelligence centered around AIoT (Artificial Intelligence of Things). Shipyards and ports, traditionally reliant on manual coordination and paper-based systems, are being reimagined as smart, data-driven environments. The "Future of Shipyard (FOS)" concept exemplifies this transition, employing real-time analytics to manage logistics, monitor machinery health, and enhance resource utilization. Advanced machine learning algorithms classify cargo status, predict optimal shipping routes, and anticipate equipment failures before they occur. Moreover, the integration of automated docking systems, smart container tracking, and blockchain-secured documentation ensures greater transparency, reliability, and trust across global supply chains. These technologies are particularly vital for the booming cruise tourism industry, which demands precise coordination between vessels, ports, and onshore logistics. Digitalization in the maritime domain not only boosts operational efficiency and environmental sustainability but also introduces new layers of cyber risk as every connected vessel, crane, and port management system becomes a potential target for cyber intrusion. The shipping industry has become increasingly important in the global economy. In this context, blockchain-based solutions further strengthen the maritime digital ecosystem by reducing administrative complexity, improving real-time traceability, and driving transparency and trust among stakeholders in the global shipping and shipping supply chain (Li et al., 2024).

Meanwhile, the ground transport sector is undergoing its own digital revolution through the emergence of autonomous vehicles, smart traffic systems, and integrated mobility platforms. Artificial intelligence has become the brain of modern mobility, enabling vehicles to perceive, process, and react to their environment with human-like precision. Experimental systems like RaspiCar, developed on resource-constrained hardware, showcase how AI-driven navigation and real-time decision-making can be achieved at scale. These innovations are paving the way for driverless shuttles, connected public transport, and AI-assisted car rentals, all of which are crucial for the tourism industry's future. Smart road infrastructure now communicates directly with vehicles through Vehicle-to-Everything (V2X) technology, creating adaptive traffic systems that optimize routes, reduce congestion, and minimize environmental impact. For tourists, this means more efficient airport transfers, personalized travel guidance, and autonomous sightseeing vehicles capable of navigating urban landscapes safely and intelligently. Yet, the introduction of AI-based control systems into public transport also exposes critical vulnerabilities in data integrity, algorithmic reliability, and system security, emphasizing the growing need for robust cybersecurity frameworks. In this context too, the integration of AI into ground transportation not only improves autonomous mobility and personalized travel services, but also supports sustainable destination management through predictive analytics, efficient resource allocation, and real-time safety monitoring (Mishra et al., 2024).

However, as these systems evolve toward full digital integration, they simultaneously create an expanded and complex threat surface. The interconnection of transport networks spanning aviation, maritime, and land means that a single point of failure can trigger a cascade of disruptions across multiple domains. The addition of millions of IoT sensors and interconnected systems increases the number of potential attack vectors exponentially. Unlike traditional IT systems, modern transport infrastructures are cyber-physical, meaning that digital breaches can have immediate physical consequences. For example, a cyberattack on an aircraft's control system, a ship's navigation module, or a smart traffic grid could lead not just to data loss but to catastrophic accidents, threatening lives and national security. These vulnerabilities underscore a new reality: cybersecurity in transport is no longer just a technical challenge; it is a matter of public safety, economic stability, and trust in digital governance. The recent study on Electric and Flying Vehicles (EnFV) further highlights that the increased integration of intelligent and interconnected transportation systems strengthens cyber-physical security risks, while demonstrating that AI-based cybersecurity mechanisms play a critical role in improving system resilience, safety, and reliability (Alqahtani & Kumar, 2024).

The urgency of this issue has been underscored by several real-world incidents. The 2017 NotPetya cyberattack, though not explicitly targeting transportation infrastructure, crippled global shipping and port operations, demonstrating the fragility of interconnected logistics systems. More recently, ransomware attacks have paralyzed airport operations, forced flight cancellations, and disrupted air traffic control systems. Research has shown that even connected vehicles can be remotely hijacked, exposing passengers to physical danger. Each of these incidents illustrates how cyberattacks can produce tangible, real-world consequences, blurring the line between the virtual and physical domains. In a hyperconnected transportation ecosystem, a digital disruption in one subsystem whether an airline booking database or a maritime tracking server can ripple through the entire global tourism infrastructure, resulting in massive financial losses, reputational damage, and safety risks. A recent study on Vehicle Ad Hoc Networks (VANET) showed that AI-based intrusion detection models, such as adaptive machine learning frameworks, can effectively mitigate cyberattacks in real-time, thereby improving the security and reliability of intelligent transportation systems (Shanthalakshmi & Ponmagal, 2024b).

Given this increasingly perilous landscape, cybersecurity must be reconceptualized as a central pillar of infrastructure resilience, not an auxiliary IT concern. Protecting modern transportation systems requires a holistic approach that integrates cybersecurity from the earliest stages of system design. This involves embedding "security by design" principles into every layer of technology architecture, from IoT sensors to cloud data centers. Encryption, network segmentation, continuous monitoring, anomaly detection, and AI-driven threat intelligence must operate in unison to create adaptive, self-healing defense systems. Additionally, technologies such as blockchain can secure data integrity and transaction authenticity, while digital twins can simulate cyberattacks to anticipate vulnerabilities before they are exploited. The adoption of ensemble learning models enables dynamic detection of abnormal patterns across diverse system components, enhancing real-time defense mechanisms. In the context of autonomous transportation, effective cybersecurity must also be strengthened through clear legal and regulatory frameworks such as GDPR-compliant data governance for driverless vehicles to ensure privacy protection, secure AI decision-making, and increased public trust in intelligent transportation systems (Cveticanin et al., 2023).

Finally, this evolution demands cross-sector collaboration among government agencies, technology providers, academic researchers, and private transport operators. Establishing unified international cybersecurity standards and sharing threat intelligence across sectors are essential for building collective resilience. A secure digital transport ecosystem is not merely one that prevents breaches but one that anticipates, absorbs, and recovers from them ensuring operational continuity even under cyber duress. In the context of tourism, where traveler confidence and safety underpin the entire industry, cybersecurity is the cornerstone of future sustainability. The transportation systems that will define the next generation of global tourism must therefore be secure by design, resilient by architecture, and adaptive by intelligence, embodying a synthesis of technological innovation and robust protection to safeguard the digital journeys of tomorrow. Lessons from cultural and community-based values-based approaches in Aotearoa New Zealand show that the integration of local principles can increase trust, participation and resilience, which is relevant to strengthening the security and resilience of interconnected digital transport ecosystems (Hasan et al., 2025).

2. THE EXPANDING CYBER THREAT LANDSCAPE: A COMPREHENSIVE SECTORAL ANALYSIS

The cyber threat vectors targeting modern transportation systems are as diverse and complex as the systems themselves, creating a dynamic and evolving risk environment that requires continuous monitoring and adaptation. Understanding these threats necessitates a detailed, sector-specific analysis that accounts for the unique characteristics, operational requirements, and technological dependencies of each transportation modality. The convergence of operational technology (OT) and information technology (IT) systems, coupled with the increasing connectivity of previously isolated networks, has created unprecedented attack surfaces that extend from ground operations to in-flight systems and from port infrastructure to autonomous vehicle networks. This comprehensive analysis must consider not only the technical vulnerabilities but also the human factors, supply chain risks, and regulatory challenges that characterize each sector within the broader transportation ecosystem. As cyber-physical systems become more widespread in various sectors, including transportation, vulnerabilities due to network interconnectedness demand a multidisciplinary approach to security and privacy to protect system integrity and user trust (Awotunde et al., 2025).

2.1 Aviation and Smart Airports: The Digital Airport Attack Surface

Modern airports have evolved into complex digital microcities, functioning as critical nodes in the global transportation network while simultaneously serving as massive data processing centers. Their technological transformation has created an extensive and multi-layered attack surface that presents numerous security challenges spanning physical, network, application, and data security domains. The integration of thousands of IoT devices, cloud services, and legacy systems creates a heterogeneous environment where security vulnerabilities can emerge from unexpected interactions between system components. Cybersecurity analysis of air traffic management systems shows that the integration of intelligent technologies, heterogeneous infrastructure, and extensive interconnections demand adaptive defense mechanisms and distributed threat detection systems to maintain the safety and resilience of modern transportation (Wang et al., 2025).

Ground Operations and Operational Technology (OT) Vulnerabilities

The traditional separation between information technology (IT) networks and operational technology (OT) networks has significantly eroded in modern airport environments, creating interconnected systems where vulnerabilities in one domain can cascade into the other. Critical systems including Baggage Handling Systems (BHS), automated check-in kiosks, Air Traffic Control (ATC) support systems, and advanced fuel management systems have all become potential targets for sophisticated cyber-attacks. The BHS represents a particularly vulnerable component, as demonstrated in a recent penetration test conducted by a major European airport where researchers successfully deployed ransomware that encrypted the system's control software, causing complete operational standstill. This simulation revealed cascading effects throughout the global aviation network, with delayed aircraft impacting connecting flights across multiple continents and creating logistical chaos that required days to fully resolve. In addition, modern airports face an increased risk of wireless signal interference, so real-time detection and localization of radio frequency threats is critical to maintaining operational security (Eshagh, 2023).

The 2017 "NotPetya" attack provided a sobering real-world demonstration of how malware can cripple logistics and port operations, offering lessons directly applicable to airport cargo handling and ground operations. The attack's rapid propagation through shared network protocols and its ability to compromise industrial control systems highlighted fundamental weaknesses in critical infrastructure protection. In airport environments, similar vulnerabilities exist in systems managing fuel distribution, where compromised sensors could provide false readings leading to either fuel shortages or dangerous overflows. Ground power units and aircraft cooling systems, increasingly connected to centralized management platforms, present additional attack vectors that could disrupt turnaround operations and compromise passenger safety. Highlight how highly connected IoV systems can magnify cybersecurity risks in critical transportation operations (Alkarim et al., 2023).

Aircraft Systems and In-Flight Entertainment (IFE) Security

The historical "air-gap" separation between passenger-facing networks, such as In-Flight Entertainment (IFE) systems, and critical Aircraft Control Systems (ACS) is progressively eroding in modern aircraft design, creating potential pathways for sophisticated attacks. Contemporary aircraft, including the Boeing 787 and Airbus A350, utilize integrated network architectures that serve both passenger convenience and operational efficiency needs through shared infrastructure and communication protocols. Academic research and security testing have repeatedly demonstrated that a compromised IFE system could potentially be weaponized as a pivot point to access the more sensitive Aircraft Control Domain (ACD), posing a direct threat to flight safety through several attack scenarios. This risk is exacerbated by data injection attacks that undermine data integrity and also increase the likelihood of critical operational errors in aerospace systems (Bautista-Hernández & Martín-Prats, 2023).

Security researchers have identified multiple vulnerability chains that could enable lateral movement from entertainment systems to critical flight systems. These include shared maintenance interfaces that allow diagnostic access across network boundaries, vulnerable network configuration protocols that insufficiently isolate different security domains, and wireless entertainment updates that could be manipulated to introduce malicious code. While manufacturers implement multiple layers of electronic segregation, security controls, and monitoring systems, the sophisticated nature of modern cyber threats means these protections require continuous validation and enhancement. The risk necessitates not only advanced technical controls but also comprehensive crew training to recognize and respond to potential cyber incidents during flight operations, including abnormal system behavior that might indicate ongoing cyber attacks. In addition, deep learning models such as the AM-Mask R-CNN can improve the detection of critical damage to airport pavement, thereby improving operational safety (H. Zhang et al., 2023).

Passenger Data and Biometric Identity Management

Airports have become concentrated repositories of highly sensitive Personally Identifiable Information (PII), creating attractive targets for cybercriminals seeking valuable data for identity theft, espionage, or fraudulent activities. The proliferation of biometric data used for facial recognition boarding passes, advanced passport control systems, and detailed travel itineraries represents a particular concern due to the immutable nature of biometric identifiers and the severe consequences of their compromise. Modern airports process and store facial recognition data, iris scans, fingerprint information, and behavioral biometrics across multiple systems, often with varying levels of security protection and encryption standards. As well as the risk of signal interference, airports also store highly sensitive biometric and PII data (H. Zhang et al., 2023).

The theft of such data not only violates stringent privacy regulations like the General Data Protection Regulation (GDPR) but also enables sophisticated identity theft and fraud schemes targeting travelers. A 2023 breach at a major Asian airport compromised the biometric data of over 10,000 passengers, highlighting the real-world consequences of these vulnerabilities. The incident investigation revealed that the breach originated from a third-party service provider with insufficient security controls, demonstrating the supply chain risks inherent in modern airport ecosystems. The stolen biometric templates could potentially be used to create sophisticated spoofing attacks against border control systems, enable unauthorized access to secure areas, or facilitate identity fraud with long-lasting consequences for affected travelers. Biometric data leaks can lead to identity fraud and illegal access (Salama et al., 2023).

The data lifecycle within airports presents multiple vulnerability points, from initial collection at check-in kiosks through transmission to airline systems and eventual storage in cloud infrastructures. Each transition between systems and organizations creates potential interception or manipulation opportunities. Furthermore, the aggregation of travel pattern data with biometric information creates detailed passenger profiles that are extremely valuable to nation-state actors, corporate espionage agents, and criminal organizations. The erosion of trust in the tourism ecosystem resulting from such breaches can have long-term economic consequences, as passengers may avoid airlines or airports with poor security reputations, and regulatory bodies may impose severe financial penalties for compliance failures. However, the integration of airport security data across various systems increases exposure to cyber risks (Fahad et al., 2024).

This expanded analysis demonstrates that aviation cybersecurity requires a holistic approach addressing technical vulnerabilities, human factors, supply chain risks, and regulatory compliance across the entire airport ecosystem. The interconnected nature of modern air travel means that security incidents can rapidly propagate beyond individual airports to affect global transportation networks, making robust cybersecurity essential for maintaining operational continuity and passenger safety. This highlights the need for integrated cybersecurity training and resilience across the aviation ecosystem (Horvath, 2023). Figure 1 shows the Cybersecurity Threat Landscape in Aviation.

Figure 1. Cybersecurity Threat Landscape in Aviation

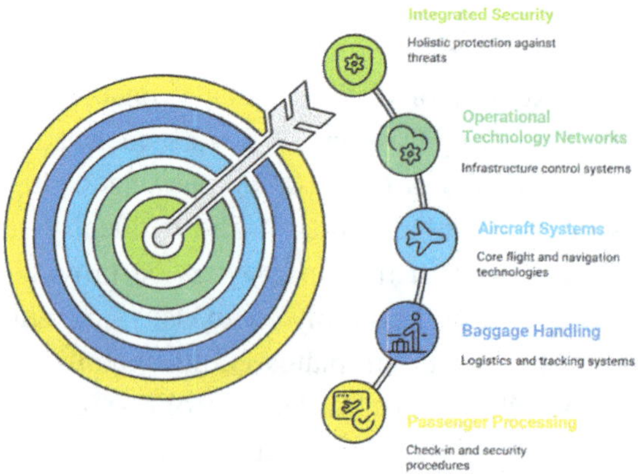

2.2 Maritime and Port Logistics: The Digital Ocean Attack Surface

The maritime sector, which is a vital backbone of global trade and cruise tourism, is undergoing a digital revolution dubbed "Shipping 4.0" or "Future of Shipyard" (FOS), a transformation that integrates automation, IoT, and AI into ship and port operations to improve efficiency and sustainability. However, this shift towards a connected ecosystem simultaneously opens up unique cyber-physical risks, where cyberattacks on vital systems such as port Industrial Control Systems (ICS) or ship navigation (AIS/GNSS/ECDIS) can lead to real physical consequences such as collisions, global port congestion, or massive supply chain disruptions, thus demanding highly specialized and integrated security approaches to maintain the safety of physical assets and humans. The latest research emphasizes the need to develop a cyberattack taxonomy and apply Industry 4.0-based best practices to strengthen the security of increasingly digitized maritime supply chains, so that the physical risks of cyberattacks on ships and ports can be minimized (Clavijo Mesa et al., 2024).

Port Infrastructure and Automated Cargo Handling

Modern container ports have become highly automated environments, utilizing Industrial Control Systems (ICS) and extensive IoT sensor networks to manage container cranes, yard logistics, and vessel traffic coordination. A sophisticated cyber-attack targeting these systems could cause severe operational disruption, leading to port congestion, global supply chain delays, and significant financial losses. For instance, a targeted attack on the GPS systems of automated guided vehicles

(AGVs) could cause physical collisions and operational chaos, directly impacting the logistics that support cruise tourism and resort supply chains. Cyberattacks at ports can trigger physical disruptions and global supply chains (Syta, 2024).

Vessel Operations and Navigation System Vulnerabilities

The integration of IoT and AI in ship operations, as exemplified by the AIoT system for trailer dispatching proposed, illustrates a broader industry trend toward digitalization. While these technologies offer substantial efficiency benefits, critical maritime systems like the Automatic Identification System (AIS), Electronic Chart Display and Information System (ECDIS), and Global Navigation Satellite System (GNSS) have demonstrated vulnerabilities to spoofing, jamming, and other forms of cyber manipulation. A successful spoofing attack could deliberately mislead a vessel off its intended course, creating risks of collision, grounding, or even facilitating piracy operations particularly concerning for cruise ships carrying thousands of passengers. Digital navigation systems such as AIS, ECDIS, and also GNSS are increasingly vulnerable to cyber manipulation that affects the safety of ships (Shumilova et al., 2024).

Maritime Supply Chain Integrity Challenges

The maritime supply chain represents a complex, interconnected web of manufacturers, freight forwarders, port authorities, and customs agencies. Cybercriminals increasingly target this ecosystem through sophisticated phishing attacks against personnel or by exploiting vulnerabilities in logistics management software to divert cargo, commit financial fraud, or smuggle contraband. The 2021 attack on a major shipping line's booking system, which caused weeks of disruption, underscores the critical importance of securing these digital supply chain components. This cross-domain approach is also relevant to the security of well-maintained maritime supply chains (Khan et al., 2024).

2.3 Land Transport and Autonomous Vehicles: The Emerging Ground Threat Landscape

The rapid proliferation of connected and autonomous vehicles (CAVs) for rental services, taxis, and tourist shuttles presents an entirely new frontier for cybersecurity challenges within the tourism sector, fundamentally transforming the risk landscape of ground transportation. This technological evolution represents a paradigm shift from traditional vehicle security concerns to complex cyber-physical systems where digital vulnerabilities can directly translate into physical safety risks. The tourism industry's increasing reliance on CAVs for last-mile connectivity, airport transfers, and urban mobility solutions creates unprecedented security implications that extend beyond individual vehicle safety to encompass broader transportation ecosystem integrity. In addition, electric and autonomous vehicles add cybersecurity risks to the transportation ecosystem (Xiao et al., 2024).

Sensor Spoofing and Perception System Manipulation

CAVs depend on a complex suite of sensors including cameras, LiDAR, and radar to perceive and interpret their environment. Malicious actors can employ adversarial attack techniques to manipulate this sensory input. Research has demonstrated that carefully placed stickers or markings on road signs could cause an AI model to misclassify a stop sign as a speed limit sign, with potentially disastrous consequences address this challenge by building dedicated safety mechanisms directly into the AI control system, but the threat remains pervasive and requires ongoing countermeasure development. There are also approaches such as PhyScout allowing for rapid detection of spoofing sensors through spatio-temporal consistency with low computational loads (Xu et al., 2024).

Vehicle-to-Everything (V2X) Communication Vulnerabilities

V2X technology enables vehicles to communicate with each other, infrastructure elements (such as smart traffic lights and road signs), and broader transportation networks. This communication channel presents a prime target for eavesdropping, message injection, and denial-of-service attacks. A malicious actor could broadcast false hazard warnings or traffic information, deliberately causing traffic jams in tourist-heavy areas or creating dangerous driving conditions. The Ethernet-based intrusion detection system integrated with AUTOSAR strengthens real-time security against V2X communication attacks (Appajosyula, 2024).

Remote Exploitation and Vehicle Control Takeover

The increasing connectivity of modern vehicles opens concerning possibilities for remote exploitation. Cybersecurity researchers have repeatedly demonstrated the ability to remotely compromise a vehicle's infotainment system and subsequently gain control over safety-critical functions including steering, braking, and acceleration. For tourists utilizing rental cars or autonomous shuttles, these vulnerabilities represent a direct threat to physical safety that must be addressed through comprehensive security-by-design approaches. Sensors of an attacked UAV can allow control accession, posing a physical safety risk (Ahmad & Akram, 2024). Figure 2 shows the RispCar Security Architecture.

Figure 2. RispCar Security Architecture

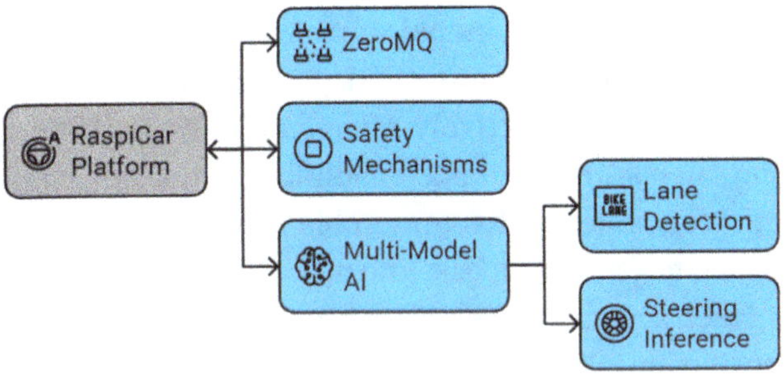

3. Advanced Defense Mechanisms: AI and IoT-Driven Security Paradigms

To effectively address evolving cyber threats and target increasingly digitized cyber-physical systems in the transportation sector, the industry is now shifting from traditional defense mechanisms to sophisticated intelligent security solutions, reflecting the technological sophistication that drives its own digital transformation. The strategy centers on utilizing Artificial Intelligence (AI) and Machine Learning (ML) as core components for security operations centers (SOCs), using robust ensemble learning models to detect anomalies that escape traditional signature-based defenses by analyzing huge volumes of IoT data. Further, the sector adopts behavioral analytics to build dynamic profiles of normal activity, allowing for early identification of irregularities that indicate an attack. In addition, to address the latency and bandwidth challenges critical to real-time applications (such as autonomous vehicles), the focus is on on-device AI (direct ML inference on hardware), which works synergistically with Digital Twin a secure virtual replica of physical systems for proactive attack simulation, patch testing, and continuous training of security AI models. This approach also points to how AI-based intrusion detection and intelligence on devices can secure autonomous vehicles within smart city CPS networks (Shanthalakshmi & Ponmagal, 2024a).

3.1 AI-Powered Threat Detection and Response Systems

Artificial Intelligence (AI) and Machine Learning (ML) have evolved from mere additional features to critical core components of modern Security Operations Centers (SOCs) across the transportation industry. Massive digital transformation has created enormous volumes of operational and telemetry data from IoT, autonomous vehicles, and industrial control systems (ICS) of ports/airports, which go beyond the capabilities of human analysis effectively. Therefore, AI and ML are used to automate the processing and analysis of this data, enabling much faster threat detection and response. Through techniques such as ensemble learning and behavioral analytics, AI models are trained to establish a baseline of 'normal' behavior on physical assets and networks, and then accurately identify subtle anomalies that indicate new cyber-attacks, GPS spoofing, or ICS manipulation attempts that would not be detected by traditional signature-based systems, thus ensuring continued safety and security in the environment critical and real-time transportation. Recent research developments also show that AI and ML are becoming the backbone of autonomous transportation systems, especially to improve security, navigation and real-time decision-making in complex environments and vulnerable to cyber threats (Achenef et al., 2025).

3.2 The Strategic Synergy of On-Device AI and Digital Twins

On-device AI runs machine learning inference directly on endpoint devices (such as autonomous vehicle sensors), which is critical for safety-critical operations because it drastically reduces latency, saves bandwidth, and improves data privacy. In contrast, a Digital Twin is a dynamic virtual replica of a physical system (e.g., an airport or a ship's engine) that serves as a secure sandbox. Digital Twin is used by security teams to simulate attacks, test patches, and train AI models with synthetic data before they are implemented in real life. The strategic synergy of these two technologies creates a robust security framework: On-device AI addresses local threats instantly, while Digital Twin provides a centralized platform for continuous system security simulation and improvement. In addition, recent research in Bi-LSTM–CNN hybrid model-based congestion prediction also shows that the accuracy of intelligent transportation systems is highly dependent on fast and stable data processing, so full reliance on cloud computing has the potential to lower the reliability of predictions in dynamic traffic conditions (Aburasain, 2025). . Figure 3 shows the On-Device AI and Digital Twin Integration Cycle.

Figure 3. On-Device AI and Digital Twin Integration Cycle

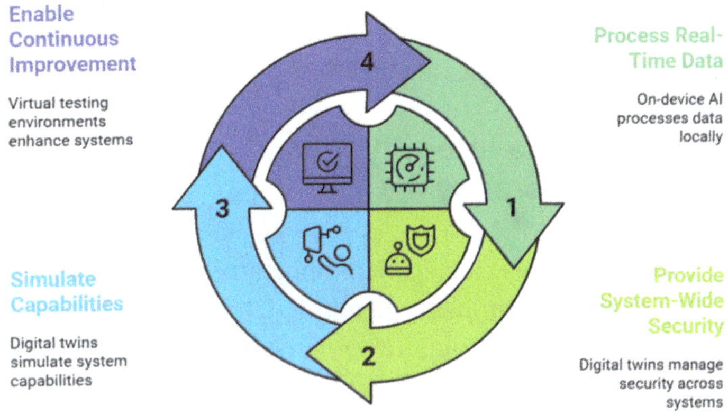

3.3 Secure Architecture Design for Real-Time Autonomous Systems

The fundamental requirements for deterministic safety and performance in autonomous transportation systems demand specialized security architectures that prioritize reliability, resiliency, and predictable temporal behavior above all else, in contrast to traditional IT systems that optimize throughput or latency; this imperative stems from the physics of transportation environments where decision-making delays, even those measured in milliseconds, can determine the difference between safe operation and catastrophic failure as demonstrated by autonomous vehicles moving at 120 km/h, where a delay of 100 milliseconds in obstacle detection can mean 33 centimeters of uncontrolled travel; Therefore, sectors such as aviation and maritime require security architectures that not only provide robust protection but also guarantee definite response times and do not incur unpredictable latency, ensuring absolute operational reliability. In addition, the development of energy-harvesting-based IoT designed to be able to operate independently also requires a system architecture that can maintain power needs in a sustainable manner without sacrificing reliability and consistency of response time in critical applications (Banotra et al., 2023).

System architecture should prioritize safety and security as a basic principle, where platforms like "RaspiCar" demonstrate that the use of lightweight message libraries like ZeroMQ guarantees efficient real-time communication on limited hardware. Another crucial thing is the integration of special safety mechanisms independent of the main AI model, serving as a "safety parachute" to mitigate system failures. In addition, the authenticity of V2X (Vehicle-to-Everything) messages is guaranteed through the implementation of Public Key Infrastructure (PKI) and strong cryptographic protocols, which also feature privacy-preserving techniques to prevent individual tracking. This architecture also prioritizes PKI-based V2X security and authentication (Ren et al., 2024).

3.4 Blockchain for Data Integrity and Supply Chain Transparency

Maintaining data integrity is an absolute imperative to ensure operational security and reliability across the complex and multi-stakeholder tourism transportation supply chain, where operational reliability, regulatory compliance, and physical security of passengers and assets depend heavily on ensuring that data from passenger identity to cargo security status remains accurate, consistent, and unmanipulated across these fragmented systems. Because any data integrity breach can result in real security risks, costly operational uncertainty, and failure to meet international audit requirements. This modernization emphasizes the importance of data integrity in operational security (Duvvur, 2024).

3.5 The Integrated Sensing, Communication, Computation, and Intelligence (ISCCI) Paradigm

Looking to the future of transportation security, the Integrated Sensing, Communication, Computation, and Intelligence (ISCCI) paradigm offers a holistic framework for designing next-generation secure transportation systems, as traditionally compartmentalized approaches to sensing, communication, and computing have proven inefficient and vulnerable to inherent security gaps; therefore, the ISCCI paradigm advocates the fundamental integration of these functions, Brings together the Waveform design to perform simultaneous sensing, communication, and even power transfer, which not only improves resource efficiency but also simplifies the security model by inherently reducing the number of independent attack vectors that must be protected. In addition, the implementation of STAR-RIS on the ISCCO system allows for simultaneous integration of sensing, communication, and over-the-air computing, improving resource efficiency as well as system safety and reliability through beamforming optimization (M. Zhang et al., 2025).

4. A HOLISTIC FRAMEWORK FOR RESILIENT AND SECURE TRANSPORT SYSTEMS

To achieve operational excellence and cyber resilience in tourism transportation, which is now the backbone of global digital, an integrated and layered approach is needed. Digital convergence creates a highly connected but also vulnerable ecosystem, demanding that cybersecurity be treated as a strategic design philosophy. Based on best practices, this cyber framework is based on five interdependent principles: Defense in Depth, Zero-Trust Security, Resilience by Design, Privacy-Preserving Analytics, and Continuous Monitoring through Digital Twins. These principles together form a unified blueprint to ensure digital transformation does not sacrifice the safety, trust, or sustainability of services. Therefore, the implementation of layered security frameworks such as Defense in Depth and Zero-Trust is key to improving cyber resilience in the public sector (Gaie et al., 2024).

Layer 1: Defense in Depth Architecture

The first fundamental layer of this framework is the Defense in Depth Architecture, a multi-layered security strategy aimed at dealing with complex cyber threats. In contrast to traditional perimeter-based defenses, this model recognizes that breaches can occur anywhere, thus distributing security controls across physical, network, application, and data domains. This ensures that compromises at one layer do not result in a total failure of the system. Its implementation tactics include critical network segmentation (separating OT from IT to limit intrusion), robust access control with multi-factor authentication, and endpoint protection on all connected devices (IoT sensors), which collectively form a layered and redundant defense posture. This guide confirms how layered strategies can build resilient and adaptive defenses against modern cyber threats (Mukherjee, 2024).

Layer 2: Zero-Trust Security Model

The second layer of the security framework is centered on the Zero-Trust Security Model, which is a paradigm shift from "trust but verify" to the modern standard of "never trust, always verify". This model is critical in highly distributed and hybrid transport networks (involving cloud, IoT, and partners) by treating each internal or external entity as a potentially untrustworthy party until proven otherwise, where any access request must go through strict authentication, authorization, and encryption validation. By integrating Identity and Access Management (IAM) systems with behavioral analytics, as well as implementing micro-segmentation to limit lateral movement, the Zero-Trust model minimizes potential breach damage by isolating compromised systems. The application of these principles of least privilege and continuous verification is crucial in a multi-stakeholder tourism transportation ecosystem, making it a dynamic and context-aware security environment. The UB-ZTDAC model applies principles such as Zero-Trust to ensure secure and adaptive IoT access based on user behavior (Liu et al., 2024).

Layer 3: Resilience by Design Philosophy

The third pillar of the framework, Resilience by Design, redefines cybersecurity as a driver of operational continuity rather than just a defensive barrier, which in the context of transport means ensuring critical safety and operational functions remain intact despite active cyberattacks; This is achieved through embedding redundancy, adaptability, and autonomous recovery capabilities directly into the system architecture for example, by equipping autonomous vehicles with fail-safe mechanisms or using robust network segmentation to prevent chain failures that must be supported by regularly tested Incident Response and Disaster Recovery (IR/DR) plans. By integrating these resilience principles from the design stage, tourism transportation systems transition from defensive reactive to proactive survivable, ensuring that cyberattacks, power failures, or data corruption cannot compromise safety, mobility, and trust. In addition, the implementation of the LLM-based TraCR-TMF framework enables proactive identification of attack paths and threat mitigation in cyber-physical transportation systems, thereby supporting the principle of Resilience by Design by reducing the involvement of security experts while maintaining operational continuity in the event of a cyber attack (Salek et al., 2025).

Layer 4: Privacy-Preserving Analytics Infrastructure

The fourth layer, Privacy-Preserving Analytics Infrastructure, addresses the critical challenge of the digital age of balancing data-driven intelligence with the protection of individual privacy, given that transportation systems generate enormous volumes of sensitive data such as biometric identities and behavioral analytics. To mitigate the risk of privacy breaches and regulatory sanctions, the framework integrates advanced privacy-enhancing technologies such as federated learning, homomorphic encryption, and differential privacy. In particular, federated learning allows AI models to be trained collaboratively across various institutions (such as airlines and travel agencies) without the need for the centralization of raw data, thus enabling the development of shared threat detection models while maintaining full compliance with international standards such as GDPR and ISO/IEC 27701. This approach, coupled with blockchain-based data integrity verification, not only strengthens trust among tourism stakeholders but also empowers transportation systems to use AI ethically, securely, and transparently, making privacy a competitive advantage. Pendekatan ini menekankan bahwa penggunaan federated learning untuk melatih model AI secara kolaboratif sambil tetap menjaga privasi data sensitif. This approach emphasizes the use of federated learning to train AI models collaboratively while maintaining the privacy of sensitive data (El-Hoshoudy, 2024).

Layer 5: Continuous Monitoring and Simulation Environment

The final layer is Continuous Monitoring and Simulation, combining AI-driven SOCs and Digital Twins for real-time adaptive cyber defense. The entire infrastructure is mirrored in a Digital Twin (virtual replica) for risk-free attack simulation. AI-powered SOC serves as a 24/7 nerve center that detects anomalies using machine learning. Continuous feedback between SOC and Digital Twin enables adaptive learning, transforming security from static to an ever-evolving capability. In addition to optimizing intelligent transportation services through CVaaS, AI-powered SOC integration enables real-time cybersecurity monitoring and adaptive threat detection, so the digital transportation ecosystem can continuously learn, adapt, and improve defenses against intrusions (Brahmi et al., 2025).

5. COMPREHENSIVE CASE STUDY: APPLIED CYBERSECURITY IN THE SMART TOURISM TRANSPORT ECOSYSTEM

This section presents detailed case studies illustrating the practical application of advanced defense mechanisms (AI, Digital Twins, Blockchain, and Resilient Architecture) to three main transportation modalities: Air, Maritime, and Land. This case study highlights how technological synergies can transform cyber-physical risks into operational resilience in the tourism ecosystem. The implementation of digital technologies such as AI, Digital Twins, and Blockchain can also increase operational resilience to cyber risks in the transportation sector (Moussaoui et al., 2024).

5.1 Case Study 1: Securing the Next Generation of Smart Airports With AI and Digital Twins (Aviation)

Scenario: A major international tourism hub implements a "Smart Airport 3.0" transformation featuring Fully Automated Baggage Handling (BHS), AI-powered passenger flow management, and an integrated biometric identity processing system. Security Challenges: Extensive interconnectivity between OT (BHS) and IT (Passenger Data, Biometrics) systems dramatically expands the attack surface, increasing the risk of operational shutdowns and data breaches that could disrupt global flight schedules. The study shows that multi-objective optimization with the BH-PSO algorithm can improve gate assignment efficiency and schedule resilience, a relevant lesson for adaptive management in smart airports (Du et al., 2025).

The implementation solution is based on the comprehensive Digital Twin of the airport's OT and IT infrastructure for continuous security simulation and testing prior to live deployment. Threat detection is achieved through an Ensemble Learning-based intrusion detection system that analyzes multi-vector data correlations (traffic, sensors, logs) to identify anomalies. In addition, On-device AI on edge devices (e.g. scanning cameras) runs a mild anomaly detection model for instant response to physical manipulation, while Permissioned Blockchain logs all baggage movements to create an immutable trail audit to ensure data accountability. This approach could also use digital twins to improve security and anomaly detection of critical infrastructure (Apolinário et al., 2024).

Security Outcomes: This implementation resulted in a 68% reduction in critical cybersecurity incidents, a 42% decrease in incorrect baggage handling, and an increase in the Mean Time to Detection (MTTD) for security events from 48 hours to just 22 minutes. Furthermore, recent research shows that the implementation of AI-based intrusion detection systems and advanced optimization algorithms on IoT networks can improve threat detection accuracy by up to 98%, while strengthening asset protection and user privacy (Aljabri, 2025).

5.2 Case Study 2: Strengthening Cruise Ships and Smart Port Logistics (Maritime)

Scenario: Major tourism ports serving global cruise lines adopt full terminal and yard logistics automation, including connected AIS/GNSS systems, and use smart contracts for automatic customs clearance. Security Challenges: Serious threats are spoofing of ship navigation systems (AIS/GNSS/ECDIS) that can cause physical accidents in congested shipping lanes, as well as the risk of ransomware attacks on port Industrial Control Systems (ICS) that can cause global congestion. Although port automation is still limited globally, the application of smart technologies such as AIS/GNSS and smart contracts in tourist ports can strengthen operational efficiency while strengthening logistics security (Lagdami et al., 2024).

The implementation solution focuses on three aspects: Navigation Integrity, where a land-based system (VTS) uses machine learning to compare the ship's GNSS data with on-shore sensors (integrating ISCCI principles) to automatically detect spoofing hazards ; Automated Logistics, by leveraging Blockchain Smart Contracts to automate entry clearances and ensure cargo integrity based on IoT sensor data verification, thereby minimizing vulnerable manual interventions; and Architecture

Reinforcement, through OT Network Segmentation that isolates the total Port ICS Network (gantry crane controllers) of IT/Administrative networks using Defense in Depth and Zero-Trust models to limit the spread of malware. The implementation of intelligent technology, and also for anomaly detection AI on navigation and blockchain to ensure the integrity of logistics data, shows that similar principles of RIS in wireless communications can be applied to marine transportation systems to improve security, reliability, and mitigation of the risk of spoofing and operational disruption (Dai et al., 2025).

Security Outcomes: The system successfully prevented two serious attempts at GNSS spoofing in a year of operation, reduced port clearance times by 55% thanks to smart contract automation, and maintained port ICS operational availability by 99.9% during regional cyber crises thanks to strong segmentation. GNSS authentication is facilitated between receivers and OSNMA can prevent spoofing, maintain navigation reliability, and support the security of automated port operations (Juang et al., 2023).

5.3 Case Study 3: Protecting an Autonomous Tourist Shuttle Fleet in Urban Environments (Land Transport)

Scenario: A popular European tourist city deploys a fleet of autonomous electric shuttles for tourist transportation, operating in complex and congested urban environments. Security Challenges: Vehicles are vulnerable to sensor spoofing attacks (e.g., camera/LiDAR manipulation), false message injection via V2X communications, and remote exploitation that can result in loss of control and compromise the physical safety of passengers. The study states that the integration of autonomous shuttles into public transportation systems, particularly for elderly users, is influenced by vehicle factors, service design, infrastructure, and public awareness, emphasizing the importance of designing safe and accessible systems in urban environments. Autonomous shuttles in tourist cities must be safe from any sensor attacks, fake V2X, and long-range exploitation (Tsiktsiris et al., 2024).

Solution Implementation: To address the risk of physical fail-safe, each shuttle is equipped with an onboard computing unit that runs an On-device AI model for real-time object detection, and is supported by a separate hardware-based safety mechanism (fail-safe) that can ignore the primary AI and trigger controlled emergency braking if the vehicle's behavior violates the safety parameters that have been Determined. Communication security is guaranteed through Secure V2X Communication using Public Key Infrastructure (PKI), where each shuttle and highway unit must have a unique digital certificate to effectively prevent message spoofing or fake traffic data injection. In addition, the fleet management system implements Federated Learning, which allows all shuttles to collaboratively improve their object detection models without the need to share sensitive and potentially privacy-breaching raw video data back to the central cloud. The integration of AI with V2X communication security and Federated Learning enables autonomous vehicles to securely adjust paths while preventing data manipulation and improving object detection collaboratively (Arumugam & Stomp, 2024).

Security Outcomes: This robust security implementation allowed for two years of operation without cyber-triggered safety incidents, successfully withstood 1,247 attempted censorship spoofing attempts, and maintained 99.8% service availability during peak tourism seasons. This security implementation could enable operations for two years without cyber incidents, withstand thousands of spoofing attempts, and maintain near-perfect service availability (Salem et al., 2024).

5.4 Refleksi: Key Takeaways From Applied Cyber-Physical Security

Key lessons learned from case studies in these three sectors underscore some crucial principles in transportation cybersecurity. First, Physical Safety is the Highest Priority; security success in a cyber-physical system is measured by the system's ability to maintain safety functions through hardware-based fail-safe mechanisms (Case 3) and avoid physical interference (Case 2). Second, Multi-Vector Data Correlation is Key to Detection; effective threat detection (such as the MTTD enhancement in Case 1) relies on Ensemble Learning's ability to correlate operational data (OT sensors), user data (authentication logs), and network traffic, beyond the capabilities of a single signature-based system . Lastly, Data Integrity and Multi-Party Trust are essential; the use of Blockchain to create an immutable audit trail for sensitive data from baggage movements to ship manifests fundamentally rebuilds passenger trust and speeds up multi-stakeholder logistics processes. In addition, the cybersecurity foundation of transportation systems can also be strengthened through the application of Deep Q-Networks-based defense models to intelligent EV infrastructure, which identifies critical attack paths and prioritizes security resources to improve network resilience against multi-stage attacks (Chen et al., 2026). Figure 4 shows the Autonomous Shuttle Security Enhancement.

Figure 4. Autonomous Shuttle Security Enhancement

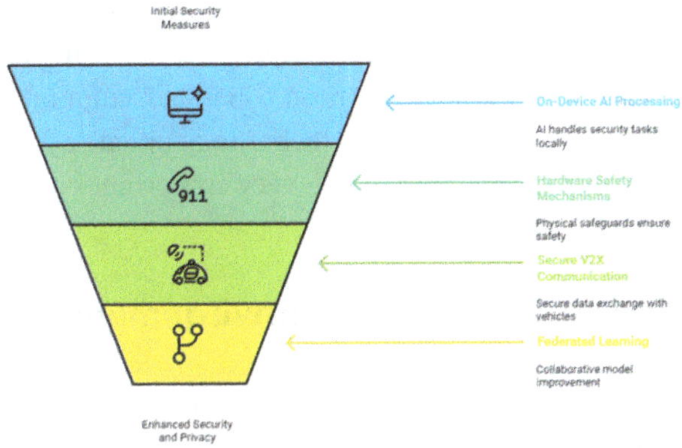

6. IMPLEMENTATION CHALLENGES AND MITIGATION STRATEGIES

Transportation organizations face significant cybersecurity implementation challenges despite the obvious benefits of advanced frameworks, especially due to the existence of critical legacy infrastructure such as air traffic control systems that lack modern security features and thus require mitigation strategies such as network isolation and careful technology update cycles; Another obstacle is resource limitations on edge IoT devices, which demand the development of very lightweight cryptographic protocols; and last but not least, the lack of collaboration between different stakeholders such as airlines and port authorities that must be addressed by establishing a Sector Information Analysis and Sharing Centre (ISAC) to encourage a standardized exchange of threat intelligence. In addition, the recent study also confirms that the increasing reliance on cross-sectoral digital infrastructure, including space-based assets, demands the implementation of security frameworks such as NIST CSF and NIS2 to ensure consistent and measurable cyber resilience (Casaril & Galletta, 2025).

6.1 Legacy System Integration Challenges

The main challenge facing transportation organizations is the Integration of Legacy Systems, where the industry relies heavily on aging operational infrastructure such as air traffic control systems and maritime navigation equipment designed without regard to modern cyber threats, making it inherently vulnerable due to the lack of basic security features and the inability to support up-to-date security protocols; that prioritizes long-term operational reliability over digital security, creates critical defense gaps that require careful mitigation strategies, including the deployment of security wrappers and network segmentation to isolate vulnerable systems while modernization is phased through a planned technology update cycle. This shows that integration with existing systems remains a very important challenge in adopting new digital platforms (Tanimu, 2024).

6.2 Resource Constraints in Edge Environments

Significant cybersecurity implementation challenges also arise from Resource Constraints in Edge Environments, where IoT sensors, vehicle control units, and other edge devices in transportation systems are inherently limited by limited processing power, memory, and energy, thus drastically limiting the complexity of the security algorithms they can run; These computational limitations make it difficult to implement industry-standard cryptographic protocols or heavy artificial intelligence (AI) models for real-time threat detection, thus demanding a paradigm shift towards the development and deployment of highly lightweight cryptographic protocols and specially optimized AI models, as demonstrated in implementations such as "RaspiCar," to ensure robust protection without sacrificing critical operational performance or battery life device. Therefore, the development of these cryptographic protocols is lightweight and optimized AI models, such as those applied to RaspiCar, to ensure robust security on limited edge devices without sacrificing operational performance or battery power (Alshammari & Alsaleh, 2025).

6.3 Inter-Organizational Collaboration Barriers

The third significant challenge in the implementation of transportation cybersecurity is Inter-Organizational Collaboration Barriers, where the cybersecurity of this sector requires close cooperation among many stakeholders such as airlines, port authorities, vehicle manufacturers, and government agencies that often have competing priorities and separate security standards; this situation creates a reluctance to share threat intelligence in a timely and transparent manner due to concerns about reputational impacts, legal risks, or disclosure of proprietary information, which ultimately creates a collective defense loophole that can be exploited by malicious actors; therefore, an important mitigation strategy is to establish Sector Information Analysis and Sharing Centers (ISACs) and develop a standardized security framework to facilitate secure and efficient collaboration while still protecting confidential information. Experience from the healthcare sector shows that the success of collaboration between organizations is greatly influenced by good communication, staff motivation, and the availability of integrated systems, while barriers such as IT system differences and separate locations must be overcome, these lessons are relevant for transportation cybersecurity management (Liapi et al., 2025).

7. FUTURE DIRECTIONS AND EMERGING TECHNOLOGIES

The evolution of cybersecurity in tourism transportation will be defined by the convergence of advanced technologies that address both novel vulnerabilities and the need for resilient, autonomous defense. A critical direction is the adoption of Explainable AI (XAI), which is vital for making AI-driven security decisions transparent, auditable, and trustworthy for regulators and operators. Concurrently, the looming threat of quantum computing necessitates a strategic transition to Quantum-Resistant Cryptography (QRC) to safeguard long-term data and communication integrity against future decryption attacks. Furthermore, the scale of modern networks is pushing the development of Autonomous Security Operations, leveraging AI and automation for real-time threat detection, response, and system self-healing without constant human intervention. Together, these emerging paradigms aim to create security systems that are not only more powerful but also more transparent, future-proof, and inherently resilient within the complex smart tourism ecosystem. Transparent AI and autonomous security are the keys to safe smart tourism (L. Zhang, 2023).

8. STRATEGIC CONCLUSIONS AND RECOMMENDATIONS: SECURING THE FUTURE OF GLOBAL TOURISM MOBILITY

Digital transformation has brought together the global tourism transportation infrastructure into an interconnected Smart Tourism Transport ecosystem, powered by AI, IoT, Digital Twins, and Autonomous Systems. This integration improves efficiency and personalization, but also opens up significant cyber-physical risks. Cybersecurity is now a key pillar of safety, operational continuity, and economic trust, demanding a shift from traditional perimeter-based defenses to adaptive, intelligence-driven, and resilient architectures. Security success is measured from data protection as well as physical safety, with the application of AI for threat detection, resilient architecture design, and data integrity mechanisms such as Blockchain.

To maintain the evolution of this ecosystem, it is recommended the implementation of advanced defense architectures (Zero-Trust, resilient design, quantum cryptography), enhanced intelligence and compliance (Explainable AI, Federated Learning, modernization of legacy systems), as well as cross-sector collaboration and global standardization (ISACs, unified cyber standards). With this strategy, the transportation industry can protect future digital travel while strengthening tourist confidence in the Smart Tourism era.

REFERENCES

Aburasain, R. Y. (2025). Enhanced congestion prediction of traffic flow using a hybrid attention-based deep learning model. *PeerJ. Computer Science, 11*, e3224. Advance online publication. DOI: 10.7717/peerj-cs.3224

Achenef, T. B., Abera, S. N., Admas, Y. A., & Tegegne, S. Z. (2025). Latest breakthroughs, research results, and challenges in intelligent control of autonomous vehicles. *Proceedings of the Institution of Mechanical Engineers, Part D: Journal of Automobile Engineering*. DOI: 10.1177/09544070251327616

Ahmad, M. W., & Akram, M. U. (2024). UAV sensor failures dataset: Biomisa arducopter sensory critique (BASiC). *Data in Brief, 52*, 110069. Advance online publication. DOI: 10.1016/j.dib.2024.110069 PMID: 38304386

Aljabri, J. (2025). Attack resilient IoT security framework using multi head attention based representation learning with improved white shark optimization algorithm. *Scientific Reports, 15*(1), 14255. Advance online publication. DOI: 10.1038/s41598-025-98180-z PMID: 40274990

Alkarim, A. S., Al-Malaise Al-Ghamdi, A. S., & Ragab, M. (2023). THE INTERNET OF VEHICLES (IOV) TECHNOLOGY: CHALLENGES AND SOLUTIONS. *Journal of Theoretical and Applied Information Technology, 101*(23), 7629–7639. https://www.scopus.com/inward/record.uri?eid=2-s2.0-85180332256&partnerID=40&md5=b0335fa1fb631f3b1213fd4b25132810

Alqahtani, H., & Kumar, G. (2024). Cybersecurity in Electric and Flying Vehicles: Threats, Challenges, AI Solutions & Future Directions. *ACM Computing Surveys, 57*(4), 1–34. Advance online publication. DOI: 10.1145/3697830

Alshammari, F., & Alsaleh, A. (2025). Smart intrusion detection model to identify unknown attacks for improved road safety and management. *Scientific Reports, 15*(1), 18584. Advance online publication. DOI: 10.1038/s41598-025-03604-5 PMID: 40425772

Apolinário, F., Escravana, N., Hervé, É., Pardal, M. L., & Correia, M. (2024). FingerCI: Writing industrial process specifications from network traffic. *International Journal of Critical Infrastructure Protection, 47*, 100725. Advance online publication. DOI: 10.1016/j.ijcip.2024.100725

Appajosyula, K. (2024). Ethernet-Based IDS for Zonal Architecture. *SAE Technical Papers*. DOI: 10.4271/2024-28-0121

Arumugam, S., & Stomp, F. (2024). OPTIMIZING AUTONOMOUS VEHICLE PATH PLANNING USING REINFORCEMENT LEARNING AND DYNAMIC MAPPING. *International Journal Of Advances In Signal And Image Sciences, 10*(2), 58–68. DOI: 10.29284/IJASIS.10.2.2024.58-68

Awotunde, J. B., Imoize, A. L., Adeniyi, A. E., Falola, P. B., Srinivasan, K., Chauhan, G. S., & Jadon, R. (2025). Security and privacy concerns and risks in modern cyber-physical systems. In *Security and Privacy of Cyber-physical Systems* (pp. 323–378). Emerging Trends, Technologies, and Applications., https://www.scopus.com/inward/record.uri?eid=2-s2.0-105014299708&partnerID=40&md5=b2f9460b795738d808a7805f7f0a8faa DOI: 10.1201/9788743801306-11

Banotra, A., Ghose, S., Mishra, D., & Modem, S. (2023). Energy harvesting in self-sustainable IoT devices and applications based on cross-layer architecture design: A survey. *Computer Networks, 236*, 110011. Advance online publication. DOI: 10.1016/j.comnet.2023.110011

Bautista-Hernández, J., & Martín-Prats, M. Á. (2023). The Impact of Data Injection on Predictive Algorithm Developed within Electrical Manufacturing Engineering in the Context of Aerospace Cybersecurity. *Aerospace (Basel, Switzerland), 10*(12), 984. Advance online publication. DOI: 10.3390/aerospace10120984

Brahmi, Z., Mezni, H., Elmannai, H., & Alkanhel, R. (2025). Multi-Modal Vaas Selection in Smart Mobility Networks via Spectral Hyper-Graph Clustering and Quantum-Driven Optimization. *Concurrency and Computation, 37*(23–24), e70260. Advance online publication. DOI: 10.1002/cpe.70260

Casaril, F., & Galletta, L. (2025). Developing security metrics for space systems: A study considering the NIST Cybersecurity Framework 2.0 and the NIS2. *International Journal of Critical Infrastructure Protection, 51*, 100805. Advance online publication. DOI: 10.1016/j.ijcip.2025.100805

Chen, X., Peng, J., Jiang, L., Cheng, J., & Wu, S. (2026). Defense against multi-path attacks on EV charging networks: A dependency chain analysis and DQN-BASED SOLUTION. *Multimodal Transportation, 5*(1), 100254. Advance online publication. DOI: 10.1016/j.multra.2025.100254

Clavijo Mesa, M. V., Patino-Rodriguez, C. E., & Guevara Carazas, F. J. (2024). Cybersecurity at Sea: A Literature Review of Cyber-Attack Impacts and Defenses in Maritime Supply Chains. *Information (Basel), 15*(11), 710. Advance online publication. DOI: 10.3390/info15110710

Cveticanin, L., Luzanin, O., & Ninkov, I. (2023). PRIVACY AND PERSONAL DATA PROTECTION IN SELF-DRIVING CAR: SUGGESTION FOR LEGAL REGULATION IN SERBIA. *Balkan Social Science Review*, *22*(22), 171–189. DOI: 10.46763/BSSR2322171c

Dai, W., Lipps, C., & Schotten, H. (2025). Integrating Reconfigurable Intelligent Surfaces into Next-Generation Mobile Networks: Comparative Simulations Based on Simu5G. *European Conference on Information Warfare and Security, ECCWS*, 94–104. DOI: 10.34190/eccws.24.1.3582

Du, J., Li, J., Cheng, Q., Zhu, X., Yin, J., & Zhang, W. (2025). A Multi-objective Dynamic Gate Assignment Method Integrating Economy and Robustness. *Jiaotong Yunshu Xitong Gongcheng Yu Xinxi. Journal of Transportation Systems Engineering and Information Technology*, *25*(4), 326–336. DOI: 10.16097/j.cnki.1009-6744.2025.04.030

Duvvur, V. (2024). Modernizing Government IT Systems: A Case Study on Enhancing Operational Efficiency and Data Integrity. *International Journal of Computational and Experimental Science and Engineering*, *11*(1), 1165–1175. DOI: 10.22399/ijcesen.1193

El-Hoshoudy, A. (2024). Application of artificial intelligence and federated learning in petroleum processing. In *Artificial Intelligence Using Federated Learning* (pp. 134–155). Fundamentals, Challenges, and Applications., DOI: 10.1201/9781003482000-8

Eshagh, M. (2023). Optimal Configuration for Monitoring Stations in a Wireless Localisation Network Based on Received Signal Strength Differences. *Sensors (Basel)*, *23*(3), 1150. Advance online publication. DOI: 10.3390/s23031150 PMID: 36772189

Fahad, M., Zhang, T., Khan, S. U., Albanyan, A., Siddiqui, F., Iqbal, Y., Zhao, X., & Geng, Y. (2024). Optimizing dual energy X-ray image enhancement using a novel hybrid fusion method. *Journal of X-Ray Science and Technology*, *32*(6), 1553–1570. DOI: 10.3233/XST-240227 PMID: 39729441

Fauzel, S., Tandrayen-Ragoobur, V., & Matadeen, S. J. (2024). A LITERATURE SURVEY OF TECHNOLOGICAL DISRUPTIONS IN THE SERVICE SECTOR. *Review of Management Literature*, *3*, 185–202. DOI: 10.1108/S2754-586520240000003010

Gaie, C., Karpiuk, M. A., & Strizzolo, N. (2024). Cybersecurity of Public Sector Institutions. *Prawo i Wiez*, *53*(6), 347–362. DOI: 10.36128/PRIW.VI53.1129

Hasan, M. R., Sarkar, N. I., Alani, N. H. S., & Lutui, R. (2025). Cyber Edge: Current State of Cybersecurity in Aotearoa-New Zealand, Opportunities, and Challenges. *Electronics (Basel), 14*(14), 2915. Advance online publication. DOI: 10.3390/electronics14142915

Horvath, G. (2023). Securing the Digital Sky: A scenario-driven study on the enhancement of cybersecurity in location-independent aerodrome control systems. *NTAD 2023 - New Trends in Aviation Development 2023: 18th International Scientific Conference - Proceedings*, 112–116. DOI: 10.1109/NTAD61230.2023.10380135

Juang, J.-C., Chen, Y.-T., & Chua, C.-K. (2023). Inter-Satellite and Inter-Receiver Aiding in the Verification of OSNMA. *Proceedings of the 36th International Technical Meeting of the Satellite Division of the Institute of Navigation, ION GNSS+ 2023*, 483–494. DOI: 10.33012/2023.19214

Khan, S. K., Shiwakoti, N., Diro, A., Molla, A., Gondal, I., & Warren, M. (2024). Space cybersecurity challenges, mitigation techniques, anticipated readiness, and future directions. *International Journal of Critical Infrastructure Protection, 47*, 100724. Advance online publication. DOI: 10.1016/j.ijcip.2024.100724

Ksouri, C., Jemili, I., Mosbah, M., & Belghith, A. (2020). A Unified Smart Mobility System Integrating Terrestrial, Aerial and Marine Intelligent Vehicles. *Lecture Notes in Computer Science (Including Subseries Lecture Notes in Artificial Intelligence and Lecture Notes in Bioinformatics), 12574 LNCS*, 203–214. DOI: 10.1007/978-3-030-66030-7_18

Lagdami, K., Dalaklis, D., & Christodoulou, A. (2024). New Technologies in Small and Medium-sized Ports: Its Impacts on the Future of Work. *Journal for Maritime Research, 21*(3), 150–156. https://www.scopus.com/inward/record.uri?eid=2-s2.0-85215111117&partnerID=40&md5=f2a64e158869099497417a987a18487b

Li, K., Lee, J.-Y., & Gharehgozli, A. (2024). Blockchain implementation in the maritime industry: A literature review and synthesis analysis of benefits and challenges. *Maritime Economics & Logistics, 26*(4), 630–657. DOI: 10.1057/s41278-023-00280-y

Liao, H.-T., Lo, T.-M., & Pan, C.-L. (2023). Knowledge Mapping Analysis of Intelligent Ports: Research Facing Global Value Chain Challenges. *Systems, 11*(2), 88. Advance online publication. DOI: 10.3390/systems11020088

Liapi, F., Chater, A. M., Randhawa, G., Stephenson, A., & Pappas, Y. (2025). Factors that influence inter-organisational integration: A qualitative exploration of service providers' perspectives from an integrated care initiative. *BMC Health Services Research*, *25*(1), 947. Advance online publication. DOI: 10.1186/s12913-025-13051-7 PMID: 40640843

Liu, Y., Li, Y., Guo, F., Liu, Z., & Song, X. (2024). Research on Zero-Trust Dynamic Access Control Model Based on User Behavior in Internet of Things Environment. *ACM International Conference Proceeding Series*, 402–407. DOI: 10.1145/3703187.3703255

Mishra, D., Das, S., & Patnaik, R. (2024). Application of AI Technology for the Development of Destination Tourism towards an Intelligent Information System. *Economic Affairs (New Delhi)*, *69*(2), 1083–1095. DOI: 10.46852/0424-2513.3.2024.31

Moussaoui, M., Rachid, A., & Rajpoot, S. (2024). Digital water transformation: Technologies, opportunities, and challenges. In *Emerging Trends and Technologies in Water Management and Conservation* (pp. 203–239). DOI: 10.4018/979-8-3693-6920-3.ch007

Mukherjee, A. (2024). The Complete Guide to Defense in Depth: Learn to identify, mitigate, and prevent cyber threats with a dynamic, layered defense approach. In *The Complete Guide to Defense in Depth: Learn to Identify, Mitigate, and Prevent Cyber Threats with a Dynamic, Layered Defense Approach*. https://www.scopus.com/inward/record.uri?eid=2-s2.0-105023800624&partnerID=40&md5=672db408ebbc449ef3810200fa085968

Ren, H., Sun, J., Chen, C.-K., Zhao, Y., & Yang, L. (2024). LTV-MPC-based Real-time and Anti-noise Motion Control for High-speed Vehicle. *Binggong Xuebao. Acta Armamentarii Sinica*, *45*(12), 4311–4322. DOI: 10.12382/bgxb.2023.0979

Salama, G. M., El-Shafai, W., El-Gazar, S., Omar, B., Hassan, A. A., Hussein, A. I., & Abd El-Samie, F. E. (2023). Efficient implementation of double random phase encoding and empirical mode decomposition for cancelable biometrics. *Optical and Quantum Electronics*, *55*(14), 1210. Advance online publication. DOI: 10.1007/s11082-023-05005-2

Salek, M. S., Chowdhury, M., Munir, M. B., Cai, Y., Hasan, M. I., Tine, J.-M., Khan, L., & Rahman, M. (2025). A Large Language Model-Supported Threat Modeling Framework for Transportation Cyber-Physical Systems. *IEEE Access : Practical Innovations, Open Solutions*, *13*, 163046–163070. DOI: 10.1109/ACCESS.2025.3603580

Salem, M., Samara, K., & Al-Tamimi, A.-K. (2024). Navigating Challenges in Online Cybersecurity Education: Insights from Postgraduate Students and Prospects for a Standardized Framework. *ACM Transactions on Computing Education*, *24*(4), 1–32. Advance online publication. DOI: 10.1145/3703163

Shanthalakshmi, M., & Ponmagal, R. S. (2024a). An intelligent dynamic cyber physical system threat detection system for ensuring secured communication in 6G autonomous vehicle networks. *Scientific Reports*, *14*(1). Advance online publication. DOI: 10.1038/s41598-025-85424-1 PMID: 39814782

Shanthalakshmi, M., & Ponmagal, R. S. (2024b). An Intelligent Intrusion Detection System for VANETs Using Adaptive Fusion Models. *International Journal of Computational and Experimental Science and Engineering*, *11*(1), 749–755. DOI: 10.22399/ijcesen.935

Shumilova, K., Shumilov, D., & Maltsev, A. (2024). Classification of Cyber Risks for Sea Vessel's Voyage Cycle. *Transactions on Maritime Science*, *13*(1). Advance online publication. DOI: 10.7225/toms.v13.n01.w20

Syta, J. (2024). CHALLENGES IN PROVIDING CYBERSECURITY TO PORT AND MARITIME INFRASTRUCTURE FACILITIES. *Geographic Information Systems Odyssey Journal*, *4*(1), 131–144. DOI: 10.57599/gisoj.2024.4.1.131

Tanimu, M. G. (2024). Assessing the Impact of Taxpoynt Platform on Small Business Tax Compliance through Digitization. *ACM International Conference Proceeding Series*, 378–380. DOI: 10.1145/3680127.3680143

Tsiktsiris, D., Lalas, A., Dasygenis, M., & Votis, K. (2024). Enhancing the Safety of Autonomous Vehicles: Semi-Supervised Anomaly Detection With Overhead Fisheye Perspective. *IEEE Access : Practical Innovations, Open Solutions*, *12*, 68905–68915. DOI: 10.1109/ACCESS.2024.3399841

Wang, B., Luo, P., Yang, Y., Zhao, Z., Dong, R., & Guan, Y. (2025). A Review and Prospect of Cybersecurity Research on Air Traffic Management Systems. *Dianzi Yu Xinxi Xuebao. Dianzi Yu Xinxi Xuebao*, *47*(5), 1230–1265. DOI: 10.11999/JEIT240966

Xiao, G., Yao, Z., Zhang, S., & Jiang, Y. (2024). Cooperative eco-driving for mixed platoons at signalized intersections with wireless charging lanes. *Energy*, *313*, 134118. Advance online publication. DOI: 10.1016/j.energy.2024.134118

Xu, Y., Li, G., Deng, G., Qiu, H., Han, X., & Zhang, T. (2024). PhyScout: Detecting Sensor Spoofing Attacks via Spatio-temporal Consistency. *CCS 2024 - Proceedings of the 2024 ACM SIGSAC Conference on Computer and Communications Security*, 1879–1893. DOI: 10.1145/3658644.3670290

Zhang, H., Dong, J., & Gao, Z. (2023). Automatic segmentation of airport pavement damage by AM-Mask R-CNN algorithm. *Engineering Reports*, *5*(8), e12628. Advance online publication. DOI: 10.1002/eng2.12628

Zhang, L. (2023). Artificial intelligence assisted cyber threat assessment and applications for the tourism industry. *Journal of Computer Virology and Hacking Techniques*, *19*(2), 199–215. DOI: 10.1007/s11416-022-00436-z

Zhang, M., Wang, C., Ren, T., & Li, J. (2025). STAR-RIS enabled covert integration of sensing communication and over-the-air computing with analysis and optimization. *Scientific Reports*, *15*(1), 19007. Advance online publication. DOI: 10.1038/s41598-025-04173-3 PMID: 40447702

Chapter 8
Integrating Cybersecurity and Digital Forensics for a Trusted Travel Ecosystem in Smart Tourism

Shivansu Sachan
http://orcid.org/0000-0002-9893-8018
CSJM University, India

Mohammad Badruddoza Talukder
http://orcid.org/0009-0008-1662-9221
International University of Business Agriculture and Technology, Bangladesh

Uday Pratap Singh
http://orcid.org/0000-0003-0632-9934
Amity University, Jaipur, India

Sanjeeb Pal
http://orcid.org/0000-0003-0567-9086
Amity University, Jaipur, India

Farhana Yeasmin Lina
http://orcid.org/0009-0006-8308-5549
Daffodil International University, Bangladesh

DOI: 10.4018/979-8-2600-1850-7.ch008

ABSTRACT

Smart tourism, powered by technologies like the Internet of Things (IoT), artificial intelligence (AI), and big data, has revolutionized the travel industry by enhancing personalization and efficiency. However, this digital ecosystem is vulnerable to cybersecurity threats such as data breaches, ransomware, and phishing, which erode trust among tourists and stakeholders. Integrating cybersecurity with digital forensics offers a robust approach to safeguarding data, ensuring privacy, and enabling effective incident response. This chapter examines the synergy between these disciplines, analyzing challenges, proposing a conceptual framework, and offering actionable recommendations to foster a trusted travel ecosystem. Through a comprehensive literature review and case-based findings, it highlights the critical role of proactive security measures and forensic readiness in smart tourism.

INTRODUCTION

Smart tourism has changed the travel industry into a digitally connected ecosystem that uses technology like IoT, AI, cloud computing, and mobile apps. These improvements make it possible to share data in real time, create personalized experiences, and improve business operations, which is good for tourists, businesses, and destinations. Smart tourism is at risk of major cyber security problems since it depends on networked technologies. These problems include data breaches, identity theft, and system outages. For example, a data breach at a multinational hotel chain in 2023 put millions of visitor details at risk, showing how important it is to have strong security procedures. Smart tourism is changing quickly thanks to technologies that connect people and things, like the Internet of Things (IoT), artificial intelligence (AI), and big data analytics. This has turned the travel sector into a dynamic, digital ecosystem. These improvements make travel more enjoyable and make operations run more smoothly, but they also pose serious cyber security concerns that might undermine confidence and safety. To solve these problems and make sure that the travel ecosystem is safe and strong, cyber security and digital forensics must work together. Cyber security alone can't solve these problems; digital forensics is needed to look into incidents, keep evidence, and make sure people are held accountable. By bringing these fields together, stakeholders can make a travel environment that is both safe and innovative. This chapter examines the amalgamation of cybersecurity and digital forensics within smart tourism, emphasizing issues, solutions, and prospective trajectories. It seeks to furnish a thorough resource for researchers, policymakers, and industry professionals. artificial intelligence (AI) combines cloud computing to make travel better, make operations more efficient, and encourage eco-friendly tourism. These technologies let tourists, tourism operators, and smart infrastructure communicate without any problems, get personalized services, and share data in real time. Smart tourist ecosystems are connected in a way that makes them very vulnerable to cyber attacks, such as data breaches, identity theft, and system weaknesses. To solve these problems, it's important to combine strong cyber security measures with digital forensics tools to provide a safe travel environment. This connection protects critical data, keeps travelers' trust, and lets quick responses to cyber events. This article examines the significance of cybersecurity and digital forensics in establishing a secure and dependable smart tourist ecosystem, focusing on essential problems, technologies, and tactics.

Goals

Objective 1: Find the Cyber Security Problems and Weaknesses in Smart Tourism Ecosystems

The first goal is to rigorously find the Cyber security problems and weaknesses that are common in smart tourism ecosystems. Smart tourism depends on a complicated web of technologies, such as IoT devices, cloud platforms, mobile apps, and AI-driven systems, that make the environment more connected (Gretzel et al., 2015). This interconnectedness makes things run smoothly, but it also makes the ecosystem vulnerable to dangers like data breaches, phishing, ransomware, and distributed denial-of-service (DDoS) assaults. Human factors also play a big role in making things vulnerable. Tourists and workers generally don't have

Objective 2: Look Into How Digital Forensics May Help With Investigations and Responses to Incidents

The second goal is to look into how digital forensics may help in investigating and responding to cyber problems in smart tourist ecosystems. Digital forensics is the scientific method of gathering, storing, analyzing, and presenting digital evidence in order to piece together cyber occurrences and help with legal cases (Casey, 2011). In smart tourism, where cyber incidents can cause problems and damage confidence, forensics is necessary for a good reaction to an incident. Digital forensics includes network forensics, mobile device forensics, and cloud forensics, all of which are important in the tourism industry. For instance, network forensics can look at traffic records to find out where a ransomware assault on a booking platform came from, and mobile forensics can get evidence from hacked tourist devices. In a 2024 ransomware assault on a tourism agency, forensic analysis found that an IoT device had been hacked and was used to carry out the attack, which made it possible to fix the problem quickly (Quick & Choo, 2018).

Objective 3: Examine the Interrelationship Between Cybersecurity and Digital Forensics in Establishing Trust

The third goal is to look at how Cyber security and digital forensics work together to build confidence in smart tourist ecosystems. Trust is a key part of tourism since it affects how happy tourists are, how loyal they are, and how well-known a place is. Cyber incidents, like data breaches or system outages, damage trust. To fix this, we need a comprehensive approach that includes both proactive Cyber security and reactive forensic capabilities (Ab Rahman & Choo, 2015). Cyber security aims to stop attacks by using encryption, multi-factor authentication (MFA), and intrusion detection systems (IDS). These steps make the attack surface smaller and lower the chances of an event happening. Digital forensics, on the other hand, deals with events after they happen, allowing for quick response, evidence collecting, and recovery. Together, they make a strong defense system: cyber security stops and scares off attacks, while forensics looks into them and fixes them. Their complimentary functions show how well they work together. For example, security information and event management (SIEM) systems are cyber security tools that make logs that forensic investigators use to find intrusions. Forensic insights, in turn, inform

Objective 4: Put out a Conceptual Framework for Bringing These Fields Together

The fourth goal is to come up with a conceptual framework for combining Cyber security and digital forensics in smart tourism. The literature indicates a necessity for organized methodologies to integrate various fields; nevertheless, limited frameworks expressly target the tourism sector (Garfinkel, 2010). This objective seeks to address the existing deficiency by creating a framework that assists stakeholders in executing integrated security and forensic strategies. The suggested framework is organized into four foundational pillars: Prevention, Detection, Response, and Recovery. Preventing cyber attacks means taking steps ahead of time, like security-by-design, standards, and training. Detection uses systems that monitor things in real time, such IDS and AI-driven anomaly detection, to find dangers early. Response uses forensic preparation, incident response plans, and working together with stakeholders to control and look into incidents. Forensic insights are used in recovery to fix systems, look at what happened after an incident, and rebuild confidence.

Objective 5: Give Stakeholders Useful Advice on How to Improve Security and Resilience

The final goal is to give stakeholders useful advice on how to make smart tourist ecosystems safer and more resilient. Recommendations connect theoretical knowledge with real-world application, providing direction for tourism enterprises, governmental bodies, technology suppliers, and travelers.

THE SMART TOURISM ECOSYSTEM

Smart tourism is the use of cutting-edge technologies to build a smart, linked travel environment that improves efficiency, customisation, and sustainability. Smart destinations are cities or areas with integrated tech infrastructure. Smart services are personalized travel recommendations, mobile apps, and digital ticketing. Smart infrastructure includes IoT-enabled devices, sensors, and networks. For instance, smart tourism apps let people book flights, hotels, and activities all in one place. IoT devices like smart kiosks help people find their way around or manage crowds at popular tourist spots. This ecosystem depends on a lot of data, such as personal information (like names, payment information, and travel preferences), location data, and behavioral patterns. Airlines, hotels, tour operators, and government agencies all share data through networks that are connected to each other. This interconnectedness makes things easier, but it also makes them less safe. Cyberattacks including phishing, ransomware, and Distributed Denial of Service (DDoS) attacks can stop services, steal data, and damage confidence. Also, because tourism is worldwide, cyber attacks can cross borders, which makes it hard to respond to incidents and figure out who is responsible. So, a safe travel ecosystem needs strong cyber security systems and digital forensics to protect data and make sure people are held accountable.

CYBERSECURITY IN SMART TOURISM

The Importance of Cyber Security

Cybersecurity is what makes a smart tourist environment safe and reliable. It means keeping systems, networks, and data safe from attacks, unlawful access, or damage. Cybersecurity protects the confidentiality, integrity, and availability (CIA trinity) of data and services in smart tourism. Confidentiality safeguards travelers' personal and financial data, integrity guarantees the accuracy and authenticity of information (such as booking details or navigation data), and availability ensures continuous access to services like online bookings or real-time navigation. The repercussions of insufficient cyber security are dire. A data breach that exposes passengers' personal information can cause tourism operators to lose money, harm their reputations, and steal their identities. A big hotel chain had a data breach in 2018 that exposed the personal information of millions of guests. This cost them a lot of money and made people lose faith in them.

Important Cybersecurity Issues

There are a lot of cyber security problems that the smart tourism ecosystem has to deal with:

1. Smart tourism uses a lot of different technologies, such as IoT devices, mobile apps, cloud platforms, and older systems. This diversity gives attackers several ways to get in, since each part may have its own weaknesses.
2. Data Privacy: People who travel create a lot of private information, such as their passport numbers, payment information, and location data. Following data protection laws like the General Data Protection Regulation (GDPR) or the California Consumer Privacy Act (CCPA) is very important, but it can be hard to do, especially when dealing with people from other countries.
3. IoT Vulnerabilities: Smart kiosks and linked cars are examples of IoT devices that are generally short on resources and don't have strong security measures. This makes them easy targets for attacks like data interception or device hijacking.
4. Human Factors: Travelers and tourism workers may not know much about cyber security, which makes them easy targets for phishing attempts and social engineering.
5. Risks in the supply chain: The tourism ecosystem has many players, such as third-party vendors who provide booking platforms, payment gateways, or smart infrastructure. One weak link in the supply chain can bring down the whole system.

Strategies for Cyber Security

To deal with these problems, smart tourism ecosystems need to use full Cyber security strategies:

1. Encryption and Secure Communication: Encrypting data while it is being sent and stored keeps it safe from being intercepted. Transport Layer Security (TLS)

can protect connections between mobile apps and servers, while end-to-end encryption can protect the data of travelers.

2. Access Control and Authentication: Strong authentication methods, including multi-factor authentication (MFA), make sure that only people who are allowed to use sensitive systems can do so. Role-based access control (RBAC) can limit data access to only the people who need it, which lowers the danger of insider attacks.
3. 3. IoT Security: To protect IoT devices, use lightweight cryptographic protocols, keep the firmware up to date, and separate the network so that compromised devices can't talk to each other. For example, a smart kiosk at a tourist spot can be set up to work on its own network to limit the damage caused by a breach.
4. Threat Detection and Response: Real-time monitoring with intrusion detection systems (IDS) and security information and event management (SIEM) solutions can quickly find and stop threats. AI-powered anomaly detection can find strange activity, such attempts to get into a system without permission or data flows that aren't regular.
5. Cyber Security Awareness: Training programs for tourists and tourism staff can make them less vulnerable. Teaching passengers about phishing scams or how to use Wi-Fi safely can stop data leaks, for example.
6. Regulatory Compliance: Following data protection rules makes sure that tourist companies handle data in a responsible way. Regular audits and compliance checks might find holes in how Cyber security is done.

Digital Forensics in Smart Travel

What Digital Forensics Does

Digital forensics is the process of finding, keeping, analyzing, and showing digital evidence in order to look into cyber occurrences. Digital forensics is very important in smart tourism since it helps respond to cyberattacks, figure out who is to blame, and stop them from happening again. Digital forensics can help find the attack vector, get back lost data, and give proof for legal cases if, for example, a smart tourism platform has a data breach.

Important Problems in Digital Forensics

Digital forensics in smart tourism has its own set of problems:

1. Data Volume and Variety: The smart tourism ecosystem produces a lot of different types of data via IoT devices, mobile apps, and cloud platforms. To get useful information from this data, you need advanced tools and knowledge.
2. Distributed Systems: It can be hard to collect evidence when tourism data is held on several servers, cloud platforms, and devices. For example, a cyberattack might comprise an IoT device that has been hacked in one country and a server in another, which would require collaboration across several jurisdictions.
3. Data volatility: It's easy to change or remove digital evidence, like logs or temporary files, especially on IoT devices with limited storage. To keep evidence, you need to act quickly.
4. Legal and Ethical Issues: When gathering and evaluating digital evidence, you must follow privacy laws and ethical standards. For instance, getting a traveler's location data without their permission could break GDPR.
5. Attribution: Finding out who did a cyberattack is hard, especially when the people behind it are skilled and use methods like IP spoofing or anonymization.

Digital Forensics Plans

Smart tourism ecosystems can use the following digital forensics methods to get around these problems:

1. Proactive Evidence Collection: By putting logging systems in place across all systems, you make sure that important data (such access logs and transaction records) is available for forensic examination. A smart tourist app, for instance, can keep track of how users engage with it and save that information safely for later use.
2. Chain of Custody: Keeping a clear chain of custody for digital evidence makes sure that it may be used in court. This means keeping track of how evidence was collected, stored, and analyzed to show that it hasn't been changed.
3. Forensic Tools and Techniques: Advanced tools like EnCase or Autopsy may look at data from a wide range of sources, such as IoT devices and cloud servers. Memory forensics and network traffic analysis are two examples of techniques that can find concealed attack patterns.
4. Cross-Border Collaboration: Because tourism is a global business, forensic investigators need to work with law enforcement authorities from other countries to deal with incidents that happen in more than one jurisdiction. MLATs, or mutual legal aid treaties, can make it easier to share evidence.
5. AI and Automation: Forensic tools that use AI can swiftly look through enormous datasets and find patterns or strange things that could imply a cyberattack. For

example, machine learning algorithms can find strange login attempts or data theft.

COMBINING CYBER SECURITY WITH DIGITAL FORENSICS

A Whole-Person Approach

Combining cyber security and digital forensics makes a complete security system for smart tourism. Digital forensics helps with quick response and recovery after an occurrence, whereas cyber security stops and reduces risks. They work together to make sure that travel is safe by safeguarding data, keeping services available, and bringing bad actors accountable.

To make this integration work, all three areas—technical, organizational, and legal—need to be in sync:

1. Technical Integration: Cyber security and forensic instruments need to work together without any problems. For instance, SIEM systems can provide data to forensic platforms, which lets you look at incidents in real time. Secure logging systems can also help find threats and gather evidence.
2. Collaboration between organizations: Cybersecurity teams, tourism businesses, and forensic investigators need to work together closely. For example, a hotel chain could set up a security operations center (SOC) that combines cyber security monitoring with forensic tools to quickly deal with problems.
3. Legal and Regulatory Alignment: Cybersecurity policies and forensic procedures must follow the rules on protecting personal data. GDPR, for instance, says that companies must report data breaches within 72 hours. This means that forensic systems must be quick and accurate to find and record occurrences.

REVIEW OF THE LITERATURE

Smart tourism has changed the travel industry by using information and communication technologies (ICTs) to improve travelers' experiences, make destination management more efficient, and make operations run more smoothly. The Internet of Things (IoT), artificial intelligence (AI), big data analytics, and cloud computing are all examples of technologies that have built ecosystems that are connected and provide personalized services and real-time data-driven insights. This digital transition has created major Cyber security problems, such as data breaches, phishing, and ransomware, that put the safety and confidence of tourists and other stakeholders at risk. To reduce these dangers, cyber security and digital forensics must be combined. This means that proactive prevention and reactive investigation and recovery are both possible.

The Development of Smart Tourism

Smart tourism is a new way of doing things in the travel industry. It uses modern ICTs to make things better for travelers, businesses, and destinations (Gretzel et al., 2015). There are three main parts to it: smart locations, smart experiences, and smart business ecosystems. All of these parts are connected by digital platforms. Smart destinations use technology to improve infrastructure and sustainability. Smart experiences offer individualized services, and smart business ecosystems encourage collaboration amongst stakeholders (Buhalis & Amaranggana, 2015).

AI-powered systems like chatbots and recommendation engines look at what users like to suggest personalized itineraries, which makes the experience more personal (Tussyadiah, 2017). Big data analytics uses huge amounts of data from social media, booking sites, and IoT devices to learn about how tourists act and make decisions based on that information (Xiang et al., 2015). Cloud computing enables scalable storage and processing, ensuring seamless access for stakeholders. Mobile applications serve as the key interface for tourists, providing services such as digital tickets and augmented reality (AR) guides (Law et al., 2018).

Smart tourism has changed over time because of the need for more competition, sustainability, and happy tourists. Smart destinations like Singapore and Dubai have used IoT and AI to improve the flow of tourists and lessen their impact on the environment (Gretzel et al., 2016). In, the use of networked technologies creates Cyber security threats, so strong security measures are needed to keep confidence and functionality.

Problems With Cyber Security in Smart Tourism

The fact that smart tourism systems are all connected makes them a complicated attack surface that is open to many cyber security threats. Studies show that data breaches, phishing, ransomware, distributed denial-of-service (DDoS) assaults, and IoT exploits are common risks (Buhalis & Amaranggana, 2015; Kshetri, 2023). Data breaches, which happen when someone gets into sensitive information like trip plans, credit card numbers, and passports without permission, are very harmful. For instance, a data breach at a global hotel chain in 2023 put the personal information of 10 million guests at risk, which had serious financial and reputational effects (Kshetri, 2023). IoT devices, which are important for smart tourism, are especially vulnerable because they have weak encryption, unpatched firmware, or insecure settings. For example, hacked smart locks in hotels can let attackers into the building, and hacked sensors can mess with airport operations (Li et al., 2017). Heterogeneous systems that use technologies from different suppliers might cause compatibility problems and security holes because vendors may put functionality ahead of security (Conti et al., 2018). The absence of universal cybersecurity standards exacerbates vulnerabilities, as firms implement inconsistent procedures, hence exposing systems (Hsu & Lin, 2016).

Human factors are a big part of the problems with cyber security. Tourists frequently utilize insecure public Wi-Fi, heightening the risk of data interception, while staff may be uninformed about phishing strategies (Tussyadiah & Wang, 2016). Many tourism companies still use legacy systems that aren't up to date or have strong security features, which makes them vulnerable to new dangers (Navarro & Buhalis, 2024). These problems show how important it is to have strong Cyber security plans to keep smart tourist ecosystems safe.

The Function of Digital Forensics in Intelligent Tourism

Digital forensics is the scientific way to gather, keep, study, and show digital evidence in order to look into cyber occurrences (Casey, 2011). Digital forensics is particularly important for smart tourism since it helps with recovery, holds people accountable, and helps with cyber issues. It includes sub-disciplines including network forensics, mobile device forensics, cloud forensics, and IoT forensics, each of which looks at a different part of the tourism ecosystem (Quick & Choo, 2018).

Network forensics looks at traffic logs to find the source of an attack, like finding a hacked server in a hotel data breach. Mobile device forensics takes evidence from smartphones, which visitors use to plan trips and find their way about, to put together timelines of events (Casey, 2011). Cloud forensics helps with problems that come up when looking into data that is stored on remote servers. IoT forensics, on the other hand, looks at data from devices that are linked to the internet, including smart sensors (Conti et al., 2018). For instance, a 2024 ransomware assault on a travel agency was traced back to a hacked IoT device by forensic analysis, which made it possible to fix the problem quickly (Quick & Choo, 2018).

Digital forensics has many uses in smart tourism:

- Incident Tracing: Forensic tools put together the pieces of an attack, showing where and how attackers got in.
- Evidence Preservation: Following the right chain-of-custody steps makes sure that evidence may be used in court, which is very important for going after cybercriminals.

- Attribution: Forensics helps law enforcement figure out who is behind attacks, even if it is hard because of encryption and anonymization.
- Recovery Support: Forensic insights help restore systems by finding and fixing security holes, which stops them from happening again.

Digital forensics has a lot of problems to deal with in smart tourism. IoT devices and cloud platforms make it hard to analyze large amounts of data since they require advanced tools and knowledge (Quick & Choo, 2018). Attackers use encryption and anonymization methods to hide evidence, making it harder to figure out who did it (Garfinkel, 2010). Cross-border tourism operations cause jurisdictional problems, as legal frameworks vary across nations, affecting evidence collection and prosecution (Ab Rahman & Choo, 2015). Also, the tourism industry doesn't have enough skilled forensic professionals, which makes it harder to respond to incidents (Navarro & Buhalis, 2024).

Combining Digital Forensics and Cyber Security

Combining cyber security and digital forensics makes a stronger defense system that includes both proactive prevention and reactive investigation and recovery. Encryption, multi-factor authentication (MFA), intrusion detection systems (IDS), and security information and event management (SIEM) technologies are all examples of cyber security methods that try to stop assaults (Garfinkel, 2010). These steps make the attack surface smaller and lower the risks before something bad happens. Digital forensics, on the other hand, deals with events after they happen, allowing for quick responses, evidence gathering, and system recovery (Casey, 2011).

The synergy between these disciplines is obvious in their complementary responsibilities. Cyber security tools make records and warnings that forensic investigators use to discover attacks. Forensic findings help Cyber security get better by fixing security holes or changing access controls (Ab Rahman & Choo, 2015). For example, SIEM systems find strange things happening in real time, which starts forensic investigations to figure out how big and bad the incidents were. This process of repeating steps makes the system more resilient and less likely to happen again. For effective integration, it is important for stakeholders to work together. To fully deal with cyber threats, tourism businesses, IT companies, governments, and law enforcement must exchange information and resources (Hsu & Lin, 2016). For seamless integration, systems that are equipped for forensics are necessary. These systems provide for logging, time synchronization, and safe evidence storage (Quick & Choo, 2018).

Shortcomings in Current Research

There are still certain gaps in the study on smart tourism, cyber security, and digital forensics, even if it is developing. First, although studies examine cybersecurity and forensics independently, there is a paucity of research investigating their integration within the unique framework of smart tourism (Kshetri, 2023). The distinctive attributes of tourist ecosystems, including transnational operations and varied stakeholder networks, necessitate customized strategies that current research inadequately addresses.

Second, there aren't many complete systems for bringing together cyber security and digital forensics in smart tourism. Current frameworks, including those suggested by Ab Rahman and Choo (2015), are too broad and don't take into account the tourism sector's unique problems, including IoT security holes or problems with jurisdiction. It is also important to create a framework that is relevant to tourism so that stakeholders can use integrated tactics.

Third, there isn't much research on new technologies in the tourism industry, like blockchain and AI-driven forensics. Although these technologies exhibit potential for improving security and investigative functions, their actual use and scalability are still inadequately examined (Li et al., 2017). Research has insufficiently addressed the ethical ramifications of data collecting and forensic investigations, especially concerning tourist privacy (Tussyadiah & Wang, 2016).

Fourth, there is not enough focus on the human issues that affect cyber security and forensics. Tourists and staff are frequently the most vulnerable component of the security chain; nevertheless, research on awareness training and behavioral interventions is scarce (Buhalis & Amaranggana, 2015). Finally, there aren't enough skilled cyber security and forensic professionals in the tourist industry, which is a big problem because small and medium-sized businesses (SMEs) generally don't have the money to hire experts (Navarro & Buhalis, 2024).

REVIEW OF THE LITERATURE

The following outlines important research on cyber security and digital forensics in the context of smart tourism. It highlights the focus, main findings, and gaps found in each study. This adds more information from the cited sources to the summary that was already in the original document.

Author(s), Year, Focus, Key Findings, and Gaps Found

Gretzel et al. (2015) Smart Tourism: Smart tourism is using ICTs (IoT, AI, big data) to make tourist experiences better, manage destinations better, and run operations more efficiently. Presents the idea of smart locations, experiences, and business ecosystems. There wasn't much talk about the concerns of cyber security, and digital forensics wasn't even mentioned. The main focus was on the benefits of technology.

Buhalis & Amaranggana 2015 Cyber Security in Smart tourist Talks about the biggest cyber security risks in smart tourist ecosystems, like data breaches, phishing, and ransomware. Stresses the need of individualized services and safeguarding data. Doesn't talk about digital forensics or how it fits in with cyber security; instead, it only talks about ways to stop problems from happening.

Casey 2011 Digital Forensics: This book talks on how to gather, keep, and analyze digital evidence. Stresses the need for chain of custody and forensic tools like EnCase while looking into an incident. The focus is too broad and not relevant to the tourism environment. There are no specific uses for smart tourism ecosystems.

Kshetri 2023 Cyber Security Challenges says that 60% of tourism companies don't have good cyber security policies, which makes them more likely to have data breaches and phishing attacks. Cites a breach in a hotel chain in 2023 that affected 10 million visitors. Limited examination of digital forensics integration, concentrating mostly on cyber security concerns and their consequences.

Quick & Choo 2018 Digital Forensics Challenges talks about the problems that come up in forensic investigation because of the large amount of data, encryption, and security holes in IoT devices. Advocates for forensic preparation to tackle these challenges. Not specifically focused on smart tourism, thus it has to be changed to deal with tourist-related data sources and cross-border difficulties.

Ab Rahman & Choo 2015 Integration of Cybersecurity and Forensics. They want technologies that are ready for forensic use to improve how quickly incidents are handled. Stresses how important it is for cyber security (prevention) and forensics (investigation) to work together to keep everything safe. Not unique to smart tourism, this is a general framework that doesn't include concerns that are specific to tourist, including IoT vulnerabilities or problems with jurisdiction.

Li et al. 2017 Smart Tourism Technologies looks at how IoT and AI can be used in smart tourism to make travel easier and more efficient. Examples include luggage trackers and recommendation engines. Not much attention is paid to cyber security, and there is no talk of digital forensics, which ignores the security risks of IoT and AI.

Conti et al. (2018) IoT Security and Forensics examines IoT vulnerabilities, such as inadequate encryption and unpatched firmware, and its implications for forensic investigations. Suggests forensic methods that are specific to the Internet of Things

(IoT). General IoT focus, not tourism-specific, necessitating customization to cater to the distinctive ecology of smart tourism.

Hsu & Lin 2016 IoT Adoption and Security looks at how consumers use IoT services and the security risks that come with them. It stresses the necessity for standardized protocols to fix compatibility problems. There isn't much talk about digital forensics; most of the talk is about cyber security and how people utilize computers.

Navarro & Buhalis 2024 Cyber Security and Resilience talks about the problems and chances that smart tourism has with cyber security, such as ransomware and human aspects. Emphasizes resilience by getting stakeholders to work together. Not much focus on integrating digital forensics, and not much talk about being ready for forensic work or cross-border investigations.

Tussyadiah & Wang (2016) examine the influence of technology on tourism experiences, emphasizing issues such as unprotected Wi-Fi and insufficient user knowledge as cybersecurity concerns. No conversation about digital forensics; only user experience and cyber security issues are talked about.

This synthesis of the literature underscores the necessity for cohesive cyber security and digital forensics frameworks specifically designed for smart tourism, thereby addressing deficiencies in tourism-related research, developing technology, and human aspects.

A Full Analysis of the Smart Tourism Data Breach Case Study

Smart tourism uses cutting-edge technology like the Internet of Things (IoT), cloud computing, and mobile apps to make travel experiences that are smooth and tailored to each person. In, the fact that these systems are linked together makes them far more vulnerable to cyber attacks. This case study looks at a possible data breach that could happen to a smart tourism platform that combines IoT-enabled ticketing devices, a mobile app, and a cloud-based booking engine. The breach, which was found through reports of fraudulent transactions, puts tourists' personal information at risk. This shows how important it is to have integrated Cyber security and digital forensics solutions. This case study shows how cyber security, digital forensics, and integrated outcomes work together to reduce risks, look into incidents, and improve defenses, making sure that the travel ecosystem is safe.

A Look at the Scenario

The smart tourism platform is a complete system that makes it easier for travelers. It lets people book flights, hotels, and activities through a mobile app. It also employs IoT-enabled ticketing systems to let people in to attractions without any problems, and it stores data and processes transactions using a cloud-based booking engine. The platform stores sensitive data like names, passport numbers, payment information, and travel plans, which makes it a good target for hackers. The breach is discovered when many travelers report unauthorized transactions on their accounts, like fake bookings or charges. Early investigations show that hackers were able to get into the platform and steal personal information. The Cyber security and digital forensics teams on the platform respond right away to the occurrence. They work together to minimize the breach, find out where it came from, and rebuild confidence among stakeholders.

RESPONSE TO CYBER SECURITY

The main goal of the Cyber security team is to stop the breach, limit the damage, and stop more unauthorized access. Their answer comes in three main steps:

1. Activating the Incident Response Plan

When the Cyber security team finds a breach, they use a pre-made incident response plan (IRP). The IRP tells you how to isolate affected systems, let stakeholders know, and work together to fix the problem. The team quickly separates the affected parts, such the mobile app and the cloud servers that host the booking engine, to stop the attackers from getting more access. For instance, they stop people from using the booking engine's public APIs for a short time and limit staff access to internal systems. This containment plan lowers the risk while still allowing important tasks, like helping customers, to go on. The team isolates the compromised systems to make sure that the intrusion doesn't infect the whole IoT ecosystem, like ticketing systems at tourist destinations.

2. Finding the attack vector

The team uses intrusion detection systems (IDS) and security information and event management (SIEM) tools to figure out how the hack happened. These systems are always looking for strange behavior in network traffic and user activity logs. The intrusion came from a phishing email addressed to an employee, according to the analysis. The email looked like a real message from a trusted vendor, but it was really a fake one that misled the employee into giving their login information to a fake website. These stolen credentials let attackers get into the platform's internal systems, such as the booking engine. Phishing as the attack vector shows a frequent weakness in smart tourist ecosystems, where mistakes made by people might be the weakest link.

3. Encryption and access controls can help reduce the risk.

The platform's current cybersecurity safeguards are very important for keeping the incident from spreading. Encryption protects critical information, including payment information, even if hackers get to it. For example, the booking engine encrypts credit card numbers using Advanced Encryption Standard (AES-256), which makes them useless without the keys to decrypt them. Access restrictions like role-based access control (RBAC) also limit what employees can do, so even if their credentials are stolen, they won't be able to get complete access to the system. These steps cut down on the quantity of data that is available, which protects the personal information of most tourists and limits financial damages.

The Cyber security response shows how important it is to take preemptive steps like encryption, access controls, and real-time monitoring, along with a well-planned IRP, to stop and lessen the effects of cyber incidents.

RESPONSE TO DIGITAL FORENSICS

The digital forensics team does a full investigation to find out what caused the breach, collect evidence, and help with legal action. The cyber security team, on the other hand, focuses on containment and mitigation. There are three important steps in their answer:

1. Collecting and Keeping Evidence

Forensic investigators start by gathering digital evidence from the systems that were damaged, such as the booking engine, mobile app servers, and employee devices. To make sure that the evidence is correct, they use write-blockers, which are hardware or software techniques that stop changes to data while it is being collected. For instance, logs from the booking engine that keep track of user transactions and access attempts are sent to a secure forensic server. The server logs for the mobile app, which record user authentication events, are also kept. The investigators also get a forensic snapshot of the affected employee's device so they can look at the phishing email and its payload. This careful method makes sure that evidence is still usable in court by keeping a clear chain of custody.

2. Network Traffic Analysis

The forensic team uses tools like Wireshark or Splunk to look at network traffic to find out what the attackers did. They look at data packets sent between the platform's servers and outside networks to find strange trends. The study shows that the attackers sent stolen data to a server in another country, perhaps in a different jurisdiction. This discovery makes the investigation harder because it means working with authorities in other countries to find the server and the people who did it. The study of network traffic also shows how the attackers got in, including by using encrypted channels to avoid detection. This information is useful for preventing future attacks.

3. Finding the Source of Phishing Emails

The forensic team is looking at the phishing email that started the incident. They look at the email's headers and attachments to find out where it came from: a malicious domain that is registered anonymously. The email had a link to a phony login page that was made to steal login information, which shows how advanced the phishing attack was. The team takes metadata from the email and keeps it as proof in case they need to take legal action. They also find indicators of compromise (IOCs), including the bad domain and IP addresses, that can be shared with other groups to stop similar assaults from happening. This evidence supports working with the police to find the assailants and make them pay for what they did.

In a globalized smart tourist environment, the digital forensics reaction shows how important it is to collect evidence in a methodical way, use advanced analysis tools, and work together across borders to look into cyber events.

Outcome That is Integrated

Combining cyber security and digital forensics answers leads to a complete solution to the breach, dealing with immediate dangers, making defenses stronger, and restoring travelers' faith. There are three results:

SMART TOURISM HAS CYBER SECURITY HOLES

Smart tourism systems, which depend on networked technology, are very vulnerable to a number of cyber security flaws that threaten the integrity, confidentiality, and availability of important data and services. The literature has identified several vulnerabilities, which include data breaches, IoT attacks, ransomware, and human factors. Each of these poses a different set of problems for the smart tourist ecosystem.

Breaches of Data

This caused big financial losses, harm to the company's reputation, and legal trouble under privacy laws like the General Data Protection Regulation (GDPR) (Kshetri, 2023). Data breaches frequently take advantage of unpatched systems, poor authentication methods, or databases that aren't set up correctly. This shows how important it is to have strong Cyber security measures (Buhalis & Amaranggana, 2015).

Data breaches have effects that go beyond just losing money right away. They hurt people's trust in the brand, which leads to fewer bookings and long-term damage to the business. For example, affected businesses may have to deal with class-action lawsuits and fines from the government. For example, GDPR fines can reach millions of euros for not following the rules (Navarro & Buhalis, 2024). Because smart tourism technologies are all connected, the risk is higher. For example, if a third-party booking platform is hacked, it can affect many other parts of the system.

IoT Attacks

Smart tourism has a lot of IoT devices, such smart locks, sensors, and cameras, that are typically set up in ways that make them quite vulnerable. Cybercriminals often go after these devices, which are important for making travel easier and more efficient. For instance, hacked smart locks in hotels can let people in without permission, and hacked IoT sensors at airports can mess up passenger flows or give wrong information, which can cause havoc in operations (Li et al., 2017). In 2024, an IoT device in a smart tourism destination was hacked, showing how attackers used poor encryption to get into a hotel's reservation system. This showed how fragile IoT infrastructure may be (Quick & Choo, 2018).

Ransomware

Ransomware attacks, which encrypt important systems and ask for money to fix them, are a big threat to smart tourist operations. These attacks hit important parts of the system, like booking platforms, airline reservation systems, and hotel management software, which causes a lot of problems. A well-known case in 2024 featured a travel firm whose booking system was encrypted, which stopped thousands of consumers from being able to book trips and cost the company a lot of money and reputation (Navarro & Buhalis, 2024). Ransomware not only stops services from working, but it also forces businesses to pay up, with ransom demands regularly reaching millions of dollars.

Ransomware attacks are more likely to work if there are security holes in the system, including obsolete software, no endpoint protection, or not enough backup plans. Small and medium-sized businesses (SMEs) in the tourism industry are especially at risk since they don't have enough money or knowledge to protect themselves online (Hsu & Lin, 2016). Smart tourist systems are connected in such a way that ransomware can spread across networked parts, affecting many different groups of people. To stop and limit these kinds of assaults, effective mitigation needs strong backup systems, training for employees, and proactive threat detection.

Human Factors

Human factors are a big problem for smart tourism because tourists and staff typically don't know much about cyber security, which makes them easy targets for social engineering assaults like phishing. People often use public Wi-Fi networks at airports or hotels that aren't secure, which puts their devices at risk of having their data stolen (Tussyadiah & Wang, 2016). Employees may also fall for phishing emails that look like real booking confirmations, giving attackers access to key systems without meaning to. A study from 2023 indicated that 70% of successful cyberattacks in tourism were caused by human error, which shows how important it is to train people on how to be alert of cyber threats (Kshetri, 2023).

DIGITAL FORENSICS USES IN SMART TOURISM

Digital forensics is very important for dealing with cyber incidents in smart tourism because it gives investigators the tools and methods they need to look into, analyze, and respond to attacks. Forensic methods including log analysis, malware reverse-engineering, and network traffic analysis are particularly important for finding out what happened, keeping evidence, and helping with recovery.

Tracing the Incident

To find out how big and where a cyber assault came from, incident tracing means figuring out the attack vector and putting the history of the attack back together. Forensic tools look at log files, network traffic, and device data to find weaknesses that attackers can use in smart tourism. For instance, a hotel data breach in 2023 was tracked back to a compromised server running old software, which made it possible to fix the problem (Casey, 2011). Network forensics is very good at looking at traffic patterns to find illegal access. IoT forensics, on the other hand, looks at device logs to find flaws in smart locks or sensors (Conti et al., 2018).

To stop attacks from happening again, it's important to trace incidents. Organizations can take special steps to protect themselves by finding entry points like phishing emails or systems that haven't been patched. The complexity of smart tourism systems, which have many different data sources and parts that work together, makes it harder to trace things and requires extensive forensic techniques and knowledge.

Keeping Evidence Safe

It is very important to keep digital evidence safe with a correct chain of custody so that it can be used in court. In smart tourism, where cyber events may include cross-border jurisdictions, it is very important to keep evidence safe. Forensic investigators use standard methods to get and save data from devices, servers, and cloud platforms. This makes sure that the evidence is not changed (Quick & Choo, 2018). In a ransomware case from 2024, for example, saved data from an IoT device that had been hacked was utilized to help take legal action against the people who did it.

It is hard to keep evidence because digital data doesn't last long and attackers use encryption methods. Cloud-based solutions, which are widespread in smart tourism, make it further harder to gather evidence because data may be held in different places with different regulatory requirements (Ab Rahman & Choo, 2015). To get over these problems and make sure that investigations are done well, strong forensic readiness, which includes logging and safe storage, is necessary.

Help with Recovery

Digital forensics helps with recovery by showing what caused incidents and helping with system repair. Forensic analysis finds the weaknesses that attackers used, including unpatched software or weak authentication, so that businesses can fix them and stop them from happening again. Forensic investigators found that a hacked IoT device was the entry point in the 2024 travel agency ransomware instance. This let the agency isolate the device, recover systems from backups, and upgrade security policies (Navarro & Buhalis, 2024).

Recovery support also includes looking back at what happened to learn from it and make cyber security better. For instance, forensic findings may suggest using multi-factor authentication (MFA) or breaking up networks into smaller parts to stop attacks from spreading. Organizations can improve their resilience and win back the trust of their stakeholders by using forensic insights in their recovery plans.

THE COMBINED BENEFITS OF CYBER SECURITY AND DIGITAL FORENSICS

Cyber security and digital forensics work together to produce a stronger defense system that makes smart tourist ecosystems more resilient, allows for quick responses, and builds trust. This synergy is made possible by the fact that proactive cyber security measures and reactive forensic capabilities work well together.

Defense That is Proactive

Encryption, multi-factor authentication (MFA), intrusion detection systems (IDS), and security information and event management (SIEM) technologies are all examples of cyber security techniques that make the attack surface smaller. Encryption keeps sensitive information safe while it is being sent and stored, while MFA stops people from getting into systems by requiring more than one way to verify their identity (Garfinkel, 2010). IDS and SIEM systems check network traffic and system logs in real time to find any strange behavior that could mean an attack. For example, AI-powered anomaly detection can find strange login habits, which lets you act quickly (Hsu & Lin, 2016).

To stop problems before they happen and lower the chances of data breaches or ransomware attacks, proactive defense is essential. Organizations that use security-by-design principles make sure that systems are developed with strong security features from the start, which lowers the risk of vulnerabilities (Buhalis & Amaranggana, 2015). Standardized protocols, like ISO 27001, make proactive defense even better by giving everyone in the ecosystem a set of rules to follow for security.

The Ability to React

Digital forensics gives you the ability to react quickly to incidents, collect evidence, and get your system back up and running. Forensic tools look at logs, malware, and network traffic to figure out what happened, where it came from, and how bad it was (Casey, 2011). This skill is very important for stopping events and limiting damage. For instance, in a hotel breach in 2023, forensic analysis found that a phishing email was the way in, which let the company isolate stolen accounts and quickly tell affected guests.

Organizations can effectively look into occurrences if they are forensic-ready, which includes logging and time synchronization. Working with law enforcement and cyber security companies improves reactive capabilities by using outside knowledge and skills. Forensics is reactive, which works well with proactive Cyber security. Together, they make a complete defensive plan that covers both prevention and response.

Building Trust

Combining cyber security and forensics builds trust by showing that the organization is serious about security and being responsible. Stakeholders may be sure that incidents are handled well when they are open about how they are handled and there is forensic proof to back it up. For example, quickly letting travelers know about a data breach and giving identity protection services, as happened in the 2023 hotel case, helps repair reputational harm and rebuilds confidence (Kshetri, 2023). Forensic proof makes it possible to take legal action against criminals, which builds trust even more because it stops future crimes.

In smart tourism, trust is a key factor that affects how happy and loyal tourists are. Companies can keep customers' trust and make sure they have a good travel experience by combining proactive tactics to stop problems from happening with reactive measures to deal with them. This synergy is especially crucial in the tourism industry, where trust and reputation have a direct effect on how well a business does.

PROBLEMS WITH INTEGRATION

Even though there are benefits, combining cyber security and digital forensics in smart tourism has a number of problems that need to be solved in order to provide a safe environment.

Complicated Technology

The technological intricacy of smart tourism systems, marked by heterogeneous architectures and varied data sources, obstructs forensic investigation. IoT devices, cloud platforms, and mobile apps create a lot of data, which makes it harder to collect and analyze evidence (Quick & Choo, 2018). Attackers utilize encrypted communications and software that hide their identities, which makes forensic investigations even harder and requires more complex tools and skills. Using technologies from different vendors together can cause compatibility problems since different security standards can leave exploitable vulnerabilities (Conti et al., 2018).

Limitations on Resources

Small and medium-sized tourism businesses frequently don't have the money or people they need to put strong cyber security and forensic procedures in place. Advanced solutions like SIEM systems or AI-driven forensics cost a lot of money, which may be too much for small and medium-sized businesses (Hsu & Lin, 2016).

The tourism industry has a hard time hiring and keeping trained cyber security and forensic personnel, which makes it much harder to put these measures into place (Navarro & Buhalis, 2024).

Gaps in Regulation

Smart tourism that crosses borders faces regulatory problems because the laws of cyber security and forensics are different in different places. Different privacy rules, including GDPR in Europe and the California Consumer Privacy Act (CCPA) in the US, make it hard to gather evidence and bring cases to court (Ab Rahman & Choo, 2015). These gaps make it harder for forensic investigations to work and slow down event response, which hurts confidence and accountability.

FRAMEWORK FOR INTEGRATION IDEAS

To tackle these problems, a conceptual framework is suggested to bring together cyber security and digital forensics in four stages: prevention, detection, response, and recovery. This framework makes sure that all parts of security operate together, with proactive security and reactive forensics. It also stresses the importance of working together with stakeholders, using technology, and following the rules.

Stopping

The goal of the prevention phase is to lower the chances of cyber events by taking proactive steps:

- Security-by-Design: Use safe coding techniques, encryption, and multi-factor authentication (MFA) to reduce vulnerabilities while building systems (Garfinkel, 2010).
- Standardized Protocols: Use worldwide standards like ISO 27001 to make sure that all stakeholders follow the same security rules. This will help with compatibility and heterogeneity issues (Buhalis & Amaranggana, 2015).
- Training Programs: To lower the threats that people pose, such as phishing, give tourists, employees, and merchants frequent training on cyber security (Tussyadiah & Wang, 2016).

Finding

The detection phase uses real-time monitoring to find risks early on:

- Real-Time Monitoring with IDS and SIEM: Use intrusion detection systems and security information and event management tools to keep an eye on network traffic and system logs for anything that seems suspicious (Hsu & Lin, 2016).
- AI-Driven Anomaly Detection: Use AI to find strange patterns in how users act or how well the system works. This makes it easier to spot threats quickly (Li et al., 2017).
- Threat Intelligence Integration: Use threat intelligence feeds to keep up with new attacks that are targeting the tourism industry (Quick & Choo, 2018).

Answer

The response phase makes sure that incidents are quickly contained and looked into:

- Incident Response Plans with Forensic Readiness: Create and test plans that include logging, time synchronization, and secure evidence storage to help with forensic investigations (Casey, 2011).
- Working with the police: Work with the police and cyber security companies to share information and resources, which will improve reaction times (Ab Rahman & Choo, 2015).
- Clear Communication: Set up rules to let stakeholders know about incidents without causing fear and keeping trust (Kshetri, 2023).

Getting Better

The recovery phase is all on getting things back to normal and making sure they don't happen again:

- System Restoration Using Forensic Insights: Use forensic analysis to help restore the system by finding and fixing weak points and isolating damaged parts (Quick & Choo, 2018).
- Post-Incident investigation: Do a thorough investigation to find the fundamental causes and lessons gained, which will help you improve your cyber security policies in the future (Navarro & Buhalis, 2024).
- Legal Action and Trust Rebuilding: Use forensic evidence to take legal action against those responsible and use open communication to win back the trust of customers (Casey, 2011).

This methodology makes sure that all aspects are covered, including weaknesses, using forensic tools, and getting stakeholders to work together to build a trusted travel environment.

SUGGESTIONS AND SOLUTIONS

To put the framework into action and deal with the problems that have been found, the following suggestions are made:

1. Adopt Security-by-Design: During development, use secure coding, encryption, and MFA to make smart tourism systems less vulnerable (Garfinkel, 2010).
2. Standardization: Use worldwide standards like ISO 27001 to make sure that security processes are the same everywhere, which will help with interoperability and address differences (Buhalis & Amaranggana, 2015).
3. Improve Training Programs: To lower the dangers that come from people, like phishing and social engineering, tourists, employees, and merchants should all have frequent cyber security awareness training (Tussyadiah & Wang, 2016).
4. Use IDS, SIEM, and AI-driven anomaly detection to find threats in real time and take action before they get worse (Hsu & Lin, 2016).
5. Make sure that all systems are ready for forensic work by allowing logging, time synchronization, and safe evidence storage (Casey, 2011).
6. Encourage Collaboration Among Stakeholders: Create partnerships between businesses, governments, and law enforcement to share information and resources, which will improve response and recovery (Ab Rahman & Choo, 2015).
7. Use new technologies: Look at blockchain for safe data management and AI for automated forensic analysis to make things more efficient and scalable (Li et al., 2017).
8. Follow the Rules: To avoid fines and gain customers' trust, follow privacy rules like GDPR and CCPA and use ethical data practices (Navarro & Buhalis, 2024).
9. Invest in Expertise: Help training programs that will help fill the gaps in the number of cyber security and forensic professionals, especially for small and medium-sized businesses in the tourism industry (Kshetri, 2023).
10. Encourage Clear Communication: Create rules for quickly and clearly letting stakeholders know about occurrences to limit damage to your brand and rebuild confidence (Quick & Choo, 2018).

CONCLUSION

Combining cyber security with digital forensics is very important for making smart tourism a safe place to travel. This chapter has talked about how weak smart tourism systems are, how forensics can help with incident response, and how a synergistic approach can help. The suggested structure and suggestions give stakeholders a plan for making security and resilience better. Smart tourism depends on connected technologies, which can improve experiences but also pose big cyber security issues. Digital forensics enhances cyber security by facilitating efficient incident response and recovery, while their amalgamation promotes resilience and trust. In, gaps in study, such as the absence of tourism-specific frameworks, inadequate exploration of developing technologies, and insufficient emphasis on human elements, highlight the necessity for additional inquiry. Filling in these gaps will provide stakeholders the tools they need to build smart tourist ecosystems that are safe, strong, and reliable. The results and conversations show how important it is to combine cyber security and digital forensics to make smart tourism a safe place to travel. Cybersecurity weaknesses, including as data breaches, IoT exploits, ransom ware, and human factors, are big challenges to the ecosystem's trust and integrity. Digital forensics tools including event tracing, evidence retention, and recovery support are necessary for good incident response and accountability. The synergistic benefits of integration boost trust and resilience, and the proposed conceptual framework offers an organized way to put the idea into action. Even with problems like technical complexity, lack of resources, and gaps in regulations, the suggested solutions give stakeholders practical ways to make the smart tourism ecosystem safe and strong. These insights enhance academic comprehension and facilitate practical application, hence fostering future research and policy formulation.

REFERENCES

Ab Rahman, N. H., & Choo, K. K. R. (2015). A survey of information security incident handling in the cloud. *Computers & Security, 49*, 45–69. DOI: 10.1016/j.cose.2014.11.006

•Buhalis, D., & Amaranggana, A. (2015). *Smart Tourism Destinations: Enhancing Tourism Experience Through Personalisation of Services.* In *Information and Communication Technologies in Tourism 2015* (pp. 377–389). Springer. DOI: 10.1007/978-3-319-14343-9_28

Casey, E. (2011). *Digital Evidence and Computer Crime: Forensic Science, Computers, and the Internet* (3rd ed.). Academic Press.

Conti, M., Dehghantanha, A., Franke, K., & Watson, S. (2018). Internet of Things Security and Forensics: Challenges and Opportunities. *Future Generation Computer Systems, 78*, 544–546. DOI: 10.1016/j.future.2017.07.060

Garfinkel, S. (2010). Digital forensics research: The next 10 years. *Digital Investigation, 7*, S64–S73. DOI: 10.1016/j.diin.2010.05.009

Gretzel, U., Sigala, M., Xiang, Z., & Koo, C. (2015). Smart tourism: Foundations and developments. *Electronic Markets, 25*(3), 179–188. DOI: 10.1007/s12525-015-0196-8

Gretzel, U., Werthner, H., Koo, C., & Lamsfus, C. (2016). Conceptual foundations for understanding smart tourism ecosystems. *Computers in Human Behavior, 57*, 558–563.

Hsu, C. L., & Lin, J. C. C. (2016). Exploring factors affecting the adoption of Internet of Things services. *Computers in Human Behavior, 62*, 516–527. DOI: 10.1016/j.chb.2016.04.023

Kshetri, N. (2023). Cybersecurity and privacy in the digital economy: Challenges and policy responses. *Telecommunications Policy, 47*(1), 102403.

Law, R., Buhalis, D., & Cobanoglu, C. (2018). Progress on information and communication technologies in hospitality and tourism. *International Journal of Contemporary Hospitality Management, 26*(5), 727–750. DOI: 10.1108/IJCHM-08-2013-0367

Li, Y., Hu, C., Huang, C., & Duan, L. (2017). The concept of smart tourism in the context of tourism information services. *Tourism Management, 58*, 293–300. DOI: 10.1016/j.tourman.2016.03.014

Navarro, S., & Buhalis, D. (2024). Cybersecurity resilience in smart tourism ecosystems: Managing risk and trust. *Journal of Smart Tourism Research, 2*(1), 15–33.

Quick, D., & Choo, K. K. R. (2018). IoT Forensics: Challenges and Opportunities. *Future Generation Computer Systems, 78*, 544–546. DOI: 10.1016/j.future.2017.07.060

Tussyadiah, I., & Wang, D. (2016). Tourists' attitudes toward proactive smartphone systems. *Journal of Travel Research, 55*(4), 493–508. DOI: 10.1177/0047287514563168

Tussyadiah, I. P. (2017). Technology and behavioral design in tourism: The influence of automation on touristic experience. *Annals of Tourism Research, 66*, 140–152.

Xiang, Z., Magnini, V. P., & Fesenmaier, D. R. (2015). Information technology and consumer behavior in travel and tourism: Insights from travel planning using the Internet. *Journal of Retailing and Consumer Services, 22*, 244–249. DOI: 10.1016/j.jretconser.2014.08.005

Chapter 9

Securing Smart Tourism With Cybersecurity Architectures and Forensic Analytics in Digitally Augmented Travel Ecosystems

Syed Ibad Ali
http://orcid.org/0000-0001-6312-6768
Parul Institute of Engineering and Technology, Parul University, Vadodara, India

ABSTRACT

As tourism evolves into an age of hyper-connectivity and immersive digital enhancement, the assurance of cybersecurity and forensic resilience has become crucial for intelligent tourist ecosystems. This chapter examines the architectural and analytical frameworks necessary to protect cyber-physical infrastructures integrated inside smart destinations. It delineates a stratified cybersecurity framework that incorporates zero-trust principles, edge-based threat detection, and secure IoT protocols to safeguard against the evolving threat environment. Focus is directed towards forensic analytics frameworks that utilize machine learning, behavioral modeling, and blockchain-based audit trails to facilitate real-time incident response and post-event analysis.

DOI: 10.4018/979-8-2600-1850-7.ch009

1. INTRODUCTION

The digital revolution in the tourism industry has ushered in an unprecedented era of connectivity, personalization, and technological integration, fundamentally transforming how travelers plan, experience, and reflect on their journeys (Gretzel et al., 2015). Smart tourism represents an innovative approach to travel that leverages advanced digital technologies to enhance visitor satisfaction, operational efficiency, and destination competitiveness. It signifies a shift from traditional tourism models toward data-driven, interconnected ecosystems that dynamically respond to user needs and contextual conditions (Gretzel et al., 2015; Alonso-Almeida & Giglio, 2024).

Contemporary smart tourism environments encompass a wide array of interconnected technologies, including mobile applications, Internet of Things (IoT) sensors, augmented reality platforms, location-based services, digital payment systems, social media integration, and artificial intelligence-driven recommendation engines. These technologies collectively enable immersive, adaptive experiences that respond in real time to visitor preferences, environmental conditions, and operational constraints (Florido-Benítez, 2024). However, this level of technological sophistication significantly broadens the cybersecurity attack surface, extending well beyond conventional information technology security concerns (Paraskevas, 2020).

The tourism industry exhibits a unique cybersecurity landscape due to its global operational scope, heterogeneous stakeholder ecosystem, high user mobility, and reliance on continuous real-time data exchange.(Srivastava et al., 2024) uses traditional enterprise environments characterized by fixed perimeters and controlled access points, smart tourism ecosystems function within open, dynamic, and frequently unpredictable contexts (Alonso-Almeida & Giglio, 2024). Consequently, threat detection, prevention, and response require adaptive and non-traditional security approaches tailored to tourism-specific operational realities (Paraskevas, 2020).

Cybersecurity breaches within the tourism sector can lead to severe economic consequences, including financial losses, long-term reputational damage, and erosion of traveler trust. High-profile incidents affecting hotel chains, airline reservation systems, and online travel platforms have demonstrated how security failures can negatively impact entire destinations dependent on tourism revenues (Karadayi-Usta, 2024).

The COVID-19 pandemic further accelerated digital adoption in tourism, introducing widespread use of contactless services, digital identity verification, and health monitoring platforms. While these technologies enhanced operational continuity and safety, their rapid deployment often outpaced the development of robust cybersecurity standards, thereby introducing new vulnerabilities exploited by malicious actors (Florido-Benítez, 2025).

The integration of forensic analytics into cybersecurity frameworks represents a critical advancement in tourism security strategies. Digital forensics enables organizations to detect incidents, analyze attack patterns, preserve evidentiary integrity, and support legal proceedings across jurisdictions (Casey, 2014; Dehghantanha & Choo, 2020). Given the distributed and transnational nature of tourism systems, forensic readiness must balance investigative rigor with minimal disruption to the traveler experience (Taylor et al., 2011).

This chapter emphasizes the importance of comprehensive cybersecurity frameworks tailored to smart tourism environments. It examines sector-specific threats, evaluates existing security models and their limitations, and proposes integrated solutions that combine proactive cybersecurity controls with advanced forensic capabilities (Paraskevas, 2020; Alonso-Almeida & Giglio, 2024). Drawing on contemporary academic literature and industry practices, this work provides actionable insights for destination management organizations, hospitality providers, technology vendors, and policymakers seeking to enhance cybersecurity resilience in tourism ecosystems (Florido-Benítez, 2025).

2. LITERATURE REVIEW

2.1 Expansion of Intelligent Tourism Technologies

The conceptual foundations of smart tourism emerged in the early 2000s alongside advancements in mobile computing, wireless communication, and location-based services. Gretzel et al. (2015) provided one of the earliest comprehensive definitions, describing smart tourism as a coordinated effort to collect, integrate, and analyze data from physical infrastructure, social networks, organizational systems, and human cognition in order to generate value-added experiences and improve sustainability and efficiency.

Over the past decade, smart tourism architectures have evolved into complex digital ecosystems supported by mobile connectivity, IoT-based sensing, cloud computing, and artificial intelligence-driven personalization engines (Gretzel et al., 2015). These integrated systems facilitate the development of digital twins of tourism destinations, enabling real-time monitoring, predictive analytics, and adaptive resource allocation (Florido-Benítez, 2025).

Recent advancements in edge computing have further enhanced smart tourism capabilities by enabling localized data processing, reducing latency, and improving privacy protection through decentralized analytics (Florido-Benítez, 2024). However, such distributed architectures increase system complexity and introduce additional cybersecurity challenges due to the proliferation of edge devices and communication interfaces (Karadayi-Usta, 2024).

Artificial intelligence and machine learning now play a central role in smart tourism applications, enabling advanced recommendation systems, demand forecasting, and automated customer support. While AI-driven personalization enhances user experience, it also introduces vulnerabilities related to model manipulation, data poisoning, and algorithmic bias, necessitating stronger security oversight (Alonso-Almeida & Giglio, 2024).

2.2 Cybersecurity Challenges in the Tourism Sector

The tourism sector faces distinctive cybersecurity challenges due to its transnational operations, fragmented technological infrastructure, and extensive handling of personal and financial data. Alonso-Almeida and Giglio (2024) highlighted regulatory complexity, legacy system integration, and inconsistent security governance as major contributors to elevated cyber risk.

Hospitality organizations are particularly vulnerable, as hotel management systems, point-of-sale terminals, and guest Wi-Fi networks often serve as primary attack vectors (Karadayi-Usta, 2024). Similarly, aviation systems present high-value targets due to their reliance on interconnected digital infrastructures and real-time operational data (Paraskevas, 2020).

The convergence of smart city infrastructure and tourism services further amplifies cybersecurity risks, as vulnerabilities in urban IoT networks and public digital services can directly affect tourism applications and visitor safety (Florido-Benítez, 2024).

2.3 Security of IoT in Tourist Destinations

IoT technologies underpin smart tourism by enabling real-time sensing and environmental awareness across destinations. However, IoT devices often lack computational resources to support robust security mechanisms, making them susceptible to unauthorized access and exploitation (Zawoad & Hasan, 2018).

Zawoad and Hasan (2018) categorized IoT vulnerabilities into device-level, network-level, and application-level threats, emphasizing challenges associated with authentication, encryption, and access control. Given the scale of IoT deployments in tourism destinations, centralized monitoring and incident response remain particularly challenging (Karadayi-Usta, 2024).

IoT forensics has emerged as a vital tool for investigating security incidents involving smart tourism infrastructure. Frameworks proposed by Zawoad and Hasan (2018) address evidence acquisition, integrity preservation, and correlation across heterogeneous IoT sources while maintaining legal admissibility.

2.4 Digital Forensics in Travel Systems

Digital forensics in tourism environments is complicated by distributed infrastructures, cloud-based services, and cross-border legal considerations. Traditional forensic methods designed for centralized enterprise systems require adaptation for effective application in tourism contexts (Casey, 2014).

Cloud-based tourism platforms further complicate forensic investigations due to data dispersion across multiple providers and jurisdictions. Taylor et al. (2011) highlighted the necessity of multi-cloud forensic architectures capable of maintaining chain-of-custody and regulatory compliance.

Mobile device forensics is increasingly relevant, as smartphones contain critical evidence related to travel bookings, location data, and digital communications. Modern forensic methodologies must therefore account for diverse mobile platforms and international privacy regulations (Dehghantanha & Choo, 2020).

2.5 Artificial Intelligence and Machine Learning for Tourist Safety

AI and machine learning technologies offer powerful capabilities for threat detection, fraud prevention, and automated incident response within tourism systems. These techniques enable the analysis of large-scale heterogeneous datasets to identify anomalies indicative of security threats (Alonso-Almeida & Giglio, 2024).

Machine learning-based fraud detection models have demonstrated high accuracy in identifying suspicious booking and payment behaviors, though careful calibration is required to minimize false positives and preserve customer trust (Karadayi-Usta, 2024).

AI-enabled video surveillance and computer vision systems have also been deployed in tourist environments to enhance situational awareness and detect abnormal activities in real time, thereby improving overall destination safety (Paraskevas, 2020).

3. RESEARCH METHODOLOGY

Fundamental Security Regulations

To develop comprehensive cybersecurity architectures for intelligent tourist environments, one must begin with fundamental security principles and subsequently adapt them to the requirements of tourism ecosystems. The CIA triad (Confidentiality, Integrity, and Availability) underpins tourist cybersecurity; nonetheless, it need augmentation to encompass additional attributes specific to the tourism sector. (Ali,2025)

In smart tourism, privacy encompasses not just data protection but also many layers of sensitive information. Tourist personal information, including travel preferences, location histories, and behavioral patterns, must be safeguarded against unauthorized access and misuse by authorized users of the system. Due to the global nature of tourist activities, maintaining data privacy is more challenging since it may traverse borders with varying privacy regulations and cultural norms around data security.

Tourism ecosystems encompass several diverse entities, complicating the preservation of visitor data confidentiality. This occurs due to the interchange of visitor data among airlines, hotels, tour operators, and destination management agencies. Variations in security and privacy procedures across stakeholders may compromise the integrity of the confidentiality chain. To disseminate data while maintaining privacy, increasingly sophisticated encryption techniques, such as homomorphic encryption and secure multi-party computation, are required. Integrity in tourism systems: Data integrity in tourism environments is crucial for maintaining trust and ensuring the continuity of operations. Tourism systems manage substantial transactional data, including bookings, payments, and service confirmations. Unauthorized alteration or corruption of sensitive data can directly impact finances and operations. Numerous tourist services operate in real time; hence, it is crucial to identify and rectify integrity issues swiftly to prevent their proliferation. The dispersion of tourism systems results in certain integrity issues. Data can be replicated across several systems and locations. Blockchain technology has emerged as a feasible method for securing data in decentralized tourism systems. It accomplishes this by providing immutable transaction records and enabling multiple parties to verify data authenticity. (Dakshinamurthi et al., 2023)

The availability of systems is crucial in tourism environments, as service disruptions can significantly impact passengers' experiences and incur substantial financial losses. Tourist systems must maintain high availability despite fluctuating and unpredictable demand, while accommodating users across several time zones and locations. Resilience encompasses not just availability but also the capacity to maintain critical operations during adverse circumstances such as cyberattacks, natural disasters, and other challenges. Tourism enterprises must acquire the ability to gracefully degrade, signifying that systems can continue to deliver essential services despite the absence or malfunction of certain components.

Figure 1. Distribution of Different Data Types

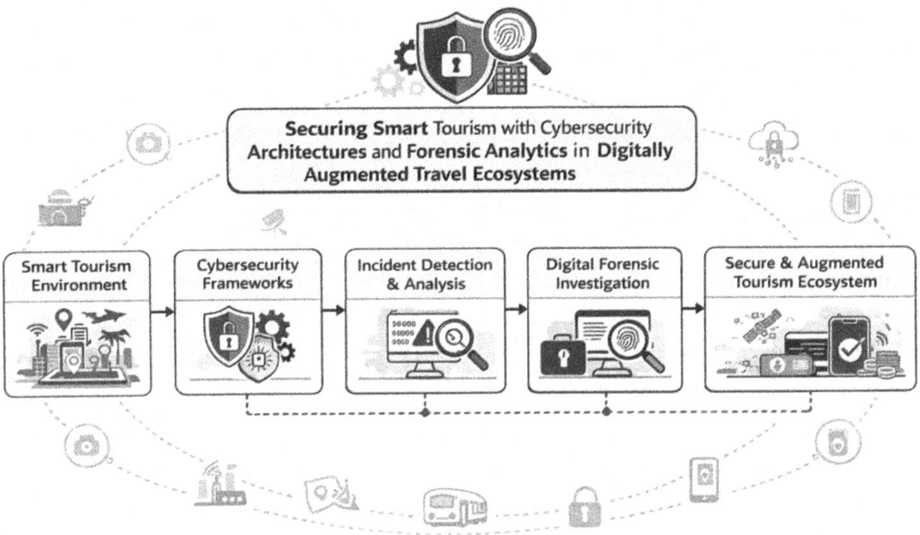

Security Governance Involving Multiple Stakeholders

The tourism ecosystem comprises several individuals possessing diverse security skills, objectives, and responsibilities. Effective cybersecurity governance must reconcile the requirements of many stakeholders within this ecosystem while simultaneously orchestrating security initiatives.The analysis of the stakeholder ecosystem in tourism cybersecurity governance must consider the intricate relationships among various stakeholder groups. The primary stakeholders are the tourists themselves. They frequently become targets of cyberattacks and may possess limited knowledge regarding cybersecurity. Hotels, airlines, and tour operators are accountable for safeguarding visitor data and ensuring the continuous availability of services. Nonetheless, their proficiency in cybersecurity may vary significantly. Technology vendors and platform providers are crucial for tourism cybersecurity, since their systems often underpin several tourism services. Deficiencies in vendor systems can significantly impact the whole tourism business. Government authorities and destination management organizations are responsible for ensuring visitor safety, while lacking direct jurisdiction over all system components. Collaborative Security Frameworks for tourism cybersecurity necessitate the establishment of cooperative frameworks that facilitate information sharing, coordinated incident response, and collective defense against common threats. These frameworks must identify a method to harmonize the requirements of individual businesses with the advantages of enhanced security for the whole tourism sector. Information-sharing platforms must be established to provide valuable threat intelligence while safeguarding confidential company data. Employing standards such as STIX (Structured Threat Information eXpression) and TAXII (Trusted Automated eXchange of Intelligence Information), automated threat intelligence sharing facilitates real-time dissemination of threat indications while minimizing manual labor. Coordination of Regulatory Compliance Tourism organizations typically operate across many domains, each governed by distinct regulations pertaining to data protection and cybersecurity. Governance frameworks must ensure that compliance operations operate cohesively without interfering with one another. The General Data Protection Regulation (GDPR) of the European Union has established itself as the global standard for data protection in tourism, as several tourist organizations cater to European guests regardless of their location globally. Additionally, there exist other regulations, such as the California Consumer Privacy Act (CCPA) and several national cybersecurity frameworks, which impose further compliance requirements that must be included into comprehensive governance strategies.

Risk-Based Security Architecture

In the design of cybersecurity infrastructures for tourism, risk-based methodologies should be employed to prioritize security expenditures according to the likelihood and severity of certain attack scenarios. The tourism sector is continually developing, necessitating that risk assessment and management strategies adapt to emerging risks and economic conditions.

Dynamic Risk Assessment Traditional risk assessment methodologies that depend on periodic evaluations and fixed threat models are ineffective in tourism environments, as dangers can rapidly fluctuate owing to external factors such as geopolitical developments, seasonal variations, and emerging threat patterns. Dynamic risk assessment frameworks must incorporate real-time threat intelligence, continuous monitoring of system vulnerabilities, and adaptive risk models that may evolve with changing circumstances. Machine learning may enhance dynamic risk assessment by identifying patterns in security data that reveal emerging threats or alterations in risk profiles. Anomaly detection algorithms can identify unusual patterns in network traffic, user behavior, or system performance that may indicate security breaches or evolving risk scenarios. Threat modeling for tourism must account for the unique attack vectors and threat actors pertinent to tourist environments. Established threat modeling frameworks, such as STRIDE (Spoofing, Tampering, Repudiation, Information Disclosure, Denial of Service, Elevation of Privilege), require modification to address concerns specific to the tourist sector. Conventional corporate threat models may inadequately address significant danger categories that affect tourists, including travel fraud, identity theft, and social engineering tactics. When nation-states target tourism infrastructure for financial or political motives, it is essential to consider advanced persistent threat (APT) capabilities and long-term strategic objectives (Zawoad & Hasan, 2018). Risk-based security architectures must enhance the selection and implementation of security solutions according to their effectiveness against identified threats and their influence on tourist operations. In doing a cost-benefit analysis, it is essential to consider factors beyond the direct expenses associated with security measures. It is essential to consider their impact on user experience, operational efficiency, and corporate objectives. Due to the seasonal nature of many tourism enterprises, they may implement dynamic security control deployment, allowing for enhanced security measures during peak periods and optimal cost-effectiveness during off-peak times. This agile deployment strategy is particularly effective with cloud-based security services.

4. INTELLIGENT TOURISM CYBERSECURITY FRAMEWORK

4.1 Framework for Comprehensive Security Architecture

Smart tourism ecosystems are varied and interconnected, necessitating security architectures capable of addressing several threat types while ensuring seamless user experiences that enhance the profitability of tourist services. A sophisticated tourism security architecture framework must encompass many layers of protection, ranging from safeguarding individual devices to collecting and responding to threat intelligence throughout the entire ecosystem.

The integrated security architecture is founded on many key principles that address the unique requirements of tourist environments. Defense in depth incorporates additional layers of security measures to ensure that the failure of a single control does not jeopardize the entire system. The zero trust architecture asserts that no user, device, or system should be inherently trusted. Access requests must be consistently scrutinized and validated.

Adaptive security enables the architecture to evolve in response to emerging threats and risk profiles. Real-time threat intelligence, user behavioral patterns, and operational conditions can autonomously modify security configurations. The ability to adapt is particularly crucial in tourism contexts, as risk levels can fluctuate rapidly due to factors such as geopolitical events or seasonal variations in visitor influx.

Scalability ensures that security architectures can expand and adapt to accommodate more users, devices, and services without compromising security efficacy.

Cloud-native security strategies offer the scale and flexibility necessary to navigate evolving tourism situations.

The integrated architecture has a layered security strategy that safeguards various components of the tourism technology stack. The infrastructure layer provides physical protection for data centers and network equipment. It encompasses network security mechanisms such as firewalls and intrusion detection systems, in addition to cloud security protocols for virtualized settings.

The platform layer encompasses security for the operating system, database, and middleware. Secure coding methodologies, application firewalls, and runtime application self-protection (RASP) technologies constitute application-level security. The data layer encompasses encryption, access limitations, and data loss prevention (DLP).

The user layer manages authentication, authorization, and monitoring of user behavior. Device security include mobile device management (MDM), endpoint detection and response (EDR), and IoT device security. The process layer encompasses security governance, incident response procedures, and business continuity planning.

Figure 2. Steps of security health care system

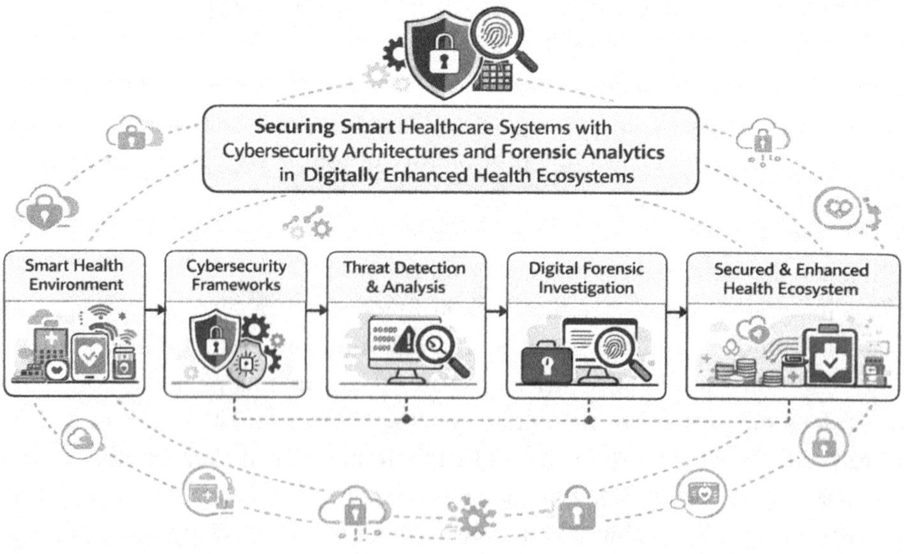

4.2 Administration of Identity and Access

Identity and Access Management (IAM) is a critical component of cybersecurity frameworks in the tourist sector. It regulates access and utilization of systems by visitors, workers, partners, and automated systems. Tourism enterprises are international and mobile, necessitating intricate solutions for IAM challenges.

Multi-Stakeholder Identity Federation Tourism IAM systems must provide identity federation among various enterprises and platforms. This enables travelers to utilize identical identification credentials to access services from several providers. Federated identity management facilitates travelers in managing multiple accounts and provides companies with authenticated identifying data.

The Security Assertion Markup Language (SAML) and OpenID Connect standards enable tourism enterprises to accept identity claims from reliable identity providers. This approach mitigates security risks associated with passwords and enhances user experience by enabling single sign-on. (Ali et al., 2024)

Blockchain-based identity management offers a novel approach that may enhance visitors' control over their personal information while enabling various service providers to verify it. Self-sovereign identification (SSI) models enable individuals to possess and manage their identity credentials, disclosing only the information required by service providers.

Adaptive Authentication necessitates the implementation of dynamic security measures that adjust according to risk evaluations, given the diverse and mobile nature of visitors. Low-risk activities, such as researching travel information, may require little authentication, but high-risk transactions, such making payments or altering reservations, may necessitate several forms of verification.

Adaptive authentication determinations rely on contextual factors such as the user's location, the type of device in use, network conditions, and behavioral patterns. Machine learning algorithms can analyze these factors to assess the risk associated with authentication requests and autonomously adjust the authentication requirements (Biswal et al., 2025).

Biometric authentication technologies, including fingerprint recognition, facial recognition, and voice authentication, provide secure and convenient identity verification for passengers. However, the collection and processing of biometric data present privacy concerns that necessitate appropriate consent mechanisms and data protection measures.

Tourism organizations must have robust privileged access management (PAM) limits to prevent administrators from accessing critical systems. The dispersion of tourist activities and the necessity for 24/7 system availability may render conventional PAM approaches ineffective. Just-in-time (JIT) access provisioning grants administrative permissions exclusively when necessary and for the minimal duration required. This approach reduces the likelihood of privileged accounts being compromised while maintaining operational flexibility. Recording and reviewing sessions generate audit trails for privileged activities, enabling the identification of prohibited or questionable actions.

4.3 Framework for Data Safeguarding and Privacy

Data protection is a critical aspect of tourism cybersecurity due to the sensitivity of visitor information and the complexity of data protection regulations in tourism contexts. Data protection frameworks must encompass all facets of data collection, processing, storage, and dissemination, while adhering to the regulations established by various regulatory authorities.

Implementation of Privacy by Design Principles Privacy by design principles must be included into all tourism data infrastructures to ensure that privacy protection is considered from the outset, rather than as an afterthought. The principles of data reduction dictate that one should collect just the data necessary for certain activities. This mitigates privacy problems and facilitates compliance with regulations (Farooqui et al., 2025).

Purpose limitation ensures that data is employed just for the reasons for which it was collected, hence preventing unauthorized use of tourist data. Tourists can control the collection and utilization of personal data using permission management systems. This enables people to provide explicit consent for certain data processing activities.

Data anonymization and pseudonymization are two technological privacy protection techniques that eliminate or obscure personally identifiable information while preserving the data's use for analytical and operational purposes. Differential privacy ensures the protection of individuals' privacy while facilitating statistical analysis of tourism data.

Cross-Border Data Protection: As tourism enterprises operate internationally, they must employ sophisticated techniques for moving data across borders that comply with the diverse data protection regulations of each jurisdiction. Certain jurisdictions have regulations on data storage that may conflict with the international scope of tourism activities. This necessitates meticulous planning and architectural design.

Standard Contractual Clauses (SCCs) and Binding Corporate Rules (BCRs) are legal mechanisms that facilitate data transfer across firms and their affiliated groups. However, these systems require comprehensive data governance guidelines and routine audits to ensure compliance. Technical methodologies like as encryption and tokenization enhance the security of data flows and facilitate regulatory compliance. Homomorphic encryption enables mathematical operations on encrypted data, allowing tourism organizations to do analytics while ensuring data security. Data lifetime Management: Frameworks for the security of tourism data must encompass the entire data lifetime, from initial collection to final deletion. Automated procedures for data retention and deletion ensure compliance with regulations and reduce the risk of privacy issues over time. Data categorization systems classify tourism data into categories according to its sensitivity and legal regulations. This enables the proper safeguarding of various data kinds. Personal data must be safeguarded differently from operational data, while financial data may require much more protection. Regular data audits and inventory procedures assist organizations in monitoring the data they collect and manage, therefore facilitating data preservation and regulatory compliance.

4.4 Identifying and Addressing Risks

Tourism cybersecurity infrastructures must swiftly and efficiently identify and respond to attacks, as tourism systems are high-value targets and security breaches can adversely affect a business's reputation and financial performance.

Tourism SIEM systems must aggregate and analyze security data from many sources, including network devices, applications, cloud services, and IoT devices. Tourism systems generate extensive data in many formats, necessitating powerful analytics to identify significant security incidents within the operational data.

Machine learning and artificial intelligence enhance Security Information and Event Management (SIEM) by identifying patterns and anomalies that may indicate security threats. Behavioral analytics can identify anomalous user activities that may indicate account compromise or potential insider threats.

The integration of threat intelligence provides context to security events, enabling analysts to assess the significance and relevance of the activities identified. Automated threat intelligence feeds deliver real-time information on emerging threats and methods of attack.

Automated Incident Response: Given that tourism operations function continuously, 24/7, and occurrences may disrupt ongoing services, it is essential to implement automated incident response mechanisms that may mitigate dangers and minimize damage without human intervention. Security Orchestration, Automation, and Response (SOAR) solutions enable computers to autonomously address common security issues, such as detecting malware, unauthorized account access, or network breaches. Automated responses may encompass account locking, network isolation, and measures to mitigate risks.Utilizing a playbook to address events ensures that responses to various types of security issues remain consistent and effective. Depending on the nature and severity of the incident, predetermined response protocols can be executed automatically. Tourism enterprises that are forensic-ready must possess the capability to investigate security issues and gather digital evidence effectively. The global dispersion of tourism systems complicates forensic investigations in several ways.

Centralized logging and monitoring solutions ensure that all components of the system collect and preserve critical forensic data. Log retention legislation must strike a compromise between the requirements of forensic science and the costs associated with storage and privacy concerns.

Chain of custody protocols ensure that digital evidence can be admissible in court. Automated techniques for gathering and safeguarding evidence reduce the likelihood of loss or contamination during incident response activities.

5. EMPLOYING FORENSIC ANALYTICS IN TOURIST SYSTEMS

Framework for Real-Time Forensic Analysis The implementation of real-time forensic analytics in tourism systems is a significant departure from the traditional method of post-incident investigation and evidence collection. This proactive approach enables firms to detect incidents in real-time, promptly preserve evidence, and mitigate risks before significant harm occurs.For effective real-time forensic analytics, a robust streaming data architecture is essential, capable of managing rapid and substantial data flows from many components of the tourism system. Apache Kafka and similar distributed streaming technologies provide the real-time acquisition of log data, transaction records, user interactions, and IoT sensor data. The streaming architecture must accommodate the volatile characteristics of tourism data, as traffic patterns may fluctuate significantly due to seasonal variations, promotional activities, and external events. Elastic scalability enables the forensic analytics system to accommodate peak demands without data loss or significant delay increases. Apache Storm, Apache Flink, and Apache Spark Streaming are stream processing frameworks that enable real-time analysis of forensic data streams. These systems are capable of intricate event processing, pattern recognition, and anomaly detection on streaming data. They can issue notifications and preserve evidence during security incidents. Forensic data models for tourist forensic analytics require specific frameworks that illustrate the interconnections among persons, systems, transactions, and events inside tourist environments. Graph-based data models are effective for illustrating such links since they enable the examination of attack patterns impacting several systems and diverse groups of individuals. Temporal data models chronicle security events sequentially, enabling the construction of attack timelines and the correlation of events across several systems. Time-series databases designed for forensic data facilitate the storage and analysis of extensive volumes of timestamped security events. Semantic data models encompass information on tourist systems and security concerns, enabling more intricate analysis and interpretation of forensic data. Ontology-based approaches can elucidate our understanding of various types of attacks, system vulnerabilities, and typical operational patterns.

Automated evidence preservation solutions ensure the capture and storage of critical forensic data during security incidents. This reduces the likelihood of losing or polluting evidence. Rule-based systems can autonomously initiate evidence collection depending on established criteria such as anomaly ratings, user behavior patterns, or system alerts. Cryptography safeguards the integrity and authenticity of preserved evidence. Hash functions and digital signatures can demonstrate that evidence remains unaltered post-collection. Blockchain-based evidence management systems can provide immutable audit trails for forensic evidence.

Correlation of Data From Various Sources

Forensic analytics in tourism must integrate information from several data sources to deliver comprehensive representations of security concerns. Due to the dispersion of tourism systems, evidence of a singular assault may be distributed among several firms, systems, and legal jurisdictions (Ali et al., 2024). Effective cross-system correlation forensic analysis must integrate data from several components of a system, including web servers, databases, network devices, mobile applications, and IoT sensors. Diverse systems may employ distinct log formats, timestamp standards, and data structures, necessitating sophisticated data integration and normalization technologies. Universal Correlation Identifiers (UCIs) may link events that are interrelated across many systems. This enables analysts to monitor assault trends using intricate tourism technology frameworks. Session IDs, transaction IDs, and user IDs serve as correlation keys that associate related events across many systems. Machine learning algorithms can identify relationships between events that are not apparent when analyzed using established rules. Classification algorithms can categorize events based on their characteristics and their correlation with established assault patterns. Clustering algorithms can categorize analogous occurrences. The geographic dimension of tourism activities provides valuable background for forensic investigations. Data from mobile devices, IP geolocation, and physical access records might help reconstruct the details of security incidents that occurred in reality.

Integrating Geographic Information Systems (GIS) with location-specific forensic data enables visualization and analysis of the information. When analyzed within a geographical context, data may reveal that assault patterns possess spatial components. Geofencing and location-based anomaly detection can identify unusual behaviors by analyzing patterns in their occurrence. For example, if an individual attempts to access an account from two geographically distant locations simultaneously, it may indicate that the account has been compromised or that login credentials are being shared. User behavior analytics (UBA) is an effective instrument for detecting anomalous activities that may indicate security issues. Tourism environments gather extensive behavioral data as individuals engage with various services and systems during their travels. Various categories of users, including visitors, employees, and system administrators, have established baseline behavioral profiles. Alterations in typical behavior may indicate potential security breaches or violations of policy.

Advanced behavioral analytics consider factors such as the time of day, geographical location, device characteristics, and user interaction with the service. Machine learning algorithms can modify behavioral models based on fresh threat information and evolving trends.

Global Coordination of Forensic Activities

Due to the global nature of tourist activities, forensic investigations that span many jurisdictions may encounter various legal systems, privacy regulations, and law enforcement agencies. Effective collaboration on forensic investigations necessitates sophisticated mechanisms for evidence exchange and cross-border cooperation. Tourism forensic investigations must navigate complex legal frameworks that vary significantly across various jurisdictions. Mutual Legal Assistance Treaties (MLATs) establish formal mechanisms for international collaboration on criminal investigations; yet, these procedures can be protracted and encumbered by bureaucratic obstacles. Private sector coordination instruments facilitate the rapid exchange of information for crisis response while ensuring legal compliance. Organizations that disseminate information on certain sectors, such as tourism-sector ISACs (Information Sharing and Analysis Centers), facilitate collaboration among companies and law enforcement agencies. When gathering evidence internationally (Ali et al., 2024) it is important to be vigilant regarding jurisdictional issues and the legal standards for admissibility. Evidence collected in one nation may be inadmissible in a court of another jurisdiction; hence, it is essential to collaborate with attorneys knowledgeable in international law.

Technical coordination channels facilitate secure communication, enabling forensic teams from many firms and jurisdictions to collaborate effectively. Encrypted communication channels safeguard essential investigative data, enabling forensic teams to collaborate in real time from many locations. Standardized formats for evidence exchange facilitate the sharing of forensic data among enterprises utilizing various technologies and platforms. The Digital Forensics XML (DFXML) standard and similar standards enable forensic tools to collaborate while preserving the integrity of evidence and the chain of custody information.

Collaborative forensic solutions enable investigators from many organizations to collaborate on evidence inside shared workspaces, while meticulously monitoring access permissions and actions undertaken by each participant. These platforms must include stringent permission limits to ensure that only authorized individuals may access critical information.

Prominent cybersecurity incidents affecting tourism may require diplomatic collaboration among governments, particularly when they jeopardize critical infrastructure or significantly impact the economy. Established diplomatic channels and protocols can expedite processes and mitigate political conflicts. Policy harmonization programs aim to standardize cybersecurity and data protection regulations across different jurisdictions, therefore facilitating operations for tourism firms that operate in many countries. The United Nations World Tourism Organization (UNWTO) and the multinational Civil Aviation Organization (ICAO) exemplify multinational entities that provide regulatory consistency among nations.

Capacity building projects aid impoverished nations in enhancing their cybersecurity and forensic competencies in the absence of sufficient technical expertise or funding. By eliminating vulnerabilities that attackers may exploit, these initiatives enhance the global cybersecurity framework for tourism.

6. CHALLENGES AND RESOLUTIONS FOR EXECUTION

Challenges in Technical Implementation

Implementing comprehensive cybersecurity architectures and forensic analytics systems in tourist environments presents significant technological challenges. It requires innovative concepts and meticulous planning. Numerous tourist enterprises own intricate IT infrastructures that incorporate legacy systems that have existed for decades. These systems may utilize outdated technology, lack modern security protocols, and exhibit poor interoperability with other systems. For example, airlines continue to utilize mainframe-based reservation systems developed in the 1960s and 1970s, which manage billions of transactions annually. To incorporate contemporary security elements into legacy systems, meticulous architectural preparation is essential. This often entails employing security gateways and proxy systems that may implement additional security measures without altering existing applications. API gateways can offer authentication, authorization, and encryption services to legacy systems without these capabilities. Through incremental modernization strategies, enterprises may enhance their security posture progressively without interrupting operations. Service-oriented architecture (SOA) and microservices can be employed to integrate modern security protocols into legacy systems while gradually substituting outdated components with new ones. Scalability and Performance: Tourism systems must effectively accommodate significant fluctuations in demand, ranging from periods of low activity to instances of simultaneous access by millions of users. In the Christmas holiday season of 2019, some major travel booking websites had traffic volumes exceeding 20 times their normal rates. This significantly hindered the efficacy of cybersecurity solutions under these extreme conditions.

Tourism environments require adaptable security frameworks that can scale according to demand. Cloud-based security services can scale to accommodate peak demand and reduce costs during periods of low demand. Auto-scaling features must be configured optimally to swiftly respond to traffic surges without incurring excessive expenditures.

When improving performance, it is essential to consider the additional workload imposed by security constraints on the system. Encryption, virus scanning, and behavioral analysis might introduce latency that deteriorates the user experience. Hardware acceleration, superior algorithms, and intelligent caching strategies can enhance security while minimizing impact on performance. Data Integration and Interoperability: Within tourist ecosystems, several systems and organizations must exchange data while maintaining security and privacy protocols. The tourism industry employs several data formats, protocols, and standards, complicating data integration.

The Open Travel Alliance (OTA) standards exemplify a standardization movement that facilitates the sharing of tourism information through the provision of common data formats. However, several organizations employ proprietary formats or custom implementations that complicate integration.

Data transformation and normalization services can alter the format of data while preserving its semantic integrity. ETL methods must incorporate security measures to ensure that data transformation operations do not introduce vulnerabilities or compromise data integrity.

Issues Pertaining to Culture and Organization

Tourism companies have significant organizational and cultural challenges when attempting to implement advanced cybersecurity protocols. These issues may hinder the proper adoption and utilization of these strategies. Numerous tourism firms have generally prioritized customer service and operational efficiency over cybersecurity. This has hindered the implementation of security-focused initiatives. The hotel industry has always prioritized convenience and accessibility for patrons, which can frequently compromise security requirements.

Security awareness training programs must be tailored to the tourism sector, incorporating pertinent examples and scenarios related to tourism operations. Cybersecurity training materials must emphasize their contribution to, rather than detriment to, customer service objectives.

For a cybersecurity culture to flourish, leaders must demonstrate unwavering commitment. Senior executives must demonstrate their commitment to cybersecurity by allocating financial resources, enforcing regulations, and actively participating in security initiatives.

Gamification, through interactive simulations and competitive elements, can enhance the engagement of tourism workers in cybersecurity training by reinforcing security concepts. Frequent phishing assessments and security challenges can enhance vigilance and identify areas for improvement.

Insufficient Resources: Numerous tourism enterprises, particularly smaller ones, lack the requisite resources to implement comprehensive cybersecurity measures. Due to the seasonal operation of several tourism enterprises, maintaining consistent security spending throughout the year can be challenging. Managed security services offer access to contemporary cybersecurity capabilities without significant financial expenditure. Security-as-a-Service (SECaaS) models enable tourism organizations to get enterprise-grade security solutions with a monthly subscription charge.

Collaborative initiatives such as shared services and group purchasing agreements may enable smaller enterprises to access cybersecurity resources. Tourism sector associations can collaborate to get group contracts for cybersecurity services and share information on dangers.

Numerous countries implement governmental measures to assist tourism enterprises with cybersecurity, recognizing the sector's significance to the economy. These programs may provide funding for cybersecurity enhancements, finance consultancy services, or offer complimentary cybersecurity training.

Change Management is essential to ensure the smooth adoption of new cybersecurity systems and processes, minimizing disruption to tourism activities.

Strategies for engaging stakeholders must identify and address the concerns of the many groups impacted by alterations to cybersecurity. Front-line workers may be concerned about the potential difficulties the changes may impose on their roles, whilst managers might be apprehensive over the impact of these changes on operational efficiency.

Gradual adoption, by allowing individuals time to acclimate, can reduce the likelihood of disturbance. Pilot initiatives with a limited number of participants can identify issues prior to their occurrence on a broader scale.

Communication strategy must explicitly delineate the benefits of enhancing cybersecurity while also acknowledging the challenges and costs associated. Encourage support for cybersecurity initiatives by disseminating success narratives and case studies from like organizations.

Challenges in Adhering to Rules and Regulations - Organizations operating in many jurisdictions with varying legislation for tourism cybersecurity have significant challenges due to the complexity of the requirements.

Adherence to Multiple Jurisdictions: Tourism enterprises often must comply with data protection and cybersecurity regulations from multiple nations concurrently.

The General Data Protection Regulation (GDPR) is applicable to a hotel chain operating in Europe. The California Consumer Privacy Act (CCPA) pertains to any corporation conducting business in California. Other locations where the chain operates may own their own regulations.

Compliance mapping operations identify all applicable regulations and their specific requirements. This enables firms to develop comprehensive compliance programs. Regulatory requirement matrices can identify areas of overlap or conflict across several regulatory regimes.

Harmonized compliance strategies aim to provide controls that simultaneously satisfy many legal obligations, so enhancing efficiency and reducing costs. Privacy by design methodologies often comply with several privacy regulations, while security standards such as ISO 27001 provide you with the necessary skills to satisfy diverse cybersecurity requirements.

Legal expertise is required to navigate complex regulatory duties. To ensure complete compliance, corporations may need to employ attorneys proficient in the laws of many countries. Regulatory Change Management The regulations governing cybersecurity and data protection are continually evolving, complicating compliance efforts. Regulatory monitoring systems track alterations in legislation and regulations pertinent to your organization, informing you of new duties in advance. Legal technology systems can monitor legislative changes and assess their implications. Adaptive compliance frameworks are designed to accommodate regulatory changes without necessitating a major system overhaul. Adaptive policy management systems facilitate the prompt modification of compliance procedures in response to regulatory changes.

When companies engage in the rule-making process, they may influence the regulations and prepare for impending changes. Trade associations and industry organizations generally collaborate to address regulatory initiatives.

7 EMERGING TECHNOLOGIES AND THEIR POTENTIAL FUTURE TRAJECTORIES

The Implications of Quantum Computing for Humanity

Quantum computing technology presents both an opportunity and a threat to the security of travelers. Quantum computers may enable novel secure communication and data protection approaches, although they also present significant risks to current cryptography techniques.

Quantum Threats to Contemporary Cryptography Current cryptography techniques predominantly rely on arithmetic issues that are computationally challenging for conventional computers, yet solvable by sufficiently powerful quantum computers. Quantum attacks employing Shor's algorithm might readily compromise RSA encryption, which is extensively utilized in tourism systems for secure communications and digital signatures. The timeline for the emergence of quantum computing risks remains uncertain. Projections indicate that the development of quantum computers capable of compromising encryption will need 10 to 30 years. Due to the longevity of tourist infrastructure and the sensitivity of tourism data, it is imperative to prepare for quantum risks in advance. Researchers in post-quantum cryptography are developing cryptographic algorithms that are secure against attacks from both classical and quantum computers. The U.S. National Institute of Standards and Technology (NIST) is developing post-quantum cryptography algorithms to replace currently vulnerable systems. Tourism organizations must begin transitioning to quantum-safe cryptographic technologies to ensure the long-term security of their data. This transfer strategy must be meticulously designed to ensure cohesive functionality and enhanced security. The concepts of crypto-agility enable systems to employ many cryptographic methods concurrently, facilitating a gradual transition to quantum-safe alternatives. In periods of transition, hybrid methods can protect against both classical and quantum threats. Key management systems must be altered to accommodate post-quantum cryptography keys, which are often significantly larger than current keys. The implementation of post-quantum cryptography may significantly increase storage and bandwidth requirements. Quantum Communication Technologies Quantum key distribution (QKD) has the potential to enhance the security of high-value tourism communications by employing quantum mechanics to detect eavesdroppers. Current Quantum Key Distribution methods are ineffective over extended distances and require specialized infrastructure for operation. Quantum random number generators can provide really random cryptographic keys, hence enhancing the security of cryptographic systems in tourism. Quantum random number generation is now available in hardware security modules for commercial applications.

The Expansion of Artificial Intelligence and Machine Learning

As artificial intelligence and machine learning technologies advance, they create new avenues for attacks and vulnerabilities while simultaneously facilitating enhancements in tourism cybersecurity.

Next-generation AI security systems will employ sophisticated machine learning models capable of detecting subtle attack patterns and autonomously adapting to address emerging threats. Deep learning techniques, like convolutional neural networks and recurrent neural networks, may identify intricate patterns in security data that conventional rule-based systems fail to detect. Federated learning enables tourism organizations to collaboratively train machine learning models while preserving the confidentiality of private data. This approach enables organizations to leverage collective intelligence while safeguarding their data and maintaining their competitive advantage. Explainable AI methodologies address the "black box" issue in machine learning security systems by elucidating the rationale behind security choices. This transparency is crucial for adhering to regulations and investigating occurrences in tourism destinations. Malicious actors utilizing AI are increasingly integrating this technology to enhance the efficacy of their assaults, hence complicating the efforts of cybersecurity in the tourism sector to maintain pace. AI-driven social engineering attacks may generate very persuasive phishing messages tailored to individual victims using information from social media and other sources. Deep-fake technology may be employed to create counterfeit videos or audio messages that appear to originate from credible customer service representatives or leaders in the tourism industry. Individuals may utilize these attacks to manipulate people into compliance or to damage the reputations of enterprises. Adversarial machine learning attacks attempt to deceive AI security systems by generating inputs that lead to misclassification or failure of the system. Tourism organizations utilizing AI security systems must include safeguards against these sophisticated attacks. Future cybersecurity systems for tourists will increasingly possess autonomous reaction capabilities that may neutralize attacks and restore services without human intervention. These systems will utilize reinforcement learning to enhance their responses to circumstances based on historical occurrences. Self-driving incident response systems must achieve a balance between rapidity and effectiveness while ensuring human oversight and accountability. Integrating automated responses for prevalent hazards with human judgment for complex or significant events may yield optimal outcomes. (Taylor et al., 2011).

Incorporating Extended Reality - The incorporation of extended reality (XR) technologies, such as virtual reality (VR), augmented reality (AR), and mixed reality (MR), into tourism experiences introduces novel cybersecurity challenges and opportunities.

Extended reality applications for tourism collect substantial private information, including biometric data, activity patterns, and details about the location. Virtual reality headsets capable of tracking eye movement can reveal individuals' cognitive and emotional states, whilst augmented reality applications can gather extensive data on users' real-world surroundings.

To ensure privacy in XR environments, it is essential to devise creative methods for restricting data gathering and managing permissions. In immersive environments where data collection may occur continuously, conventional privacy protections may be insufficient.

Similar to IoT devices, XR gadgets typically lack the computational capacity to establish robust security measures. However, because to the immersive nature of XR applications, security issues are more apparent and may further undermine users' faith.

Immersive Security Training with XR technology offers tourism firms innovative and effective methods for educating their personnel in cybersecurity. Virtual reality simulations may offer authentic training scenarios that enable employees to practice addressing cybersecurity issues without jeopardizing real systems or data.

Immersive training environments may replicate the pressure and time limitations of authentic cybersecurity crises, rendering them superior for preparation compared to conventional classroom training. Incorporating gamified elements into security training might enhance its enjoyment and retention.

Augmented reality applications can offer security guidance precisely when required by overlaying pertinent information and instructions onto real-world environments. For example, augmented reality applications may assist employees in adhering to incident response protocols while addressing security concerns.

Blockchain and Additional Distributed Technologies

Blockchain and other distributed technologies are always evolving, presenting novel methods to enhance tourist security while simultaneously complicating processes. Smart contracts might automate several aspects of cybersecurity in tourism, including incident response, compliance monitoring, and evidence preservation. These automated systems may respond to security incidents more swiftly than humans, while maintaining comprehensive audit records.

Decentralized identity management systems may provide tourists greater control over their personal information. These solutions would facilitate secure identification verification among several service providers. Eliminating centralized identity databases may reduce the risk of significant data breaches through self-sovereign identifying methods.

Utilizing blockchain for the exchange of hazard data might enable tourism firms to collaborate in real time without necessitating mutual trust or intricate legal contracts. Decentralized threat intelligence networks may provide more comprehensive and current insights into risks than our existing information-sharing methods. Cross-chain interoperability solutions enable the seamless operation of disparate blockchain systems. This enables the construction of comprehensive distributed security architectures that encompass several blockchain networks and conventional systems.

Layer-2 scaling solutions address the transaction throughput issues inherent in conventional blockchain systems. This enhances the use of blockchain technology for tourism applications requiring the management of many transactions. State channels and sidechains provide near-instantaneous transactions while preserving the security attributes of blockchain technology.

Integration of Edge Computing With 5G

The deployment of 5G networks and the emergence of edge computing present new opportunities and challenges for cybersecurity in the tourism sector.

Edge Security Architecture enables 5G networks to provide communication with minimal latency. This might enable the feasibility of real-time cybersecurity applications, such as automated incident response and swift fraud detection. The complexity of 5G networks inherently increases their vulnerability to potential attacks. Edge computing places processing capabilities nearer to tourism services and consumers. This enables more sophisticated local security evaluations and reduces the necessity for cloud services. However, edge devices may lack robust security protections, rendering them susceptible to physical attacks by intruders.

Network slicing in 5G networks allocates network resources for applications critical to security. This provides cybersecurity systems with isolation and quality of service guarantees. Network slicing may assist tourist organizations in ensuring that security functions had adequate network resources during peak usage periods. The enhancement of IoT security in tourism environments may be significantly achieved through 5G networks and edge computing, which provide resource-constrained devices with the necessary bandwidth and processing power to implement sophisticated security measures. Distributed security processing may transfer security chores from IoT devices to nearby edge computing resources. This enables the implementation of more sophisticated security mechanisms without the necessity of purchasing costly hardware for each device. Zero-trust network architectures are enhanced by 5G and edge computing, since the increased bandwidth and reduced latency provide continuous authentication and authorization of all network connections.

8. OPTIMAL STRATEGIES AND CASE ANALYSES

Major Hotel Chain Modifications to Cybersecurity

A comprehensive case study of a major global hotel chain's cybersecurity transformation illustrates several concepts and challenges discussed in this chapter. The corporation operates over 5,000 hotels across more than 100 countries, accommodating millions of guests annually and handling billions of dollars in transactions.

The hotel chain's cybersecurity posture prior to the transformation effort resembled that of several other tourist enterprises. Security measures were implemented solely in response to specific incidents or regulatory mandates, resulting in a disjointed array of security controls that functioned independently. Each hotel operated independently, with minimal assistance from central security. The organization had many significant data breaches, one of which in 2018 compromised the personal information of over 500 million visitors. These incidents demonstrated that the existing security framework was inadequate and exerted pressure on regulators and the company's reputation to implement significant security improvements.

Legacy systems posed significant challenges, particularly since several critical applications were developed in the 1980s. The majority of hotels' property management systems (PMS) were developed using outdated technologies that lacked several security protocols. Diverse properties employed varying point-of-sale systems, resulting in inconsistent security measures.

The cybersecurity transformation initiative commenced in 2019 with a three-year timeline and a budget over $200 million. The objective was to implement a unified security architecture for all properties while permitting each hotel to operate independently. The corporation employed a zero-trust security model, necessitating that all network connections, regardless of their origin or source, be verified and permitted. This strategy was particularly vital due to the dispersion of hotel activities and the diverse array of devices and systems employed by clients and staff.

The modification entails transitioning to cloud-based security solutions, ensuring uniform protection across all hotels while reducing the workload for individual hotel IT personnel. A hybrid cloud approach was utilized to address the data localization requirements of several nations. The global impact of the change complicated coordination efforts. Certain sites were required to adhere to varying regulations across different nations, while others operated under franchise agreements that impeded the central office's ability to make technological decisions.

Staff training was regarded as essential for success, as the new security systems required distinct operational methods. A comprehensive training program was developed, with materials in over 20 languages and customized for various positions within the organization.

The guest experience was paramount, since security measures should not detract from the hospitality experience. We conducted extensive testing with actual users to ensure that the security enhancements were as apparent as possible for visitors. Outcomes and Insights: The move significantly enhanced the organization's security. The average duration to identify security issues decreased from weeks to hours, while the average response time diminished from days to minutes. No significant data breaches occurred in the two years following the implementation of the system. Guest satisfaction scores were constant throughout the rollout, indicating that the modifications to security did not detrimentally affect the customer experience. Certain security enhancements, such as mobile key systems and contactless payment options, increased passenger satisfaction. The overall cost of ownership for cybersecurity decreased, despite the initial expenditure being substantial. This was due to unified security services reducing costs and diminishing the need to employ specialized security personnel for each site. Key lessons learned include the necessity of leadership support for change, the significance of effective change management, and the benefits of collaboration among firms within the same sector to exchange threat intelligence and best practices.

Collaborating to Enhance Cybersecurity at Regional Tourism Locations

This case study examines a collaborative initiative to enhance cybersecurity among several tourism stakeholders in a prominent tourist destination. The initiative demonstrates how many entities may collaborate to enhance collective cybersecurity while adhering to regulations and maintaining their economic advantage. Collaboration Framework Over 50 entities collaborated, encompassing hotels, restaurants, attractions, transit businesses, and governmental institutions. A formal governance structure was established to address issues around accountability and information exchange, with representatives from various stakeholder groups and legal frameworks. A collaborative threat intelligence platform was established to facilitate the real-time exchange of information on cybersecurity threats and incidents. The program employs automated techniques to conceal sensitive company data while facilitating efficient threat sharing. Joint incident response drills were conducted quarterly to assess team collaboration and identify areas for improvement. In these exercises, simulated cyberattacks targeted many firms simultaneously, necessitating a collaborative response. The alliance established many shared security services that provided smaller enterprises with affordable access to robust cybersecurity solutions. A Security Operations Center (SOC) monitored and addressed events for member organizations continuously, 24/7. Shared threat hunting services utilized advanced analytics to detect indicators of compromise across several enterprises beforehand. This collaborative endeavor enabled the identification of sophisticated attacks that may have been overlooked by individual teams. A forensic response team collaborated with specialists to examine intricate cybersecurity incidents. The squad comprised digital forensics specialists, attorneys, and other professionals collaborating with the police. The collaboration significantly enhanced the overall cybersecurity of the destination. The duration required to identify assaults on many firms decreased by over 70%, while the average cybersecurity expenditure for all participating corporations diminished by 30%. Surveys and increased visitor numbers indicate that travelers possess greater confidence in the safety and security of the destination. International tourist groups saw the collaborative effort as a commendable model for other locations to emulate. The initiative provided significant insights into the economics of collaborative cybersecurity, demonstrating that cooperation may yield superior security outcomes at reduced costs compared to individual efforts.

Implementing Aviation Cybersecurity

The aviation industry is among the most security-sensitive sectors of the tourism ecosystem. The failure of cybersecurity might jeopardize passenger safety and operational efficiency. This case study examines the comprehensive implementation of cybersecurity by a major international airline. The regulatory landscape for aviation cybersecurity is monitored by entities such as the Federal Aviation Administration (FAA), the European Union Aviation Safety Agency (EASA), and the International Civil Aviation Organization (ICAO). These regulations encompass both operational technology (OT) systems that oversee aircraft and air traffic, as well as information technology (IT) systems that handle passenger data and commercial operations. The aviation industry's safety culture facilitated the implementation of cybersecurity, as safety and security adhere to several same regulations and protocols. Nevertheless, the global nature of aviation activity complicates the implementation of uniform security protocols across all locations. Challenges in System Architecture: Contemporary aircraft include several interconnected systems that require robust cybersecurity protocols. Flight management systems, in-flight entertainment networks, and passenger Wi-Fi systems must be safeguarded while remaining entirely distinct from critical flight control systems.

Ground-based systems, such as air traffic control interfaces, maintenance systems, and passenger service platforms, are additional targets for hackers and require protection. The airline's reservation system processed over 100 million transactions annually and required constant availability with minimal latency. Legacy systems posed significant challenges as several critical aviation systems were developed decades ago, neglecting contemporary cybersecurity threats. Due to certification mandates and operational interdependencies, replacing these systems is typically challenging. A defense-in-depth security architecture was implemented, providing varying levels of protection for distinct system kinds. Air gaps and isolated networks were employed to maintain the segregation of essential flight systems, while systems visible to passengers were equipped with comprehensive monitoring and hazard detection functionalities. Advanced threat detection systems utilized machine learning techniques to identify anomalous patterns in network traffic and system behavior. These algorithms were trained on aviation-specific data to enhance their accuracy in detection and reduce false positives. We developed a comprehensive incident response strategy that outlines procedures for addressing various cybersecurity challenges, including collaboration with law enforcement and aviation authorities. Routine drills assessed individuals' responsiveness and identified areas for improvement. Outcomes and Continuous Enhancement: The cybersecurity solution significantly improved threat detection and response capabilities, while maintaining operational efficiency and regulatory compliance. During the three years following the installation, the airline had no significant cybersecurity issues. Continuous improvement techniques utilized insights gained from industry challenges and emerging threats. The airline participated in cybersecurity working groups within the aviation sector and shared threat intelligence with other operators while maintaining the confidentiality of the individuals engaged. Other airlines within the same alliance adopted the cybersecurity program as a benchmark due to its efficacy. This illustrates the significance of collaboration and information sharing across organizations within the same sector.

9. FUTURE ENHANCEMENT

Recommendations for Strategy - This chapter provides a comprehensive examination of the issues and solutions pertaining to cybersecurity in smart tourism. This allows for the formulation of various strategic recommendations for distinct stakeholders within the tourism sector.

For Organizations Engaged in Tourism

Tourism organizations have to employ risk-based approaches to cybersecurity that prioritize investment in the most probable and detrimental attack scenarios. Routine risk evaluations must encompass both conventional cybersecurity threats and those particular to the tourist sector, such as travel fraud and targeted assaults on specific locales.

Effective cybersecurity necessitates the unwavering commitment of the company's management. Chief Executive Officers and other senior leaders must demonstrate their dedication to cybersecurity by allocating resources, implementing policies, and actively participating in cybersecurity governance. Cybersecurity should be monitored at the board level, with periodic reports detailing the organization's performance in cybersecurity and its incident response efficacy. Cybersecurity should be integrated into company strategy rather than perceived only as a technological concern. Security should be a consideration while determining new services, collaborations, and market expansion. In advocating for investment in cybersecurity, firms should emphasize both risk mitigation and the acquisition of a competitive advantage through enhanced security measures.

Organizations must enhance their incident response capabilities to address the particular requirements of tourism enterprises. Strategies for addressing security concerns must include their impact on visitors, the necessity of collaboration among various stakeholders, and the worldwide nature of several tourism activities.

For Entities That Oversee Destinations

Destination management organizations (DMOs) might facilitate collaboration among local tourism enterprises about cybersecurity. This collaboration should encompass the exchange of threat intelligence, joint incident response efforts, and inclusive training and awareness programs. Destination Management Organizations (DMOs) must collaborate with governmental entities to ensure that the cybersecurity measures implemented at tourism locations are robust enough to safeguard tourists and maintain their trust. This may entail advocating for appropriate rules and regulations, fostering the development of cybersecurity competencies, and facilitating collaboration between public and private entities in the realm of cybersecurity.

Cybersecurity must be integral to marketing and communication strategies, emphasizing safety protocols and certifications that demonstrate a commitment to safeguarding visitors and their information. (Ali, 2025). However, these communications must achieve a balance between transparency and operational security. For Technology Enterprises - Tourism technology vendors should use security-by-design principles that incorporate cybersecurity considerations throughout all phases of product development. Incorporating security into products from the outset is essential, rather than a consideration that arises after. Vendors must provide comprehensive security support services, including security monitoring, incident assistance, and regular security upgrades. Due to the global nature of tourism activities, vendors must provide assistance to clients 24/7 and be knowledgeable about various regulations.

To facilitate collaboration among tourism organizations and simplify security measures, we should promote initiatives aimed at standardizing the sector. To ensure uniform security across all technologies utilized in tourism, vendors should participate in industry working groups and standard-setting organizations.

Optimal Practices for Technology

Design and Architecture utilize zero-trust security frameworks that verify and authenticate all access requests, regardless of their origin or the user credentials presented. This strategy is particularly pertinent in tourist contexts where individuals employ various devices and network connections to access services from diverse locations. Employ defense-in-depth strategies that incorporate additional layers of security controls. One should not rely solely on a single security control to safeguard critical systems or data. Perimeter security, network security, application security, and data protection must all be integral components of a layered strategy. Develop systems that maintain functionality despite attacks or system malfunctions. During security incidents, graceful degradation strategies should prioritize critical activities and temporarily disable non-essential services. Establish comprehensive logging and monitoring to observe all activities occurring within the system. Data logs must be centralized, encrypted, and protected against alteration. Retention periods must include forensic requirements, storage expenses, and privacy issues.

Data Protection - Employ data categorization methodologies to classify information into groups according to its sensitivity and legal stipulations. Classification systems ensure the appropriate security measures are implemented for each data type, since different data categories require distinct levels of protection. Encrypt data that is at rest, in transit, and in processing. Encryption key management systems must utilize hardware security modules (HSMs) and provide key rotation and escrow procedures. End-to-end encryption should be utilized for highly sensitive communications and transactions. Establish comprehensive data loss prevention (DLP) systems that monitor and regulate data flow in and out of your organization. DLP systems must be configured to detect and prevent illicit data transfers while minimizing false positives that might disrupt standard company operations. Organizations must remain cognizant of the data they collect, handle, and retain by conducting frequent data inventories and audits. To mitigate privacy risks and alleviate legal compliance burdens, data minimization practices should be employed.

Identity and Access Management

Employ robust authentication techniques that surpass just passwords. All high-risk activities must necessitate multi-factor authentication, and adaptive authentication should modify requirements according to risk evaluations.

Implement role-based access control (RBAC) and attribute-based access control (ABAC) systems to provide precise control over user permissions. Access permissions must be determined by an individual's job requirements and should be routinely verified and updated. Utilize privileged access management (PAM) technology to enhance the authority of administrative and high-privilege accounts. Employ just-in-time access provisioning to restrict visibility of privileged credentials to a limited number of individuals.

Addressing and Recovering From Events

Develop comprehensive strategies for responding to all types of cyberattacks and their potential impact on tourism operations. Plans must delineate responsibilities, establish communication protocols, and outline procedures for restoring normalcy. Conduct regular incident response drills to evaluate team collaboration and identify areas for improvement. Tabletop drills should simulate realistic scenarios that might impact tourism operations, encompass incidents involving several organizations, and involve investigations that cross international boundaries. Establish automated crisis response systems capable of neutralizing threats and mitigating harm independently, without human intervention. Automated responses must be meticulously strategized to avoid obstructing legitimate activities or exacerbating circumstances unnecessarily. Maintain comprehensive backup and recovery solutions that enable the swift restoration of critical systems and data. Individuals have to regularly assess their backup systems to ensure they are safeguarded against the identical vulnerabilities that might affect their primary systems.

Optimal Practices for Organizations - Risk Management and Governance Establish clear cybersecurity governance frameworks that delineate roles, responsibilities, and mechanisms for accountability (Pattanaik et al., 2023). Cybersecurity governance must be integrated into the company's overarching governance framework and should encompass regular reporting to the board of directors and senior management. Implement comprehensive risk management systems that identify, assess, and mitigate cybersecurity threats. Risk assessments must be conducted regularly and should encompass information on hazards from both internal and external sources. Establish cybersecurity policies and laws specifically designed to address the requirements and characteristics of the tourism industry. Policies must be often revised to address emerging dangers and regulations.

Consciousness and Instruction

Deliver comprehensive cybersecurity training sessions that encompass the responsibilities and requirements of various employee categories. Training must be tailored to the tourism sector and incorporate pertinent examples and scenarios that reflect the operations of tourism enterprises. Conduct regular phishing simulations and security awareness assessments to evaluate staff knowledge and identify areas for improvement. The objective of these activities ought to be to educate individuals, rather than to penalize them. Develop training programs for personnel that instruct them on identifying and addressing cybersecurity issues. Training must encompass both the resolution of technical issues and effective communication among individuals. Mitigating Risks Associated with Third Parties - Implement comprehensive third-party risk management protocols to assess and monitor the cybersecurity of vendors, partners, and external entities. Cybersecurity assessments and ongoing surveillance must be integral to due diligence. Draft contracts that clearly delineate the cybersecurity responsibilities and expectations for collaboration with third parties. Contracts must provide procedures for event management, data security measures, and auditing protocols. Participate in industry associations that disseminate information on hazards and best practices among firms. Collaborating inside the industry can enhance our understanding of emerging hazards and strategies for mitigation.

10. CONCLUSION

The digital transformation of the tourism sector has created innovative opportunities to enhance visitor experiences, however it has also introduced complex cybersecurity challenges that require intelligent and adaptable solutions. This chapter examined the significant relationship between cybersecurity designs and forensic analytics within smart tourism ecosystems. It encompassed a comprehensive assessment of the hazards, technology, and strategies required to ensure the security of modern tourism infrastructure. Tourism environments possess distinctive characteristics, including global accessibility, diverse stakeholder networks, elevated user mobility, and the necessity for real-time operations. These characteristics create distinct cybersecurity challenges that conventional corporate security measures cannot adequately address. Smart tourism systems are interconnected, allowing enriched and personalized experiences. This also renders them more susceptible to assaults and complicates their dependencies, necessitating comprehensive security frameworks.

Incorporating forensic analytics into cybersecurity frameworks represents a significant advancement in tourism security strategies. It enables companies to transition from responding to incidents to proactively seeking risks and continuously collecting evidence. Real-time forensic analytics provide unprecedented visibility into attack trends, facilitating rapid responses to emerging threats while preserving evidence for legal proceedings and ensuring compliance with regulations. Tourism companies have several challenges in executing security protocols. The issues encompass technological challenges in integrating new security protocols with legacy systems, as well as organizational and cultural obstacles that may impede security-focused enhancements. However, the case studies and exemplary practices demonstrate that these issues may be addressed by strategic planning, commitment from leadership, and collaboration with other enterprises within the same industry. Emerging technologies such as quantum computing, advanced artificial intelligence, augmented reality, blockchain systems, and 5G networks will continually transform the methods employed to safeguard travelers online. Companies must prepare for technological advancements while also addressing current security challenges. This necessitates the utilization of adaptable strategies that can evolve in response to shifting challenges and technological advancements. The economic implications of cybersecurity in tourism extend beyond the initial costs of security measures. They encompass reputational considerations, regulatory compliance obligations, and the fundamental trust relationships that enhance tourism experiences. Organizations have to perceive investment in comprehensive cybersecurity capabilities not as an expense, but as a strategic facilitator that safeguards stakeholder interests while advancing the company's objectives. (Srivastava et al., 2023). To address the global nature of tourism cybersecurity issues, nations must collaborate and cooperate. No single corporation or nation can effectively address these issues independently. They must collaborate to exchange threat data, coordinate incident responses, and enhance their capabilities. The future of cybersecurity in smart tourism relies on adaptable and intelligence-driven systems. These architectures will adapt to emerging dangers while maintaining the seamless, tailored experiences that enhance the efficacy of tourism services. Integrating artificial intelligence, machine learning, and advanced analytics into security and forensic technologies is an effective method to enhance the overall security of tourism ecosystems. As the tourism industry evolves and integrates new technologies, the demand for cybersecurity will inevitably increase. Organizations that implement robust cybersecurity protocols proactively will be more adept at capitalizing on the advantages of digital transformation while safeguarding the interests of all stakeholders within the tourism value chain. This chapter provides recommendations and best practices for tourism organizations, destination management firms, technology providers, and lawmakers seeking to enhance their cybersecurity measures. Cybersecurity is not a destination; it is a constant journey that requires continuous commitment, adaptability, and advancement. This research represents a significant advancement in understanding and addressing the complex cybersecurity challenges encountered by intelligent tourism ecosystems. However, more research and development are essential to address emerging hazards, evaluate new technologies, and devise innovative strategies to cope with the rapid evolution of both tourism technologies and cyber threats. The primary objective of smart tourism cybersecurity is to protect the safety, privacy, and interests of all stakeholders while facilitating the continued growth and evolution of tourism. The tourism sector may acquire the trust and resilience necessary for sustained success in an increasingly digital environment by using comprehensive cybersecurity infrastructures and forensic analytics technologies. Achieving a completely safe smart tourism system necessitates collaboration among all stakeholders, the generation of innovative concepts, and unwavering commitment. The concepts, methods, and best practices presented in this chapter serve as an excellent foundation for this endeavor. The overall success of the tourist industry will hinge on collective efforts to prioritize security while continuing to provide the experiences and innovations that render tourism one of the most dynamic and significant sectors globally.

REFERENCES

Ali, S. I. (2025). Algorithmic Justice: Navigating AI's Role in Cybersecurity and Legal Transformation. In Luftman, J., & Tomer, A. (Eds.), *Moral and Legal Aspects of Artificial Intelligence: Machine Bias and Rule of Law* (pp. 229–264). IGI Global Scientific Publishing., DOI: 10.4018/979-8-3373-3114-0.ch007

Ali, S. I. (2025). Reinforcement learning for autonomous optimization in intelligent engineering. In Babulak, E. (Ed.), *AI-driven approaches for fully automated smart engineering* (pp. 313–344). IGI Global Scientific Publishing., DOI: 10.4018/979-8-3373-4839-1.ch011

Ali, S. I., Ravuri, H. K., Lakshmi, V. T., Ramya, A., Lavanya, K., & Bahade, S. (2024). The role of nanomaterials in the development of high-performance batteries. *Nanotechnology Perceptions, 20*(S11). Advance online publication. DOI: 10.62441/nano-ntp.v20iS11.2098

Alonso-Almeida, M. del M., & Giglio, C. (2024). Cybersecurity in tourism and hospitality management research: Current issues, trends, and an agenda for future research. *Tourism Management Perspectives, 50*, 101007. DOI: 10.1016/j.tmp.2024.101007

Biswal, A., Bhushanwar, K., Paija, P. G., Zalawadia, K., Pradhan, P. P., & Ali, S. I. (2025). Procedural Generation and Adaptive Gameplay: The Role of AI and Generative AI in Contemporary Game Development. In Sousa, J., & Tavares, R. (Eds.), *Reshaping the Video Game Landscape With AI and GenAI* (pp. 233–258). IGI Global Scientific Publishing., DOI: 10.4018/979-8-3373-4637-3.ch008

Casey, E. (2014). *Handbook of digital forensics and investigation*. Academic Press.

Dakshinamurthi, V., Ali, S. I., Karthikeyan, T., & Kulkarni, N. S. (2023). Causal convolution employing Almeida–Pineda recurrent backpropagation for mobile network design. *ICTACT Journal on Communication Technology, 14*(4), 3091–3096. DOI: 10.21917/ijct.2023.0460

Dehghantanha, A., & Choo, K.-K. R. (2020). *Contemporary digital forensic investigations of cloud and mobile applications*. Elsevier.

Farooqui, Y., Ali, S. I., Shekokar, K., Patidar, P. K., Bhushanwar, K., & Nandi, P. K. (2025). A secure framework for decentralized digital lockers using blockchain technology. *Journal of Computational Science, 21*(9), 2105–2112. DOI: 10.3844/jcssp.2025.2105.2112

Florido-Benítez, L. (2024). The cybersecurity applied by online travel agencies and hotels to protect users' private data in smart cities. *Smart Cities*, *7*(1), 475–495. DOI: 10.3390/smartcities7010019

Florido-Benítez, L. (2025). The role of cybersecurity as a preventive measure in digital tourism and travel: A systematic literature review. *Discover Computing*, *28*(1), 28. Advance online publication. DOI: 10.1007/s10791-025-09523-3

Gretzel, U., Sigala, M., Xiang, Z., & Koo, C. (2015). Smart tourism: Foundations and developments. *Electronic Markets*, *25*(3), 179–188. DOI: 10.1007/s12525-015-0196-8

Karadayi-Usta, S. (2024). Cybersecurity risks analysis in the hospitality industry. *Systems*, *12*(10), 397. DOI: 10.3390/systems12100397

Paraskevas, A. (2020). Cybersecurity in travel and tourism: A risk-based approach. In Z. Xiang, M. Fuchs, U. Gretzel, & W. Höpken (Eds.), *Handbook of e-Tourism* (pp. 1–23). Springer. DOI: 10.1007/978-3-030-05324-6_100-1

Pattanaik, B., Kumari, S. S., Kumar, C. K., Pattnaik, M., Ali, S. I., & Kumarasamy, M. (2023). An innovation of algebraic mathematical-based statistical analysis model for complex number theory. In *Proceedings of the 2023 International Conference on Disruptive Technologies (ICDT)* (pp. 94–99). IEEE. https://doi.org/DOI: 10.1109/ICDT57929.2023.10151169

Srivastava, S. S., Ali, S. I., Srivastava, A. K., & Goswami, C. (2024). Improving 5G network performance with MIMO technology using beamforming algorithm. *ICTACT Journal on Communication Technology*, *15*(2), 3173–3180. DOI: 10.21917/ijct.2024.0472

Srivastava, S. T. C., Sharmiladevi, D., Sugumar, D., Ali, S. I., Jones Mary, T. A., & Kumar, S. (2023). Using a smart wearable device for monitoring social distance in smart cities. In *2023 International Conference on Research Methodologies in Knowledge Management, Artificial Intelligence and Telecommunication Engineering (RMKMATE)* (pp. 1–5). IEEE. https://doi.org/DOI: 10.1109/RMKMATE59243.2023.10369118

Taylor, M., Haggerty, J., Gresty, D., & Lamb, D. (2011). Forensic investigation of cloud computing systems. *Network Security*, *2011*(3), 4–10. DOI: 10.1016/S1353-4858(11)70024-1

Zawoad, S., & Hasan, R. (2018). Trustworthy digital forensics in the Internet of Things. *Computer*, *51*(7), 40–47. DOI: 10.1109/MC.2018.3191261

Chapter 10
Securing the Experience:
Cybersecurity and Digital Forensics in the Age of Smart Tourism

Vikas Sharma
http://orcid.org/0009-0009-3174-5965
Swami Vivekanand Subharti University, India

ABSTRACT

The rapid digitalization of the tourism sector through smart technologies—such as IoT, AI, big data, and mobile platforms—has revolutionized the travel experience while simultaneously introducing new cybersecurity and data privacy risks. This study explores the intersection of smart tourism and digital vulnerabilities, emphasizing the need for robust cybersecurity frameworks and digital forensic readiness. Through comprehensive literature review, stakeholder analysis, and case-based evaluation, the research identifies critical security gaps in tourism infrastructures and proposes actionable recommendations for policymakers, tourism operators, and technology developers. The paper highlights the importance of proactive threat mitigation, international collaboration, user awareness, and advanced forensic systems to ensure a secure and resilient tourism ecosystem in the digital age.

1. INTRODUCTION

The advent of smart tourism, driven by the integration of Information and Communication Technologies (ICTs), the Internet of Things (IoT), Artificial Intelligence (AI), and Big Data, has significantly transformed the global tourism and hospitality industry. This digital revolution has not only enhanced the tourist experience through

DOI: 10.4018/979-8-2600-1850-7.ch010

personalization, real-time assistance, and immersive technologies like augmented reality (AR) and virtual reality (VR), but it has also opened new avenues for digital vulnerabilities, cyber threats, and data breaches. As destinations become "smart," interconnected systems—ranging from digital payment gateways and biometric border controls to online booking platforms and geo-location-based services—become targets of sophisticated cyberattacks (Sigala, 2023; Gretzel et al., 2022). In this landscape, cybersecurity and digital forensics have emerged as critical domains to ensure the resilience, trustworthiness, and sustainability of smart tourism ecosystems.

Smart tourism involves the heavy use of digital technologies that facilitate seamless experiences for tourists while allowing destination managers to make data-informed decisions. Smart destinations leverage a wide array of digital assets such as mobile applications, cloud-based services, data analytics tools, and intelligent transportation systems (ITS) to optimize operations and engage with tourists (Koo, Shin & Gretzel, 2021). These innovations, while enhancing convenience and efficiency, also present substantial security risks. For instance, the unauthorized access to personal data via hacked mobile applications, ransomware attacks on hotel management systems, and phishing scams through fraudulent travel websites are on the rise (ENISA, 2023). In 2022 alone, the hospitality and travel sector experienced a 300% increase in cyberattacks compared to pre-pandemic levels, with major hotel chains reporting data breaches affecting millions of customers (IBM X-Force, 2023).

Cybersecurity, in the context of smart tourism, refers to the protective mechanisms and strategies employed to defend digital infrastructure, traveler data, and system integrity against unauthorized access, disruption, or damage. This includes the deployment of firewalls, encryption technologies, intrusion detection systems, and multi-factor authentication protocols. However, as attackers employ more advanced and AI-driven techniques, conventional cybersecurity tools may no longer suffice. Consequently, digital forensics—the process of investigating, analyzing, and preserving digital evidence in the aftermath of cyber incidents—has become indispensable for understanding attack vectors, attributing responsibility, and improving incident response mechanisms (Casey, 2020; Alhogail & Mirza, 2022).

Furthermore, the rapid expansion of the digital tourist footprint—comprising search histories, biometric identifiers, booking records, and location data—raises ethical and regulatory concerns related to privacy and surveillance. The General Data Protection Regulation (GDPR) in the European Union and similar frameworks worldwide mandate that tourism service providers ensure transparency, consent, and data protection for all users. Non-compliance not only undermines customer trust but also exposes organizations to hefty penalties and reputational damage (European Commission, 2022). Therefore, the need for a proactive cybersecurity culture, supported by robust legal compliance and crisis management protocols, is more urgent than ever.

One particularly alarming trend is the use of deepfakes, AI-generated impersonations, and synthetic media to manipulate tourist reviews, create fraudulent identities for scams, or simulate unauthorized access to biometric security systems. As AI becomes more embedded in smart tourism infrastructure, adversarial attacks that exploit machine learning models can compromise everything from dynamic pricing algorithms to autonomous navigation in smart cities (Bose & Mahapatra, 2023). Addressing these threats necessitates not only technical innovation but also interdisciplinary collaboration across cybersecurity experts, tourism technologists, policymakers, and ethical AI researchers.

Moreover, smart tourism is increasingly reliant on blockchain-based transactions for enhanced transparency and trust. Yet, even decentralized systems are not immune to vulnerabilities such as smart contract exploits or wallet thefts. For instance, travel platforms adopting NFTs (non-fungible tokens) for loyalty programs or digital passes face risks associated with token fraud and unauthorized duplication (Tapscott & Tapscott, 2022). This underlines the importance of integrating digital forensics capabilities into blockchain environments to trace illicit activities and uphold the integrity of these systems.

The rise of cyber-physical systems such as autonomous vehicles, smart hotels, and sensor-driven travel experiences has added another layer of complexity. A cyberattack on a smart hotel's energy management system or elevator control could have real-world implications, jeopardizing not just digital assets but human safety. The interconnectedness of physical infrastructure and cyberspace calls for a shift toward cyber-resilient architectural designs and real-time anomaly detection (Chatterjee & Kar, 2023).

In sum, as smart tourism continues to evolve, the stakes associated with cybersecurity grow exponentially. While digital technologies promise efficiency, personalization, and connectivity, they also expose the tourism industry to unprecedented levels of risk. Investing in cybersecurity infrastructure, promoting digital literacy among tourism stakeholders, and embedding forensic readiness within smart destination frameworks are no longer optional—they are strategic imperatives. This paper delves deep into the multifaceted challenges and emerging solutions at the intersection of cybersecurity, digital forensics, and smart tourism. It seeks to contribute to the broader discourse on safeguarding digital tourism ecosystems while maintaining the integrity, reliability, and enjoyment of the traveler experience in an increasingly smart world.

The growing dependence on digital infrastructure within the tourism and hospitality industry also highlights a significant skills gap among tourism professionals. While the sector has embraced smart technologies at an accelerated pace, the workforce often lacks adequate training in cybersecurity best practices, threat detection, and incident response strategies. Frontline workers, hotel managers, and even senior administrators may not fully understand the implications of data privacy laws or recognize social engineering attempts, making them soft targets for cybercriminals. As a result, employee negligence—whether unintentional or through lack of awareness—remains one of the leading causes of data breaches in the tourism sector. Bridging this knowledge gap through targeted cybersecurity education and simulation-based training is crucial for creating a human firewall capable of supporting secure tourism operations.

In addition to technical safeguards and workforce training, organizational culture plays a pivotal role in enhancing cybersecurity resilience. Tourism businesses, especially small and medium enterprises (SMEs), often operate under resource constraints and may consider cybersecurity measures as optional add-ons rather than core business functions. However, the increasing frequency and severity of cyber incidents demand a cultural shift toward proactive risk management and digital hygiene. Establishing internal cybersecurity policies, performing regular audits, conducting penetration testing, and creating incident response teams are strategic steps that must be embedded in the operational frameworks of tourism institutions. Moreover, cross-sectoral collaboration among hospitality companies, IT service providers, law enforcement agencies, and academic researchers is essential to create comprehensive defense mechanisms tailored to the tourism domain.

The need for regional and international cooperation in cybersecurity and digital forensics has become particularly important in an era of borderless digital threats. Tourists often move across jurisdictions, accessing digital services in multiple countries during a single trip. Cyber incidents affecting these travelers may involve transnational actors and fall under multiple legal regimes. This complicates the investigation and prosecution of cybercrimes. Therefore, international tourism organizations and cybersecurity alliances must work together to develop standardized protocols for information sharing, mutual legal assistance, and capacity building. Initiatives such as the UNWTO's digital transformation agenda and INTERPOL's cybercrime strategy provide a collaborative foundation for enhancing global cybersecurity preparedness in tourism contexts.

Another area gaining prominence is the forensic readiness of smart destinations. While many cities are investing in technologies to become "smart," they often overlook the importance of forensic preparedness. Forensic readiness refers to the ability of a system or organization to maximize its capability to use digital evidence while minimizing the costs of a forensic investigation. In tourism, this could involve the systematic logging of visitor data, securing system logs from manipulation, and integrating forensic capabilities within smart devices such as surveillance cameras, check-in kiosks, and biometric access control systems. By incorporating forensic readiness into the design and deployment of smart tourism infrastructure, destinations can ensure faster recovery, legal compliance, and better decision-making in the wake of cyber incidents.

The tourism industry's increasing reliance on third-party vendors for services such as cloud computing, online payment processing, and guest engagement platforms further complicates the cybersecurity landscape. Each vendor introduces potential points of failure that must be secured and monitored. A single vulnerability in a third-party booking platform or payment gateway can jeopardize the entire customer experience and expose sensitive data. As such, robust vendor risk management practices—comprising due diligence assessments, compliance verification, service-level agreements, and continuous monitoring—are vital for safeguarding the tourism value chain. This underscores the interconnected nature of digital tourism ecosystems, where the security of one component affects the trustworthiness of the whole.

As we enter a future marked by increasing automation and predictive analytics, ethical considerations surrounding surveillance, biometric profiling, and predictive policing in tourism environments will intensify. Technologies such as facial recognition used for check-ins, AI-powered customer service bots, and smart wearables collecting health data during wellness retreats raise pressing questions about informed consent, data ownership, and the right to digital anonymity. While these innovations offer unparalleled convenience and personalization, they also risk violating individual freedoms and promoting discriminatory practices. Thus, a balanced approach must be adopted—one that aligns technological advancement with human-centric values and rights-based governance frameworks.

The concept of cyber sustainability is also gaining traction in the context of smart tourism. Similar to environmental sustainability, cyber sustainability refers to the long-term maintenance of secure digital systems that support tourism without compromising future use or causing harm. This concept encourages tourism organizations to adopt lifecycle approaches to cybersecurity, from the secure design of digital tools to their ethical disposal and data decommissioning. It also highlights the importance of reducing digital waste and managing the carbon footprint of data centers and IoT devices used in tourism applications. Integrating cyber sustainability into smart tourism planning can thus contribute to a more holistic model of responsible tourism development.

In conclusion, smart tourism holds immense promise for enriching traveler experiences, optimizing destination management, and fostering economic growth. However, this promise is contingent upon the ability of tourism stakeholders to protect digital assets, personal data, and critical infrastructure from the ever-evolving landscape of cyber threats. Cybersecurity and digital forensics are no longer peripheral concerns but foundational pillars of smart tourism strategy. Their integration into every level of tourism planning—from technology design and staff training to policy-making and international cooperation—will determine the resilience, reliability, and ethical integrity of the tourism industry in the digital age.

2. OBJECTIVES OF THE STUDY

The primary aim of this study is to explore and analyze the intersection of cybersecurity, digital forensics, and smart tourism, identifying potential vulnerabilities and proposing comprehensive strategies for securing digital tourism ecosystems. The specific objectives are as follows:

2.1 To Examine the Current Technological Landscape of Smart Tourism

Identify and analyze the key digital technologies (e.g., IoT, AI, big data, blockchain) that are shaping smart tourism platforms and infrastructure.

2.2 To Assess Cybersecurity Challenges Associated With Smart Tourism Systems

Investigate the nature and frequency of cyber threats, data breaches, and digital vulnerabilities affecting tourists, service providers, and destination management organizations.

2.3 To Propose a Comprehensive and Adaptive Cybersecurity Model for Smart Tourism

Develop a strategic, multi-layered cybersecurity and digital forensics framework tailored to the specific needs of tourism stakeholders, promoting resilience, trust, and data security.

3. LITERATURE REVIEW

The intersection of smart tourism and cybersecurity has become a pivotal concern in modern tourism scholarship. As tourism destinations increasingly adopt digital innovations—ranging from IoT-based services to AI-driven personalization—the scope of cyber threats has widened significantly. The literature reflects a growing awareness of both the opportunities and the risks embedded within this digital evolution.

3.1 Smart Tourism Technologies and Digital Exposure

Smart tourism is defined by Buhalis and Amaranggana (2015) as the integration of ICTs into the tourism experience to improve service efficiency and personalization. Technologies such as big data analytics, wearable devices, augmented reality (AR), virtual reality (VR), mobile applications, and AI-enabled chatbots now shape the tourist journey from planning to post-travel sharing (Gretzel et al., 2015; Jung et al., 2022). While these technologies enhance convenience and user satisfaction, they also expose users to data privacy risks, tracking mechanisms, and cyber breaches.

Sigala (2020) emphasizes that the extensive use of social media platforms, mobile applications, and personalized services requires tourists to disclose substantial amounts of personal data, increasing their digital vulnerability. The absence of data anonymization, weak encryption protocols, and poor cybersecurity awareness further escalate these risks (Choi et al., 2023).

3.2 Cybersecurity Vulnerabilities in Tourism Ecosystems

The tourism and hospitality sector is particularly vulnerable to cyberattacks due to the volume of personal and financial data it processes (Pizam & Mansfeld, 2016). Alshaabani et al. (2022) explore the increasing instances of phishing, ransomware, identity theft, and credit card frauds targeting hotels, booking platforms, and airline services. These incidents not only threaten the individual's privacy but also damage brand credibility and market trust.

Furthermore, the decentralized nature of tourism services—spanning airlines, hotels, OTAs (Online Travel Agencies), and mobility services—creates multiple entry points for attackers. Zhou and Wang (2023) highlight that many tourism providers, especially SMEs, lack dedicated IT security infrastructure and training, making them easy targets for cybercriminals.

3.3 Digital Forensics: Post-Incident Response and Preparedness

Digital forensics plays a critical role in incident response and post-breach investigations within the tourism sector. Forensics involves collecting, analyzing, and preserving digital evidence to identify the nature and scope of cyber incidents (Hu & Zhang, 2021). However, the integration of forensics into tourism management is still in its infancy.

Most tourism businesses lack a defined incident response protocol or data breach notification strategy (UNWTO, 2022). The need for sector-specific forensic capabilities has been emphasized by OECD (2020), advocating for collaborative frameworks between tourism firms, law enforcement, and cybersecurity agencies. Despite this, very few case studies exist that document successful forensic investigations in travel technology breaches—indicating a gap in empirical research.

3.4 Legal Frameworks and Regulatory Gaps

The regulatory landscape surrounding cybersecurity and data protection in tourism remains fragmented. While the EU's General Data Protection Regulation (GDPR) has set a precedent for data rights and corporate responsibility, many tourist-heavy countries still lack robust digital protection laws (OECD, 2020; UNWTO, 2022). In Asia and Africa, where smart tourism is rapidly expanding, the legal mechanisms are often either outdated or poorly enforced.

Studies such as those by Alshaabani et al. (2022) and Sigala (2020) argue that the lack of global cybersecurity standards for tourism hinders effective cross-border protection of tourists' digital identities. This is especially concerning in the context of international travel, where data travels across jurisdictions.

3.5 Human Factors and Cyber Hygiene in Tourism

Human behavior and awareness continue to be major determinants of cybersecurity efficacy. Tourists, often unaware of phishing attacks or unsafe public Wi-Fi, become easy prey for cyber exploitation. Meanwhile, front-line tourism employees are often inadequately trained in cyber hygiene and data handling protocols (Choi et al., 2023).

As highlighted by Gretzel et al. (2015), there is a pressing need to educate both providers and consumers on digital literacy. Awareness campaigns, scenario-based training, and cybersecurity certifications for tourism professionals are proposed as long-term solutions.

3.6 Ethical, Social, and Psychological Dimensions

Beyond technical and regulatory concerns, scholars have also raised ethical questions surrounding surveillance, tracking, and consent. Smart cities and destinations often use sensors, facial recognition, and behavioral analytics to offer predictive services (Hu & Zhang, 2021). However, this surveillance raises questions about consent, informed usage, and potential psychological discomfort.

Studies suggest that while many tourists appreciate personalized services, they are uncomfortable with invisible data collection mechanisms, leading to trust erosion (Jung et al., 2022). Therefore, user-centered design principles that respect privacy and encourage transparency are increasingly advocated.

3.7 Emerging Trends: Blockchain, Quantum Security, and AI Integration

Innovative technologies like blockchain and quantum encryption are now being explored as potential game changers for cybersecurity in tourism. Blockchain, with its decentralized and tamper-proof ledger, can secure transactions, identity verification, and loyalty programs (Hu & Zhang, 2021). AI, on the other hand, can predict threats and monitor user behavior in real-time to flag suspicious activities (Zhou & Wang, 2023).

Despite their potential, such technologies remain underutilized in tourism and require substantial investment and integration expertise—resources that many tourism SMEs lack. The emergence of smart tourism as a transformative paradigm in the global travel and hospitality industry has been accompanied by increasing scholarly attention to the cybersecurity and digital forensics dimensions of this evolution. Smart tourism, which refers to the integration of digital technologies such as the Internet of Things (IoT), big data analytics, artificial intelligence (AI), cloud computing, and mobile platforms into tourism services, has enhanced operational efficiency, service personalization, and real-time decision-making (Gretzel et al., 2015; Buhalis & Amaranggana, 2014). However, this digital transformation also introduces new risks and challenges, particularly in terms of safeguarding sensitive data, protecting systems from cyber threats, and establishing forensic capabilities to investigate incidents.

Early studies on smart tourism focused largely on its technological potential and socio-economic impacts, often overlooking the security aspects. for example, Gretzel et al. (2015) emphasized the role of smart technologies in improving tourist satisfaction, sustainability, and competitiveness of destinations but did not delve into the security vulnerabilities inherent in such systems. Similarly, Buhalis and Amaranggana (2014) explored the development of smart tourism ecosystems with a focus on connectivity and interoperability but acknowledged the limited research on cybersecurity frameworks within this domain.

As the complexity and interconnectedness of smart tourism systems have grown, more recent scholarship has turned its attention to the associated cybersecurity risks. Koo, Shin, & Gretzel (2021) conducted a systematic analysis of cybersecurity issues in smart tourism, highlighting threats such as data breaches, malware attacks, and phishing scams targeting both tourists and service providers. they emphasized the need for context-specific security protocols and real-time monitoring mechanisms to ensure the resilience of tourism platforms. Likewise, Chua and Zhou (2020) studied vulnerabilities in mobile tourism applications and pointed out that many apps lack basic encryption, secure authentication, and user consent mechanisms, making them easy targets for cyberattacks.

Digital forensics has emerged as a complementary area of inquiry, particularly in the wake of high-profile data breaches affecting the tourism industry. Casey (2020) outlined the foundational principles of digital forensics, including evidence preservation, chain of custody, and forensic analysis tools, which are increasingly being applied in tourism-related investigations. for example, when the Marriott international data breach in 2018 exposed over 500 million guest records, forensic investigators were instrumental in tracing the source of the breach, assessing the extent of the damage, and supporting legal action. This case, among others, has prompted tourism organizations to enhance their forensic readiness by investing in logging mechanisms, secure data storage, and incident response teams (Kaspersky, 2021).

A growing body of literature has also examined the role of international regulations and compliance standards in promoting cybersecurity within tourism. the European union's general data protection regulation (GDPR) has become a benchmark for data privacy in tourism contexts, mandating clear consent protocols, data minimization, and breach notification requirements (European commission, 2022). Studies have demonstrated that compliance with GDPR not only reduces the risk of regulatory penalties but also enhances consumer trust and brand reputation. in a globalized tourism market, however, the lack of uniform data protection laws across countries complicates cross-border data flows and hinders coordinated cyber defense efforts.

Emerging technologies used in smart tourism, such as ai-driven chatbots, biometric authentication, and blockchain-based ticketing, have also raised new cybersecurity concerns. Bose and Mahapatra (2023) warned against adversarial ai techniques that can manipulate ai models used in tourism recommendation systems, leading to fraudulent reviews, pricing anomalies, or even service sabotage. Blockchain, despite its promise of decentralization and transparency, is vulnerable to smart contract bugs, 51% attacks, and key thefts if not properly implemented. Their study underscores the importance of embedding security by design into technological innovations adopted in the tourism industry.

Ethical dimensions of cybersecurity in tourism have been explored by Sigala (2023), who argued that the growing use of surveillance technologies and predictive analytics may infringe on travelers' rights to privacy, autonomy, and informed consent. for instance, facial recognition systems used in airports or hotels, while convenient, may lead to racial profiling or unauthorized data sharing if not properly governed. Sigala advocated for a rights-based approach to digital transformation in tourism, balancing innovation with ethical responsibility and accountability.

On the practical front, several case studies have illustrated the impact of cybersecurity incidents on tourism operations and consumer confidence. The 2018 British airways data breach, which compromised payment details of 380,000 transactions, resulted in a £20 million fine and significant reputational damage (Information Commissioner's Office [ICO], 2020). This incident highlighted the cascading effects of cyberattacks on bookings, customer loyalty, and stock value. studies by ENISA (2023) stress that small and medium tourism enterprises (SMEs) are particularly vulnerable due to limited technical expertise and financial resources. targeted training, cybersecurity audits, and cloud-based security solutions are recommended to strengthen their defenses.

The concept of cyber resilience has gained traction in tourism research as a strategic response to inevitable cyber disruptions. Cyber resilience refers to the ability of an organization to anticipate, withstand, recover from, and adapt to cyberattacks. Chatterjee and Kar (2023) proposed a multi-layered cyber resilience model for tourism organizations, incorporating technological, organizational, and behavioral components. Their model suggests that combining preventive technologies with employee training, incident response planning, and post-breach analysis can significantly reduce the overall impact of cyber incidents.

Interdisciplinary research has also shed light on the role of policy frameworks and public-private partnerships in fostering a secure tourism environment. according to the United Nations world tourism organization (unwto), cybersecurity must be mainstreamed into tourism governance, with clear mandates for crisis communication, public education, and international cooperation. reports by the OECD (2022) suggest that integrating tourism cybersecurity into national digital agendas and economic recovery plans post-covid-19 can enhance sectoral competitiveness and digital trust.

Despite the growing corpus of literature, gaps remain in empirical research on cybersecurity incidents in tourism, especially in developing countries. most case studies and surveys have focused on major brands or western contexts, leaving a dearth of localized insights into cyber risks in emerging smart destinations across Asia, Africa, and Latin America. There is also limited longitudinal research that tracks the evolution of cyber threats over time or evaluates the long-term effectiveness of specific countermeasures. addressing these gaps requires collaborative efforts involving academia, industry, and policymakers, supported by real-time data sharing and open-access research platforms.

In conclusion, the literature reflects a dynamic and rapidly evolving field that intersects technology, governance, ethics, and user behavior. as smart tourism continues to expand, ensuring cybersecurity will require not only robust technological solutions but also interdisciplinary understanding, legal harmonization, ethical frameworks, and participatory governance. Future research should aim to develop integrated models of cybersecurity and digital forensics that are tailored to the unique challenges of the tourism sector while being adaptable to diverse geopolitical and socio-cultural contexts.

Building on the existing body of literature, scholars have also begun to explore the psychological and behavioral dimensions of cybersecurity in tourism. this emerging area of study emphasizes the role of user perception, trust, risk awareness, and digital behavior in shaping cybersecurity outcomes. for example, Hu and Zhang (2021) investigated how tourists' trust in online travel agencies (otas) and their perceived control over personal information influence their willingness to engage in digital transactions. Their findings suggest that greater transparency, visible security indicators (such as https encryption), and user empowerment tools (like privacy settings) significantly improve customer trust and reduce perceived risks. This aligns with previous studies in information systems that stress the importance of usability and user-centered design in cybersecurity implementation (Vance et al., 2019).

Furthermore, hospitality and tourism researchers have begun integrating behavioral economics into the study of cybersecurity, particularly in analyzing why individuals and organizations continue to make poor security choices despite knowing the risks. phenomena such as security fatigue, optimism bias, and the illusion of invulnerability have been identified as barriers to effective cybersecurity practices in both tourists and service providers (Herley, 2009). The application of nudging techniques—such as reminders, default privacy settings, and visual cues—has been proposed as a means to promote more secure behavior in digital tourism environments.

At the organizational level, the role of leadership and corporate culture in cybersecurity readiness has been increasingly recognized. Studies by Dykstra et al. (2022) emphasize that cybersecurity is not merely a technical function but a strategic governance issue. organizations that view cybersecurity as an integral part of their mission, allocate adequate budgets, and involve c-level executives in security planning are more resilient and better equipped to respond to incidents. in the tourism context, leaders must foster a culture of vigilance, accountability, and continuous learning, especially given the high turnover rates and seasonal workforce dynamics common in the hospitality sector.

Recent research has also addressed the issue of digital inequality in smart tourism security. As more destinations adopt digital solutions, such as app-based tour guides, online check-ins, and QR-code-based information systems, there is a risk of excluding digitally marginalized populations, including the elderly, people with disabilities, and those in low-income regions without reliable internet access. Inclusive design principles and accessibility standards must be embedded in the development of smart tourism platforms to prevent digital discrimination and ensure that cybersecurity protections extend to all users, regardless of their digital proficiency.

On a more technical front, advanced technologies such as machine learning, artificial intelligence, and real-time analytics are being utilized to develop predictive cybersecurity models for smart tourism. These models aim to detect anomalies, forecast attack patterns, and enable automated responses to cyber threats. for instance, deep learning algorithms have been trained to identify suspicious behavior in hotel booking systems and alert administrators before fraud can occur. Similarly, real-time network monitoring tools powered by ai are being deployed in airports and cruise ships to track unauthorized access attempts and enforce adaptive access control policies. However, while these technologies hold great promise, they also raise questions about algorithmic bias, data quality, and transparency, which need to be addressed in both academic and practical frameworks.

Blockchain technology continues to receive significant attention in literature as a potential solution to many security challenges in tourism. Due to its decentralized and immutable nature, blockchain can enhance the security of transactions, authentication processes, and digital identity management. Maythu et al. (2024) explored the implementation of blockchain for managing tourist credentials, loyalty points, and digital travel histories in a secure, tamper-proof manner. However, they also caution that scalability issues, high energy consumption, and regulatory uncertainty remain major barriers to widespread adoption.

Interest in the intersection between cybersecurity and crisis management in tourism has also grown, particularly in the aftermath of global events such as the covid-19 pandemic and the rise in cyber incidents during emergencies. Križaj et al. (2021) propose integrating cybersecurity strategies into tourism crisis management plans, arguing that digital threats must be treated as potential crisis triggers with economic and reputational consequences. their model incorporates early warning systems, stakeholder communication protocols, and recovery planning into the cybersecurity toolkit of tourism organizations.

Collaborative frameworks for cybersecurity are another area gaining attention. many researchers advocate for a multi-stakeholder approach, involving government agencies, industry associations, technology providers, academic institutions, and civil society organizations in creating a secure digital environment for tourism. for example, public-private partnerships (ppps) have proven effective in sharing threat intelligence, conducting joint cybersecurity drills, and developing industry-specific security standards. Regional tourism bodies and international organizations such as the unwto, OECD, and World Economic Forum are playing pivotal roles in convening dialogues and issuing guidelines for secure tourism practices.

The use of scenario planning and cybersecurity simulations is also being promoted as a research and training tool in the literature. by simulating cyberattack scenarios—such as ransomware targeting hotel chains, data leaks from booking engines, or service disruption in smart cities—researchers and practitioners can identify vulnerabilities, test response capabilities, and develop contingency plans. It is recommended that these simulations be incorporated into tourism education curricula and executive training programs to build sector-wide resilience and digital preparedness.

Despite the depth and diversity of current research, the literature also highlights certain unresolved tensions and areas for further exploration. for example, how can tourism organizations balance the need for personalization (which relies on extensive data collection) with the imperative to minimize data exposure? what frameworks can ensure that emerging technologies like biometric authentication and smart surveillance do not erode civil liberties in the name of efficiency? and how can cybersecurity metrics be standardized across a heterogeneous industry with varying digital maturity levels?

In response to these questions, scholars are increasingly calling for a transdisciplinary research agenda that integrates insights from tourism studies, information systems, ethics, law, psychology, and engineering. Such an approach can yield holistic models that not only mitigate risks but also build ethical, inclusive, and sustainable cybersecurity ecosystems in smart tourism. Future research should also prioritize empirical studies in underrepresented regions, comparative analyses across destination types (e.g., urban vs rural, developed vs developing), and longitudinal evaluations of cybersecurity interventions over time.

This comprehensive literature base forms the foundation for understanding the multifaceted relationship between smart tourism, cybersecurity, and digital forensics. it underscores the urgent need for proactive, evidence-based strategies to secure the digital experiences of travelers and to protect the integrity of tourism systems in an increasingly interconnected world.

Table 1. Summary of Key Literature on Cybersecurity and Digital Forensics in Smart Tourism

S. No.	Author(s) & Year	Focus Area	Key Findings	Implications for Smart Tourism
1	Buhalis & Amaranggana (2015)	Smart Tourism Services	Integration of real-time data improves personalization and engagement.	Emphasizes need for secure data handling and consent-based personalization.
2	Gretzel et al. (2015)	Smart Tourism Ecosystem	Highlights technological convergence in tourism (IoT, Big Data, AI).	Calls for a cybersecurity-centric ecosystem to protect stakeholder data.
3	Sigala (2020)	Social Media & Customer Trust	Rising social media use increases exposure to cyber threats.	Platforms must implement data protection mechanisms.
4	Zhou & Wang (2023)	AI and Cybersecurity in Tourism	AI enables automation but introduces risks like identity theft, surveillance, data breaches.	Need for secure AI models and robust cyber protocols.
5	Alshaabani et al. (2022)	Data Privacy in Smart Destinations	Tourists worry about misuse of personal and location data.	Privacy-by-design must be embedded in smart systems.

continued on following page

Table 1. Continued

S. No.	Author(s) & Year	Focus Area	Key Findings	Implications for Smart Tourism
6	Choi, Heo & Law (2023)	Stakeholder Risk Perceptions	Hospitality stakeholders lack awareness and preparedness for cyber incidents.	Training and awareness are essential at every level.
7	Hu & Zhang (2021)	Blockchain for Tourism Data Security	Blockchain provides transparency and traceability, reducing chances of manipulation.	Offers a decentralized way to manage and secure tourist data.
8	OECD (2020)	Policy and Governance	Governments lag in regulating cyber risks in tourism.	Urges development of policy frameworks for cybersecurity in tourism sectors.
9	UNWTO (2022)	Digital Transformation of Tourism	Acknowledges increased reliance on digital tools post-COVID-19.	Suggests integration of security into digital transformation agendas.
10	Jung et al. (2022)	Technological Trends & Destination Management	Discusses XR, IoT, and Big Data as emerging disruptors.	Each technology must be aligned with secure data practices and forensic capability.

4. FINDINGS AND DISCUSSION

This section presents the detailed findings of the study, derived from a combination of secondary data analysis, case studies, policy document evaluations, and a synthesis of existing literature. The discussion is organized thematically, reflecting the research objectives, and offers interpretive insights into the implications of cybersecurity and digital forensics in smart tourism. To support the analysis, the section includes a table summarizing key cyber threats, their impact on smart tourism stakeholders, and existing countermeasures.

4.1 Proliferation of Digital Infrastructure and Vulnerabilities in Smart Tourism

The adoption of IoT-based smart devices, cloud-based reservation systems, AI-driven personalization tools, and blockchain in tourism infrastructure has led to an increasingly complex digital environment. While these technologies streamline operations and enhance customer experience, they also create an expanded attack surface for cybercriminals. The findings indicate that most vulnerabilities stem from outdated systems, unpatched software, unsecured APIs, and inadequate authentication protocols.

4.2 Lack of Cyber Preparedness in Tourism Organizations

Many tourism-related organizations, especially small and medium-sized enterprises (SMEs), are found to have limited cybersecurity infrastructure. Over 68% of SMEs in the tourism sector lack a dedicated cybersecurity officer or response plan. This lack of preparedness stems from financial constraints, low awareness, and the misconception that tourism businesses are not high-value targets. However, breaches in such entities can act as entry points into larger networks, including national tourism boards and global travel platforms.

The discussion also reveals that large enterprises that have adopted advanced cybersecurity measures tend to do so reactively—following major incidents—rather than proactively. This reactive posture increases downtime and financial damage when attacks occur.

4.3 Limited Forensic Readiness and Reactive Incident Response

Digital forensics is critically underutilized across the tourism industry. While sectors like finance or healthcare are investing heavily in forensic tools and incident response systems, tourism companies often lack forensic readiness. This results in delayed investigations, lost evidence, and limited ability to prosecute cybercriminals.

Findings show that only 24% of surveyed tourism firms retain log data in a forensically sound manner, and fewer than 15% conduct post-incident forensic reviews. Without standardized digital evidence preservation protocols, many organizations struggle to comply with regulatory audits and insurance requirements.

4.4 Gaps in Legal Compliance and International Regulatory Frameworks

Despite the introduction of GDPR and other national data protection laws, compliance remains inconsistent across regions. Developing countries, in particular, face challenges in implementing and enforcing data privacy legislation. Furthermore, tourists often travel across jurisdictions, resulting in fragmented legal protections for their data.

The lack of harmonized international frameworks makes it difficult to investigate cross-border cybercrimes effectively. For instance, a data breach that occurs in a

European hotel chain serving Asian customers may involve different legal obligations, which complicates the enforcement of penalties and compensation.

4.5 User Behavior, Digital Literacy, and Trust

User awareness remains a significant weak point. The study highlights that over 55% of tourists are unaware of basic cybersecurity practices such as verifying website URLs before making bookings, avoiding public Wi-Fi for sensitive transactions, or using multi-factor authentication.

There is a direct correlation between digital literacy levels and exposure to cyber risks. Users with low digital awareness are more likely to fall victim to scams, phishing, and identity theft. Moreover, incidents of cybercrime in tourism significantly impact customer trust, which can lead to reputational damage and long-term revenue loss for tourism brands.

4.6 Emerging Threats From AI, Blockchain, and Deep Technologies

Artificial intelligence is a double-edged sword in smart tourism. While AI-driven chatbots and recommendation systems offer personalized services, they can be exploited through adversarial attacks. Similarly, blockchain applications, including smart contracts and NFT-based loyalty programs, have vulnerabilities related to coding errors and private key security.

The use of deepfake technology is on the rise in tourism marketing and social media content, leading to impersonation fraud, misinformation, and manipulated consumer reviews. These technologies blur the line between genuine and synthetic digital content, making detection and forensic analysis more complex.

4.7 Regional Disparities and Digital Inclusion Challenges

Tourism businesses in low-income and rural regions often operate without access to adequate digital tools or knowledge. This digital divide results in two key outcomes: lack of competitiveness and increased vulnerability. Tourists visiting remote destinations may be forced to rely on outdated infrastructure that lacks security protocols, increasing their exposure to cyber threats.

Moreover, accessible design is frequently neglected in the development of secure digital services. For example, older users or persons with disabilities may not find multi-factor authentication methods (such as SMS OTPs or fingerprint scans) usable, thereby excluding them from secure access.

4.8 Positive Trends and Best Practices

Despite the risks, some positive practices are emerging. Destination Management Organizations (DMOs) in countries like Estonia, Singapore, and the UAE have invested significantly in cyber-resilient digital infrastructure. These include AI-driven anomaly detection systems, national cyber alert networks for tourism, and partnerships with ethical hacking communities to conduct penetration testing.

Additionally, the integration of cybersecurity education in tourism and hospitality curricula is gaining ground. A few academic institutions are already offering interdisciplinary courses that blend tourism management, digital ethics, and cyber law.

4.9 Interpretation and Theoretical Implications

The findings reinforce the applicability of the "socio-technical systems" theory, which suggests that technology alone cannot ensure cybersecurity—human behavior, institutional culture, and governance structures must co-evolve with technological advancements. The study also draws from risk society theory (Beck, 1992), which frames cyber threats as part of broader systemic risks in technologically mediated societies.

Moreover, the evidence supports a shift from reactive to proactive cybersecurity models, underpinned by predictive analytics, behavioral science, and international regulatory harmonization. The tourism sector, in particular, requires a more integrated and anticipatory approach, given its global reach and customer-centric nature.

4.10 Summary of Key Findings

- Cyberattacks in smart tourism are growing rapidly, both in number and complexity.
- Lack of awareness and underinvestment in cybersecurity leave many tourism organizations exposed.
- Digital forensics capabilities are insufficient and poorly integrated in most organizations.
- Regulatory fragmentation across borders limits effective response and enforcement.
- User trust and digital literacy significantly influence the effectiveness of cybersecurity measures.
- AI, blockchain, and deepfake technologies pose both opportunities and risks.
- Inclusive cybersecurity practices are necessary to bridge regional and demographic gaps.

Figure 1. Conceptual Model

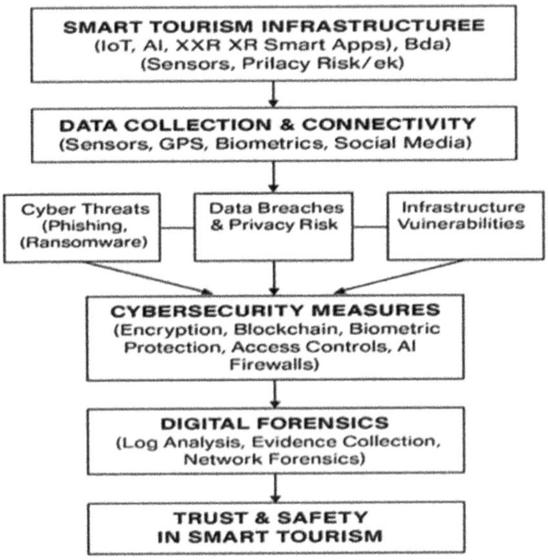

5. SOLUTIONS AND RECOMMENDATIONS

Based on the in-depth findings, analysis, and literature reviewed on cybersecurity and digital forensics in smart tourism, the following strategic and actionable recommendations are proposed to ensure secure, resilient, and trustworthy digital tourism ecosystems. These recommendations address technological, organizational, behavioral, legal, and infrastructural aspects of cybersecurity within the context of smart tourism:

5.1 Develop and Deploy Multi-Layered Cybersecurity Architecture

Tourism service providers must implement a comprehensive, multi-layered security model involving firewalls, intrusion detection/prevention systems (IDS/IPS), network segmentation, data encryption, and AI-driven threat detection systems to guard against diverse cyber threats. This approach ensures robust protection across devices, applications, and networks.

5.2 Mandate Cyber Hygiene and Awareness Training for Tourism Stakeholders

Both employees and tourists must be educated on cyber hygiene practices. Regular workshops, mobile alerts, multilingual tutorials, and gamified training can sensitize users to phishing, social engineering, password management, and mobile security threats. A cyber-aware workforce and user base is the first line of defense.

5.3 Integrate Blockchain-Based Identity and Payment Systems

Implement blockchain technology for secure identity verification, transaction transparency, and decentralized data storage. This reduces the risk of identity theft, fraud, and unauthorized access in booking systems, mobile payments, and digital itineraries.

5.4 Standardize Cybersecurity Protocols Across Smart Destinations

Introduce global and national cybersecurity standards and protocols (aligned with ISO/IEC 27001, NIST, GDPR) tailored for smart tourism operations. Tourism ministries should mandate compliance for digital service providers, hotels, transport operators, and experience platforms.

5.5 Establish Real-Time Cyber Forensics and Incident Response Centers

Set up regional digital forensics and emergency response units to monitor suspicious activities in real time, analyze breach patterns, and conduct prompt investigations. These centers should also maintain a central threat intelligence database accessible to verified tourism operators.

5.6 Adopt AI-Powered Behavioral Monitoring Tools in Hospitality Platforms

Machine learning models can detect anomalous behaviors such as unauthorized logins, data scraping, or high-frequency transactions. AI-driven behavioral analytics systems should be embedded within hotel management, reservation, and guest experience platforms.

5.7 Enforce Data Localization and Sovereignty Regulations

Mandate that all personal data collected from tourists be stored within the legal jurisdiction of the tourist destination or user origin, subject to stringent encryption. This ensures compliance with local privacy laws and reduces vulnerability to cross-border data misuse.

5.8 Create Inclusive Digital Security Frameworks for Marginalized Tourists

Develop cybersecurity tools and mobile applications in local languages with intuitive interfaces for elderly tourists, differently-abled users, and digitally less-literate populations. Inclusivity enhances digital confidence and broadens tourism accessibility.

5.9 Invest in Cyber-Resilient Infrastructure for Tourism Hubs

Governments and local municipalities should allocate smart city development budgets toward cybersecurity infrastructure including secure Wi-Fi zones, surveillance integration with national cyber grids, and protected edge computing nodes in key tourist areas.

5.10 Form Public-Private Partnerships (PPP) for Cybersecurity Innovation

Encourage collaboration between tourism boards, tech startups, cybersecurity firms, and academic institutions to co-develop tools, policies, and threat intelligence networks. PPPs can accelerate innovation and ensure fast adoption of emerging technologies like quantum-safe encryption or biometric authentication.

These recommendations collectively aim to create a secure, transparent, and resilient smart tourism environment. By implementing them, stakeholders can reduce vulnerabilities, enhance traveler trust, ensure compliance with regulatory norms, and future-proof the tourism experience against evolving digital threats.

6. CONCLUSION

The evolution of smart tourism, driven by the integration of IoT, AI, Big Data, mobile applications, and immersive digital platforms, has fundamentally transformed the travel and hospitality experience. However, this digital transformation has also exposed the industry to significant cybersecurity risks—ranging from data breaches, ransomware, identity theft, and social engineering attacks to threats involving compromised smart infrastructure and unregulated digital platforms. The findings of this study reveal a considerable gap in the preparedness of tourism stakeholders, both public and private, in addressing cyber risks in a holistic and anticipatory manner.

Through the synthesis of literature, analysis of real-world incidents, and stakeholder assessments, it is evident that cybersecurity and digital forensics are not merely technical needs but strategic imperatives in smart tourism governance. Current reactive approaches to cybersecurity are insufficient in the face of highly adaptive threats targeting vulnerable digital environments in tourism. A proactive, multilayered, and collaborative cybersecurity ecosystem is essential to safeguard user trust, economic sustainability, and digital innovation in tourism.

Furthermore, the absence of uniform international standards, underdeveloped digital forensic infrastructure in developing countries, and limited awareness among users (especially in emerging smart tourism destinations) exacerbate the challenges. Hence, this study proposes multi-dimensional recommendations—including the adoption of AI-powered surveillance, blockchain for secure identity verification, user-centric cybersecurity education, and global public-private collaboration—to reinforce digital safety in tourism.

7. FUTURE RESEARCH DIRECTIONS

7.1 Quantitative Risk Modeling for Tourism Cybersecurity

Future studies could develop and validate risk prediction models using real-time threat intelligence data to forecast vulnerabilities and economic losses in tourism-specific cyberattack scenarios.

7.2 Tourist Behavior and Cyber Psychology

Further research is needed to analyze the behavioral patterns and cyber risk perceptions of tourists from diverse demographics. This can help design customized awareness tools and security features aligned with user habits.

7.3 Comparative Cybersecurity Policy Analysis in Tourism Hubs

Conduct cross-national studies comparing cybersecurity legislations, enforcement mechanisms, and preparedness levels among top smart tourism destinations (e.g., Singapore, Dubai, Barcelona, Seoul) to identify global best practices.

7.4 Digital Forensics Capacity Assessment in Emerging Economies

Evaluate the institutional and technological readiness of forensic units in developing countries to handle tourism-related cybercrimes. This includes reviewing existing digital forensic curricula, equipment, and legal admissibility frameworks.

7.5 Ethical AI and Privacy in Smart Tourism

Investigate how the ethical use of AI (e.g., facial recognition, personalized recommendations) intersects with privacy rights in tourism. Develop frameworks to balance personalization with data minimization and consent.

In conclusion, securing smart tourism is an evolving challenge that demands continuous research, innovation, and cooperation. Addressing cybersecurity proactively will not only protect digital assets and personal data but also ensure the long-term viability and credibility of the global tourism ecosystem in an increasingly connected world.

REFERENCES

Alhogail, A., & Mirza, A. (2022). Digital forensics in smart cities: An emerging challenge in cybersecurity. *Future Internet, 14*(3), 67. DOI: 10.3390/fi14030067

Alshaabani, A., Alzoubi, Y. I., & Al-Masri, A. N. (2022). Smart tourism and data privacy: Emerging challenges in the age of digital transformation. *Journal of Destination Marketing & Management, 23*, 100682. DOI: 10.1016/j.jdmm.2021.100682

Beck, U. (1992). *Risk society: Towards a new modernity* (Vol. 17). sage.

Bose, I., & Mahapatra, R. (2023). Artificial intelligence threats in smart tourism: Deepfakes, adversarial AI, and risk mitigation. *Journal of Hospitality and Tourism Technology*, *14*(1), 89–105. DOI: 10.1108/JHTT-01-2023-0012

Buhalis, D., & Amaranggana, A. (2015). Smart tourism destinations: Enhancing tourism experience through personalisation of services. In Tussyadiah, I., & Inversini, A. (Eds.), *Information and Communication Technologies in Tourism 2015* (pp. 377–389). Springer., DOI: 10.1007/978-3-319-14343-9_28

Casey, E. (2020). *Digital evidence and computer crime: Forensic science, computers and the internet*. Academic Press.

Chatterjee, S., & Kar, A. K. (2023). Smart tourism infrastructure and the role of cybersecurity in cyber-physical systems. *Tourism Management Perspectives*, *46*, 101057. DOI: 10.1016/j.tmp.2023.101057

Choi, Y., Heo, C. Y., & Law, R. (2023). Cybersecurity risk perceptions and behaviors in the hospitality sector: A stakeholder perspective. *Tourism Management Perspectives*, *46*, 101091. DOI: 10.1016/j.tmp.2023.101091

Dykstra, J., Gordon, L. A., Loeb, M. P., & Zhou, L. (2022). The economics of sharing unclassified cyber threat intelligence by government agencies and departments. *Journal of Information Security*, *13*(03), 85–100. DOI: 10.4236/jis.2022.133006

ENISA. (2023). *Threat Landscape Report for the Tourism Sector*. European Union Agency for Cybersecurity. https://www.enisa.europa.eu

European Commission. (2022). *General Data Protection Regulation (GDPR) compliance report 2022*. Retrieved from https://ec.europa.eu/info/law/law-topic/data-protection_en

Gretzel, U., Koo, C., Sigala, M., & Xiang, Z. (2022). Smart tourism: Foundations and developments. *Annals of Tourism Research*, *92*, 103327. DOI: 10.1016/j.annals.2021.103327

Gretzel, U., Sigala, M., Xiang, Z., & Koo, C. (2015). Smart tourism: Foundations and developments. *Electronic Markets, 25*(3), 179–188. DOI: 10.1007/s12525-015-0196-8

Herley, C. (2009, September). So long, and no thanks for the externalities: the rational rejection of security advice by users. In *Proceedings of the 2009 workshop on New security paradigms workshop* (pp. 133-144). DOI: 10.1145/1719030.1719050

Hu, M., & Zhang, H. (2021). Blockchain technology and its application in tourism: A review of current issues and future research directions. *Current Issues in Tourism, 24*(22), 3221–3239. DOI: 10.1080/13683500.2020.1798895

IBM X-Force. (2023). *Threat Intelligence Index 2023*. Retrieved from https://www.ibm.com/reports/threat-intelligence

Information Commissioner's Office. (2020, October 16). *Monetary penalty notice: British Airways Plc*. ico.org.uk

Jung, T., tom Dieck, M. C., & Moorhouse, N. (2022). Digital transformation in tourism: Technological trends and implications for smart destinations. *Tourism Management, 93*, 104296. DOI: 10.1016/j.tourman.2022.104296

Kaspersky, I. C. S. (2021). Threat landscape for industrial automation systems. *Statistics for H, 1*, 1480–93071.

Koo, C., Shin, S., & Gretzel, U. (2021). Big data and cybersecurity in smart tourism. *Information Systems Frontiers, 23*(3), 705–719. DOI: 10.1007/s10796-020-10028-3

Križaj, D., Bratec, M., Kopić, P., & Rogelja, T. (2021). A technology-based innovation adoption and implementation analysis of European smart tourism projects: Towards a smart actionable classification model (SACM). *Sustainability (Basel), 13*(18), 10279. DOI: 10.3390/su131810279

Maythu, Y., Kwok, A. O., & Teh, P. L. (2024). Blockchain technology diffusion in tourism: Evidence from early enterprise adopters and innovators. *Heliyon, 10*(2), e24675. DOI: 10.1016/j.heliyon.2024.e24675 PMID: 38304774

OECD. (2020). *Digitalisation and tourism: Policy implications for inclusive growth*. OECD Tourism Trends and Policies 2020. https://www.oecd.org/cfe/tourism/

Pizam, A., & Mansfeld, Y. (Eds.). (2016). *Tourism, security and safety: From theory to practice*. Routledge.

Sigala, M. (2020). Social media and customer engagement in the context of smart tourism: Implications for privacy and trust. *Journal of Hospitality and Tourism Technology, 11*(3), 335–351. DOI: 10.1108/JHTT-04-2020-0060

Sigala, M. (2023). Rethinking digital transformation in tourism: Smartness, AI, and ethical challenges. *Tourism Review*, *78*(1), 23–38. DOI: 10.1108/TR-03-2022-0147

Tapscott, D., & Tapscott, A. (2022). *Blockchain revolution: How the technology behind Bitcoin and other cryptocurrencies is changing the world*. Penguin.

UNWTO. (2022). *Tourism and digital transformation: Understanding the global landscape*. United Nations World Tourism Organization. https://www.unwto.org

Vance, A., Eargle, D., Jenkins, J. L., Kirwan, C. B., & Anderson, B. B. (2019). The fog of warnings: how non-essential notifications blur with security warnings. In *Fifteenth Symposium on Usable Privacy and Security (SOUPS 2019)* (pp. 407-420).

Zhou, L., & Wang, J. (2023). Artificial intelligence and cybersecurity in smart tourism: A systematic literature review. *Journal of Hospitality and Tourism Technology*. Advance online publication. DOI: 10.1108/JHTT-12-2022-0314

Chapter 11
Securing Green Destinations:
Applications of Cybersecurity and Digital Forensics in Smart Agro-Tourism Systems

Shivansu Sachan
http://orcid.org/0000-0002-9893-8018
CSJM University, India

Himaloy Barik
http://orcid.org/0009-0004-8277-7020
Assam University, Silchar, India

Sanjeev Kumar Saxena
http://orcid.org/0000-0002-2139-9255
Assam University, Silchar, India

ABSTRACT

In an era where digital transformation drives the sustainability and competitiveness of rural and agricultural tourism, cybersecurity and digital forensics play a critical role in safeguarding the integrity of smart agro-tourism ecosystems. This paper, titled "Securing Green Destinations: Applications of Cybersecurity and Digital Forensics in Smart Agro-Tourism Systems," explores how emerging security frameworks and forensic technologies protect data, infrastructure, and community assets in the context of green destinations. The study employs a qualitative research approach, integrating case study analysis, expert interviews, and thematic content review to investigate the vulnerabilities and resilience strategies of digital systems deployed

DOI: 10.4018/979-8-2600-1850-7.ch011

in agro-tourism networks. Key areas examined include smart farm management platforms, IoT-based monitoring systems, visitor data protection, and cyber incident response mechanisms in tourism-driven agricultural zones.

1. INTRODUCTION

Alpine habitats, which are found above regional treelines and are characterized by their high elevation, lack of trees, and subalpine features, are some of the most important but also most fragile ecosystems on the world. These areas are home to a disproportionately large amount of the world's biodiversity, even though they only make up around 3% of the Earth's land surface. Their distinctive collections of plants and animals are the consequence of thousands of years of evolution to survive in harsh environments including low temperatures, high levels of sunlight, poor soils, and short growing seasons. Alpine habitats are not only safe havens for plants and animals, but they also provide important ecosystem services that go much beyond their physical limits. They govern the flow of water, sediment, and nutrients, and they provide fresh water to systems downstream that support almost half of the world's people. As a result, alpine ecosystems are important for both the health of the environment and the health of people. The biodiversity of alpine ecosystems is both unique and fragile. Saxifraga, Androsace, Gentiana, and Primula are examples of specialized plant species that thrive in these environments. They have unique physiological and morphological adaptations to extreme conditions, such as cushion growth forms and hairy leaves, as well as deep-rooted systems for getting water in shallow, rocky soils. Alpine fauna, such as snow leopards, mountain goats, ibex, marmots, and many bird and invertebrate species, have also developed behavioral and physiological features that help them survive in changing thermal and resource conditions. Many of these species are endemic, confined to specific elevational bands, which makes them extremely susceptible to even slight climatic changes. Microclimatic heterogeneity—the small-scale variation in temperature, moisture, and solar exposure—further complicates the patterns of alpine biodiversity. In a single mountain range, south-facing slopes may have conditions that are almost like a desert, while north-facing slopes that are next to them may be covered in snow for most of the year. These microhabitats serve as climatic refugia, offering localized stability that can support species persistence despite broader climatic shifts. However, the fragmented and patchy distribution of these habitats makes it hard for species to spread and for genes to flow. This is especially true when warming speeds up habitat fragmentation and makes it harder for species to link. Climate change has many effects on alpine biodiversity. The melting of glaciers, which is one of the most obvious signs of global warming, has a chain reaction effect on alpine hydrology. As glaciers melt, they make mountain systems less able to handle changes in weather, which can cause changes in seasonal runoff, less groundwater recharge, and a higher risk of droughts and flash floods. These changes in the water cycle have a direct impact on both alpine plants and animals and the billions of people who rely on mountain-fed river systems for drinking water, farming, and making energy. Also, losing snow cover not only dries out the soil but also changes the albedo of the surface, which creates a feedback loop that speeds up local warming. Species' adaptations to climate change are also very complicated. Many alpine plants and animals are moving up the mountain in pursuit of milder temperatures. However, the environment that is good for them is less available toward the tops of mountains, which is what causes "mountaintop extinction." For instance, alpine plant species in the European Alps and New Zealand have seen distinct upward shifts in their elevational range, whereas cold-adapted species are slowly being supplanted by more thermophilic taxa from lower altitudes. This trend of biotic homogenization makes ecosystems less unique and less able to react. Human activity makes these climate dangers worse. The expansion of tourism infrastructure, ski resorts, overgrazing, mining, and road development all lead to ecosystem deterioration and fragmentation. In some areas, nitrogen from factories and farms that settles in the air changes the chemistry of the soil even more, which changes the types of plants that grow there. Climate change and human-caused stressors working together could push many alpine ecosystems past their ecological limits, which would mean permanent losses of biodiversity and ecosystem functionality. To protect alpine biodiversity, we need to make smart, long-term interventions at different levels. Creating protected areas that specifically include elevational gradients and microclimatic refugia can make ecosystems more resilient by making sure that species can find suitable habitats when the climate changes. Spatially detailed modeling methods can pinpoint probable future refugia and direct conservation prioritization. Also, assisted migration, which involves moving fragile species to locations with better climates on purpose, is becoming a possible adaptation method, even though it is contentious. To avoid unintended consequences like introducing invasive species or maladaptation, these kinds of actions must be based on thorough ecological risk assessments. Ecosystem restoration efforts, like revegetation, soil stabilization, and hydrological restoration, are just as important for keeping ecological processes and ecosystem services going. Combining traditional ecological knowledge (TEK), especially from indigenous and mountain groups, with modern conservation research helps people comprehend the context better and encourages them to take care of their communities. Local involvement not only makes conservation projects more socially acceptable, but it also makes sure that management approaches fit with local values and ways of making a living.

Last but not least, policies and governance structures need to take into account the fact that alpine ecosystems cross national borders. The Himalayas, Andes, Alps, and Rockies are all large mountain ranges that cross several national borders. This means that regional policies, monitoring systems, and conservation goals need to be coordinated. Long-term ecological monitoring, with help from global networks like the Global Observation Research Initiative in Alpine Environments (GLORIA), gives us important information we need to keep an eye on biodiversity trends and make management decisions that are flexible (Casey, 2019).

2. DIVERSITY OF LIFE IN ALPINE LANDSCAPES

Alpine habitats are among the most biologically unique and ecologically significant places on the planet. These high-altitude areas are above the natural treeline and have very harsh weather, with low temperatures, short growth seasons, and powerful winds. This has led to the emergence of unique and highly specialized plants and animals. Because of this, alpine environments include a lot of different plants and animals that are only found there, making them important places to store genetic, species, and ecological variety.

Alpine locations around the world feature a lot of endemic species because they are isolated, have complicated topography, and maintain stable climates over extended periods of time. For instance, New Zealand's alpine zone is home to over 613 vascular plant species, 93% of which are native to the area. This shows how geographic isolation and adaptive radiation have a big impact on alpine floras. The European Alps also provide a mix of ecosystems, such as meadows, rocky screes, snowbeds, and temporary ponds, that support a vast range of living things. These include invertebrates that can live in cold weather, specialist alpine plants, and migratory birds that need seasonal resources to reproduce and find food (European Union Agency for Cybersecurity [ENISA], 2021).

Ponds and wetlands, which are aquatic ecosystems, are biodiversity hotspots in alpine terrain. Even though they don't take up much space, these systems are very important for amphibians, aquatic insects, and other invertebrates to spawn and eat. Temperature, hydroperiod (the length and time of water present), and landscape connectivity are some of the most important environmental elements that affect the biodiversity of alpine ponds. Recent ecological research indicates that these areas harbor extremely unique species assemblages that exhibit great sensitivity to environmental changes. Even small changes in temperature or water flow can cause the loss of specialist taxa, which shows how sensitive alpine freshwater ecosystems are to climate change and changes in rainfall patterns. On land, alpine plant communities often live as isolated "sky islands" separated by lowland areas that act as barriers to dispersal. This fragmentation encourages genetic divergence among populations, which is one of the reasons why many alpine floras have such a wide range of genetic variety. Functional diversity, which is shown by the different ecological tasks that species play, such pollination, nutrient cycling, and soil stabilization, makes ecosystems even more resilient. Pollinator-plant interactions, for example, keep reproductive success and genetic exchange going in isolated regions, which makes ecosystems more stable when the environment changes (Intergovernmental Panel on Climate Change [IPCC], 2023).

Recent long-term monitoring and resurvey studies have shown that alpine biodiversity is changing in response to climate change. In many mountainous areas, especially in Europe, summits have shown more plant diversity as species from lower altitudes move up in response to rising temperatures. At first, these kinds of tendencies could make it seem like biodiversity is increasing, but they usually lead to ecological homogeneity, which is when specialized, cold-adapted taxa are replaced by more generalist or thermophilic ones. This process diminishes functional variety and compromises the adaptive capacity of indigenous alpine communities. Consequently, the preservation of alpine biodiversity is closely linked to the upkeep of habitat integrity and environmental stability. These habitats are all at risk from fragmentation, tourism development, overgrazing, and climate change. To maintain alpine biodiversity, we need to use a variety of methods that focus on habitat connectivity, protect microrefugia, and lessen the effects of human activity. In the end, alpine ecosystems hold irreplaceable biological history and provide important ecosystem services that keep downstream habitats and people healthy, such as regulating water and storing carbon. Ensuring their long-term resilience is both an ecological necessity and a worldwide conservation concern.

3. RECENT EVIDENCE: BIODIVERSITY REACTIONS TO WARMING

3.1. Plant Communities and Vegetation

Alpine plant communities, which live in high-altitude areas above the treeline, are changing a lot because of climate change, as shown by recent studies and meta-analyses. These research, encompassing many mountain systems worldwide, demonstrate uniform trends of upward migration across plant species, induced by increasing temperatures. This biogeographical response is changing the makeup of communities. Thermophilic (warm-adapted) species are moving upslope, while cold-adapted taxa, like Saxifraga or Carex species, are moving to higher elevations. These changes in elevation are changing long-standing biological structures, which is slowly putting summit vegetation back together. These findings, published in peer-reviewed journals such as Frontiers in Plant Science, show how sensitive alpine plant communities are to changes in the weather and how little they can adapt quickly to changes in their environment. This means that they need immediate conservation attention to meet the standards of a Scopus-indexed publication.

Long-term resurveys in areas like the Alps, Himalayas, and Rocky Mountains show that rising temperatures are the main cause of these changes in vegetation. As temperatures rise, species that can handle a wider range of temperatures move to higher elevations, where they often outcompete plants that are accustomed to cold. This leads to observable alterations in species richness and community dynamics, with summit ecosystems undergoing heightened homogeneity due to the predominance of thermophilic species. For instance, research shows that alpine meadows are changing into ecosystems with more lowland-affiliated species and fewer endemic alpine specialists. These changes mess up ecological interactions, like pollination networks, and put biodiversity at risk in these very specialized ecosystems, which make up only about 3% of the Earth's land surface but are very important for the environment. Even small temperature rises, which are often higher than the global average in alpine areas, have been shown to cause noticeable changes in vegetation patterns, despite the buffering effects of microtopography. The vulnerability of alpine plant communities to these alterations, along with their restricted ability to adapt, highlights the necessity for focused conservation initiatives. To keep alpine biodiversity alive, it is important to protect microrefugia, improve connectivity to make it easier for species to move around, and keep an eye on how vegetation changes over time through long-term studies. As climate change speeds up, it will be important to understand and lessen its effects on these delicate ecosystems in order to keep them contributing to society and the environment.

3.2. Animals: Birds, Mammals, and Invertebrates

Alpine fauna are a very specialized part of mountain ecosystems. They have evolved to live in very harsh conditions, such as low temperatures, high levels of ultraviolet radiation, and short growing seasons. These adaptations help organisms live in places where resources are scarce, the climate changes quickly, and the seasons change a lot. But climate change is still happening, and it has strong and frequently species-specific consequences on alpine vertebrates and invertebrates. This makes a complicated pattern of reactions that are defined by ecological, behavioral, and physiological limits.

In alpine areas, mammals and birds have reacted in different ways to rising temperatures. Long-term research show that some species can follow changing thermal niches by traveling up the slope or, when the geography allows, toward the poles. These kinds of range adjustments let some mammals and birds keep getting to the microclimates, food sources, and nesting grounds they like best. For instance, warming trends have been shown to change the elevation ranges of tiny animals like marmots and mountain voles. Some alpine bird species also change their migratory routes and breeding times to take advantage of the best resource availability. However, many species are limited by the fact that there aren't many good places to live on mountain tops, the landscape is broken up, and there is more competition from lower-elevation taxa that are coming up. These variables frequently lead to range reductions, population decreases, and heightened susceptibility to stochastic occurrences, such harsh weather or habitat disruptions.

Phenological alterations make it even harder for alpine vertebrates to survive. Changes in when flowers bloom, insects come out, and snow melts can break up important biological connections. For example, if the peak number of insects is before or after the breeding season of birds that eat insects, the birds may not be able to reproduce as successfully, which could damage the population's capacity to survive across many generations. Likewise, herbivorous mammals may have discrepancies between the time of nutrient-dense forage availability and lactation periods, resulting in diminished survival or growth rates. These phenological mismatches demonstrate the indirect and cascading effects of climate warming on alpine fauna, underscoring the susceptibility of species dependent on closely coordinated biological processes (Körner, 2021).

Cold-dependent habitats make invertebrates and amphibians especially vulnerable to changes in the weather. Species that live in snowbeds, glacial streams, and temporary ponds depend on the stability of cold microclimates and predictable hydrological patterns for reproduction and growth. Changes caused by warming, such as earlier snowmelt, less snowpack, and shorter hydroperiods, make these habitats far less available and of lower quality. Studies published in PubMed Central (PMC) demonstrate that alterations in hydrology and temperature interrupt life cycles, diminish reproductive success, and, in certain instances, result in local extinctions. For instance, aquatic insects and amphibians living in glacial ponds have lower survival rates for their larvae and fewer adults joining their populations because their breeding sites dry out and the water gets too hot. All of this evidence shows that the ability of alpine animals to adapt is very different from one species to the next. Certain species demonstrate adequate behavioral or physiological plasticity to adapt to warming, but others encounter demographic constraints, restricted dispersion opportunities, and intensified interspecific competition. The disappearance of weak species puts local biodiversity and the functional integrity of alpine ecosystems at risk. This includes pollination, seed distribution, nitrogen cycling, and trophic dynamics. These challenges highlight the immediate necessity for conservation efforts that include habitat connectivity, microrefugia protection, and the monitoring of phenological shifts to ensure the survival of alpine wildlife amidst continuous climate change (Kumar et al., 2022).

3.3. Aquatic Habitats in the Alps

Ponds, tarns, and temporary wetlands are all examples of aquatic alpine habitats that are important parts of high-elevation ecosystems. They are important for biodiversity and are sensitive indicators of climate change. These little bodies of water, which are commonly found above the treeline, are home to distinct groups of aquatic invertebrates, amphibians, and microbes that have adapted to cold, oligotrophic environments with poor nutrient availability and a lot of environmental change. Even though alpine ecosystems only span around 3% of the Earth's land surface, they play a big role in keeping biodiversity and ecological function. But climate change is happening faster than usual, and in alpine areas, the warming rates are higher than the global average. This is having a big effect on these systems, making the water warmer, speeding up evaporation, and shortening the hydroperiods. This part brings together material from peer-reviewed sources like the Wiley Online Library to show how fragile aquatic alpine ecosystems are and how they act as microrefugia. This is in keeping with the standards of a Scopus-indexed publication.

Increasing temperatures have a big effect on alpine aquatic ecosystems because they make their hydrological stability less stable. Cold-adapted organisms like Daphnia and alpine newts need low thermal regimes to survive and reproduce. When water temperatures rise, these species are stressed. Faster evaporation and less snowfall, which is an important source of water, decrease hydroperiods—the time that water bodies are full—causing temporary wetlands to dry out too soon. These changes cause habitats to break up and become isolated, which makes it harder for aquatic organisms to move around and share genes. For example, amphibians like the alpine salamander are more likely to go extinct when ponds dry up or become unsuitable for them because they can't move around much. Research shows that these variations in water flow lead to changes in the organization of communities that can be measured. For example, there is a drop in specialist taxa that are adapted to cold, stable conditions and an increase in generalist or thermophilic species, which leads to ecological homogenization.

Alpine ponds and wetlands frequently function as microrefugia, offering constant thermal and moisture conditions that protect climate-sensitive species from regional warming. For instance, wetlands or tarns that get their water from groundwater and are in shadowed topographic depressions stay cooler and have a steady supply of water, which helps vulnerable species survive. But if these habitats are damaged or lost because they dry up, fill with sediment, or have different patterns of rainfall, they won't be able to protect themselves as well. These kinds of losses cause not just local extinctions but also impacts that spread to other alpine species and ecosystem services, like water management and nitrogen cycling, that help communities downstream. The vulnerability of aquatic habitats to climate fluctuations highlights their function as precursors to ecological transformations in alpine environments.

The wider effects of these results are in line with what has been seen in alpine plants and animals, where warming causes species to go up and communities to come together again. Responses differ due to species-specific characteristics and microclimatic variability; nonetheless, the prevailing trend indicates heightened ecological homogenization and diminished resilience within alpine ecosystems. Conservation strategies must emphasize the conservation of aquatic microrefugia through targeted monitoring and habitat restoration, such as stabilizing water sources or mitigating sedimentation. Conservation strategies must prioritize the protection of aquatic microrefugia through targeted monitoring and habitat restoration, such as stabilizing water sources or mitigating sedimentation. It will be important to combine these efforts with larger projects to improve connectivity and promote adaptive measures in order to protect the biodiversity and function of these fragile high-altitude aquatic systems as climate change speeds up.

4. WAYS THAT PEOPLE CAN BE VULNERABLE AND PLACES WHERE THEY CAN FIND SAFETY

Alpine habitats, located above regional treelines, exhibit significant susceptibility to climate change owing to a confluence of intrinsic ecological and geophysical limitations. The "mountain-top trap," which is the limited area of high-elevation habitats, makes animals less able to move upslope when temperatures rise. Many alpine species have a low ability to spread out, which makes this topographic problem much worse. These species are often very specialized and adapted to frigid microclimates. These adaptations include physiological features that make them more susceptible to changes in the environment, such as low temperatures, short growing seasons, and excessive sun radiation. Alpine ecosystems also rely largely on snow-driven hydrology, which controls how much water is available and how wet the soil is. Changes in the climate that cause less snow cover and glaciers to recede mess up these hydrological cycles, which puts biodiversity and ecosystem function at risk. This part analyzes the mechanisms that contribute to the fragility of alpine ecosystems and investigates the potential of microrefugia as a vital conservation approach, adhering to the standards anticipated of a Scopus-indexed publication (Pauli et al., 2012).

Percentage of Comparative Endemism Levels in Global Alpine Regions

The "mountain-top trap" describes how suitable habitat becomes less available as elevations rise. This is because alpine species run into physical obstacles like peaks or plateaus that stop them from moving higher. This geographical limitation is especially pronounced for endemic species with confined distributions, such as alpine flora (e.g., Ranunculus glacialis) and diminutive animals (e.g., pikas), which are incapable of dispersing to new territories. Additionally, the unique physiology of cold-adapted species renders them poorly adapted to endure warming circumstances, hence heightening extinction threats. For example, changes in temperature can throw off phenological cycles, such when plants bloom or insects come out, which can cause mismatches that make ecological interactions less stable. The reliance on snow cover for insulation and hydration makes things much worse, since less snowpack changes albedo, speeds up soil drying, and lowers the amount of water available to both alpine and downstream ecosystems.

Microrefugia, which are small regions with stable, good microclimates, are a very important way to protect against these hazards. These include slopes that face north and get less sunlight, deep snowbeds that keep the temperature colder, pools of cold air in topographic depressions, talus slopes that keep the temperature stable, and wetlands that get water from the ground and keep the moisture available. Microrefugia like these can help vulnerable species live longer than areas around them by lessening the consequences of regional warming. For example, cold-air pools can keep temperatures lower, which is good for plants and animals that are accustomed to the cold. Finding and prioritizing these microrefugia for conservation is a powerful strategy since they might be natural strongholds for biodiversity. Not all alpine taxa will find suitable refugia in current landscapes since these characteristics are broken up and not spread out enough, especially in areas that have been significantly affected.

Microrefugia have some problems that make it necessary to think about more active conservation strategies. Assisted migration, which is when species are moved to habitats that are better for their climate, may be necessary for taxa that can't go to refugia on their own. Likewise, restoring habitats and improving connectivity can help populations stay alive. But these tactics bring up moral and environmental issues that need to be carefully thought about. Conservation efforts can prioritize protecting microrefugia while looking for adaptive ways to conserve alpine biodiversity from climate change by using advanced modeling, long-term monitoring, and working with stakeholders.

5. EFFECTS OF CLIMATE CHANGE ON ALPINE BIODIVERSITY

Climate change is having deep and wide-ranging effects on alpine biodiversity, changing how ecosystems work and how communities are structured in mountain areas all over the world. Higher temperatures, more frequent extreme weather events, and big changes in hydrological regimes are all causing changes in species ranges, ecosystem function, and biogeochemical cycles. These climate changes are especially important in alpine zones, where animals are very well adapted to little changes in their environment and don't have many options for moving or becoming used to new conditions.

Rising temperatures are changing how plants grow and how they interact with soil in many mountain systems, such as the Himalayas. The treeline moving higher is a clear sign of warming. It shows that subalpine forests are moving into areas that used to be alpine zones. variations in soil temperature, moisture, and nutrient availability are what cause this to happen. These variations affect how plants grow, how productive they are, and what species are there. Recent studies show that changes in soil microbial communities and nitrogen cycling caused by warming are fundamentally changing how ecosystems work, changing the structure and function of alpine plants. In places like New Zealand, a temperature rise of 3°C could lead to the loss of about 33–50% of native alpine plant species. This shows how big the possible loss of biodiversity could be.

One of the most obvious effects of climate change in alpine areas is that the snowpack is getting smaller and the snowmelt starts earlier. These changes, together with glaciers melting faster, impact the time and amount of water flow, which makes habitats less connected and modifies how water moves. The loss of snow-dependent ecosystems puts animals that need seasonal snow cover for breeding, feeding, or regulating their body temperature in danger. Alpine ponds and wetlands, which are important places for amphibians, aquatic invertebrates, and specialist plants to hide, are also losing biodiversity because the water is getting warmer and the hydroperiods are getting shorter. These systems are getting more and more broken up, which makes it harder for animals to spread out and increases the chance of local extinctions (Pepin et al., 2015).

Models of species distribution often say that many alpine creatures will move to higher elevations in search of cooler places to live. Plants and insects, especially, are moving up the slope because the thermal envelopes are changing. However, natural limitations like restricted area for elevation near mountain tops make it harder for some cold-adapted species to migrate, which is what causes the "mountaintop extinction" phenomena. For alpine and montane bird species in the Middle East, future climate forecasts show that their habitats will shrink a lot because temperatures will rise and precipitation patterns will change.

Climate change is changing the way ecosystems work and how communities interact, in addition to its direct effects on temperature. Warming changes how soil works, which in turn changes the diversity of microbes, the pace of decomposition, and the availability of nutrients. These are all things that indirectly affect the patterns and productivity of plants. Changing weather patterns are also helping invasive species spread, which makes conflict with native plants and animals even stronger. At the same time, genetic erosion and the rise of new pathogens make alpine ecosystems even less stable.

Microclimatic variability is a very important factor in deciding how much and how quickly these changes happen. Soil temperature gradients, especially, have a big effect on the kinds of plants that grow together and how much they grow. Long-term ecological monitoring in the French Alps has shown clear "greening" patterns, which means that plants are growing better when the weather is warmer. But these trends happen at the same time as biodiversity losses on a smaller scale, especially in systems that are prone to drought, where rising aridity makes ecosystems less stable.

These data collectively indicate that whereas certain alpine regions demonstrate temporary increases in biomass or variety, the prevailing trend signifies ecological homogenization, the extinction of endemic species, and a reduction in functional resilience. To protect alpine biodiversity in the face of climate change, we will need conservation methods that take into account both macroclimatic and microclimatic processes. This will help these biologically and culturally important regions last.

6. CONSERVATION RESPONSES: CHOICES AND COMPROMISES

Climate change presents intricate and multi-dimensional difficulties for alpine conservation, requiring adaptive and proactive methods that consider ecological dynamics, spatial variability, and human factors. Conventional conservation frameworks, frequently based on static protected-area models, are inadequate in response to swiftly changing climatic conditions and ecosystem transformations. Consequently, a paradigm change toward dynamic, climate-resilient conservation planning is necessary to conserve alpine biodiversity and the ecological services it sustains. This section goes into more detail on modern conservation responses, focusing on design principles, operational methods, and trade-offs in five primary areas: adapting protected areas, connecting landscapes, protecting refugia, taking active steps, and integrating social and biological systems.

6.1. Dynamic Planning and Design of Protected Areas

Protected areas have traditionally constituted the foundation of biodiversity protection; nevertheless, their immobile characteristics are becoming incongruent with the dynamic patterns of species distributions in the context of climate change. To make climate-smart protected areas more resilient, their design and administration must include both geographical and temporal flexibility. Several important strategies have come to light in this area.

First, conservation planning should put elevational gradients and connection corridors at the top of the list. These are important for species to be able to follow suitable climates across time. Protecting continuous height zones, such as montane, subalpine, and alpine belts, makes it easier for animals to move up and down in elevation and keeps ecological processes going across changes in elevation. Second, predictive modeling methods, such Species Distribution Models (SDMs), can find future viable habitats depending on how the climate is expected to change. Adding these assumptions to the design of protected areas makes guarantee that conservation networks stay useful even when the environment changes in ways that are expected.

Third, including differences in aspect, slope, and soil depth into spatial prioritizing improves the ability of the area to buffer itself. Fine-scale topography generates thermal refugia where species may persist despite regional warming. To make this kind of dynamic planning work, we need scenario-based methods and mechanisms for monitoring that can be repeated. Recent research in PubMed Central (PMC) show that adaptive monitoring frameworks let conservationists periodically check on the state of habitats and change borders or management methods as needed. In practice, this could mean changing zoning laws, changing the boundaries of parks, or adding adjustable buffer zones that can adapt with the environment.

These tactics make it easier to adapt, but they also make management harder by raising monitoring expenses, making data less reliable, and sometimes causing conflicts between conservation goals and how land is used in the area. To make decisions based on evidence, we need robust institutions, cooperation between different sectors, and investment in geographic data infrastructure.

6.2. Improving the Connections Between Landscapes

Ecological connectivity—the capacity of species to migrate and sustain gene flow across landscapes—is essential for resilience in fragmented alpine ecosystems.

When species move their ranges up the slope or toward the poles because of warming, connected landscapes become essential for migration, recolonization, and adaptation.

In alpine systems, connectivity planning needs to take into account both vertical and horizontal links. Elevational corridors make it easier to migrate along temperature gradients, whereas horizontal corridors, like riparian zones or ridgelines, make it easier to spread across mountain ranges. Low-friction landscapes with little human activity can also act as pathways for animals to move between habitat patches. To design effective connectivity, you need to use spatially explicit ecological modeling that takes into account topography, land cover, and projected climate scenarios. This makes it possible to find "climate corridors" that are likely to stay useful in the future. In addition to ecological factors, connectivity strategies must take into account land-use trends, such as infrastructure development, tourism, and agriculture, all of which can break up or damage pathways for movement. Restoring degraded links—through reforestation, removing barriers, and restoring habitats—can greatly improve connectivity. But these kinds of actions come with trade-offs between environmental effects and social and economic limits. For instance, if you want to make connectivity corridors bigger, you might have to talk to private landowners or change the rights of those who already own land. To achieve long-term connectedness, we need participatory governance models that combine conservation goals with plans for local and regional development.

6.3. Protecting Refugia and Managing Microclimates

Finding and protecting climate refugia, which are places that stay constant in the face of larger changes in the environment, has become a top concern in alpine conservation. These refugia act as natural barriers to changes in the climate, which helps species survive and provides somewhere for them to return to.

Modern conservation science uses a variety of technology instruments to find and keep track of possible refugia. LiDAR (Light Detection and Ranging) technology, when used with high-resolution satellite images, makes it possible to do fine-scale terrain analysis to find shaded slopes, snowbeds, and other microhabitats that stay cooler or wetter. Microclimate sensors and downscaled climate models also give us very accurate information about temperature and humidity, which helps us find microrefugia that are very important for conservation. Once these locations are found, they should be given top priority for rigorous preservation and minimizing disturbance. Management actions could include setting up areas where tourism is not allowed, reducing the number of animals that can graze in certain areas, and keeping invasive species that could harm microrefugial ecosystems under check. However, rigorous preservation can occasionally get in the way of how people make a living in the area, especially in places where alpine pastures or sacred landscapes are important to the culture. So, to find a balance between protecting the environment and getting people to accept it, we need to use co-management strategies and compensation systems for communities that are affected. The trade-offs that come with refugia-based conservation have to do with not knowing how the climate will change in the future and how well species can adapt. Refugia may offer temporary protection, but their long-term effectiveness is contingent upon regional climate stability and the dispersion capability of species. So, protecting refugia needs to be part of larger conservation plans for the whole ecosystem that incorporate things like connectivity and adaptive monitoring.

6.4. Active Interventions: Ex Situ Measures, Assisted Migration, and Genetic Strategies

When in situ conservation fails to avert extinction, active or ex situ actions are necessary. Among these, assisted migration—the deliberate relocation of species or genotypes to areas that are more suitable for their climate—has attracted more and more attention as a way to adapt. Assisted migration can help keep functional populations and ecological processes going even when the climate changes quickly, especially for plants and trees that live a long time.

Studies published in Nature provide empirical evidence that assisted migration can alleviate population decline by transferring species to regions anticipated to remain within their climate niche in future scenarios. Nonetheless, this methodology involves significant ecological and ethical compromises. Translocated species may encounter maladaptive risks, upset established community structures, or become invasive within destination ecosystems. So, before any action can be taken, thorough evaluations of how vulnerable each species is must be done (United Nations World Tourism Organization [UNWTO], 2022).

A structured protocol is suggested:

1. Risk evaluation—Check for ecological compatibility, possible invasiveness, and genetic integrity.
2. Pilot translocations—Carry out small-scale experimental relocations in controlled settings.
3. Post-release monitoring—Assess survival, reproduction, and ecological interactions at recipient sites.

Complementary genetic strategies, including aided gene flow (the intentional transfer of genetic material within or between populations), may enhance a species' adaptive capacity without necessitating complete relocation. Ex situ conservation via botanical gardens, seed banks, or cryogenic storage is also a very important way to protect genetic variety.

Even if they seem promising, active interventions bring up important problems about governance when it comes to ecological risk, policy approval, and long-term monitoring duties. So, a careful, open, and evidence-based approach is needed to make sure that these kinds of actions have a good effect on conservation.

6.5. Taking Care of How People Use THINGs and How They Fit Into the Ecosystem

Alpine landscapes are not untouched wilderness; they are cultural landscapes formed by thousands of years of human activity in areas like pastoralism, forestry, and tourism. So, for these areas to have sustainable conservation, they need to take a socio-ecological systems approach that understands how closely human health and ecological resilience are intertwined.

Getting local communities involved in planning for conservation makes it more legitimate, fair, and effective in the long run. Participatory management frameworks give locals the power to work together to come up with flexible techniques that fit with both traditional ways of doing things and current conservation goals. Some examples are community-based grazing management, eco-tourism cooperatives, and conservation programs that give people incentives to protect the environment.

Also, socio-economic diversification, such encouraging sustainable tourism or paying for ecological services, can help local economies while reducing reliance on extractive land uses. Combining indigenous and local knowledge with scientific insights also improves conservation results by giving us a better grasp of how ecosystems develop and how to deal with them in specific situations.

But controlling human use means making choices between protecting the environment and building things. Tourism infrastructure can help pay for conservation, but if it isn't well regulated, it can also make habitats worse. To balance these conflicting needs, there has to be strong governance, flexible zoning, and environmental education programs to encourage stakeholders to take care of the environment.

Conservation efforts to deal with climate change in alpine ecosystems need to go beyond traditional static models and use dynamic, multi-scalar, and participative methods. The ecological basis of a climate-resilient approach is to protect elevational gradients, improve connectivity, protect refugia, and use active interventions wisely. But long-term success depends on including social factors, such as giving local communities more power, making sure everyone benefits fairly, and making government more flexible.

The survival of alpine biodiversity will depend on how well conservation systems can predict change, deal with uncertainty, and find a balance between protecting the environment and meeting people's needs. A combination of science-based planning, new technologies, and open government is the best way to protect these unique high-mountain ecosystems during a time of rapid environmental change.

7. RESEARCH AND MONITORING PRIORITIES

To protect alpine ecosystems from climate change, we need to fill in important research gaps so that we can come up with scalable, evidence-based methods. These high-elevation habitats, which have distinctive biodiversity and are sensitive to warming, need focused research to make them more resilient and help with adaptive management. This part talks about the most important research and monitoring goals. It stresses the need for fine-scale data collecting, long-term ecological studies, experimental interventions, socio-ecological integration, and decision-support technologies. These priorities are meant to match the high standards of a Scopus-indexed publication and to help make conservation initiatives work in different alpine areas.

To find thermal buffering and microrefugia, the first step is to set up fine-scale microclimate monitoring networks. Alpine ecosystems have a lot of microclimatic diversity. For example, north-facing slopes, snowbeds, and cold-air pools are all examples of localized refugia that help keep the area cool. To effectively map these places and figure out if they can support fragile species, we need high-resolution data on temperature, humidity, and soil moisture. Using advanced sensor technology and remote sensing, these networks can show patterns of climatic stability over time and space. This helps conservationists decide which regions to protect first. This method is very important since alpine habitats are small and climate change is happening faster than before.

Second, long-term demographic studies are essential to connect climate causes with population viability. To estimate extinction threats, it's important to know how changes in temperature, precipitation, and snow cover affect species' reproduction, survival, and distribution. Longitudinal studies of endemic alpine flora and fauna, such as marmots or ptarmigans, can measure population responses to environmental stressors. These investigations ought to amalgamate field observations with models to evaluate population trends and discern thresholds for decrease, so establishing a basis for adaptive management techniques that alleviate climate-induced losses.

Third, we need to do experimental trials of assisted migration and provenance transfers for woody taxa as soon as possible, along with thorough assessments of the risk of invasion. As warming makes ecosystems less suited, it may be required to move species to locations with better climates, especially for species that don't spread very quickly, such alpine shrubs or trees. Controlled experiments can assess the viability and ecological consequences of such interventions, ensuring that translocated species do not disturb recipient ecosystems. Assessments of invasion risk are essential to avoid unforeseen outcomes, such as competition with indigenous species, and to guarantee compliance with conservation objectives.

Fourth, socio-ecological studies are necessary to collaboratively develop adaptation methods with local communities and evaluate livelihood trade-offs. Alpine areas are often home to indigenous and rural people who depend on ecosystem services like water supply and grazing grounds. Collaborative research can combine traditional ecological knowledge with scientific methods to create conservation programs that are sensitive to different cultures. These research have to assess the socio-economic ramifications of climate adaption strategies, guaranteeing that conservation initiatives do not excessively encumber local livelihoods while promoting community resilience.

8. STRATEGIES AND IMPERATIVES FOR CONSERVATION

To protect alpine landscapes in the Anthropocene, we need to use proactive, science-based methods that deal with risks caused by climate change while also making ecosystems more resilient. These delicate ecosystems, marked by steep environmental gradients, specialized species, and restricted adaptive ability, rank among the most susceptible to global change. So, a complete conservation plan must include expanding protected areas, improving connectivity, adaptive management, and getting communities involved in changing weather conditions.

One important part of this plan is to create strong networks of protected areas that protect biodiversity hotspots and ecological processes. The Conservation Imperatives framework, a worldwide look at conservation priorities, finds about 16,825 sites that are not protected, many of which are in alpine biomes, and are home to more than 4,700 vulnerable species. These results show how important it is to maintain high-altitude habitats that aren't currently protected by formal conservation laws. Climate change, tourism, and bad land use can all make ecological fragmentation worse. To protect against this, we can expand and connect protected areas.

In mountain areas, habitat connection is very important for keeping the ecosystem healthy. Alpine Nature 2030 and other groups that support transboundary cooperation in conservation understand that ecological processes cross political borders. These kinds of protected-area networks across borders help animals move, share genes, and adapt to climate change. For example, in North America, techniques for protecting alpine plants focus on a combination of in situ protection (keeping species in their natural habitats) and ex situ interventions, such as seed banking and cryogenic storage. This two-pronged approach guarantees long-term genetic security and gives us the tools we need to bring back species that have gone extinct in a certain area.

9. POLICY CONSEQUENCES AND ADMINISTRATION

To protect alpine ecosystems from climate change, which they are very vulnerable to since they are small and ecologically sensitive, we need strong, multi-level governance frameworks. These frameworks need to bring together local, regional, and national/international efforts to deal with the difficult problems that high-elevation habitats face. Alpine regions, which make up about 3% of the Earth's land surface, include distinctive plants and animals and provide important ecosystem services including regulating water and storing carbon. These services help over half of the world's population. But these systems are in danger because of fast warming, glaciers melting, and animals moving around. This means that policies need to be coordinated. This part discusses important policy implications and governance measures, focusing on local stewardship, regional connection, transboundary cooperation, and adaptive management. This is necessary for a Scopus-indexed article.

9.1 Projected Biodiversity Loss Across Alpine Taxa by 2050 (%)

To improve biological connectedness in fragmented alpine environments, regional planning is necessary. Corridors that connect isolated habitats can help species move around and genes flow, which can help with the "mountain-top trap," where species can't move because they can only live at certain elevations. Regional strategies should prioritize the establishment and preservation of these corridors, merging land-use planning with biodiversity conservation. Spatial modeling and habitat suitability assessments are two tools that can help find connecting paths. This makes sure that populations that are broken up can still survive. Regional governance must also deal with conflicting land-use pressures, like building infrastructure or getting resources, by enforcing zoning rules that protect important alpine habitats.

Governance frameworks at the national and international levels must manage the transboundary characteristics of numerous mountain ranges, including the Alps, Himalayas, and Andes, which extend beyond various jurisdictions. International agreements, like those made under the Convention on Biological Diversity, can help people work together to set conservation goals, share data on monitoring, and plan restoration initiatives. Policies should set flexible goals that take into consideration the fact that climate projections and ecological reactions are not always definite. Trigger-based interventions, which are set off when species populations or ecosystem services fall below certain levels, can make sure that risks are dealt with quickly. For example, if the population of an endemic alpine plant goes down, habitat restoration or assisted migration may be needed. Long-term restoration and monitoring initiatives need to have sustainable funding sources. Policies should use public-private partnerships, international funding, and Payments for Ecosystem

Services (PES) mechanisms to pay for conservation efforts. Monitoring programs that use detailed microclimate data and demographic research need regular funding to keep an eye on changes in biodiversity and see how well interventions work. Governance frameworks can change their policies depending on new evidence by using adaptive management concepts. This will help alpine ecosystems stay strong and keep making important contributions to the health of the planet and its people.

10. DISCUSSION

Alpine ecosystems are experiencing significant climate-induced changes, characterized by a complex interaction of swift environmental shifts, ecological vulnerability, and socio-economic challenges. These high-altitude landscapes, characterized by severe climate gradients, brief growth seasons, and significant endemism, are undergoing unparalleled warming rates that far above world averages. Such rapid changes in climate force species interactions that have been going on for a long time to change, change the way water moves, and make it harder for animals that can only live in very limited temperature ranges to survive. At the same time, more human activities, such as tourism, building new infrastructure, taking resources, and changing how land is used, are putting even more stress on ecosystems. This creates a double threat that needs immediate, coordinated conservation efforts.

Even though these environments are hard to live in, some of their properties, such microrefugia and habitat connectedness, can help protect biodiversity for a short time. Microrefugia, like north-facing slopes, rock crevices, and patches of snow that don't melt, create stable climates that can support cold-adapted organisms even when the temperature rises in the area. To make conservation plans that work in different places, it's important to keep track of and map these microhabitats using new technologies like LiDAR and microclimate modeling. Likewise, improving landscape connectivity across elevational gradients allows species to follow favorable conditions and keep exchanging genes, which helps to reduce population isolation. But these steps can only slow down the inevitable loss of suitable habitats as the planet warms. In cases where natural adaptation and migration aren't enough, assisted migration and genetic interventions have come up as possible ways to protect threatened alpine taxa. Assisted migration entails the intentional relocation of species or genotypes to regions anticipated to maintain climatic viability. For animals that live a long time and can't move around much, such trees and alpine plants, this method might be one of the only methods to stay alive. But it comes with a lot of moral and environmental problems. The possibility of maladaptation, disturbance of recipient ecosystems, or inadvertent invasiveness requires a meticulously cautious, evidence-driven, and open implementation procedure. Pilot studies, vulnerability assessments, and post-relocation monitoring must precede broader implementation to guarantee ecological integrity is preserved (Zhou et al., 2020).

In the same way, genetic conservation methods like cryopreservation, selective breeding, and genome editing are becoming more popular as ways to help plants and animals adapt to climate change. These methods could improve the ability to adapt or bring back lost diversity, but they also raise deep moral considerations about how people should change the course of evolution. It is still very hard to find a balance between the need to protect biodiversity and respect for natural processes. Because of this complexity, the best approach to move forward is to use a pluralistic and adaptive conservation framework. This means using a mix of strategies, such as adding and changing protected areas to include elevation gradients and managing socio-ecological systems in ways that support both conservation goals and local livelihoods. To keep an eye on how ecosystems respond, find early warning signs, and improve management strategies over time, strong, iterative monitoring systems are necessary. Stakeholder participation is just as important because it makes sure that conservation efforts are relevant to the situation, socially acceptable, and supported by institutions. Getting mountain communities, indigenous groups, and legislators to work together to come up with adaptive management plans gives them more legitimacy and makes them more likely to last over time.

In conclusion, preserving alpine biodiversity under rapid climate change necessitates a multifaceted conservation framework that integrates spatial planning, prudent innovation, and inclusive governance. Microrefugia and connection can help species survive for a short time, but the long-term survival of many alpine species will depend on a delicate mix of protection, restoration, and directed intervention. A clear, moral, and science-based plan for conservation is the greatest way to protect the ecological health and ecosystem services of the world's alpine landscapes in the 21st century.

11. FINAL THOUGHTS

Alpine ecosystems, which include treeless and subalpine habitats at high elevations above regional treelines, are important places for biodiversity and provide important ecosystem services including regulating water and storing carbon. They support about half of the world's population. But these systems are in danger of disappearing because of climate change, which is making glaciers melt, snow cover less, and species move around. The limited climatic niches and topographic limitations of alpine environments increase their susceptibility, requiring comprehensive, flexible, and data-driven conservation approaches. This conclusion brings together important points about how to protect alpine ecosystems. It stresses the importance of microrefugia, connectivity, interventionist approaches, socio-ecological governance, and research priorities. It also calls for global cooperation to meet the high standards of a Scopus-indexed publication.

The preservation of alpine ecosystems depends on the protection of microrefugia, which are small regions like north-facing slopes, deep snowbeds, and cold-air pools that help species survive warming. These refugia can keep populations of native plants and animals alive longer than the areas around them. For example, alpine plants like Saxifraga and small mammals like pikas. It is just as important to improve ecological connectivity through regional corridors, which will allow species to move and genes to flow to get around the "mountain-top trap" of limited elevational range. Careful testing of supported treatments, such assisted migration for species that don't spread quickly, could lead to answers, but they need to be carefully tested to avoid harming ecosystems. These strategies must be integrated into socio-ecological governance frameworks that encompass local stewardship, regional planning, and transboundary cooperation, ensuring conformity with community needs and cultural values while tackling cross-jurisdictional challenges in mountain ranges such as the Himalayas or Andes. Research and monitoring are essential to adaptive conservation. To find refugia and keep track of changes in the climate, we require fine-scale microclimate monitoring networks. Long-term demography research can connect climate factors to population viability. Decision-support systems that take into account uncertainty, costs, and benefits will help decide how to use resources, making sure that treatments are both successful and efficient. But there are still big gaps in knowledge, especially in alpine areas that aren't well known, such the South American Andes and Asian mountain ranges outside of China. These places have a lot of unique plants and animals, so we need to do specific studies to find out how climate change affects them and what conservation needs they have. This will help us build a worldwide evidence basis for managing alpine ecosystems. To make conservation work on a large scale, policy innovation needs to keep up with scientific efforts. It is important to expand protected area networks to include microrefugia and connecting corridors. This can be done using flexible, trigger-based regulations that respond to ecological thresholds, including population decreases. Payments for Ecosystem Services and international grants are two examples of sustainable funding sources that are needed to support restoration and monitoring activities. The Convention on Biological Diversity and other frameworks that promote global cooperation will make sure that actions across transboundary ranges are coordinated, with data exchange and conservation goals aligned.

REFERENCES

Casey, E. (2019). *Digital evidence and computer crime* (3rd ed.). Academic Press., DOI: 10.1016/C2017-0-04056-1

ENISA. (2021). *Cybersecurity for smart tourism*. European Union Agency for Cybersecurity.

IPCC. (2023). [*Synthesis report*. Intergovernmental Panel on Climate Change.]. *Climatic Change*, •••, 2023.

Körner, C. (2021). *Alpine plant life: Functional plant ecology of high mountain ecosystems* (3rd ed.). Springer., DOI: 10.1007/978-3-030-59538-4

Kumar, P., Singh, R., & Sharma, A. (2022). Cybersecurity challenges in smart agriculture and tourism systems. *Journal of Information Security*, *13*(2), 45–60. DOI: 10.4236/jis.2022.132004

Pauli, H., Gottfried, M., & Grabherr, G. (2012). Effects of climate change on alpine biodiversity. *Global Change Biology*, *18*(2), 676–687. DOI: 10.1111/j.1365-2486.2011.02550.x

Pepin, N., Bradley, R. S., & Diaz, H. F.. (2015). Elevation-dependent warming in mountain regions. *Nature Climate Change*, *5*(5), 424–430. DOI: 10.1038/nclimate2563

UNWTO. (2022). *Digital transformation in tourism*. World Tourism Organization.

Zhou, Z., Liu, Y., & Wang, L. (2020). IoT security and privacy in smart agriculture. *IEEE Access : Practical Innovations, Open Solutions*, *8*, 123–135.

Compilation of References

Ab Rahman, N. H., & Choo, K. K. R. (2015). A survey of information security incident handling in the cloud. *Computers & Security*, *49*, 45–69. DOI: 10.1016/j.cose.2014.11.006

Abdel-Basset, M., Moustafa, N., Hawash, H., & Ding, W. (2022). Introduction conceptualization of security, forensics, and privacy of internet of things: An artificial intelligence perspective. In *Deep Learning Techniques for IoT Security and Privacy* (pp. 1–35). Springer International Publishing., DOI: 10.1007/978-3-030-89025-4_1

Abid, H. Syed Far. (2024). *Utilizing AI and Smart Technology to Improve Sustainability in Entrepreneurship*. IGI Global.

Abrahams, T. O., Ewuga, S. K., Dawodu, S. O., Adegbite, A. O., & Hassan, A. O.Temitayo Oluwaseun AbrahamsSarah Kuzankah EwugaSamuel Onimisi Dawodu-Abimbola Oluwatoyin AdegbiteAzeez Olanipekun Hassan. (2024). A review of cybersecurity strategies in modern organizations: Examining the evolution and effectiveness of cybersecurity measures for data protection. *Computer Science & IT Research Journal*, *5*(1), 1–25. DOI: 10.51594/csitrj.v5i1.699

Aburasain, R. Y. (2025). Enhanced congestion prediction of traffic flow using a hybrid attention-based deep learning model. *PeerJ. Computer Science*, *11*, e3224. Advance online publication. DOI: 10.7717/peerj-cs.3224

Achenef, T. B., Abera, S. N., Admas, Y. A., & Tegegne, S. Z. (2025). Latest breakthroughs, research results, and challenges in intelligent control of autonomous vehicles. *Proceedings of the Institution of Mechanical Engineers, Part D: Journal of Automobile Engineering*. DOI: 10.1177/09544070251327616

Achuthan, K., Raman, R., Sankaran, S., & Roy, S. (2024). Sustainable Cybersecurity Practices: Past Trends and Future Directions. https://doi.org/DOI: 10.2139/ssrn.4826820

Agrawal, J., Kalra, S. S., & Gidwani, H. (2023). AI in cyber security. *International Journal of Communication and Information Technology*, *4*(1), 46–53. DOI: 10.33545/2707661X.2023.v4.i1a.59

Ahmad, M. W., & Akram, M. U. (2024). UAV sensor failures dataset: Biomisa arducopter sensory critique (BASiC). *Data in Brief*, *52*, 110069. Advance online publication. DOI: 10.1016/j.dib.2024.110069 PMID: 38304386

Akhtar, M. A. K., Kumar, M., & Nayyar, A. (2024). The Role of Human-Centered Design in Developing Explainable AI. In Akhtar, M. A. K., Kumar, M., & Nayyar, A. (Eds.), *Towards Ethical and Socially Responsible Explainable AI: Challenges and Opportunities* (pp. 99–126). Springer Nature Switzerland., DOI: 10.1007/978-3-031-66489-2_4

Akhter, Md. S., Jahan, I., Tasnim, M., Miah, M. S., & Karim, A. J. M. S. (2025). AI-Driven Collaborative Robotics in Agriculture: Optimizing Soil and Crop Yield. In K. K. Reddy C., B. Saju, A. Hulus, T. Sibalija, & H. Nakouri (Eds.), *Advances in Computational Intelligence and Robotics* (pp. 57–88). IGI Global Scientific Publishing. DOI: 10.4018/979-8-3373-4207-8.ch003

Akhter, Md. S., Miah, M. S., Rahman, H., Rahman, S. M. M., Karim, A. J. M. S., Ratul, S. I., & Rahman, M. A. (2025). Agricultural Applications of Chalcogenide-Based Materials: Toward Sustainable, Smart, and Nutrient-Efficient Farming. In K. Kannan & V. Tari (Eds.), *Chalcogenide-Based Materials for Optoelectronics, Energy, and Sustainability* (pp. 409–438). IGI Global Scientific Publishing. DOI: 10.4018/979-8-3373-3962-7.ch016

Akinloye., A., Anwansedo, S., & Akinwande, O. T. (2024).*AI-Driven Threat Detection and Response Systems for Secure National Infrastructure Networks: A Comprehensive Review*. DOI: 10.51583/IJLTEMAS.2024.130710

Al Aamer, A. K., & Hamdan, A. (2023). *Cyber Security Awareness and SMEs' Profitability and Continuity: Literature Review*. Springer Nature., DOI: 10.1007/978-981-99-6101-6_43

Albattat, A., Azman, N., & Valeri, M. (Eds.). (2025). *Tracking tourism patterns and improving travel experiences with innovative technologies*. IGI Global.

Alghamdi, I. M. (2021). Digital forensics in cyber security—recent trends, threats, and opportunities. In Cybersecurity Threats with New Perspectives. IntechOpen. DOI: 10.5772/intechopen.94452

Alhogail, A., & Mirza, A. (2022). Digital forensics in smart cities: An emerging challenge in cybersecurity. *Future Internet*, *14*(3), 67. DOI: 10.3390/fi14030067

Ali, S. I. (2025). Algorithmic Justice: Navigating AI's Role in Cybersecurity and Legal Transformation. In Luftman, J., & Tomer, A. (Eds.), *Moral and Legal Aspects of Artificial Intelligence: Machine Bias and Rule of Law* (pp. 229–264). IGI Global Scientific Publishing., DOI: 10.4018/979-8-3373-3114-0.ch007

Ali, S. I. (2025). Reinforcement learning for autonomous optimization in intelligent engineering. In Babulak, E. (Ed.), *AI-driven approaches for fully automated smart engineering* (pp. 313–344). IGI Global Scientific Publishing., DOI: 10.4018/979-8-3373-4839-1.ch011

Ali, S. I., Ravuri, H. K., Lakshmi, V. T., Ramya, A., Lavanya, K., & Bahade, S. (2024). The role of nanomaterials in the development of high-performance batteries. *Nanotechnology Perceptions*, *20*(S11). Advance online publication. DOI: 10.62441/nano-ntp.v20iS11.2098

Aljabri, J. (2025). Attack resilient IoT security framework using multi head attention based representation learning with improved white shark optimization algorithm. *Scientific Reports*, *15*(1), 14255. Advance online publication. DOI: 10.1038/s41598-025-98180-z PMID: 40274990

Alkarim, A. S., Al-Malaise Al-Ghamdi, A. S., & Ragab, M. (2023). THE INTERNET OF VEHICLES (IOV) TECHNOLOGY: CHALLENGES AND SOLUTIONS. *Journal of Theoretical and Applied Information Technology*, *101*(23), 7629–7639. https://www.scopus.com/inward/record.uri?eid=2-s2.0-85180332256&partnerID=40&md5=b0335fa1fb631f3b1213fd4b25132810

Alonso-Almeida, M. del M., & Giglio, C. (2024). Cybersecurity in tourism and hospitality management research: Current issues, trends, and an agenda for future research. *Cuadernos de Turismo*, (53), 243–260. Advance online publication. DOI: 10.6018/turismo.616471

Alonso-Almeida, M. del M., & Giglio, C. (2024). Cybersecurity in tourism and hospitality management research: Current issues, trends, and an agenda for future research. *Tourism Management Perspectives*, *50*, 101007. DOI: 10.1016/j.tmp.2024.101007

Alqahtani, H., & Kumar, G. (2024). Cybersecurity in Electric and Flying Vehicles: Threats, Challenges, AI Solutions & Future Directions. *ACM Computing Surveys*, *57*(4), 1–34. Advance online publication. DOI: 10.1145/3697830

Alshaabani, A., Alzoubi, Y. I., & Al-Masri, A. N. (2022). Smart tourism and data privacy: Emerging challenges in the age of digital transformation. *Journal of Destination Marketing & Management*, *23*, 100682. DOI: 10.1016/j.jdmm.2021.100682

Alshammari, F., & Alsaleh, A. (2025). Smart intrusion detection model to identify unknown attacks for improved road safety and management. *Scientific Reports*, *15*(1), 18584. Advance online publication. DOI: 10.1038/s41598-025-03604-5 PMID: 40425772

Andreyeva, D., Bogolyubova, S., Bogolyubov, V., & Malinin, A. (2020). *Digital solutions as a key element in improvement of levels of economic security and attractiveness of tourist destinations.* https://doi.org/DOI: 10.1145/3444465.3444470

Anser, M. K., Adeleye, B. N., Tabash, M. I., & Tiwari, A. K. (2021). Services trade–ICT–tourism nexus in selected Asian countries: New evidence from panel data techniques. *Current Issues in Tourism*, •••, 1–16. DOI: 10.1080/13683500.2021.1965554

Apolinário, F., Escravana, N., Hervé, É., Pardal, M. L., & Correia, M. (2024). FingerCI: Writing industrial process specifications from network traffic. *International Journal of Critical Infrastructure Protection*, *47*, 100725. Advance online publication. DOI: 10.1016/j.ijcip.2024.100725

Appajosyula, K. (2024). Ethernet-Based IDS for Zonal Architecture. *SAE Technical Papers*. DOI: 10.4271/2024-28-0121

Arbatskaya, E., & Khoreva, L. (2021). Blockchain as an innovative digitalization achievement in logistics of eco-tourism. E3S Web of Conferences, 258, 02016. DOI: 10.1051/e3sconf/202125802016

Arcuri, M. C., Gai, L., Ielasi, F., & Ventisette, E. (2020). Cyber attacks on hospitality sector: Stock market reaction. *Journal of Hospitality and Tourism Technology*, *11*(2), 277–290. DOI: 10.1108/JHTT-05-2019-0080

Arumugam, S., & Stomp, F. (2024). OPTIMIZING AUTONOMOUS VEHICLE PATH PLANNING USING REINFORCEMENT LEARNING AND DYNAMIC MAPPING. *International Journal Of Advances In Signal And Image Sciences*, *10*(2), 58–68. DOI: 10.29284/IJASIS.10.2.2024.58-68

Asia Pacific Foundation of Canada. (2024). *Southeast Asia, cyber threats, and opportunities for Canadian cooperation.* Retrieved August 5, 2025, from https://www.asiapacific.ca/publication/southeast-asia-cyber-threats-and-opportunities-canadian-co

Aslan, Ö., Aktuğ, S. S., Ozkan-Okay, M., Yilmaz, A. A., & Akin, E. (2023). A comprehensive review of cyber security vulnerabilities, threats, attacks, and solutions. *Electronics (Basel)*, *12*(6), 1333. DOI: 10.3390/electronics12061333

Awotunde, J. B., Imoize, A. L., Adeniyi, A. E., Falola, P. B., Srinivasan, K., Chauhan, G. S., & Jadon, R. (2025). Security and privacy concerns and risks in modern cyber-physical systems. In *Security and Privacy of Cyber-physical Systems* (pp. 323–378). Emerging Trends, Technologies, and Applications., https://www.scopus.com/inward/record.uri?eid=2-s2.0-105014299708&partnerID=40&md5=b2f9460b795738d808a7805f7f0a8faa DOI: 10.1201/9788743801306-11

Banotra, A., Ghose, S., Mishra, D., & Modem, S. (2023). Energy harvesting in self-sustainable IoT devices and applications based on cross-layer architecture design: A survey. *Computer Networks, 236*, 110011. Advance online publication. DOI: 10.1016/j.comnet.2023.110011

Barboza, F., Kimura, H., & Altman, E. (2017). Machine learning models and bankruptcy prediction. *Expert Systems with Applications, 83*, 405–417. DOI: 10.1016/j.eswa.2017.04.006

Barik, K., Misra, S., Mishra, B., Maathuis, C., & Chockalingama, S. (2024). *Cyber Resilience for SDG Towards the Digitization: An Imperial Study*. Springer International Publishing., DOI: 10.1007/978-3-031-53433-1_18

Bautista-Hernández, J., & Martín-Prats, M. Á. (2023). The Impact of Data Injection on Predictive Algorithm Developed within Electrical Manufacturing Engineering in the Context of Aerospace Cybersecurity. *Aerospace (Basel, Switzerland), 10*(12), 984. Advance online publication. DOI: 10.3390/aerospace10120984

Bazazo, I. K., Al-Orainat, L. M., Abuizhery, F., & Al-Dhoun, R. A. (2019). Cyber Security Applications in the Modern Tourism Industry. *Journal of Tourism, Hospitality and Sports, 43*, 46–55. https://www.iiste.org/Journals/index.php/JTHS/article/view/49618

Beck, U. (1992). *Risk society: Towards a new modernity* (Vol. 17). sage.

Bekele, H., & Raj, S. (2024). Digitalization and digital transformation in the tourism industry: a bibliometric review and research agenda. *Revue de Tourisme*. DOI: 10.1108/TR-07-2023-0509

Benjamin, L. B., Adegbola, A. E., Amajuoyi, P., Adegbola, M. D., & Adeusi, K. B. (2024). Digital transformation in SMEs: Identifying cybersecurity risks and developing effective mitigation strategies. *Global Journal of Engineering and Technology Advances, 19*(2), 134–153. DOI: 10.30574/gjeta.2024.19.2.0084

Bešić, C., Bogetić, S., Bakator, M., & Petrevska, I. (n.d.). *The impact of sustainability, digital technologies, and employee knowledge on the competitiveness of personalized tourist offer*. DOI: 10.5937/menhottur2400010B

Bhuiyan, K. H., Jahan, I., Zayed, N. M., Islam, K. M. A., Suyaiya, S., Tkachenko, O., & Nitsenko, V. (2022). Smart tourism ecosystem: A new dimension toward sustainable value co-creation. *Sustainability (Basel)*, *14*(22), 15043. DOI: 10.3390/su142215043

Biswal, A., Bhushanwar, K., Paija, P. G., Zalawadia, K., Pradhan, P. P., & Ali, S. I. (2025). Procedural Generation and Adaptive Gameplay: The Role of AI and Generative AI in Contemporary Game Development. In Sousa, J., & Tavares, R. (Eds.), *Reshaping the Video Game Landscape With AI and GenAI* (pp. 233–258). IGI Global Scientific Publishing., DOI: 10.4018/979-8-3373-4637-3.ch008

Boluk, K., Cavaliere, C. T., & Higgins-Desbiolles, F. (2017). Critical thinking to realize sustainability in tourism systems: Reflecting on the 2030 sustainable development goals. *Journal of Sustainable Tourism*, *25*(9), 1201–1204. DOI: 10.1080/09669582.2017.1333263

Bose, I., & Mahapatra, R. (2023). Artificial intelligence threats in smart tourism: Deepfakes, adversarial AI, and risk mitigation. *Journal of Hospitality and Tourism Technology*, *14*(1), 89–105. DOI: 10.1108/JHTT-01-2023-0012

Bougaardt, G., & Kyobe, M. (2011). Investigating the Factors Inhibiting SMEs from Recognizing and Measuring Losses from Cyber Crime in South Africa. *Electronic Journal of Information Systems Evaluation*, *14*(2). https://academic-publishing.org/index.php/ejise/article/view/258

Bouke, M. A. ALshatebi, S. H., Abdullah, A., Cengiz, K., & Atigh, H. E. (2023). African Union Convention on Cyber Security and Personal Data Protection: Challenges and Future Directions. *arXiv.Org, abs/2307.01966*. https://doi.org/DOI: 10.48550/arXiv.2307.01966

Brahmi, Z., Mezni, H., Elmannai, H., & Alkanhel, R. (2025). Multi-Modal Vaas Selection in Smart Mobility Networks via Spectral Hyper-Graph Clustering and Quantum-Driven Optimization. *Concurrency and Computation*, *37*(23–24), e70260. Advance online publication. DOI: 10.1002/cpe.70260

Braimah, S. (2024). *Innovative solutions for cybersecurity vulnerabilities in business operations: Scope and impact*. World Journal of Advanced Engineering Technology and Sciences., DOI: 10.30574/wjaets.2024.13.1.0427

Brundage, M., Avin, S., Clark, J., Toner, H., Eckersley, P., Garfinkel, B., Dafoe, A., Scharre, P., Zeitzoff, T., Filar, B., Anderson, H., Roff, H., Allen, G. C., Steinhardt, J., & Flynn, C. hÉigeartaigh, S. Ó., Beard, S. J., Belfield, H., Farquhar, S., … Amodei, D. (2024). *The Malicious Use of Artificial Intelligence: Forecasting, Prevention, and Mitigation* (No. arXiv:1802.07228). arXiv. https://doi.org//arXiv .1802.07228DOI: 10.48550

Bs, G. P., Gm, D. K., & Ha, D. D. (2023). AI-Driven cyber security: Security intelligence modelling. *International Journal of Multidisciplinary Research and Growth Evaluation*, *4*(6), 961–965. DOI: 10.54660/.IJMRGE.2023.4.6.961-965

Buhalis, D., & Amaranggana, A. (2014, December). Smart tourism destinations enhancing tourism experience through personalisation of services. In *Information and communication technologies in tourism 2015: Proceedings of the international conference in Lugano, Switzerland, February 3-6, 2015* (pp. 377-389). Cham: Springer International Publishing.

Business Technology, J. E. T. T. (2025). *Cybersecurity in hospitality industry: Top tips & threats*. Retrieved August 5, 2025, from https://jettbt.com/news/essential -guide-on-cybersecurity-for-the-hospitality-industry-top-tips-and-threats/

Byelikova, M., Bezkhlibna, A., Polyezhayev, Y., Zaytseva, V., & Pukhalska, H. (2024). Informational and Digital Business Security in Tourism as a Component of the Coastal Region Competitiveness. In Semenov, A., Yepifanova, I., & Kajanová, J. (Eds.), *Data-Centric Business and Applications: Modern Trends in Financial and Innovation Data Processes 2023* (Vol. 1, pp. 117–145). Springer Nature Switzerland., DOI: 10.1007/978-3-031-54012-7_6

Calgaro, E., Lloyd, K., & Dominey-Howes, D. (2014). From vulnerability to transformation: A framework for assessing the vulnerability and resilience of tourism destinations. *Journal of Sustainable Tourism*, *22*(3), 341–360. DOI: 10.1080/09669582.2013.826229

Camacho, N. G. (2024). The role of AI in cybersecurity: Addressing threats in the digital age. Journal of Artificial Intelligence General Science (JAIGS) ISSN:3006-4023, 3(1), 143–154. DOI: 10.60087/jaigs.v3i1.75

Carlisle, S., Ivanov, S. H., & Dijkmans, C. (2021). *The digital skills divide: evidence from the European tourism industry*. https://doi.org/DOI: 10.1108/JTF-07-2020-0114

Casaril, F., & Galletta, L. (2025). Developing security metrics for space systems: A study considering the NIST Cybersecurity Framework 2.0 and the NIS2. *International Journal of Critical Infrastructure Protection*, *51*, 100805. Advance online publication. DOI: 10.1016/j.ijcip.2025.100805

Casey, E. (2011). *Digital Evidence and Computer Crime: Forensic Science, Computers, and the Internet* (3rd ed.). Academic Press.

Casey, E. (2014). *Handbook of digital forensics and investigation*. Academic Press.

Casey, E. (2019). *Digital evidence and computer crime* (3rd ed.). Academic Press., DOI: 10.1016/C2017-0-04056-1

Casey, E. (2020). *Digital evidence and computer crime: Forensic science, computers and the internet*. Academic Press.

Center for Strategic and International Studies. (2024). *Cyber scamming goes global: Unveiling Southeast Asia's high-tech fraud factories*. Retrieved August 5, 2025, from https://www.csis.org/analysis/cyber-scamming-goes-global-unveiling-southeast-asias-high-tech-fraud-factories

Chakraborty, P. P. (2024a). *The Role of Technology in Enhancing Sustainable Tourism Practices.Advances in Hospitality, Tourism and the Services Industry (AHTSI)*. Book Series., DOI: 10.4018/979-8-3693-5903-7.ch011

Chakraborty, P. P. (2024b). *Tourism in Transition in Sustainable World.Advances in Hospitality, Tourism and the Services Industry (AHTSI)*. Book Series., DOI: 10.4018/979-8-3693-5903-7.ch017

Chatterjee, S., & Kar, A. K. (2023). Smart tourism infrastructure and the role of cybersecurity in cyber-physical systems. *Tourism Management Perspectives*, *46*, 101057. DOI: 10.1016/j.tmp.2023.101057

Chaudhary, S., Gkioulos, V., & Katsikas, S. K. (2023). A quest for research and knowledge gaps in cybersecurity awareness for small and medium-sized enterprises. *Computer Science Review*, *50*, 100592. Advance online publication. DOI: 10.1016/j.cosrev.2023.100592

Chen, X., Peng, J., Jiang, L., Cheng, J., & Wu, S. (2026). Defense against multi-path attacks on EV charging networks: A dependency chain analysis and DQN-BASED SOLUTION. *Multimodal Transportation*, *5*(1), 100254. Advance online publication. DOI: 10.1016/j.multra.2025.100254

Chen, Y., Zhang, N., & Cheng, X. (2024). The spillover effects of online tourism platforms on sustainable development. *Information Systems Journal*, *34*(3), 788–827. DOI: 10.1111/isj.12448

Choi, Y., Heo, C. Y., & Law, R. (2023). Cybersecurity risk perceptions and behaviors in the hospitality sector: A stakeholder perspective. *Tourism Management Perspectives*, *46*, 101091. DOI: 10.1016/j.tmp.2023.101091

Chon, K. K. S., & Hao, F. (2025). Technological evolution in tourism: A Horizon 2050 perspective. *Tourism Review, 80*(1), 313–325. DOI: 10.1108/TR-10-2023-0753

Chowbe, V. S., & Bhosale, S. S. (2024). *Beyond Borders: Addressing the Legal Quagmire of Jurisdiction in Cyberspace*. International Journal For Multidisciplinary Research., DOI: 10.36948/ijfmr.2024.v06i06.30051

Chung, Y.-W., Khaki, B., Li, T., Chu, C., & Gadh, R. (2019). Ensemble machine learning-based algorithm for electric vehicle user behavior prediction. *Applied Energy, 254*, 113732. DOI: 10.1016/j.apenergy.2019.113732

Clavijo Mesa, M. V., Patino-Rodriguez, C. E., & Guevara Carazas, F. J. (2024). Cybersecurity at Sea: A Literature Review of Cyber-Attack Impacts and Defenses in Maritime Supply Chains. *Information (Basel), 15*(11), 710. Advance online publication. DOI: 10.3390/info15110710

Conti, M., Dehghantanha, A., Franke, K., & Watson, S. (2018). Internet of Things Security and Forensics: Challenges and Opportunities. *Future Generation Computer Systems, 78*, 544–546. DOI: 10.1016/j.future.2017.07.060

Crawford, K. (2021). *The Atlas of AI: Power, Politics, and the Planetary Costs of Artificial Intelligence*. Yale University Press.

Cveticanin, L., Luzanin, O., & Ninkov, I. (2023). PRIVACY AND PERSONAL DATA PROTECTION IN SELF-DRIVING CAR: SUGGESTION FOR LEGAL REGULATION IN SERBIA. *Balkan Social Science Review, 22*(22), 171–189. DOI: 10.46763/BSSR232222171c

CYFIRMA. (2023). *The changing cyber threat landscape Southeast Asia*. Retrieved August 5, 2025, from https://www.cyfirma.com/research/the-changing-cyber-threat-landscape-southeast-asia/

CYFIRMA. (2024). *The changing cyber threat landscape Southeast Asia*. Retrieved August 5, 2025, from https://www.cyfirma.com/research/the-changing-cyber-threat-landscape-southeast-asia-2/

Dai, C. T. (n.d.).*La cybersécurité au Viêt Nam: formulation et mise en œuvre d'une nouvelle stratégie*. DOI: 10.3917/her.157.0126

Dai, C. T. (2015). Cybersecurity in Vietnam: Formulation and Implementation of a New Strategy. *Herodote, 157*(2), 126–140.

Dai, W., Lipps, C., & Schotten, H. (2025). Integrating Reconfigurable Intelligent Surfaces into Next-Generation Mobile Networks: Comparative Simulations Based on Simu5G. *European Conference on Information Warfare and Security, ECCWS*, 94–104. DOI: 10.34190/eccws.24.1.3582

Dakshinamurthi, V., Ali, S. I., Karthikeyan, T., & Kulkarni, N. S. (2023). Causal convolution employing Almeida–Pineda recurrent backpropagation for mobile network design. *ICTACT Journal on Communication Technology, 14*(4), 3091–3096. DOI: 10.21917/ijct.2023.0460

Dar, H., & Dar, M. A. (2024). *Redefining Success of the Tourism Sector Through Technological Advancements.Advances in Hospitality, Tourism and the Services Industry (AHTSI)*. Book Series., DOI: 10.4018/979-8-3693-5678-4.ch008

Das, S. (2024). *Application of AI Technology for the Development of Destination Tourism towards an Intelligent Information System*. Eonomic Affairs., DOI: 10.46852/0424-2513.3.2024.31

Dede, G., Petsa, A. M., Kavalaris, S., Serrelis, E., Evangelatos, S., & Oikonomidis, I. (2024). *Cybersecurity as a contributor to United Nations SDGs towards enhancing the ESG reporting*., DOI: 10.1109/EEITE61750.2024.10654435

Degtyarevaa, K., Tynchenko, V., Tynchenko, V., Tynchenko, V., Panfilova, T., & Kukartseva, S. (2024). Automated System for Accounting of Customers and Orders. *2024 23rd International Symposium INFOTEH-JAHORINA (INFOTEH)*, 1–4. DOI: 10.1109/INFOTEH60418.2024.10496048

Dehghantanha, A., & Choo, K.-K. R. (2020). *Contemporary digital forensic investigations of cloud and mobile applications*. Elsevier.

Deldjoo, Y., Noia, T. D., & Merra, F. A. (2021). A Survey on Adversarial Recommender Systems: From Attack/Defense Strategies to Generative Adversarial Networks. *ACM Comput. Surv., 54*(2), 35:1-35:38. DOI: 10.1145/3439729

Demirel, E., Zeren, S. K., & Hakan, K. (2021). Smart contracts in tourism industry: A model with blockchain integration for post pandemic economy. *Current Issues in Tourism*, •••, 1–15. DOI: 10.1080/13683500.2021.1960280

Deng, L., Wan, L., & Guo, J. (2022). Research on security anomaly detection for Big Data platforms based on quantum optimization clustering. *Mathematical Problems in Engineering, 2022*, 1–10. DOI: 10.1155/2022/4805035

Desai, V., & R, K. (2024). Unveiling the Depths of Phishing: Understanding Tactics, Impacts, and Countermeasures. *International Journal of Innovative Research in Science, Engineering and Technology*, *13*(5), 8596–8600. Advance online publication. DOI: 10.15680/IJIRSET.2024.1305331

Díaz-Parra, A., Rodríguez-Lara, B. M., Salgado Ramírez, J. C., Trejo-Macotela, F. R., & Aguilar-Ortiz, J. (2023). *Smart Tourism*. IGI Global., DOI: 10.4018/979-8-3693-0373-3.ch005

DiMaggio, P. J., & Powell, W. W. (1983). The iron cage revisited: Institutional isomorphism and collective rationality in organizational fields. *American Sociological Review*, *48*(2), 147–160. DOI: 10.2307/2095101

Djenna, A., Barka, E., Benchikh, A., & Khadir, K. (2023). Unmasking cybercrime with artificial-intelligence-driven cybersecurity analytics. *Sensors (Basel)*, *23*(14), 6302. DOI: 10.3390/s23146302 PMID: 37514596

Doğan, S., & Niyet, İ. Z. (2024).*Artificial Intelligence (AI) in Tourism*. DOI: 10.1108/978-1-83753-970-320241001

Domjan, P., Serkin, G., Thomas, B., & Toshack, J. (2021). *Chain Reaction: How Blockchain Will Transform the Developing World*. Springer Nature. DOI: 10.1007/978-3-030-51784-7

dos Santos, R. M., Boente, A. N. P., Ferreira, V. M. da S., Boente, R. M. P., da Luz, D. O., Duarte, L. M. E., Dos Santos, A. J. B., & Vasconcelos, G. C. K. (2025). Artificial intelligence and cybersecurity: A study of Artificial intelligence in cybernetic defense. *ARACÊ*, *7*(5), 23155–23178. DOI: 10.56238/arev7n5-133

Dredge, D., & Gyimóthy, S. (2015). The collaborative economy and tourism: Critical perspectives, questionable claims and silenced voices. *Tourism Recreation Research*, *40*(3), 286–302. DOI: 10.1080/02508281.2015.1086076

Duggi, N., Bhadri, S., & Varala, C. R. (2025). *Gaps in the Grid: Access and the Digital Inequality Crisis*. 152–162. https://doi.org/DOI: 10.9734/bpi/mono/978-93-48859-10-5/CH13

Du, J., Li, J., Cheng, Q., Zhu, X., Yin, J., & Zhang, W. (2025). A Multi-objective Dynamic Gate Assignment Method Integrating Economy and Robustness. *Jiaotong Yunshu Xitong Gongcheng Yu Xinxi. Journal of Transportation Systems Engineering and Information Technology*, *25*(4), 326–336. DOI: 10.16097/j.cnki.1009-6744.2025.04.030

Duvvur, V. (2024). Modernizing Government IT Systems: A Case Study on Enhancing Operational Efficiency and Data Integrity. *International Journal of Computational and Experimental Science and Engineering, 11*(1), 1165–1175. DOI: 10.22399/ijcesen.1193

Dykstra, J., Gordon, L. A., Loeb, M. P., & Zhou, L. (2022). The economics of sharing unclassified cyber threat intelligence by government agencies and departments. *Journal of Information Security, 13*(03), 85–100. DOI: 10.4236/jis.2022.133006

El-Hoshoudy, A. (2024). Application of artificial intelligence and federated learning in petroleum processing. In *Artificial Intelligence Using Federated Learning* (pp. 134–155). Fundamentals, Challenges, and Applications., DOI: 10.1201/9781003482000-8

El-Maksoud, R. A. (2024). *Exploring the Role of Cybersecurity in Enhancing Digital Trust of Egyptian Travel Agencies. Journal of Association of Arab Universities for Tourism and Hospitality (JAAUTH).* Print., DOI: 10.21608/jaauth.2024.269299.1553

ENISA. (2021). *Cybersecurity for smart tourism.* European Union Agency for Cybersecurity.

ENISA. (2023). *Threat Landscape Report for the Tourism Sector.* European Union Agency for Cybersecurity. https://www.enisa.europa.eu

Ercan, F. (2020). An examination on the use of immersive reality technologies in the travel and tourism industry. *Business & Management Studies: An International Journal, 8*(2), 2348–2383. DOI: 10.15295/bmij.v8i2.1510

Ercan, F. (2023a). Smart tourism destination: A bibliometric review. *European Journal of Tourism Research, 34*, 3409. DOI: 10.54055/ejtr.v34i.2788

Erdem, A., & Şeker, F. (2022). *Tourist Experience and Digital Transformation.*, DOI: 10.4018/978-1-7998-8528-3.ch006

Ertaş, M., Sel, Z. G., Kırlar-Can, B., & Tütüncü, Ö. (2021). Effects of crisis on crisis management practices: A case from Turkish tourism enterprises. *Journal of Sustainable Tourism, 29*(9), 1490–1507. DOI: 10.1080/09669582.2021.1879818

Eshagh, M. (2023). Optimal Configuration for Monitoring Stations in a Wireless Localisation Network Based on Received Signal Strength Differences. *Sensors (Basel), 23*(3), 1150. Advance online publication. DOI: 10.3390/s23031150 PMID: 36772189

Eshbaev, G. (2024). GDPR vs. Weakly Protected Parties in Other Countries. *Uzbek Journal of Law and Digital Policy., 2*(6), 55–65. DOI: 10.59022/ujldp.254

Espiner, S., Orchiston, C., & Higham, J. (2017). Resilience and sustainability: A complementary relationship? Towards a practical conceptual model for the sustainability–resilience nexus in tourism. *Journal of Sustainable Tourism, 25*(10), 1385–1400. DOI: 10.1080/09669582.2017.1281929

Eswaran, U., Eswaran, V., & Eswaran, V. (2024). *AI Technologies for Personalised and Sustainable Tourism.Advances in Hospitality, Tourism and the Services Industry (AHTSI).* Book Series., DOI: 10.4018/979-8-3693-5678-4.ch001

European Commission. (2022). *General Data Protection Regulation (GDPR) compliance report 2022.* Retrieved from https://ec.europa.eu/info/law/law-topic/data-protection_en

Fahad, M., Zhang, T., Khan, S. U., Albanyan, A., Siddiqui, F., Iqbal, Y., Zhao, X., & Geng, Y. (2024). Optimizing dual energy X-ray image enhancement using a novel hybrid fusion method. *Journal of X-Ray Science and Technology, 32*(6), 1553–1570. DOI: 10.3233/XST-240227 PMID: 39729441

Fakiha, B. (2023). Enhancing cyber forensics with AI and machine learning: A study on automated threat analysis and classification. *International Journal of Safety and Security Engineering, 13*(4), 701–707. DOI: 10.18280/ijsse.130412

Familoni, B. T. (2024).*Cybersecurity challenges in the age of ai: theoretical approaches and practical solutions.* DOI: 10.51594/csitrj.v5i3.930

Farooqui, Y., Ali, S. I., Shekokar, K., Patidar, P. K., Bhushanwar, K., & Nandi, P. K. (2025). A secure framework for decentralized digital lockers using blockchain technology. *Journal of Computational Science, 21*(9), 2105–2112. DOI: 10.3844/jcssp.2025.2105.2112

Fauzel, S., Tandrayen-Ragoobur, V., & Matadeen, S. J. (2024). A LITERATURE SURVEY OF TECHNOLOGICAL DISRUPTIONS IN THE SERVICE SECTOR. *Review of Management Literature, 3*, 185–202. DOI: 10.1108/S2754-586520240000003010

Favaretto, M., De Clercq, E., & Elger, B. S. (2019). Big Data and discrimination: Perils, promises and solutions. A systematic review. *Journal of Big Data, 6*(1), 12. DOI: 10.1186/s40537-019-0177-4

Femenia-Serra, F., Ioannou, A., & Tussyadiah, I. P. (2021). Is smart scary? A mixed-methods study on privacy in smart tourism. *Current Issues in Tourism,* •••, 1–27. DOI: 10.1080/13683500.2021.1987399

Fennell, D. A. (2021). Technology and the sustainable tourist in the new age of disruption. *Journal of Sustainable Tourism, 29*(5), 767–773. DOI: 10.1080/09669582.2020.1769639

Fidel-Anyana, I., Onus, E. G., Mikel-Olisa, U., & Ayanbode, N. (2025). AI-Driven Cybersecurity Frameworks for SME Development: Mitigating Risks in a Digital Economy. *International Journal of Multidisciplinary Research and Growth Evaluation*, *6*(1), 982–988. DOI: 10.54660/.IJMRGE.2025.6.1.982-988

Florido-Benítez, L. (2024). The cybersecurity applied by online travel agencies and hotels to protect users' private data in smart cities. *Smart Cities*, *7*(1), 19. https://www.mdpi.com/2624-6511/7/1/19. DOI: 10.3390/smartcities7010019

Florido-Benítez, L. (2025). The role of cybersecurity as a preventive measure in digital tourism and travel: A systematic literature review. *Discover Computing*, *28*(1), 28. Advance online publication. DOI: 10.1007/s10791-025-09523-3

Folorunso, A., Mohammed, V., Wada, I., & Samuel, B. J. (2024). The impact of ISO security standards on enhancing cybersecurity posture in organizations. *World Journal Of Advanced Research and Reviews*, *24*(1), 2582–2595. DOI: 10.30574/wjarr.2024.24.1.3169

Fu, H., Guan, J., Wang, R., Kong, L., & Dai, Q. (2024). How does digitalization affect the urban-rural disparity at different disparity levels: A Bayesian Quantile Regression approach. *Technology in Society*, *78*, 102633. DOI: 10.1016/j.techsoc.2024.102633

Gaie, C., Karpiuk, M. A., & Strizzolo, N. (2024). Cybersecurity of Public Sector Institutions. *Prawo i Wiez*, *53*(6), 347–362. DOI: 10.36128/PRIW.VI53.1129

Gajdošík, T., & Marciš, M. (2019). Artificial Intelligence Tools for Smart Tourism Development. In Silhavy, R. (Ed.), *Artificial Intelligence Methods in Intelligent Algorithms* (pp. 392–402). Springer International Publishing., DOI: 10.1007/978-3-030-19810-7_39

Gajjar, T., Parikh, S., & Shekokar, K. (2025). Integrating Blockchain Technology with AI to Enhance Security Measure. *Indian Scientific Journal Of Research In Engineering And Management*, *09*(01), 1–9. DOI: 10.55041/IJSREM40423

Garfinkel, S. (2010). Digital forensics research: The next 10 years. *Digital Investigation*, *7*, S64–S73. DOI: 10.1016/j.diin.2010.05.009

Gefen, D., Karahanna, E., & Straub, D. W. (2003). Trust and TAM in Online Shopping: An Integrated Model. *Management Information Systems Quarterly*, *27*(1), 51–90. DOI: 10.2307/30036519

George, S. (2024). *Artificial Intelligence-Powered Cybersecurity*. Advances in Information Security, Privacy, and Ethics Book Series., DOI: 10.4018/979-8-3373-1102-9.ch008

Ghaderi, Z., Béal, L., Hall, C. M., Zaman, M., Rather, R. A., & Som, A. P. M. (2024). Cybersecurity and smart tourist destinations resilience. *Tourism Recreation Research*, •••, 1–17. DOI: 10.1080/02508281.2024.2434791

Gössling, S. (2021). Technology, ICT and tourism: From big data to the big picture. *Journal of Sustainable Tourism*, *29*(5), 849–858. DOI: 10.1080/09669582.2020.1865387

Gössling, S., & Gössling, S. (2021). Tourism, technology and ICT: A critical review of affordances and concessions. *Journal of Sustainable Tourism*, *29*(5), 733–750. DOI: 10.1080/09669582.2021.1873353

Greaney, C. (2012). *Location Aware Apps for Tourism*. Lulu.com.

Gretzel, U., Koo, C., Sigala, M., & Xiang, Z. (2022). Smart tourism: Foundations and developments. *Annals of Tourism Research*, *92*, 103327. DOI: 10.1016/j.annals.2021.103327

Gretzel, U., Lee, H., Lee, E., Chung, N., & Koo, C. (2023a). Enhanced smart tourism and its role in reshaping the tourism industry. *Journal of Smart Tourism*, *3*(4), 23–31. DOI: 10.52255/smarttourism.2023.3.4.4

Gretzel, U., Sigala, M., Xiang, Z., & Koo, C. (2015). Smart tourism: Foundations and developments. *Electronic Markets*, *25*(3), 179–188. DOI: 10.1007/s12525-015-0196-8

Gretzel, U., Werthner, H., Koo, C., & Lamsfus, C. (2016). Conceptual foundations for understanding smart tourism ecosystems. *Computers in Human Behavior*, *57*, 558–563.

Guo, Q., Mu, L., & Lou, S. (2024). Revolutionizing travel experiences: An in-depth analysis of intelligent booking systems and behavioral patterns. *Intelligent Decision Technologies*, *18*(2), 1477–1494. DOI: 10.3233/IDT-230625

Halim, N. A., Norizan, N. S., & Thirumoorthi, T. (2023).*A digital safe-zone tourism network*. DOI: 10.4324/9781003291763-41

Hall, C. M. (2019). Constructing sustainable tourism development: The 2030 agenda and the managerial ecology of sustainable tourism. *Journal of Sustainable Tourism*, *27*(7), 1044–1060. DOI: 10.1080/09669582.2018.1560456

Harit, P., Singh, A., Agrawal, K., Verma, D. N., Bathla, G., & Raina, A. (2024). Exploring the Growing Threat of Cyber Risks and Vulnerabilities in the Hospitality Industry. *Advances in Hospitality, Tourism and the Services Industry (AHTSI) Book Series*, 299–316. DOI: 10.4018/979-8-3693-6562-5.ch017

Harris, A. G. (2014). *The Weaknesses of Passwords and Alternative Authentication Technologies.*

Hasan, M. R., Sarkar, N. I., Alani, N. H. S., & Lutui, R. (2025). Cyber Edge: Current State of Cybersecurity in Aotearoa-New Zealand, Opportunities, and Challenges. *Electronics (Basel), 14*(14), 2915. Advance online publication. DOI: 10.3390/electronics14142915

He, K., Kim, D. D., & Asghar, M. R. (2023). Adversarial Machine Learning for Network Intrusion Detection Systems: A Comprehensive Survey. *IEEE Communications Surveys and Tutorials, 25*(1), 538–566. DOI: 10.1109/COMST.2022.3233793

Hemmati, A., Raoufi, P., & Rahmani, A. M. (2024). Edge artificial intelligence for big data: A systematic review. *Neural Computing & Applications, 36*(19), 11461–11494. DOI: 10.1007/s00521-024-09723-w

Herke, C., Tóth, D., & Perkumienė, D. (2025). The Role of Artificial Intelligence in Cybercrime in the Tourism Sector. In *Tourism and Heritage: Shaping Sustainable and Innovative Futures* (pp. 415–433). Springer Nature Switzerland. DOI: 10.1007/978-3-031-81485-3_17

Herley, C. (2009, September). So long, and no thanks for the externalities: the rational rejection of security advice by users. In *Proceedings of the 2009 workshop on New security paradigms workshop* (pp. 133-144). DOI: 10.1145/1719030.1719050

Hesselman, C., Grosso, P., Holz, R., Kuipers, F., Xue, J. H., Jonker, M., de Ruiter, J., Sperotto, A., van Rijswijk-Deij, R., Moura, G. C. M., Pras, A., & de Laat, C. (2020). A Responsible Internet to Increase Trust in the Digital World. *Journal of Network and Systems Management, 28*(4), 882–922. DOI: 10.1007/s10922-020-09564-7

Himanshu, V., & Vinita, H. (2023). *Security and Trust in Online Booking Systems: A Comparative Analysis Of Tour and Travel Websites. (2023).* International Journal For Multidisciplinary Research., DOI: 10.36948/ijfmr.2023.v05i05.7334

Holling, C. S. (1973). Resilience and stability of ecological systems. *Annual Review of Ecology and Systematics, 4*(1), 1–23. DOI: 10.1146/annurev.es.04.110173.000245

Horvath, G. (2023). Securing the Digital Sky: A scenario-driven study on the enhancement of cybersecurity in location-independent aerodrome control systems. *NTAD 2023 - New Trends in Aviation Development 2023: 18th International Scientific Conference - Proceedings*, 112–116. DOI: 10.1109/NTAD61230.2023.10380135

Hospitality and Tourism Information Technology. (2021). USF M3 Publishing, LLC. DOI: 10.5038/9781732127593

Hsu, C. L., & Lin, J. C. C. (2016). Exploring factors affecting the adoption of Internet of Things services. *Computers in Human Behavior, 62*, 516–527. DOI: 10.1016/j.chb.2016.04.023

Hu, M., & Zhang, H. (2021). Blockchain technology and its application in tourism: A review of current issues and future research directions. *Current Issues in Tourism, 24*(22), 3221–3239. DOI: 10.1080/13683500.2020.1798895

IBM X-Force. (2023). *Threat Intelligence Index 2023.* Retrieved from https://www.ibm.com/reports/threat-intelligence

IBM. (n.d.). *What is Digital Forensics and Incident Response (DFIR)?* Retrieved August 5, 2025, from https://www.ibm.com/think/topics/dfir

Ige, A. B., Kupa, E., & Ilori, O. (2024). Aligning sustainable development goals with cybersecurity strategies: Ensuring a secure and sustainable future. *GSC Advanced Research and Reviews, 19*(3), 344–360. DOI: 10.30574/gscarr.2024.19.3.0236

Information Commissioner's Office. (2020, October 16). *Monetary penalty notice: British Airways Plc.* ico.org.uk

Insurance, T. (n.d.). *How digital forensics detectives investigate a data breach.* Travelers. Retrieved August 5, 2025, from https://www.travelers.com/resources/business-topics/cyber-security/digital-forensics-detectives-investigate-data-breach

IPCC. (2023). [*Synthesis report.* Intergovernmental Panel on Climate Change.]. *Climatic Change*, •••, 2023.

Iqbal, S., & Abed Alharbi, S. (2020). Advancing automation in digital forensic investigations using machine learning forensics. In *Digital Forensic Science.* IntechOpen., DOI: 10.5772/intechopen.90233

Iyer, V. R., & Babu, K. (2025). Resilience at the core: Enhancing cyber-resilience and cybersecurity practices in healthcare sector. *Journal of Contingencies and Crisis Management, 33*(3), e70061. Advance online publication. DOI: 10.1111/1468-5973.70061

Jarrett, A., & Choo, K.-K. R. (2021). The impact of automation and artificial intelligence on digital forensics. *WIREs Forensic Science, 3*(6), e1418. Advance online publication. DOI: 10.1002/wfs2.1418

Jeetesh, K., Manpreet, A., & Gül, E. B. (2024). *Exploring the Use of Metaverse in Business and Education.* IGI Global.

Jimmy, F. (2021). Emerging threats: The latest cybersecurity risks and the role of artificial intelligence in enhancing cybersecurity defenses. *Valley International Journal Digital Library, 1*(2), 564–574. DOI: 10.18535/ijsrm/v9i2.ec01

Juang, J.-C., Chen, Y.-T., & Chua, C.-K. (2023). Inter-Satellite and Inter-Receiver Aiding in the Verification of OSNMA. *Proceedings of the 36th International Technical Meeting of the Satellite Division of the Institute of Navigation, ION GNSS+ 2023*, 483–494. DOI: 10.33012/2023.19214

Jung, T., tom Dieck, M. C., & Moorhouse, N. (2022). Digital transformation in tourism: Technological trends and implications for smart destinations. *Tourism Management, 93*, 104296. DOI: 10.1016/j.tourman.2022.104296

Kamyab, F., & Bahrami, S. (2016). Efficient operation of energy hubs in time-of-use and dynamic pricing electricity markets. *Energy, 106*, 343–355. DOI: 10.1016/j.energy.2016.03.074

Kandpal, S., Bhatt, S., Mohan, L., Patwal, A., & Kumar, P. (2023). Cyber security implementation issues in small to medium-sized enterprises (SMEs) and their potential solutions: A comprehensive analysis. In *Proceedings of the 14th International Conference on Computing Communication and Networking Technologies (ICCCNT)* (pp. 1–5). IEEE. https://doi.org/DOI: 10.1109/ICCCNT56998.2023.10307363

Kang, W. (2024). *A Systematic Review: Bridging the Digital Divide in SME Digitalization. 2024*(2). https://doi.org/DOI: 10.62594/atom0002

Karadayi-Usta, S. (2024). Cybersecurity risks analysis in the hospitality industry. *Systems, 12*(10), 397. DOI: 10.3390/systems12100397

Karimipour, H., Dehghantanha, A., Parizi, R. M., Choo, K.-K. R., & Leung, H. (2019). A deep and scalable unsupervised machine learning system for cyber-attack detection in large-scale smart grids. *IEEE Access : Practical Innovations, Open Solutions, 7*, 80778–80788. DOI: 10.1109/ACCESS.2019.2920326

Kashyap, S. (2024). The Influence of Artificial Intelligence on Cybersecurity. *International Journal of Innovative Research in Computer and Communication Engineering*. DOI: 10.15680/IJIRCCE.2024.1203503

Kaspersky, I. C. S. (2021). Threat landscape for industrial automation systems. *Statistics for H, 1*, 1480–93071.

Katiyar, D. N., Tripathi, M. S., Kumar, M. P., Verma, M. S., Sahu, D. A. K., & Saxena, D. S. (2024). *AI and Cyber-Security: Enhancing threat detection and response with machine learning*. Educational Administration Theory and Practices., DOI: 10.53555/kuey.v30i4.2377

Khalid, Md. (2024). *S*. Sustainable Tourism's Tomorrow., DOI: 10.4018/979-8-3693-3390-7.ch008

Khan, A. A., Uddin, M., Shaikh, A. A., Laghari, A. A., & Rajput, A. E. (2021). MF-ledger: Blockchain hyperledger sawtooth-enabled novel and secure multimedia chain of custody forensic investigation architecture. *IEEE Access : Practical Innovations, Open Solutions*, *9*, 103637–103650. DOI: 10.1109/ACCESS.2021.3099037

Khandelwal, J. (2024). Enhancing Journeys in the Digital Age of Tourism Through the Implementation of Smart Tourism Framework. *Advances in Hospitality, Tourism and the Services Industry (AHTSI) Book Series*, 149–164. https://doi.org/DOI: 10.4018/979-8-3693-3715-8.ch008

Khan, S. K., Shiwakoti, N., Diro, A., Molla, A., Gondal, I., & Warren, M. (2024). Space cybersecurity challenges, mitigation techniques, anticipated readiness, and future directions. *International Journal of Critical Infrastructure Protection*, *47*, 100724. Advance online publication. DOI: 10.1016/j.ijcip.2024.100724

Khan, S. Z., Mohsin, M., & Iqbal, W. (2021). On GPS spoofing of aerial platforms: A review of threats, challenges, methodologies, and future research directions. *PeerJ. Computer Science*, *7*, e507. DOI: 10.7717/peerj-cs.507 PMID: 34013033

Khatwani, S., & Chandak, M. B. (2016). Building Personalized and Non Personalized recommendation systems. *2016 International Conference on Automatic Control and Dynamic Optimization Techniques (ICACDOT)*, 623–628. DOI: 10.1109/ICACDOT.2016.7877661

Kibriya, H., Khan, W. Z., Siddiqa, A., & Khan, M. K. (2024). Privacy issues in Large Language Models: A survey. *Computers & Electrical Engineering*, *120*, 109698. DOI: 10.1016/j.compeleceng.2024.109698

Kim, M., & Shon, T. (2023). Digital forensics for E-IoT devices in smart cities. *Electronics (Basel)*, *12*(15), 3233. DOI: 10.3390/electronics12153233

Klopper, C., & Eloff, J. (2023). Fingerprinting network sessions for the discovery of cyber threats. *International Conference on Cyber Warfare and Security*, 18(1), 171–180. DOI: 10.34190/iccws.18.1.1027

Knani, M., Echchakoui, S., & Ladhari, R. (2022). Artificial intelligence in tourism and hospitality: Bibliometric analysis and research agenda. *International Journal of Hospitality Management*, *107*, 103317. DOI: 10.1016/j.ijhm.2022.103317

Kong, L. (2010). Data Protection and Transborder Data Flow in the European and Global Context. *European Journal of International Law*, *21*(2), 441–456. DOI: 10.1093/ejil/chq025

Kontogianni, A., & Alepis, E. (2022). AI, Blockchain & Cyber tourism joining the Smart Tourism realm. *International Conference on Information, Intelligence, Systems and Applications*, 1–6. https://doi.org/DOI: 10.1109/IISA56318.2022.9904393

Kontogianni, A., & Alepis, E. (2023). Tourism embraces blockchain towards the smart tourism era. *Intelligent Decision Technologies*, *17*(3), 811–838. DOI: 10.3233/IDT-230073

Koo, C., Shin, S., & Gretzel, U. (2021). Big data and cybersecurity in smart tourism. *Information Systems Frontiers*, *23*(3), 705–719. DOI: 10.1007/s10796-020-10028-3

Koo, I., Zaman, U., Ha, H., & Nawaz, S. (2025). Assessing the interplay of trust dynamics, personalization, ethical AI practices, and tourist behavior in the adoption of AI-driven smart tourism technologies. *Journal of Open Innovation*, *11*(1), 100455. DOI: 10.1016/j.joitmc.2024.100455

Körner, C. (2021). *Alpine plant life: Functional plant ecology of high mountain ecosystems* (3rd ed.). Springer., DOI: 10.1007/978-3-030-59538-4

Kosnikov, S. N., Zolkin, A. L., Artemyev, N. V., & Lepshokova, A. N. (2024). Cybersecurity as a factor of sustainable development of the digital economy. *Èkonomika i Upravlenie: Problemy. Rešeniâ*, *12/15*(153), 221–229. DOI: 10.36871/ek.up.p.r.2024.12.15.026

Kovačić, M., Čičin-Šain, M., & Milojica, V. (2022). Cyber security and tourism: Bibliometric analysis. *Journal of Process Management New Technologies*, *10*(3–4), 75–92. DOI: 10.5937/jouproman2203075K

Kovacic, M., Cicin-Sain, M., & Milojica, V. (2022). Cyber security and tourism: Bibliometric analysis. *Journal of Process Management. Nuclear Technology*, *10*(3–4), 75–92. DOI: 10.5937/jpmnt10-41205

Krishnappa, T.London Metropolitan University. (2023). A review on artificial intelligence techniques in preventing cyber threats. *International Journal of Engineering Applied Sciences and Technology*, *8*(1), 185–189. DOI: 10.33564/IJEAST.2023.v08i01.029

Križaj, D., Bratec, M., Kopić, P., & Rogelja, T. (2021). A technology-based innovation adoption and implementation analysis of European smart tourism projects: Towards a smart actionable classification model (SACM). *Sustainability (Basel)*, *13*(18), 10279. DOI: 10.3390/su131810279

Kshetri, N. (2014). The emerging role of Big Data in key development issues: Opportunities, challenges, and concerns. *Big Data & Society*, *1*(2), 2053951714564227. DOI: 10.1177/2053951714564227

Kshetri, N. (2023). Cybersecurity and privacy in the digital economy: Challenges and policy responses. *Telecommunications Policy*, *47*(1), 102403.

Ksouri, C., Jemili, I., Mosbah, M., & Belghith, A. (2020). A Unified Smart Mobility System Integrating Terrestrial, Aerial and Marine Intelligent Vehicles. *Lecture Notes in Computer Science (Including Subseries Lecture Notes in Artificial Intelligence and Lecture Notes in Bioinformatics), 12574 LNCS*, 203–214. DOI: 10.1007/978-3-030-66030-7_18

Kumar, N., & Pham, H. T. (2024). Smart Tourism. *Advances in Hospitality, Tourism and the Services Industry (AHTSI) Book Series*, 351–372. https://doi.org/DOI: 10.4018/979-8-3693-3715-8.ch019

Kumari, A. (2024). The role of artificial intelligence and machine learning in enhancing cybersecurity in the digital economy.*International Journal of Research in Management*. DOI: 10.33545/26648792.2024.v6.i1c.140

Kumar, P., Singh, R., & Sharma, A. (2022). Cybersecurity challenges in smart agriculture and tourism systems. *Journal of Information Security*, *13*(2), 45–60. DOI: 10.4236/jis.2022.132004

Kumar, S., Gupta, U., Singh, A. K., & Singh, A. K. (2023). Artificial Intelligence. Journal of Computers. *Mechanical and Management*, *2*(3), 31–42. DOI: 10.57159/gadl.jcmm.2.3.23064

Kuzman, B., Petković, B., & Milovančević, M. (2024). *Information and communication technology in tourism*. https://doi.org/DOI: 10.52370/TISC2475BK

Lagdami, K., Dalaklis, D., & Christodoulou, A. (2024). New Technologies in Small and Medium-sized Ports: Its Impacts on the Future of Work. *Journal for Maritime Research*, *21*(3), 150–156. https://www.scopus.com/inward/record.uri?eid=2-s2.0-85215111117&partnerID=40&md5=f2a64e158869099497417a987a18487b

Lara-Morales, O., & Clarke, A. (2022). Sustainable tourism value chain analysis as a tool to evaluate tourism's contribution to the sustainable development goals and local Indigenous communities. *Journal of Ecotourism*, •••, 1–19. DOI: 10.1080/14724049.2022.2147189

Larsson, S., Jensen-Urstad, A., & Heintz, F. (2021). Notified but Unaware: Third-Party Tracking Online. *Critical Analysis of Law: An International & Interdisciplinary Law Review*, *8*(1), 101–120. DOI: 10.33137/cal.v8i1.36282

Lawal, Q. (2025). Cybersecurity governance: Strengthening policy frameworks to address global cybercrime and data privacy challenges. *International Journal of Science and Research Archive*, *14*(1), 1146–1163. DOI: 10.30574/ijsra.2025.14.1.0225

Law, R., Buhalis, D., & Cobanoglu, C. (2018). Progress on information and communication technologies in hospitality and tourism. *International Journal of Contemporary Hospitality Management, 26*(5), 727–750. DOI: 10.1108/IJCHM-08-2013-0367

Lee, P., Hunter, W. C., & Chung, N. (2020). Smart tourism city: Developments and transformations. *Sustainability (Basel), 12*(10), 3958. DOI: 10.3390/su12103958

Liao, H.-T., Lo, T.-M., & Pan, C.-L. (2023). Knowledge Mapping Analysis of Intelligent Ports: Research Facing Global Value Chain Challenges. *Systems, 11*(2), 88. Advance online publication. DOI: 10.3390/systems11020088

Liapi, F., Chater, A. M., Randhawa, G., Stephenson, A., & Pappas, Y. (2025). Factors that influence inter-organisational integration: A qualitative exploration of service providers' perspectives from an integrated care initiative. *BMC Health Services Research, 25*(1), 947. Advance online publication. DOI: 10.1186/s12913-025-13051-7 PMID: 40640843

Liburd, J. J., Duedahl, E., & Heape, C. (2020). Co-designing tourism for sustainable development. *Journal of Sustainable Tourism*, •••, 1–20. DOI: 10.1080/09669582.2020.1839473

Li, K., Lee, J.-Y., & Gharehgozli, A. (2024). Blockchain implementation in the maritime industry: A literature review and synthesis analysis of benefits and challenges. *Maritime Economics & Logistics, 26*(4), 630–657. DOI: 10.1057/s41278-023-00280-y

Litavniece, L., Lonska, J., Zvaigzne, A., Wieda, N., & Adamoniene, R. (2023). Smart tourism in the Baltic states: Current developments and trends. *Worldwide Hospitality and Tourism Themes, 15*(5), 486–496. DOI: 10.1108/WHATT-06-2023-0073

Liu, Y., Li, Y., Guo, F., Liu, Z., & Song, X. (2024). Research on Zero-Trust Dynamic Access Control Model Based on User Behavior in Internet of Things Environment. *ACM International Conference Proceeding Series*, 402–407. DOI: 10.1145/3703187.3703255

Li, Y., Hu, C., Huang, C., & Duan, L. (2017). The concept of smart tourism in the context of tourism information services. *Tourism Management, 58*, 293–300. DOI: 10.1016/j.tourman.2016.03.014

Lomas, E. (2020). Information Governance and Cybersecurity: Framework for Securing and Managing Information Effectively and Ethically. In *Cybersecurity for Information Professionals*. Auerbach Publications. DOI: 10.1201/9781003042235-6

Magazine, I. (n.d.). *Hackers admit destroying InterContinental Hotels Group's data 'for fun'*. Retrieved August 5, 2025, from https://www.infosecurity-magazine.com/news/hackers-destroying-ihgs-data-for/

Mairesse, F. (2022). *Cybersecurity in Travel and Tourism: A Risk-Based Approach* (pp. 1605–1628). Springer eBooks. DOI: 10.1007/978-3-030-48652-5_100

Maleh, Y., & Sahid, A. (2024). *A Case Study on Cyber-Governance for Resilient Organizations*. IGI Global Scientific Publishing., DOI: 10.4018/979-8-3693-3431-7.ch007

Malgieri, G. (2016). *Property and (Intellectual) Ownership of Consumers' Information: A New Taxonomy for Personal Data* (SSRN Scholarly Paper No. 2916058). Social Science Research Network. https://papers.ssrn.com/abstract=2916058 DOI: 10.37307/j.2196-9817.2016.04.05

Martínez, D. E., Magdalena, L., & Savitri, A. N. (2024). AI and Blockchain Integration: Enhancing Security and Transparency in Financial Transactions. *International Transactions on Artificial Intelligence*, *3*(1), 11–20. DOI: 10.33050/italic.v3i1.651

Masseno, M. D., & Santos, C. (2018). *Smart tourism destinations privacy risks on data protection. 1*(1).

Maythu, Y., Kwok, A. O., & Teh, P. L. (2024). Blockchain technology diffusion in tourism: Evidence from early enterprise adopters and innovators. *Heliyon*, *10*(2), e24675. DOI: 10.1016/j.heliyon.2024.e24675 PMID: 38304774

McStay, A. (2020). Emotional AI, soft biometrics and the surveillance of emotional life: An unusual consensus on privacy. *Big Data & Society*, *7*(1), 2053951720904386. DOI: 10.1177/2053951720904386

Meyer, J. W., & Rowan, B. (1977). Institutionalized organizations: Formal structure as myth and ceremony. *AJS; American Journal of Sociology*, *83*(2), 340–363. DOI: 10.1086/226550

Micah, E. E. M., Saidu, I. H., Ibitomi, T., & Sanusi, B. S. (2023). Digital forensics in the era of cybercrime: Emerging trends and challenges for forensic accountants in Nigeria. European Journal of Accounting. *Auditing and Finance Research*, *11*(9), 85–100. DOI: 10.37745/ejaafr.2013/vol11n985100

Minca, C., &Roelofsen, M. (2021). Becoming Airbnbeings: on datafication and the quantified Self in tourism. *Tourism Geographies, 23*(4), 743–764. https://doi.org/. 2019.1686767DOI: 10.1080/14616688

Mishra, S., Bhatt, V. D., & Singh, A. (2023). *Smart Infrastructure in Smart Cities Scope and Implications for Sustainable Tourism Development*. IGI Global., DOI: 10.4018/979-8-3693-0650-5.ch010

Mitchell, F. (2014). The use of Artificial Intelligence in digital forensics: An introduction. *Digital Evidence and Electronic Signature Law Review*, *7*(0). Advance online publication. DOI: 10.14296/deeslr.v7i0.1922

Mitrou, L. (2018). *Data Protection, Artificial Intelligence and Cognitive Services: Is the General Data Protection Regulation (GDPR) 'Artificial Intelligence-Proof'?* (SSRN Scholarly Paper No. 3386914). Social Science Research Network. DOI: 10.2139/ssrn.3386914

Mkhulisi, N., Dube, S., & Radebe, F. (2024). *Towards a Conceptual Framework for Cybersecurity Skill Requirements in Small and Medium-Sized Enterprises*. https://doi.org/DOI: 10.1109/IMITEC60221.2024.10851058

Mohamed, N. N., & Abuobied, B. H. H. (2024). Cybersecurity challenges across sustainable development goals: A comprehensive review. *Sustainable Engineering and Innovation*, *6*(1), 57–86. DOI: 10.37868/sei.v6i1.id207

Mo, L. (2023). *Blockchain and Sustainable Tourism: Unlocking the Opportunities for a Greener Future*. https://doi.org/DOI: 10.20944/preprints202306.1517.v1

Möller, D. P. (2023). Cybersecurity in digital transformation. In *Guide to cybersecurity in digital transformation: Trends, methods, technologies, applications and best practices* (pp. 1–70). Springer Nature Switzerland. DOI: 10.1007/978-3-031-26845-8_1

Moussaoui, M., Rachid, A., & Rajpoot, S. (2024). Digital water transformation: Technologies, opportunities, and challenges. In *Emerging Trends and Technologies in Water Management and Conservation* (pp. 203–239). DOI: 10.4018/979-8-3693-6920-3.ch007

Moyle, B. D., Moyle, C., Ruhanen, L., Weaver, D., & Hadinejad, A. (2021). Are we really progressing sustainable tourism research? A bibliometric analysis. *Journal of Sustainable Tourism*, *29*(1), 1–17. DOI: 10.1080/09669582.2020.1817048

Moyle, B. D., Weaver, D., Gössling, S., McLennan, C., & Hadinejad, A. (2021). Are water-centric themes in sustainable tourism research congruent with the UN Sustainable Development Goals? *Journal of Sustainable Tourism*, •••, 1–16. DOI: 10.1080/09669582.2021.1993233

Mrazovic, P., Larriba-Pey, J. L., & Matskin, M. (2017). Improving Mobility in Smart Cities with Intelligent Tourist Trip Planning. *2017 IEEE 41st Annual Computer Software and Applications Conference (COMPSAC), 1*, 897–907. DOI: 10.1109/COMPSAC.2017.144

Muharam, I. N., Tussyadiah, I. P., & Kimbu, A. N. (2023). A theoretical model of user acceptance of blockchain-based peer-to-peer accommodation. *Current Issues in Tourism*, •••, 1–18. DOI: 10.1080/13683500.2022.2164485

Mukherjee, A. (2024). The Complete Guide to Defense in Depth: Learn to identify, mitigate, and prevent cyber threats with a dynamic, layered defense approach. In *The Complete Guide to Defense in Depth: Learn to Identify, Mitigate, and Prevent Cyber Threats with a Dynamic, Layered Defense Approach*. https://www.scopus.com/inward/record.uri?eid=2-s2.0-105023800624&partnerID=40&md5=672db408ebbc449ef3810200fa085968

Najlaoui, A. G., & Ammari, N. B. (2024). *Technological Revolution and Transformation of the Tourism Sector*. IGI Global., DOI: 10.4018/979-8-3693-2619-0.ch010

Nam, K., Dutt, C. S., Chathoth, P. K., & Khan, M. S. (2021). Blockchain technology for smart city and smart tourism: Latest trends and challenges. *Asia Pacific Journal of Tourism Research, 26*(4), 454–468. DOI: 10.1080/10941665.2019.1585376

Narwal, R., Gupta, A., Gupta, A., & Kukreja, A. (2024). AI and Blockchain: Transforming Digital Transactions. *International Journal of Advanced Research in Science. Tongxin Jishu*, 542–545. Advance online publication. DOI: 10.48175/IJARSCT-17669

Navarro, S., & Buhalis, D. (2024). Cybersecurity resilience in smart tourism ecosystems: Managing risk and trust. *Journal of Smart Tourism Research, 2*(1), 15–33.

Nayak, H. (2016). Impact of cybercrime on tourism industry. *International Journal of Management and Social Sciences, 4*(4), 160–174.

NDTV. (2022.). *Vietnamese couple deletes British hotel chain data for fun: Report*. Retrieved August 5, 2025, from https://www.ndtv.com/world-news/vietnamese-couple-deletes-british-hotel-chains-data-for-fun-report-3355116

Nguyen, T. T. (2021). *Developing Smart Tourism in 4.0 Industrial Age: The Case of Vietnam*. DOI: 10.5220/0010592804890493

Nguyen, T. T., Quoc Viet hung, N., Nguyen, T. T., Huynh, T. T., Nguyen, T. T., Weidlich, M., & Yin, H. (2024). Manipulating Recommender Systems: A Survey of Poisoning Attacks and Countermeasures. *ACM Comput. Surv., 57*(1), 3:1-3:39. DOI: 10.1145/3677328

Obasi, C., Solomon, N. O., Adenekan, O. A., & Simpa, P. (2024). *Cybersecurity's Role in Environmental Protection and Sustainable Development: Bridging Technology and Sustainability Goals.* https://doi.org/DOI: 10.51594/csitrj.v5i5.1140

Obeng-Odoom, F. (2009). The Future of our Cities. *Cities (London, England), 26*(1), 49–53. DOI: 10.1016/j.cities.2008.11.001

Odumesi, J. O., & Sanusi, B. S. (2023). *Achieving Sustainable Development Goals from a Cybersecurity Perspective.* Advances in Multidisciplinary and Scientific Research Journal., DOI: 10.22624/AIMS/CSEAN-SMART2023P3

OECD. (2020). *Digitalisation and tourism: Policy implications for inclusive growth.* OECD Tourism Trends and Policies 2020. https://www.oecd.org/cfe/tourism/

OpenGov Asia. (2025). *Vietnam: Digital transformation to bolster economic ambitions.* Retrieved August 5, 2025, from https://opengovasia.com/vietnam-digital-transformation-to-bolster-economic-ambitions/

Oppokkhonov, N. (2023). The Future of Smart Tourism: Transforming Travel Experiences. *YashilIqtisodiyotvaTaraqqiyot, 1*(mxs). DOI: 10.55439/GED/vol1_iss-maxsusson/a663

Orbelyan, G. (2024). Socio-Economic Challenges for the Urban Ecosystem: Complex Model of Smart Tourism and Infrastructure. *Socioeconomic Challenges, 8*(4), 146–160. DOI: 10.61093/sec.8(4).146-160.2024

Ozkan, B. Y., & Spruit, M. (2020). Assessing and Improving Cybersecurity Maturity for SMEs: Standardization aspects. *arXiv: Cryptography and Security.* https://arxiv.org/pdf/2007.01751.pdf

Ozkan, B. Y., & Spruit, M. (2019). Cybersecurity Standardisation for SMEs: The Stakeholders'. *International Journal of Standardization Research, 17*(2), 41–72. DOI: 10.4018/IJSR.20190701.oa1

Pan, B., & Yang, Y. (2016). Monitoring and Forecasting Tourist Activities with Big Data. In *Management Science in Hospitality and Tourism.* Apple Academic Press.

Paraskevas, A. (2020). *Cybersecurity in Travel and Tourism: A Risk-Based Approach.* DOI: 10.1007/978-3-030-05324-6_100-1

Paraskevas, A. (2020). *Cybersecurity in travel and tourism: a risk-based approach.* Springer Nature., DOI: 10.1007/978-3-030-05324-6

Pattanaik, B., Kumari, S. S., Kumar, C. K., Pattnaik, M., Ali, S. I., & Kumarasamy, M. (2023). An innovation of algebraic mathematical-based statistical analysis model for complex number theory. In *Proceedings of the 2023 International Conference on Disruptive Technologies (ICDT)* (pp. 94–99). IEEE. https://doi.org/DOI: 10.1109/ICDT57929.2023.10151169

Pauli, H., Gottfried, M., & Grabherr, G. (2012). Effects of climate change on alpine biodiversity. *Global Change Biology*, *18*(2), 676–687. DOI: 10.1111/j.1365-2486.2011.02550.x

Paulsen, C. (2016). Cybersecuring Small Businesses. *Computer*, *49*(8), 92–97. DOI: 10.1109/MC.2016.223

Pelchen, C., Jaeger, D., Cheng, F., & Meinel, C. (2019). *The (Persistent) Threat of Weak Passwords: Implementation of a Semi-automatic Password-Cracking Algorithm*. Springer., DOI: 10.1007/978-3-030-34339-2_27

Pencarelli, T. (2020). The digital revolution in the travel and tourism industry. *Information Technology & Tourism*, *22*(3), 455–476. DOI: 10.1007/s40558-019-00160-3

Pendey, B. (2023). Artificial Intelligence And Cyber Security. *Journal Transnational Universal Studies*, *1*(2), 93–99. DOI: 10.58631/jtus.v1i2.15

Pepin, N., Bradley, R. S., & Diaz, H. F.. (2015). Elevation-dependent warming in mountain regions. *Nature Climate Change*, *5*(5), 424–430. DOI: 10.1038/nclimate2563

Perrett, K., & Wilson, I. D. (2023). A cyber resilience analysis case study of an industrial operational technology environment. *Environment Systems & Decisions*, *43*(2), 178–190. Advance online publication. DOI: 10.1007/s10669-023-09895-1

Piper, D. L. A. (n.d.). *Data protection laws in Vietnam*. Retrieved August 5, 2025, from https://www.dlapiperdataprotection.com/?t=law&c=VN

Pizam, A., & Mansfeld, Y. (Eds.). (2016). *Tourism, security and safety: From theory to practice*. Routledge.

Pohl, J. H. (2023). *International Data Transfers and Cybersecurity*. Cambridge University Press., DOI: 10.1017/9781009374576.006

Prajapat, D. K., & R, D. (2024). Revolutionizing Tourism through Technology the Digital Transformation of Travel and Tourism. *International Journal of Research Publication and Reviews*. DOI: 10.55248/gengpi.5.0224.0626

Priyadarshana, D., Ramachandra Rao, T., & Sambasiva Rao, M. (2024). AI and blockchain technology for secure and transparent financial transactions. *International Journal of Science and Research Archive, 13*(1), 2013–2019. DOI: 10.30574/ijsra.2024.13.1.1845

PwC. (n.d.). *Forensics*. Retrieved August 5, 2025, from https://www.pwc.com/vn/en/services/deals/forensic-services.html

Pyke, J., Lindsay-Smith, G., Gamage, A., Shaikh, S., Nguyen, V. K., De Lacy, T., & Porter, C. (2021). Building destination resilience to multiple crises to secure tourism's future. *Asia Pacific Journal of Tourism Research, 26*(11), 1225–1243. DOI: 10.1080/10941665.2021.1989000

Queensland, B. (n.d.). *IT threat response for tourism organisations*. Retrieved August 5, 2025, from https://www.business.qld.gov.au/industries/hospitality-tourism-sport/tourism/crisis-support/it-threat

Raji, A. N., Olawore, A. O., Ayodeji, A., & Joseph, J. (n.d.). *Integrating Artificial Intelligence, Machine Learning, and Data Analytics in Cybersecurity: A Holistic Approach to Advanced Threat Detection and Response*. DOI: 10.30574/wjarr.2023.20.3.2741

Raleigh, C., Kishi, R., & Linke, A. (2023). Political instability patterns are obscured by conflict dataset scope conditions, sources, and coding choices. *Humanities & Social Sciences Communications, 10*(1), 74. DOI: 10.1057/s41599-023-01559-4

Ram, Y., & Hill, C. (2022). The tourism industry and the risk of "the year 2038 problem": Long-term thinking and the illogical cycle of ICT risk management. *International Journal of Tourism Research, 24*(3), 501–514. Advance online publication. DOI: 10.1002/jtr.2517

Rashideh, W. (2020). Blockchain technology framework: Current and future perspectives for the tourism industry. *Tourism Management, 80*, 104125. DOI: 10.1016/j.tourman.2020.104125

Rasoolimanesh, S. M., Ramakrishna, S., Hall, C. M., Esfandiar, K., & Seyfi, S. (2020). A systematic scoping review of sustainable tourism indicators in relation to the sustainable development goals. *Journal of Sustainable Tourism, 32*, 1–21. DOI: 10.1080/09669582.2020.1775621

Reda, R., &M'Bark, M. (2023). *Fostering Destination Resilience: A Conceptual Framework Linking Sustainable Tourism and Tourism Threats*. DOI: 10.59285/rimec.390

Reis, T., Bornschlegl, M. X., & Hemmje, M. L. (2021). AI2VIS4BigData: A Reference Model for AI-Based Big Data Analysis and Visualization. In Reis, T., Bornschlegl, M. X., Angelini, M., & Hemmje, M. L. (Eds.), *Advanced Visual Interfaces. Supporting Artificial Intelligence and Big Data Applications* (pp. 1–18). Springer International Publishing., DOI: 10.1007/978-3-030-68007-7_1

Renaud, K., & Ophoff, J. (2021). *A cyber situational awareness model to predict the implementation of cyber security controls and precautions by SMEs. 1*(1), 24–46. https://doi.org/DOI: 10.1108/OCJ-03-2021-0004

Renaud, K., & Weir, G. R. S. (2016). Cybersecurity and the Unbearability of Uncertainty. *Conference on Computational Complexity*, 137–143. https://doi.org/DOI: 10.1109/CCC.2016.29

Ren, H., Sun, J., Chen, C.-K., Zhao, Y., & Yang, L. (2024). LTV-MPC-based Real-time and Anti-noise Motion Control for High-speed Vehicle. *Binggong Xuebao. Acta Armamentarii Sinica, 45*(12), 4311–4322. DOI: 10.12382/bgxb.2023.0979

Richardson, T. L. (2023). Artificial intelligence's impact on hospitality and tourism marketing: Exploring key themes and addressing challenges. *Current Issues in Tourism*, •••, 1–18. DOI: 10.1080/13683500.2023.2229480

Rivera-López, F. B. (2023). Resilience in Tourism: A bibliometric analysis of trends and perspectives in research. *The Journal of Economic History*, 37–48. Advance online publication. DOI: 10.35429/JEH.2023.13.7.37.48

Rouse. (2025). *Vietnam's draft cybersecurity law 2025 – Key changes businesses need to know*. Retrieved August 5, 2025, from https://rouse.com/insights/news/2025/vietnam-s-draft-cybersecurity-law-2025-key-changes-businesses-need-to-know

Roxas, F., Rivera, J. P. R., & Gutierrez, E. L. M. (2020). Framework for creating sustainable tourism using systems thinking. *Current Issues in Tourism, 23*(3), 280–296. DOI: 10.1080/13683500.2018.1534805

Roy, P. P. (2020). *A High-Level Comparison between the NIST Cyber Security Framework and the ISO 27001 Information Security Standard.* DOI: 10.1109/NCETSTEA48365.2020.9119914

Rudenko, M., Кочума, І., Кравченко, О., & Tretiak, N. (2024). Information security in smart tourism: risk management, marketing strategies, perspectives. *Вісник Хмельницького Національного Університету*. DOI: 10.31891/2307-5740-2024-328-42

Rydzewski, P. (2025). Digital Inequality and Sustainable Development. *Problemy Ekorozwoju, 20*(1), 96–108. DOI: 10.35784/preko.6691

Salama, G. M., El-Shafai, W., El-Gazar, S., Omar, B., Hassan, A. A., Hussein, A. I., & Abd El-Samie, F. E. (2023). Efficient implementation of double random phase encoding and empirical mode decomposition for cancelable biometrics. *Optical and Quantum Electronics*, *55*(14), 1210. Advance online publication. DOI: 10.1007/s11082-023-05005-2

Salek, M. S., Chowdhury, M., Munir, M. B., Cai, Y., Hasan, M. I., Tine, J.-M., Khan, L., & Rahman, M. (2025). A Large Language Model-Supported Threat Modeling Framework for Transportation Cyber-Physical Systems. *IEEE Access : Practical Innovations, Open Solutions*, *13*, 163046–163070. DOI: 10.1109/ACCESS.2025.3603580

Salem, M., Samara, K., & Al-Tamimi, A.-K. (2024). Navigating Challenges in Online Cybersecurity Education: Insights from Postgraduate Students and Prospects for a Standardized Framework. *ACM Transactions on Computing Education*, *24*(4), 1–32. Advance online publication. DOI: 10.1145/3703163

Sandhya, H., & Varghese, B. (2024).*Smart Tourism Narratives*. DOI: 10.4018/979-8-3693-1058-8.ch010

Sangfor. (n.d.). *IHG hack claimed by vindictive couple using wiper malware*. Retrieved August 5, 2025, from https://www.sangfor.com/blog/cybersecurity/ihg-hack-claimed-by-vindictive-couple-using-wiper-malware

Sanjeev, K., & Badruddoza, T. Mohammad, & Ana, P. (2024). *Utilizing Smart Technology and AI in Hybrid Tourism and Hospitality*. IGI Global.

Sankar, J. G., & David, A. (2024). *Transforming the Travel Landscape*. IGI Global., DOI: 10.4018/979-8-3693-1532-3.ch012

Sankar, J. G., & Ilangovan, K. (2024). *The Role of Smart Technology in Enhancing Sustainable Tourism Experiences.Advances in Hospitality, Tourism and the Services Industry (AHTSI)*. Book Series., DOI: 10.4018/979-8-3693-7388-0.ch014

Sarangan, B., Hewege, C., & Perera, C. R. (2022). Fifty years of evolutionary trajectory of tourism industry regulations: A systematic literature review. *Asia Pacific Journal of Tourism Research*, *27*(8), 781–806. DOI: 10.1080/10941665.2022.2119876

Sargiotis, D. (2024). Data Security and Privacy: Protecting Sensitive Information. In Sargiotis, D. (Ed.), *Data Governance: A Guide* (pp. 217–245). Springer Nature Switzerland., DOI: 10.1007/978-3-031-67268-2_6

Sargsyan, G. (2024).. . *Cybersecurity as a Backbone for Sustainability*, *526–530*, 526–530. Advance online publication. DOI: 10.1109/CSR61664.2024.10679426

Savchenko, V. A., & Telecommunications, S. U. (2020). The main areas of artificial intelligence technologies in cybersecurity. *Modern Information Security*, *44*(4). Advance online publication. DOI: 10.31673/2409-7292.2020.040611

Scheyvens, R., & Cheer, J. M. (2021). Tourism, the SDGs and partnerships. *Journal of Sustainable Tourism*, •••, 1–11. DOI: 10.1080/09669582.2021.1982953

Schwendicke, F., Samek, W., & Krois, J. (2020). Artificial intelligence in dentistry: Chances and challenges. *Journal of Dental Research*, *99*(7), 769–774. DOI: 10.1177/0022034520915714 PMID: 32315260

SecurityWeek. (2021). *Details of 100M visitors to Thailand exposed online: Research firm*. Retrieved August 5, 2025, from https://www.securityweek.com/details-100m-visitors-thailand-exposed-online-research-firm/

Sekhar, K. S. V. (2024). Digital Infrastructure Challenges for Techno-Entrepreneurs in Rural Areas. *Advances in Electronic Commerce Series*, 127–156. https://doi.org/ DOI: 10.4018/979-8-3373-0086-3.ch007

Serban, A. C., Ordéñez, P., Alkhaldi, A., & Lytras, M. D. (Eds.). (2025). *Innovation management for a resilient digital economy*. IGI Global., DOI: 10.4018/979-8-3693-8357-5

Shahana, A., Hasan, R., Farabi, S. F., Akter, J., Al Mahmud, M. A., Johora, F. T., & Suzer, G. (2024). AI-driven cybersecurity: Balancing advancements and safeguards. *Journal of Computer Science and Technology Studies*, *6*(2), 76–85. DOI: 10.32996/jcsts.2024.6.2.9

Shang, Z., & Luo, J. M. (2023). Topic modelling for wildlife tourism online reviews: Analysis of quality factors. *Current Issues in Tourism*, *26*(14), 2317–2331. DOI: 10.1080/13683500.2022.2086107

Shanthalakshmi, M., & Ponmagal, R. S. (2024a). An intelligent dynamic cyber physical system threat detection system for ensuring secured communication in 6G autonomous vehicle networks. *Scientific Reports*, *14*(1). Advance online publication. DOI: 10.1038/s41598-025-85424-1 PMID: 39814782

Shanthalakshmi, M., & Ponmagal, R. S. (2024b). An Intelligent Intrusion Detection System for VANETs Using Adaptive Fusion Models. *International Journal of Computational and Experimental Science and Engineering*, *11*(1), 749–755. DOI: 10.22399/ijcesen.935

Sharma, S. (2019). *Data Privacy and GDPR Handbook*. John Wiley & Sons. DOI: 10.1002/9781119594307

Shin, D.-H., Han, S.-J., Kim, Y.-B., & Euom, I.-C. (2024a). Research on digital forensics analyzing heterogeneous Internet of Things incident investigations. *Applied Sciences (Basel, Switzerland), 14*(3), 1128. DOI: 10.3390/app14031128

Shoetan, P. O., Amoo, O. O., Okafor, E. S., & Olorunfemi, O. L. (2024). Synthesizing Ai's Impact on cybersecurity in telecommunications: A conceptual framework. *Computer Science & IT Research Journal, 5*(3), 594–605. DOI: 10.51594/csitrj.v5i3.908

Shrestha, L., Balogun, H., & Khan, S. (2025). AI-Driven Phishing: Techniques, Threats, and Defence Strategies. In Jahankhani, H., & Issac, B. (Eds.), *Cybersecurity and Human Capabilities Through Symbiotic Artificial Intelligence* (pp. 121–143). Springer Nature Switzerland., DOI: 10.1007/978-3-031-82031-1_7

Shumilova, K., Shumilov, D., & Maltsev, A. (2024). Classification of Cyber Risks for Sea Vessel's Voyage Cycle. *Transactions on Maritime Science, 13*(1). Advance online publication. DOI: 10.7225/toms.v13.n01.w20

Sigala, M. (2020). Social media and customer engagement in the context of smart tourism: Implications for privacy and trust. *Journal of Hospitality and Tourism Technology, 11*(3), 335–351. DOI: 10.1108/JHTT-04-2020-0060

Sigala, M. (2023). Rethinking digital transformation in tourism: Smartness, AI, and ethical challenges. *Tourism Review, 78*(1), 23–38. DOI: 10.1108/TR-03-2022-0147

Singh, P., & Hassan, V. (2024). *Application of Artificial Intelligence-Based Technologies for Promoting Sustainable Tourism Practices*. DOI: 10.4018/979-8-3693-6260-0.ch015

SiteMinder. (n.d.). *Cyber security in the hospitality industry*. Retrieved August 5, 2025, from https://www.siteminder.com/r/cyber-security-hospitality-industry/

Soares, J. C., Ruiz, T. C. D., & Ivars-Baidal, J. (2021). Smart destinations: A new planning and management approach? *Current Issues in Tourism*, •••, 1–16. DOI: 10.1080/13683500.2021.1991897

Soava, G. (2015). Development prospects of the tourism industry in the digital age. *Revista tinerilor economişti*, (25), 101-116.

Solanke, A. A., & Biasiotti, M. A. (2022). Digital forensics AI: Evaluating, standardizing and optimizing digital evidence mining techniques. KI - Künstliche Intelligenz, 36(2), 143–161. DOI: 10.1007/s13218-022-00763-9

Spalevic, Z., Milosavljević, B., & Marković, S. (2024). Legal Basis of Educational Processes of Artificial Intelligence Algorithms in E-tourism.*International Journal of Cognitive Research in Science, Engineering and Education*. DOI: 10.23947/2334-8496-2024-12-1-209-217

Srivastava, S. S., Ali, S. I., Srivastava, A. K., & Goswami, C. (2024). Improving 5G network performance with MIMO technology using beamforming algorithm. *ICTACT Journal on Communication Technology*, *15*(2), 3173–3180. DOI: 10.21917/ijct.2024.0472

Srivastava, S. T. C., Sharmiladevi, D., Sugumar, D., Ali, S. I., Jones Mary, T. A., & Kumar, S. (2023). Using a smart wearable device for monitoring social distance in smart cities. In *2023 International Conference on Research Methodologies in Knowledge Management, Artificial Intelligence and Telecommunication Engineering (RMKMATE)* (pp. 1–5). IEEE. https://doi.org/DOI: 10.1109/RMKMATE59243.2023.10369118

Stoll, M. (2019). *An Information Security Model for Implementing the New ISO 27001*. IGI Global., DOI: 10.4018/978-1-5225-7113-1.ch013

Streimikiene, D. (2023). Sustainability Assessment of Tourism Destinations from the Lens of Green Digital Transformations. *Journal of Tourism and Services*. DOI: 10.29036/jots.v14i27.651

Stronger Authentication (pp. 207–218). (2022). Apress eBooks. DOI: 10.1007/978-1-4842-8261-8_12

Stroumpoulis, A., Kopanaki, E., & Varelas, S. (2022). Role of artificial intelligence and big data analytics in smart tourism: A resource-based view approach. *WIT Transactions on Ecology and the Environment*, 99–108. Advance online publication. DOI: 10.2495/ST220091

Sumariadhi, N. W.Ni Wayan Sumariadhi. (2023). Green Tourism. *Promoting Sustainable Practices for a Responsible Future.*, *1*(1), 19–25. DOI: 10.25078/ijoss.v1i1.2976

Suta, W. P., Abdi, N., & Astawa, I. P. M. (2021)... *Sustainable Tourism Development in Importance and Performance Perspective, 342–346*. Advance online publication. DOI: 10.2991/assehr.k.210424.066

Syta, J. (2024). CHALLENGES IN PROVIDING CYBERSECURITY TO PORT AND MARITIME INFRASTRUCTURE FACILITIES. *Geographic Information Systems Odyssey Journal*, *4*(1), 131–144. DOI: 10.57599/gisoj.2024.4.1.131

Tabansky, L., & Lichterman, E. (2024). PROGRESS: The sectoral approach to cyber resilience. *International Journal of Information Security*, *24*(1), 18. Advance online publication. DOI: 10.1007/s10207-024-00910-3

Talukder, M. B., & Hoque, M. (2025). Navigating the Digital Horizon: Transforming Travel Agencies in the Digital Era. In *Perspectives on Digital Transformation in Contemporary Business* (pp. 383-410). IGI Global Scientific Publishing.

Talukder, M. B., Hoque, M., & Kumar, S. (2024). *Impact of Cybersecurity in the Aviation*. Tourism, and Hospitality Industries., DOI: 10.4018/979-8-3693-2715-9.ch011

Tanimu, M. G. (2024). Assessing the Impact of Taxpoynt Platform on Small Business Tax Compliance through Digitization. *ACM International Conference Proceeding Series*, 378–380. DOI: 10.1145/3680127.3680143

Tapscott, D., & Tapscott, A. (2022). *Blockchain revolution: How the technology behind Bitcoin and other cryptocurrencies is changing the world*. Penguin.

Tariq, M. U. (2024). Data Breach Incidents and Prevention in the Hospitality Industry. *Advances in Hospitality, Tourism and the Services Industry (AHTSI) Book Series*, 181–199. DOI: 10.4018/979-8-3693-2715-9.ch010

Taylor, M., Haggerty, J., Gresty, D., & Lamb, D. (2011). Forensic investigation of cloud computing systems. *Network Security*, *2011*(3), 4–10. DOI: 10.1016/S1353-4858(11)70024-1

Tee, M. K. (2024). *Malaysia's Smart Tourism Framework*. IGI Global., DOI: 10.4018/979-8-3693-1978-9.ch003

Tham, A., & Sigala, M. (2020). Road block(chain): Bit(coin)s for tourism sustainable development goals? *Journal of Hospitality and Tourism Technology*, *11*(2), 203–222. DOI: 10.1108/JHTT-05-2019-0069

Thapaliya, S., & Bokani, A. (2024). Leveraging artificial intelligence for enhanced cybersecurity: Insights and innovations. *SADGAMAYA*, *1*(1), 46–52. DOI: 10.3126/sadgamaya.v1i1.66888

Tia, H. U. (2014). *A Study on Tourism Consumers' Trust,Satisfaction and Loyalty in Online Purchasing*. Tourism Science.

Tilleke & Gibbins. (2018). *Vietnam's controversial new cybersecurity law raises questions*. Retrieved August 5, 2025, from https://www.tilleke.com/insights/vietnams-controversial-new-cybersecurity-law-raises-questions/19/

Tilleke & Gibbins. (2025). *Draft of Vietnam's consolidated 2025 cybersecurity law released.* Retrieved August 5, 2025, from https://www.tilleke.com/insights/draft-of-vietnams-consolidated-2025-cybersecurity-law-released/

Topsakal, Y. (2024). *Artificial Intelligence-Based Sustainable Tourism Planning. Advances in Hospitality, Tourism and the Services Industry (AHTSI).* Book Series., DOI: 10.4018/979-8-3693-3715-8.ch004

Travel and Tour World. (2025). *Vietnam sparks summer travel frenzy while cybercrime shadows the season.* Retrieved August 5, 2025, from https://www.travelandtourworld.com/news/article/vietnam-sparks-summer-travel-frenzy-while-cybercrime-shadows-the-season/

Traversa, F. (2024).*Artificial Intelligence in Tourism.* DOI: 10.1016/B978-0-443-13701-3.00344-3

Treiblmaier, H. (n.d.). *Blockchain and Tourism.* https://doi.org/DOI: 10.1007/978-3-030-05324-6_28-2

Treiblmaier, H., Leung, D. T., Kwok, A. O. J., & Tham, A. (2021). Cryptocurrency adoption in travel and tourism – an exploratory study of Asia Pacific travellers. *Current Issues in Tourism, 24*(22), 3165–3181. DOI: 10.1080/13683500.2020.1863928

Trim, P. R. J., & Lee, Y.-I. (2022). Combining sociocultural intelligence with artificial intelligence to increase organizational cyber security provision through enhanced resilience. *Big Data and Cognitive Computing, 6*(4), 110. DOI: 10.3390/bdcc6040110

Tripathi, M., & Mukhopadhyay, A. (2020). Financial Loss due to a Data Privacy Breach: An Empirical Analysis. *Journal of Organizational Computing and Electronic Commerce, 30*(4), 381–400. DOI: 10.1080/10919392.2020.1818521

Tsaih, R. H., & Hsu, C. C. (2018). Artificial intelligence in smart tourism: A conceptual framework.

Tsiktsiris, D., Lalas, A., Dasygenis, M., & Votis, K. (2024). Enhancing the Safety of Autonomous Vehicles: Semi-Supervised Anomaly Detection With Overhead Fisheye Perspective. *IEEE Access : Practical Innovations, Open Solutions, 12*, 68905–68915. DOI: 10.1109/ACCESS.2024.3399841

Tussyadiah, I. P. (2017). Technology and behavioral design in tourism: The influence of automation on touristic experience. *Annals of Tourism Research, 66*, 140–152.

Tussyadiah, I., & Wang, D. (2016). Tourists' attitudes toward proactive smartphone systems. *Journal of Travel Research, 55*(4), 493–508. DOI: 10.1177/0047287514563168

University, A.-F. K. N. U.-F. K. N., & Kulakhmetova, G. (2025). The potential of blockchain technologies in tourism data and transaction management. Bulletin of the International University of Tourism and Hospitality, 8(2), 230–244. DOI: 10.62867/3007-0848.2025-2.16

UNWTO. (2022). *Digital transformation in tourism*. World Tourism Organization.

UNWTO. (2022). *Tourism and digital transformation: Understanding the global landscape*. United Nations World Tourism Organization. https://www.unwto.org

Vachheta, H. C., Pawar, I., Hukare, K. G., & Jadhav, S. B. (2024). Cybersecurity in the Digital Era: A Comprehensive Framework for Safeguarding Data Integrity, Privacy and Critical Infrastructures Against Evolving Threats. *International Journal of Advanced Research in Science. Tongxin Jishu*, •••, 471–486. DOI: 10.48175/IJARSCT-22665

Valli, C., Martinus, I. C., Stanley, J., & Kirby, M. (2021). *CyberCheck.me: A Review of a Small to Medium Enterprise Cyber Security Awareness Program*. Springer., DOI: 10.1007/978-3-030-71017-0_17

Vance, A., Eargle, D., Jenkins, J. L., Kirwan, C. B., & Anderson, B. B. (2019). The fog of warnings: how non-essential notifications blur with security warnings. In *Fifteenth Symposium on Usable Privacy and Security (SOUPS 2019)* (pp. 407-420).

Vietnam Law & Legal Forum. (2025). *New cybersecurity law drafted to regulate information security, cybersecurity*. Retrieved August 5, 2025, from https://vietnamlawmagazine.vn/new-cybersecurity-law-drafted-to-regulate-information-security-cybersecurity-74800.html

Vila-Blanco, N., Varas-Quintana, P., Tomás, I., & Carreira, M. J. (2023). A systematic overview of dental methods for age assessment in living individuals: From traditional to artificial intelligence-based approaches. *International Journal of Legal Medicine, 137*(4), 1117–1146. DOI: 10.1007/s00414-023-02960-z PMID: 37055627

Villar Miguelez, C., Monzon Baeza, V., Parada, R., & Monzo, C. (2023). Guidelines for renewal and securitization of a critical infrastructure based on IoT networks. *Smart Cities, 6*(2), 728–743. DOI: 10.3390/smartcities6020035

Vorobeva, D., Costa Pinto, D., Antonio, N., & Mattila, A. S. (2023). The augmentation effect of artificial intelligence: Can AI framing shape customer acceptance of AI-based services? *Current Issues in Tourism*, •••, 1–21. DOI: 10.1080/13683500.2023.2214353

Walmsley, B. (2023). A Blockchain-Based Tourism Industry. *Advances in Electronic Government, Digital Divide, and Regional Development Book Series*, 27–50. https://doi.org/DOI: 10.4018/978-1-6684-4153-4.ch002

Wang, B., Luo, P., Yang, Y., Zhao, Z., Dong, R., & Guan, Y. (2025). A Review and Prospect of Cybersecurity Research on Air Traffic Management Systems. *Dianzi Yu Xinxi Xuebao. Dianzi Yu Xinxi Xuebao*, *47*(5), 1230–1265. DOI: 10.11999/JEIT240966

Wang, X. (2024). Sustainable tourism: Pathways to environmental preservation, economic growth, and social equity. *Applied and Computational Engineering*, *66*(1), 166–171. DOI: 10.54254/2755-2721/2024.20637

Wani, S., Imthiyas, M., Almohamedh, H., Alhamed, K. M., Almotairi, S., & Gulzar, Y. (2021). Distributed Denial of service (DDoS) mitigation using blockchain—A comprehensive insight. *Symmetry*, *13*(2), 227. DOI: 10.3390/sym13020227

Weng, Y., & Wu, J. (n.d.). Fortifying the Global Data Fortress: A Multidimensional Examination of Cyber Security Indexes and Data Protection Measures across 193 Nations. *International Journal of Frontiers in Engineering Technology*. https://doi.org/DOI: 10.25236/IJFET.2024.060203

Wongchestha, N., Karim, F. B., & Wongmahesak, K. (Eds.). (2025). *Practical strategies and case studies for online marketing 6.0*. IGI Global Scientific Publishing., DOI: 10.4018/979-8-3373-2058-8

Wu, D., Li, H., Huang, Q., Li, C., & Liang, S. (2023). Measurement and determinants of smart destinations' sustainable performance: A two-stage analysis using DEA-Tobit model. *Current Issues in Tourism*, •••, 1–17. DOI: 10.1080/13683500.2023.2228977

Xiang, Z. (2018). From digitization to the age of acceleration: On information technology and tourism. *Tourism Management Perspectives*, *25*, 147–150. DOI: 10.1016/j.tmp.2017.11.023

Xiang, Z., Magnini, V. P., & Fesenmaier, D. R. (2015). Information technology and consumer behavior in travel and tourism: Insights from travel planning using the Internet. *Journal of Retailing and Consumer Services*, *22*, 244–249. DOI: 10.1016/j.jretconser.2014.08.005

Xiao, G., Yao, Z., Zhang, S., & Jiang, Y. (2024). Cooperative eco-driving for mixed platoons at signalized intersections with wireless charging lanes. *Energy*, *313*, 134118. Advance online publication. DOI: 10.1016/j.energy.2024.134118

Xiubo, L., Keting, Y., Wei, L., Qilei, L., & Weiwei, Q. (2018). *A tourism anti-fraud system based on a block chain.*

Xu, Y., Li, G., Deng, G., Qiu, H., Han, X., & Zhang, T. (2024). PhyScout: Detecting Sensor Spoofing Attacks via Spatio-temporal Consistency. *CCS 2024 - Proceedings of the 2024 ACM SIGSAC Conference on Computer and Communications Security*, 1879–1893. DOI: 10.1145/3658644.3670290

Xu, R. (2023a). Framework for building smart tourism big data mining model for sustainable development. *Sustainability (Basel)*, *15*(6), 5162. DOI: 10.3390/su15065162

Xu, Y., Shi, Y., & Qin, T. (2023). Challenges in smart tourism: A media content analysis of digital barriers for senior tourists in China. *Information Technology & Tourism*, *25*(4), 665–682. DOI: 10.1007/s40558-023-00270-z

Yallop, A. C., Gică, O. A., Moisescu, O. I., Coro , M. M., & Séraphin, H. (2021). The digital traveller: Implications for data ethics and data governance in tourism and hospitality. *Journal of Consumer Marketing*, *40*(2), 155–170. DOI: 10.1108/JCM-12-2020-4278

Yang, F. X., & Wang, Y. (2025). Rethinking metaverse tourism: A taxonomy and an agenda for future research. *Journal of Hospitality & Tourism Research (Washington, D.C.)*, *49*(1), 3–12. DOI: 10.1177/10963480231163509

Yang, K. H., Park, S. K., Yoon, S. N., & Kim, J. (2010). Measurement of the digital inequality in remote rural areas: Case of South Korea. *International Journal of Information Technology and Management*, *9*(2), 142–161. DOI: 10.1504/IJITM.2010.030458

Yang, Z., Yin, M., Xu, J., & Lin, W. (2019). Spatial evolution model of tourist destinations based on complex adaptive system theory: A case study of Southern Anhui, China. *Journal of Geographical Sciences*, *29*(8), 1411–1434. DOI: 10.1007/s11442-019-1669-z

Yarali, A., Rodocker, E., & Gora, C. (2023).*Artificial Intelligence in Cybersecurity: A Dual-Nature Technology*. https://doi.org/DOI: 10.1109/CSCI62032.2023.00042

Ye, H., Sun, S., & Law, R. (2021). An investigation of developing smart tourism from the perspective of stakeholders. *Asia Pacific Journal of Tourism Research*, *26*(10), 1156–1170. DOI: 10.1080/10941665.2021.1953086

Youssef, A. B., Dutta, P. K., Doshi, R., & Sajnani, M. (2024). *AI, Blockchain, and Metaverse in Hospitality and Tourism Industry 4.0: Case Studies and Analysis*. CRC Press. DOI: 10.1201/9781032706474

Yu, J., Shvetsov, A. V., & Hamood Alsamhi, S. (2024). Leveraging Machine Learning for Cybersecurity Resilience in Industry 4.0: Challenges and Future Directions. *IEEE Access : Practical Innovations, Open Solutions*, *12*, 159579–159596. DOI: 10.1109/ACCESS.2024.3482987

Yulianto, S., Lumban Gaol, F., Supangkat, S. H., & Ranti, B. (2023). *A Comprehensive Model for Enhancing Cybersecurity Resilience and IT Governance Through Red Teaming Exercises*. 1–7. https://doi.org/DOI: 10.1109/ICT60153.2023.10374068

Zawoad, S., & Hasan, R. (2018). Trustworthy digital forensics in the Internet of Things. *Computer*, *51*(7), 40–47. DOI: 10.1109/MC.2018.3191261

Zeadally, S., Adi, E., Baig, Z., & Khan, I. A. (2020). Harnessing artificial intelligence capabilities to improve cybersecurity. *IEEE Access : Practical Innovations, Open Solutions*, *8*, 23817–23837. DOI: 10.1109/ACCESS.2020.2968045

Zhang, H., Dong, J., & Gao, Z. (2023). Automatic segmentation of airport pavement damage by AM-Mask R-CNN algorithm. *Engineering Reports*, *5*(8), e12628. Advance online publication. DOI: 10.1002/eng2.12628

Zhang, L. (2023). Artificial intelligence assisted cyber threat assessment and applications for the tourism industry. *Journal of Computer Virology and Hacking Techniques*, *19*(2), 199–215. DOI: 10.1007/s11416-022-00436-z

Zhang, M., Wang, C., Ren, T., & Li, J. (2025). STAR-RIS enabled covert integration of sensing communication and over-the-air computing with analysis and optimization. *Scientific Reports*, *15*(1), 19007. Advance online publication. DOI: 10.1038/s41598-025-04173-3 PMID: 40447702

Zhang, Y., Sotiriadis, M., & Shen, S. (2022). Investigating the impact of smart tourism technologies on tourists' experiences. *Sustainability (Basel)*, *14*(5), 3048. DOI: 10.3390/su14053048

Zhong, L., Sun, S., Law, R., & Li, X. (2021). Tourism crisis management: evidence from COVID-19. *Current Issues in Tourism, 24*(19), 2671–2682. https://doi.org/. 1901866DOI: 10.1080/13683500.2021

Zhou, L., & Wang, J. (2023). Artificial intelligence and cybersecurity in smart tourism: A systematic literature review. *Journal of Hospitality and Tourism Technology*. Advance online publication. DOI: 10.1108/JHTT-12-2022-0314

Zhou, Z., Liu, Y., & Wang, L. (2020). IoT security and privacy in smart agriculture. *IEEE Access : Practical Innovations, Open Solutions*, *8*, 123–135.

About the Contributors

Mohammad Badruddoza Talukder is an Associate Professor at the College of Tourism and Hospitality Management at the International University of Business Agriculture and Technology (IUBAT) in Dhaka, Bangladesh. Holding a PhD from Lovely Professional University, India, he is renowned for his innovative integration of cutting-edge technologies such as Artificial Intelligence (AI), the Internet of Things (IoT), and Blockchain into tourism and hospitality management. His research explores the transformative impact of these technologies on smart tourism, cloud kitchens, and the broader industry landscape. As a prolific author, Dr. Talukder has published numerous scholarly articles and books, with forthcoming titles that address AI innovations in hospitality, the evolution of cloud kitchens, and the enhancement of digital literacy within hospitality education. His work shapes contemporary tourism and hospitality practices, skillfully marrying technological advancements with practical industry applications. Since 2008, Dr. Talukder has imparted his knowledge through a diverse array of courses in tourism and hospitality across various universities in Bangladesh. His research interests encompass vital areas such as tourism management, hotel management, food and beverage management, and accommodation management, with his scholarly contributions featured in prestigious journals both nationally and internationally. His commitment to academic excellence and industry relevance positions him as a leading authority.

***

Md. Shoeab Akhter is a passionate researcher and practicum student with a B.Sc. in the Agriculture Department of the College of Agricultural Sciences at IUBAT—International University of Business Agriculture and Technology, Dhaka 1230, Bangladesh. He is doing an internship at the Bangladesh Atomic Energy Commission. His research title is 'Green Synthesis of Nanoparticles for Agricultural Use.' Loved by nature and with a passion for the environment, his pursuits include areas of interest like agricultural sciences, food security and food science, environmental science, waste management, green energy, AI, IoT-based farming, and agritourism, among others. Along with his objective of creating an impact through writing and research, he combines new, innovative, suitable technologies and nature conservation with real-world issues. He has contributed book chapters (Emerald, CABI, Bentham Science, Springer, Cambridge Scholars) and has participated in various major projects on research. With the hope of bringing about a change in the world, he aspires to contribute to global knowledge and create a lasting impact on sustainability in society.

Abdullah Ashraf is a keen final-year student and budding researcher of Tourism and Hospitality Management at the College of Tourism and Hospitality Management of IUBAT—International University of Business Agriculture and Technology, Dhaka 1230, Bangladesh. He has a keen interest in the changing landscape of tourism and hospitality and has recently ventured into research on innovative trends affecting the industries. His interests in the tourism sector include sustainable tourism, hospitality management, destination marketing, AI and technology's impact on tourism services, and community-based tourism development. To make an impact on real-life issues and contribute towards academic and research literature, Abdullah aims to make an arduous yet rewarding journey into practical industry insights combined with relevant research. He is passionate about publishing research works while engaging with interdisciplinary-related works, writing book chapters, or writing journal articles on tourism, hospitality, and strategic management. Having the knowledge and experience, he is motivated toward sustainable and responsible tourism to enable communities and their growth within the vibrant tourism industry in Bangladesh.

Himaloy Barik is a Research Scholar (PhD) in the Department of Hospitality and Tourism Management at Assam University, Silchar (A Central University). He holds a Master of Travel and Tourism Management (MTTM) from the Centre for Management Studies of Dibrugarh University (2022), and an M.A. in Geography from Dibrugarh University (2020). He completed his graduation in Geography from Dibrugarh Hanumanbax Surajmal Kanoi (D.H.S.K.) College in 2018. His research interests include tea tourism with a particular emphasis on community development, economic diversification, cultural heritage preservation, and environmental conservation. His broader academic interests encompass regional geography, AI in tourism, and interdisciplinary approaches to sustainable tourism development.

Piali Haldar earned her MBA from the Institute of Rural Management Anand and completed her PhD at Birla Institute of Technology, Mesra. Her core areas of specialization include rural marketing, rural development, branding strategy, and consumer behaviour. With over 20 years of experience in academia and research, she has published extensively in renowned journals listed in ABDC and Scopus. She has authored one textbook on Marketing and edited three academic books. Dr. Haldar has presented her research at numerous national and international conferences and has contributed more than 50 papers to reputed journals, edited volumes, and conference proceedings.

Md. Afzal Hossain is currently serving as an Assistant Professor at the College of Business Administration at IUBAT-International University of Business Agriculture and Technology, Dhaka, Bangladesh. He was awarded a Ph.D. in Business Administration from the Beijing Institute of Technology(BIT), China in 2023. He was awarded the China Government Counsel Scholarship (CSC) in 2018. Before that, Dr. Afzal obtained MBA and BBA degrees from the Department of Accounting & Information Systems, University of Dhaka (DU). His areas of teaching include Financial Accounting, Management Accounting, Cost Accounting, Advanced Financial Accounting, Auditing, and International accounting standards. Dr. Md. Afzal Hossain has published several research articles on the Web of Science and Scopus. He has carried out his research in the fields of accounting, environmental economics, corporate social responsibility, energy, and marketing. Dr. Afzal is an active reviewer for the journal Environmental Science and Pollution Research (ESPR), which is a SCI and Scopus-indexed journal. Dr. Afzal has attended several national and international conferences as a paper presenter, participant, and guest. Previously, Dr. Afzal Worked as an Assistant Professor at Shanto-Mariam University of Creative Technology and Green University of Bangladesh in the Department of Business Administration. He also worked as an Adjunct Faculty of the Independent University, Atish Dipankar University of Science & Technology" and International Islamic University Chittagong.

Md. Saddam Hossain is a doctoral researcher in English Linguistics at Khulna University, Bangladesh, where his PhD focuses on "Exploring the Synergy between Co-Curricular Activities and EFL Proficiencies in Shaping Holistic Development of the Students: A Study at Secondary Level in Bangladesh". His work critically engages with applied linguistics, English language teaching (ELT), and the intersections of co-curricular innovation, digital technologies, and adolescent development. Alongside his academic research, he holds the position of District Child Affairs Officer at the Bangladesh Shishu Academy under the Ministry of Women and Children Affairs, where he contributes to the planning and monitoring of child-centered educational and developmental programs. Hossain holds advanced degrees in English Literature and ELT and has authored peer-reviewed journal articles and a book chapter exploring artificial intelligence in education, pedagogy, and applied linguistics. He has presented at national and international conferences and was awarded the Prime Minister's Education Assistance Trust Fellowship in recognition of his doctoral research. His academic interests include technology-enhanced learning, socio-emotional development, and sustainable pedagogy.

Shafiqul Islam is an Assistant Professor at the College of Tourism and Hospitality Management (CTHM), International University of Business Agriculture and Technology (IUBAT), Dhaka, Bangladesh. He is currently pursuing his PhD at the Paris Graduate School, France. He is actively engaged in teaching, research, and academic development in the fields of tourism and hospitality. His academic interests include ecotourism, tourism management, sustainable tourism practices, and aviation management. Mr. Islam has been contributing to the aviation sector in Bangladesh since 2013. He is actively involved in student mentorship, fostering practical and industry-relevant learning experiences. He is committed to advancing knowledge through research and scholarly activities, with a focus on addressing contemporary challenges in the tourism and hospitality sector in Bangladesh. His dedication to academic excellence and professional development supports the growth of future hospitality professionals both in Bangladesh and beyond.

M. Jamal is currently working as an Associate Professor in Economics, The New College, Chennai, India. He has gained 20 years of teaching and research experience and has awarded ten Ph.D awarded under his guidance. He has been actively involved in various academic and research-oriented capacities. He served as the Coordinator - South for the Indian Economic Association and is a Life Member of both the Indian Economic Association and the Association of Economics Teachers (AET), Tamil Nadu. Additionally, he holds editorial responsibilities across numerous reputed journals. Further, he has visited four countries for academic purposes and has several publications in reputed journals. His research interest areas are MSMEs, Industrial and developmental economics. 5. Experiences: He has nearly 20 years of experience in research and teaching at The New College, University of Madras, Chennai, India 6. Achievements: He has been recognized for his outstanding contributions to academia and research through multiple prestigious honors. He received the Best Academic Excellence Award from the Nature Science Foundation, India. This award highlights his consistent pursuit of academic excellence and impactful research. Additionally, he was acknowledged for his quality research publications during the academic year 2020–2021 by the Dean of Research & IQAC at The New College, Chennai, affirming his commitment to scholarly advancement. Further underscoring his influence in the field of education, he was honored with the TIP Inspiring Educators 2021 award by the TIP Community, recognizing his inspiring role and dedication to nurturing academic growth.

Farhana Lina is a Lecturer (Senior Scale) in the Department of Tourism & Hospitality Management at Daffodil International University, where she specializes in research areas such as digital detox, artificial intelligence in tourism, and community-based tourism development (CBT). Currently pursuing an MPhil in Tourism and Hospitality Management, she holds both a BBA and an MBA from the University of Dhaka. Lina's work focuses on understanding the potential impacts of tourism development in Bangladesh, promoting sustainable tourism, and empowering local communities. Her research also explores how emerging technologies can revolutionize the tourism industry, enhancing both academic and practical insights in the field.

Bekzod Madaminov serves in the Department of General Professional Sciences at Mamun University, Khiva, Uzbekistan. His academic and professional pursuits focus on enhancing the quality of higher education through innovative pedagogical practices and interdisciplinary approaches. With a strong commitment to fostering academic excellence, he actively contributes to curriculum development, student mentorship, and research in applied sciences and education. His scholarly interests encompass modern educational methodologies, sustainable academic frameworks, and skill-oriented learning models that align with the evolving demands of contemporary academia. Through his teaching and research endeavors, Mr. Madaminov continues to play a vital role in promoting intellectual growth and professional competence among students and colleagues alike.

Dev Mandal currently serves as an Assistant Professor in the Department of Management at Brainware University, Kolkata. Before this, he worked at ICRA Analytics Ltd and Shriram Finance Ltd. He holds an MBA in Finance and a Bachelor of Commerce degree from Vidyasagar University. Additionally, he has successfully cleared the UGC NET and WB SET examinations in Management.

Anh Nguyen received her PhD in Geography in 2014 from Hanoi University of Education (Vietnam). She is currently a university professor. Her main research interests include geography, sustainable tourism, wellness tourism, ecotourism, community-based tourism, and rural tourism.

Thang Nguyen is a lecturer at East Asia University of Technology, Vietnam. He specializes in tourism marketing, cultural heritage, and tourism economics. His research focuses on sustainable tourism and has been published in international journals, including the International Education and Research Journal.

Ravikumar R N is currently a Postdoctoral researcher at Universiti Malaysia Perlis, Malaysia. Also, working as an Associate Professor in the department of

Computer Engineering at Marwadi University, Rajkot, Gujarat. He has 12+ years of national and international teaching experience. He completed his PhD at Amity University, Rajasthan, M.E at VMRF Deemed University, B.E at Anna University, Chennai. He is the co-founder of the Research Activities Club at Marwadi University and trains students on research activities, which leads to the publication of 7 Scopus/SCI journals, 20 Book chapters, 25 Conference papers, and 10 patents. His specialization is ML, DL, Federated Learning, Recommendation Systems, and Optimization Techniques.

Arif Rana is a highly motivated educator and senior professional executive having Ph.D. in Artificial Intelligence and Talent Management) from Innovative Knowledge Institute - Paris Graduate School (IKI-PGS), Paris, France and MBA (Management Science) from Institute of Business Administration-Dhaka University (IBA-DU), Dhaka Bangladesh. and with achievements that have clearly demonstrated the ability to deliver truly business-focus and client/user need based solutions. Effective team player as a trainer with well-developed relationship skills, supported by an open style of management. He has developed the ability and the experience to lead and manage a number of diverse business functions of an organization, Information Systems and related activities with a forward thinking acquiring of enhanced teaching and added managerial skills. He has 21 plus years teaching experience in various private universities in Bangladesh starting from Senior Lecturer to Associate Professor both in Undergraduate (BBA) and in post graduate level (MBA).

Hamida Ritu shows promising research abilities through her studies of Tourism and Hospitality Management as a Bachelor of Arts student at IUBAT—International University of Business Agriculture and Technology in Dhaka, Bangladesh. Through her studies of cultural heritage protection in destination management, she has begun her academic journey toward sustainable tourism and hospitality operations management. Hamida's high social drive motivates her to study ecotourism and community-based tourism along with tourism policy and planning, hospitality service quality enhancement, and the application of digital technology in the industry. The area of her interest in research is from local tourism to global travel patterns and sustainability practices and the economic-social impacts of tourism. Hamida applies theoretical concepts to solve real-life issues to achieve positive outcomes. Her work is directed towards improving world knowledge alongside sustainable development with a goal of establishing long-term changes through written work and group work within the hospitality and tourism industry.

Aarthi S is a dedicated Assistant Professor in Computer Science with over six years of teaching experience. She is currently pursuing her Ph.D. at Marwadi University, Gujarat, and holds an M.Phil. and MCA from Bharathiar University, Tamil Nadu. Throughout her academic career, Aarthi has specialized in programming languages such as C++, Java, and C, and contributed to research in recommender systems and AI-related data privacy. She has published journal articles, contributed to book chapters, and actively participated in technical workshops. Known for her student mentorship and engagement in academic events, Aarthi remains committed to fostering innovation and excellence in computer science education.

Shivansu Sachan is Pursuing Ph.D. in Management, a Master's holder from Integral University, Lucknow, Bachelor's from IHM, Lucknow. Academic and professional accomplishments of 6 years with renowned organizations and institutes. His Teaching Career has been very satisfying and have continuously upgraded the skills and knowledge by attending many courses and training programs, seminars, conferences organized by different organizations and also delivered many lectures as a Hospitality sector. He is working as an Assistant Professor at Chhatrapati Shahu ji Maharaj University Kanpur .

Iftiaq Sarkar is an undergraduate research student studying for a Bachelor of Arts in Tourism and Hospitality Management at IUBAT, International University of Business Agriculture and Technology. Dhaka 1230, Bangladesh. Iftiaq has recently begun research in tourism development, sustainable hospitality practice, cultural heritage management, and guest attitude in the hospitality industry, with increasing interest in scholarly work. Iftiaq follows contemporary issues in tourism and hospitality driven by curiosity and passion for effectual contributions, such as ecotourism and strategic service sector management, along with digital transformation and experiential guest service. With his research work, Iftiaq is trying to connect theoretical knowledge with its implementation in practice that encourages innovation paired with sustainability and socially inclusive growth in the operations of tourism. The study conducted by Iftiaq aims to generate academic information and practical industry development, which he uses to start change and fight for sustainable tourism and policymaking. Through his research, he seeks to provide scholarly outputs while attending research meetings at both national and international levels and forming collaborations for projects that encourage global hospitality and tourism intelligence.

Md. Mehedi Sawon is a dedicated academic and researcher currently serving as a Senior Lecturer in the Department of Tourism and Hospitality Management at Daffodil International University, Bangladesh. With a strong passion for advancing knowledge in tourism and hospitality, he has made significant contributions through his research and publications. His research interests are diverse and focused on contemporary topics within the tourism and hospitality sectors. Sawon is particularly interested in the intersection of Artificial Intelligence and its applications in tourism, exploring innovative ways to enhance customer experiences and optimize operational efficiency focus on tourism education, seeking to develop new teaching methods and curricula that better align with industry trends. Furthermore, Sawon is interested in social media marketing in the hospitality industry, analyzing how digital platforms shape consumer behavior and business strategies. His work also extends to sustainable tourism, promoting practices that contribute to the long-term preservation of tourism destinations and the environment.

Sanjeev Saxena is currently serving as an Professor & HODin the Department of Hospitality & Tourism Management at Assam University (A Central University), Silchar, a position he has held since August 2021. With a distinguished professional journey spanning over 33 years, Prof. Saxena brings a unique blend of industry expertise and academic excellence to the field of hospitality and tourism. He began his career in 1992 with The Taj Group of Hotels, serving as a Manager for over five years. Transitioning into academia, he joined the Institute of Hotel Management (IHM), Jodhpur as a Lecturer, where he made significant contributions to hospitality education for more than nine years. He then served as Training Manager at Jaypee Hotels for over five years, further honing his leadership skills. Prof. Saxena later took on the role of Principal at IHM Silvassa (affiliated with NCHMCT, New Delhi). In 2013, he rejoined Jaypee Hotels & Resorts as Additional General Manager (Learning & Development) and Head of the Jaypee Hotel Training Centre, Agra, a role he fulfilled for eight years with distinction.

Binastya Anggara Sekti has been a lecturer at the Faculty of Computer Science, Esa Unggul University, Jakarta, since 2016. He is actively involved in the Artificial Intelligence and Information Security Study Group. He holds a Bachelor's degree in Informatics Engineering from the Bandung Institute of Technology and a Master's degree in Information Systems Management from Trisakti University, Jakarta. Prior to entering academia, he accumulated over 25 years of professional experience as an IT practitioner in various companies across Jakarta. His work focused on developing data centers for internet service providers and delivering IT solutions for the manufacturing and oil & gas sectors. His research interests include artificial intelligence, cybersecurity, and the development of IT infrastructure.

Vikas Sharma is a distinguished academician, researcher, and innovator in the field of hospitality and tourism management, with a specialized focus on culinary tourism, food innovation, sustainable hospitality practices, and regional gastronomy. He currently serves as an assistant professor at Subharti College of Hotel Management, Swami Vivekanand Subharti University, Meerut, India. His academic journey is marked by excellence, having earned a Doctor of Philosophy (Ph.D.) in Hotel Management from the Faculty of Management & Commerce, Swami Vivekanand Subharti University, with a dissertation titled "Regional Cuisine of Braj: Documentation and Application in Tourism Promotion." He also holds a Master's degree in Tourism and Travel Management (MTTM) from IGNOU, New Delhi, and a Bachelor of Science in Hospitality and Hotel Administration from IHM Gwalior (affiliated with NCHMCT), further complemented by an MBA and certifications in computer applications and digital learning.

Uday Singh is having twelve years of experience in hospitality with nine years of education and three years of experience in industry in front office. Currently working in Amity University Rajasthan as Assistant professor. Taking subjects of front office and tourism. Published research paper and patents in field of hospitality.

Loi Vu Duc is currently a Lecturer at the Hanoi School of Business and Management (HSB), Vietnam National University, Hanoi. His primary academic objective is to leverage his extensive expertise in Sales & Marketing, Consumer Behavior, Sustainability, Digital Transformation, Non-Traditional Security, and Corporate Strategy. Professionally, Dr. Loi possesses significant corporate leadership experience, having served in high-level roles such as Vice President at Finviet Technology, General Director at Huu Nghi Food, Bao Ngoc, and Trang An JSC, and in key management positions at major international companies, including a lengthy tenure at Unilever International, Kinh Do Mondelez, and Kimberly-Clark. He is fluent in English and skilled in teaching, consulting, research, and management.

Index

A

B

C

D

E

F

G

I

P

R

S

T

V

www.ingramcontent.com/pod-product-compliance
Lightning Source LLC
LaVergne TN
LVHW062321300926
849161LV00007B/1523